Taking Stock

What is American government like today? How has it changed—and how has it remained the same—over the course of the century now coming to a close? *Taking Stock* seeks to provide the fullest and most thoughtful answers yet offered to these questions. It brings together eminent historians and political scientists to examine the past experience, current state, and future prospects of five major American public issues: trade and tariff policy, immigration and aliens, conservation and environmentalism, civil rights, and social welfare. The contributors examine the evolving nature of these issues, the reactive policies of the federal government, and the institutional devices by which these policies have been applied. Never before have these major public policy issues been explored so deeply, and with such insight, in a collaborative effort crossing disciplinary borders.

Morton Keller is Spector Professor of History at Brandeis University. His books include *The Life Insurance Enterprise, 1885–1910: A Study in the Limits of Corporate Power; Affairs of State: Public Life in Late Nineteenth Century America; Regulating a New Economy: Public Policy and Economic Change in America, 1900–1933;* and *Regulating a New Society: Public Policy and Social Change in America, 1900–1933.*

R. Shep Melnick is Thomas P. O'Neill, Jr., Professor of American Politics at Boston College. His books include *Between the Lines: Interpreting Welfare Rights* and *Regulation and the Courts: The Case of the Clean Air Act.*

WOODROW WILSON CENTER SERIES

Michael J. Lacey, editor, *Religion and Twentieth-Century American Intellectual Life*

Michael J. Lacey, editor, *The Truman Presidency*

Joseph Kruzel and Michael H. Haltzel, editors, *Between the Blocs: Problems and Prospects for Europe's Neutral and Nonaligned States*

William C. Brumfield, editor, *Reshaping Russian Architecture: Western Technology, Utopian Dreams*

Mark N. Katz, editor, *The USSR and Marxist Revolutions in the Third World*

Walter Reich, editor, *Origins of Terrorism: Psychologies, Ideologies, Theologies, States of Mind*

Mary O. Furner and Barry Supple, editors, *The State and Economic Knowledge: The American and British Experiences*

Michael J. Lacey and Knud Haakonssen, editors, A *Culture of Rights: The Bill of Rights in Philosophy, Politics and Law—1791 and 1991*

Robert J. Donovan and Ray Scherer, *Unsilent Revolution: Television News and American Public Life, 1948–1991*

William Craft Brumfield and Blair A. Ruble, editors, *Russian Housing in the Modern Age: Design and Social History*

Nelson Lichtenstein and Howell John Harris, editors, *Industrial Democracy in America: The Ambiguous Promise*

Michael J. Lacey and Mary O. Furner, editors, *The State and Social Investigation in Britain and the United States*

Hugh Ragsdale, editor, *Imperial Russian Foreign Policy*

Dermot Keogh and Michael H. Haltzel, editors, *Northern Ireland and the Politics of Reconciliation*

Joseph Klaits and Michael H. Haltzel, editors, *The Global Ramifications of the French Revolution*

René Lemarchand, *Burundi: Ethnic Conflict and Genocide*

James R. Millar and Sharon L. Wolchik, editors, *The Social Legacy of Communism*

James M. Morris, editor, *On Mozart*

Blair A. Ruble, *Money Sings: The Changing Politics of Urban Space in Post-Soviet Yaroslavl*

Theodore Taranovski, editor, *Reform in Modern Russian History: Progress or Cycle?*

Continued on page following index

Taking Stock

American Government in the Twentieth Century

Edited by
MORTON KELLER
R. SHEP MELNICK

WOODROW WILSON CENTER PRESS

AND

PUBLISHED BY THE PRESS SYNDICATE OF THE UNIVERSITY OF CAMBRIDGE
The Pitt Building, Trumpington Street, Cambridge, United Kingdom

CAMBRIDGE UNIVERSITY PRESS
The Edinburgh Building, Cambridge CB2 2RU, UK   www.cup.cam.ac.uk
40 West 20th Street, New York, NY 10011-4211, USA   www.cup.org
10 Stamford Road, Oakleigh, Melbourne 3166, Australia
Ruiz de Alarcón 13, 28014 Madrid, Spain

First published 1999

Printed in the United States of America
Typeface Sabon 10/13 pt.   *System* MagnaType™ [AG]

A catalog record for this book is available from the British Library.

Library of Congress Cataloging-in-Publication Data
Taking stock : American government in the twentieth century / edited
by Morton Keller, R. Shep Melnick.
p.   cm. – (Woodrow Wilson Center series)
ISBN 0-521-65228-6. – ISBN 0-521-65545-5 (pbk.)
1. Political planning – United States – History – 20th century.
2. United States – Politics and government – 20th century.
I. Keller, Morton. II. Melnick, R. Shep, 1951–   . III. Series.
JK468.P64T348   1999
320′.6′097309045–dc21   99-19541
                                                                              CIP

ISBN 0 521 65228 6 hardback
ISBN 0 521 65545 5 paperback

Contents

Foreword   *page* ix
    Michael J. Lacey

1 Taking Stock   1
    Morton Keller

PART I: TRADE AND TARIFF POLICY

2 Trade Policy in Historical Perspective   15
    Morton Keller
3 The Triumph of Liberal Trade: American Trade Policy
    in the Postwar Period   35
    David Vogel

PART II: IMMIGRANTS AND ALIENS

4 The Progressive State and the Legacy of Collective
    Immigrant Identities   57
    Reed Ueda
5 The Racialization of Immigration Policy   81
    Peter Skerry

PART III: CONSERVATION AND ENVIRONMENTALISM

6 The Many Faces of Conservation: Natural Resources
    and the American State, 1900–1940   123
    Donald J. Pisani

7 Risky Business: Government and the Environment after
Earth Day 156
R. Shep Melnick

PART IV: CIVIL RIGHTS

8 Since 1964: The Paradox of American Civil Rights
Regulation 187
Hugh Davis Graham
9 You Win Some, You Lose Some: Explaining the Pattern
of Success and Failure in the Second Reconstruction 219
Jennifer L. Hochschild

PART V: SOCIAL WELFARE

10 From Beginning to End: Has Twentieth-Century U.S.
Social Policy Come Full Circle? 249
Theda Skocpol

11 Conclusion: Governing More but Enjoying It Less 280
R. Shep Melnick

*Appendix: Major Environmental Statutes Enacted in the
1970s and 1980s* 307
Contributors 311
Index 315

Foreword

MICHAEL J. LACEY

"The world of public affairs is so old," Woodrow Wilson once observed, that no person can know it "who knows only that little last segment of it which we call the present." In keeping with this insight, the American program of the Woodrow Wilson International Center for Scholars, the nation's official memorial to the achievements of Wilson as a scholar and statesman, is concerned mainly with research on the history of American society and politics. It is devoted to furthering critical reflection on the relations between ideas and institutions in modern America, particularly the institutions of government. It aims to provide a forum in Washington, D.C., for the presentation and assessment of new scholarly perspectives on the American experience, and to do what it can—through its fellowships, scholarly working groups, conferences, and publications—to develop our knowledge of those long-term, fundamental, underlying issues and problems that have shaped and continue to shape our understanding of the national community.

The progress of scholarship requires collaborative creativity. One of the duties of the American program is to provide leadership for large-scale, cooperative projects that arise from time to time out of the scholarly discussions that take place among the Center's staff, its fellows, and its advisers. This volume is an example. Its editors have been long-term advisers to the program, and three of the authors whose work appears here have been fellows in recent years. The book is a product of a Center working group that met on several occasions to plan and critique the chapters that follow. Participants aimed to exploit some of the possibilities of collaboration between historians and political scientists with a shared interest in the dynamics of development that have driven the growth of the national government in the twentieth century and in the substantive effectiveness and worth of the major domains of policy that they have chosen to investigate.

Thanks are due to the editors and authors of this volume, and to all who participated in the discussion and criticism of its separate parts as they were developed.

1

Taking Stock

MORTON KELLER

"History doesn't repeat itself," Mark Twain once observed, "but it rhymes." And it is true that more than a little assonance links the issues and responses of early and late twentieth-century American government. Then, as now, there was a widespread belief that, despite the lack of major threats from abroad or economic depression at home, things were deeply wrong with the nation's government and political parties, its economic institutions, and its social system. Politically active Americans at the beginning of the century, like their counterparts at the century's end, sought policies designed to do something about political corruption and government inefficiency, the concentration of economic wealth and power in fewer and fewer hands, the condition of families and children and the provision of social welfare, the inadequacies of education and conservation of the environment, cultural and racial diversity and the size and impact of immigration, the failures of the criminal justice system, and even the ingestion of harmful substances such as liquor, drugs, and tobacco.

Then, as now, programs for change flowed not so much from the bottom up as from the top down. Intellectuals and academics, socially conscious businessmen and professionals, journalists and reformers (including a number of highly educated women) gave shape and substance to much of the reform agenda. And public life at the two ends of the century saw the rise of spokespersons for groups—women, blacks, and Native Americans then and now; the handicapped and gays and lesbians today—not previously participants in American political life.

While these advocates looked to the major political parties for support, they relied more heavily on special-purpose organizations, who lobbied politicians and tried to shape the course of public policy through media-

1

disseminated investigation and disclosure. It is worth noting that those who fear that too many Americans are "bowling alone"—that is, are insufficiently organized into voluntary associations working for the public good—look back to the early twentieth century as a golden age of that extraparty involvement.

In 1912 a third-party candidate helped to defeat an incumbent Republican president and put a Democrat in the White House. The same thing happened in 1992. Though no one would more closely equate Theodore Roosevelt and Ross Perot, this was not an entirely coincidental reprise. In both the early and late years of the twentieth century (though far more so now than then), party ties weakened, encouraging new types of leaders to make direct appeals to the public on issues that cut across traditional partisan lines.

So it is not difficult to see striking similarities between American politics and government at the two ends of this century. But it is evident as well that major changes have reshaped American politics and government over the course of the past hundred years.

The sheer scale of the public agenda today is so much larger than it was a century ago that the difference becomes a qualitative as well as a quantitative one. And there appears to be a deep underlying difference in policy purpose. At the beginning of the century the desire to restore an (imagined) American past was uppermost. Conservation, muckraking and political reform, prohibition, immigration restriction, racial segregation, and trustbusting were efforts to restore an old social and economic order, not to create a new one. In contrast, the economic policies of the New Deal and the social policies of the Great Society sought not restoration but reconstruction: to use public policy to create new conditions and new relationships.

The relative weights of government and party politics are vastly different today from the early years of the century. The courts are more interventionist; agencies, regulators, the bureaucracy, and the media are more extensive and intrusive. The money funneled through federal agencies, and the government's consequent impact on American life and work, had no counterpart in the early 1900s. Conversely, elections, parties, and the party identification of voters have a much diminished place in our public life compared to a century ago.

Values and norms—regarding race and gender, sex and the family, social welfare—have changed enormously. So too have the integuments of social and economic life. A population once defined by rural, small town, or urban residence now is primarily suburban, secondarily urban. Less than 2 percent of the workforce is on farms; a similar fraction labors in factories. White collar and service occupations now are the American norm.

So we have the paradoxical situation that the forms that public life assumed a hundred years ago powerfully resonate with us today; yet they do so across the span of a century that has seen massive economic, social, and cultural change. Given this, what larger understanding of the present state and future prospects of the American polity may be gained from a closer comparative look at how government worked in the early and late twentieth century?

We readily concede that history does not teach simple, practical lessons. But it is profoundly instructive to be reminded, and *re*-reminded, that present concerns have a deep past, and that an awareness of that past will enrich our understanding of current public policy. Linking the past and present experience of American government with major issues—particularly so when it is done with the intimacy and analytical insight of the essays in this book—is in the fullest sense an educational experience. Just as a knowledge of background, setting, and historical context inevitably adds to one's comprehension of a work of art or literature, so does the juxtaposition of the past and present record of American government make for a wiser, more sophisticated apprehension of its current state and future prospects. As the Clinton presidential crisis in 1999 demonstrated, there is a powerful tendency to dwell on the here and now of American governance without much regard for its longer, deeper currents.

The contributors to this volume have gone about the task of comparing, and drawing lessons from, the experience of a century by focusing on five major public issues. These are: tariff and trade policy, the regulation of immigration and aliens, conservation and environmentalism, civil rights, and social welfare. Others might have served as well: antitrust and business regulation; the reform of elections, Congress, and the bureaucracy; the regulation of social behavior (drinking, smoking, drug-taking, prostitution). But the ones we have chosen broadly engaged both the polity and public opinion. And each has a coherence that lends itself particularly well to an exploration of continuities and discontinuities in twentieth-century American government.

We asked historians and political scientists to examine these issues with due regard for the other discipline's concerns. We did not want to wash away the insight and understanding that is peculiar to each discipline, nor could we have done so. In this sense each essay stands on its own, speaking in its disciplinary voice—to the extent that the footnoting form customary to each field has been left undisturbed: no foolish consistency here.

No more fixed is the meaning we attach to the "beginning" and the "end" of the century. Trends and contrasts over time are what we are after. In the cases of the tariff, conservation/environmentalism, and immigration, this leads to a comparison of the late nineteenth and the first half of the twentieth centuries with the past fifty years. In the case of modern social welfare, the dictates of history tend to make the comparison more precise: the 1930s with the 1990s. Civil rights demands an even more compressed time span: from the 1940s–60s to the 1970s–90s.

Case studies of particular policies inevitably run the risk of slighting the larger historical developments that shape the contours of American life. It is not our intent to minimize the importance of depression and prosperity, war and peace, the growth of taxation and bureaucracy, the new role of the media, or significant changes in popular culture. We believe, though, that there is much to be gained by an examination of the workings of American government not from the top down—from the vantage point of these large historical forces—but from the bottom up: from the ground level of issues that directly and substantively engaged the American state. Larger developments will appear when they should appear: as part of the setting in which these issues lived their lives.

The remainder of this introduction sets the stage for the essays that constitute the core of the book. Then the essay authors will speak to you in their various voices. The editors return at the end with a conclusion that seeks to suggest what the essays tell us about the evolution, present state, and (perhaps) future shape of American government.

TRADE POLICY

The tariff, along with taxation and defense, is one of the oldest and most continuous of American issues, dating from the earliest days of the Republic. Because of this it is a particularly valuable source of insight into what has changed, and what has not, in modern American government.

In some respects, tariff-and-trade policy as an issue has altered little since the early Republic. From the beginning, a welter of commercial, manufacturing, and agricultural interests, each with its own fix on what that policy should be, has interacted with a political system—parties,

Congress, the Presidency—that responded both to those special interests and to broader public concerns.

But looked at more closely, trade policy has undergone sea changes of great and revealing scale. During the nineteenth century the tariff was an important and consistent element in the definition of party ideology. As Morton Keller observes, protection for the Republicans and free trade for the Democrats were symbols of party identity freighted not only with economic but also with ideological, sectional, even cultural meaning. That has been less and less true over the course of the twentieth century.

Nor has American trade policy been consistent—or even consistently inconsistent. A protectionist regime prevailed during the three-quarters of a century from the Civil War to the Great Depression. An open-trade regime has had comparable primacy over a comparable sweep of time from the 1930s to the present. Insofar as there is any party identity to trade policy today, it reverses the prevailing nineteenth-century norm: a mild Democratic-labor-populist protectionism, a Republican-business preference for more open trade.

But more has happened to tariff policy than the fading and fudging of its party salience. The way in which it is made has altered fundamentally. Tariff making in the nineteenth and early twentieth centuries was in the hands of Congress. Today, trade policy is the province of executive agencies, commissions, and boards, subject to occasional up-or-down Congressional votes. What was once a defining issue of party politics has become entwined in bureaucratic and regulatory processes that substantially curtail its use for partisan advantage. As David Vogel observes, an issue with substantial material consequence, one in which large numbers of people have compelling grounds for dissatisfaction with the existing open-trade regime, is strikingly resistant to partisan alignment (as the passage of the North American Free Trade Agreement and the 1996 presidential election made clear).

Here as much as anywhere, the belief that the evolution of the twentieth-century American state has been from parties and legislatures to administrative agencies seems to hold. But it is premature to assume that the traditional interplay of politics and government has disappeared because the complexities of modern life have led to new ways of implementing policy. Indeed, stirrings in the current political scene suggest that the tariff issue continues to have strong (if, at the moment, latent) partisan political potential.

This raises an important question. Does the history of trade policy suggest that the character of twentieth-century American government has been shaped primarily by alterations in its institutional *forms:* the decline of the parties, the rise of the bureaucratic-regulatory state? Or is it more proper to focus on the changing *substance* of the issue itself: on the fact that in its character and relative importance, trade policy at the end of this century is very different from what it was a hundred years ago?

In the past, it took a cataclysmic event to set American trade policy on a new course. The Civil War initiated the protectionist regime; the Great Depression, and World War II and its aftermath, set the stage for the freer trade regime that has prevailed in recent times. Would it take social upset on a comparable scale to thrust us once again into protectionism? Or is our trade policymaking, for all its bureaucratic trappings, still sensitive to political winds?

IMMIGRATION

In a number of respects immigration resembles trade as a policy issue. It too is as old as the Republic. And it has had long periods of continuity: free immigration through the nineteenth century, an increasingly restrictive regime during the early and mid-twentieth century, a more liberal policy in recent decades.

By the beginning of the twentieth century the regulation of immigration—deciding who and how many should come, and how immigrants should be treated once they came—was a major public concern. After a number of restrictive steps, a national policy of quota-based control came into place during the early 1920s. In its social consequences it was (along with prohibition) the most important policy enactment of its time.

The distractions of depression, war, and the postwar boom kept immigration off the national agenda for half a century. After the Second World War, Europe's return to prosperity and emigration restrictions in the Soviet bloc substantially reduced the pressure for large-scale flows of people from that part of the world. Instead, emigrants from Latin America and Asia clamored for admission. This coincided with the moderation of American racial prejudices. One by-product of that change was the elimination of national origins quotas in 1965 and a greater readiness to receive immigrants from the world at large. The result was the resumption, after a forty-year lapse, of large-scale immigration. From the mid-

1960s to the mid-1990s some 25 million newcomers came to the United States, three quarters of them from Asia and Latin America.

Beginning in the early 1970s the postwar economic boom ended, foreign competition (in automobiles, textiles, etc.) grew, and unemployment became an important political issue. These conditions fueled a host of economic, social, and cultural concerns about immigrants—from the vantage point of the early twentieth century, eerily familiar ones. Now, at century's end, there are signs that the issue of immigration could take on a salience comparable to that at the century's beginning. In this respect, too, it is very much like trade policy, and a comparably useful measure of what has changed, and what has persisted, in twentieth-century American government.

Reed Ueda focuses on the most distinctive aspect of immigration policy in the early years of this century: the inclination to categorize newcomers by group or racial character rather than individual qualities. Immigration restriction drew on popular xenophobia, a widely accepted and intellectually respectable belief in the racial sources of social behavior, organized labor fearful of mass immigration's threat to jobs and wage standards, and industrialists less hungry for cheap labor from abroad and more fearful of the radicalism that was supposed to come with the newcomers. Given so broad a popular base, it is not surprising that a restrictive system was readily enacted.

Peter Skerry echoes Ueda's stress on group consciousness. He focuses on the degree to which ethnic identity (in part politically crafted) has played an important role in the politics of Hispanics. But his account reveals a significant difference between the century's beginning and its end. The definition of group identity in the earlier period was primarily in the hands of the receiving society. Now it rests with the immigrant groups themselves, or at least their self-designated spokesmen. When once to be identified as a racial, ethnic, or linguistic minority carried a heavy social stigma, now it can convey considerable political and economic advantage.

The late twentieth-century revolution in racial attitudes has brought with it powerful sanctions against the kind of racism that infused the immigration issue in the early 1900s. But identity politics today raises the specter of a separatism that might lead to both a majoritarian backlash and self-destructive group isolation. Is separatism trumped by the assimilating power of contemporary popular culture? Or will immigration and group relations assume something of the social explosiveness that they had at the beginning of this century? That is the question to which the Ueda and Skerry essays address themselves.

CONSERVATION AND ENVIRONMENTALISM

The conservation of natural resources first fully entered the realm of public policy making in the early twentieth century. The nineteenth was a century of development, exploitation, and expansion, fed by the same national attitude that accepted open immigration. It was only around the turn of the century that the fear of scarcity and deprivation began to secure a foothold in the American political consciousness, and make conservation (like immigration restriction) a significant public issue.

Today, of course, the environmental movement (the change in name is suggestive: not just husbanding scarce resources, but saving an endangered ecosystem) has enormous policy weight. In part this is because of the material interests at stake. But more important is the passion and commitment of those caught up in a cause that touches on widespread anxieties in contemporary American society: not unlike the fear of a flood of newcomers that fed immigration restrictionist sentiment earlier in the century.

Environmentalism became a major public issue not because of the power of the economic interests at stake but because of its high cultural and ideological resonance. Does this matter? That is to say, do issues that are more sociocultural than economic have a distinctive political, legislative, and administrative history? Has there been a tendency, over the century, for cultural issues to occupy a more important place in national politics than more material ones? Has environmentalism in fact become a more broadly shared public concern? Or is it now, as it was a century ago, largely the property of a social elite?

The Pisani and Melnick essays cast much light on these questions. They make evident the continuities between early twentieth-century conservation and late twentieth-century environmentalism. These include the tension between conservation for use and the preservationist/environmentalist ethic, and between local interests and national policies; the frequent, and frequently distorted, use of science in policy debates; and the complex interplay of regulatory bureaucracies jockeying for power and place.

But changes in the tone, character, and outcome of this issue are no less striking. The old conservationism described by Pisani was notable for the degree to which local interests, and material concerns over scarcity and depletion—conservation for use—triumphed over the preservationist impulse. Quite the contrary is the case in the regulatory world of the new environmentalism.

Is current environmentalist milieu, in which the media, organized pressure groups, Congress, the president, the courts, and regulatory agencies engage in a complex *ronde* of policy making, implementation, and oversight, representative of American government now and in the foreseeable future? Or are there signs that tradeoffs between environmentalism and economic development, between central and local control, between government by experts, interests, and public opinion, are still very much in play? Environmentalism, like trade and immigration policy, is a litmus test for the questions of change and continuity, of elitism and democracy, that are at the core of this book.

CIVIL RIGHTS

Civil rights is the most recent of our major policy issues, and for much of the second half of the twentieth century the most hard fought and prominent. The politics of race relations have an intensity not evident in tariff or immigration debates or even in the more emotional realms of environmentalism or social welfare. This reflects the fact that race has been for American public life what class has been for many European nations: the society's great fault line.

As Hugh Davis Graham observes, the full force of civil rights as an issue burst on American public life in the second half of the twentieth century. (Aside from its legislation and its place in historical memory, the Civil War–Reconstruction interlude had little connection with the modern movement.)

The modern civil rights movement has gone through two distinct phases. The first was an assault on segregation and discrimination in politics, public accommodations, and the workplace, stretching from the Fair Employment Practice Committee of 1941 to the Civil Rights Act of 1964 and the Voting Rights Act of 1965. Since then, what Graham calls "a new social regulation" has come into prominence: affirmative action (ranging from guidelines and goals to preferences and quotas), and the extension of nondiscrimination and affirmative action to groups other than blacks—Hispanics and Asians, women, gays, the handicapped.

The civil rights legislation of the 1960s remains unchallenged. Discrimination per se has no political or legal, and greatly diminished popular, standing. But the new social regulation is a source of increasing contention. In its favor stands a powerful interlocking network of government agencies, activist pressure groups and lobbying organizations, and strong elements of support in the courts, the media, and the academy. Against it is a more diffuse public hostility to affirmative action (at least in its more assertive forms) reflected in politics, legal decisions, and state referenda.

Jennifer Hochschild asks why it is that some civil rights policies have been so successful while others have so miserably failed. Her distinction between "power to" and "power over" closely parallels Graham's distinction between the first and second phases of civil rights legislation. The former directly applied the power of the state to desegregate the armed forces, schools, and public accommodations. The latter attempted complex, indirect social engineering, which is harder to implement. Equal access to housing, fair employment practices, and affirmative action are prime examples.

Thus a common view of what has happened in civil rights appears in two distinctive formats. Graham's perspective is historical and cultural; Hochschild's approach is more schematic and focuses on how the issue fits into the American system of politics, government, and law. Together they provide insights into the present state and future prospects of civil rights as a touchstone issue of the American state.

SOCIAL WELFARE

Theda Skocpol's discussion of social policy in twentieth-century America assumes the dual obligations of the historian and the political scientist. It is both an insightful look back and a keen-eyed look around and ahead. She reminds us that social welfare did not spring full-blown from the brow of Franklin Delano Roosevelt with the Social Security Act of 1935 but had a long (and distinctively American) past. The spread of universal public schooling in the early nineteenth century was in fact a strong and consequential social welfare policy. (The same might be said of the rapid distribution of cheap or free public land.) The large-scale distribution of pensions to post–Civil War veterans also provided social welfare on a massive scale (as well as being a major political prop to the Republican party). And the passage of laws to provide mothers' pensions during the early twentieth century was a prelude to the Aid to Dependent Children provision of the Social Security Act (and a case study in post-Victorian paternalism).

This does not necessarily add up to a nascent welfare state. But it suggests that social welfare has historical parameters with considerable relevance to our own time. The localism that made the rise of public schools a concern of states and localities rather than the nation would be echoed a century and a half later in opposition to a national health system. The earlier identification of welfare with "deserving" groups—children, Civil War veterans, dependent mothers—recurred with the bestowal of benefits on World War II veterans through the G.I. Bill and on senior citizens through Medicare. A similar differentiation lay behind the recent reduction of benefits to single mothers on welfare. Even Social Security, the broadest of American social welfare enactments, was initially restricted in ways that reflected particular political interests and the stern demands of fiscal soundness.

The prospects of social welfare now and in the near future bear the weight of this historical baggage. Is it determining? Can it be overcome? Should it be overcome? These are the questions that Skocpol addresses. Her discussion of what is desirable, what is possible, and what seems unattainable is an apt and revealing commentary on Oliver Wendell Holmes's subtle admonition, which might well stand as a precept for all of the essays in this book: "Continuity with the past is only a necessity, and not a duty."

The authors of these essays do not make identical—or always compatible—arguments. Obliged to choose between scholars who are knowledgeable and those who are like-minded, we took the former. Some of the contributors are most impressed with continuity over the century, others with the extent of change. Some focus on transformations in political institutions, others on the shifting economic and social environment. Readers will no doubt take note of the historians' taste for detail and contingency, and the political scientists' penchant for abstraction and theorizing.

The editors—a historian and a political scientist—have sought in their scholarship and teaching to bring the insight and understanding of their fields into closer contact than is customary in an age of academic disciplines marching to their own, often discordant, drummers. This project is an outgrowth of that experience. It is designed not only to add to the general understanding of how American government has worked in the twentieth century, but also to show what political history and political science have to offer to—and learn from—one another. Our hope is that this interplay between the disciplinary perspectives of history and political science adds up to a whole that is something more than the sum of its parts.

I

Trade and Tariff Policy

2

Trade Policy in Historical Perspective

MORTON KELLER

Trade policy is as old as the Republic; older, if one includes the eighteenth-century English mercantilist measures (the Hat Act, the Stamp Act) that imposed restraints on American manufacturing and commerce. Once they had a nation, Americans turned quite readily to a tariff for revenue. Almost all federal revenue before the Civil War came from customs duties (and, occasionally, from the sale of public lands). Tariffs continued to yield 40 to 50 percent of federal receipts until the First World War.

The belief that the tariff was for revenue only had a secure place in the early Republic, when the economy was dominated by the production of exportable agricultural staples and a substantial Atlantic trading interest. True, there was continual tinkering with the tariff: the classic scenario of frequent and highly specific tariff bills came into being early in the nineteenth century. But the prevailing policy was to regard customs duties as a significant source of federal revenue and to set tariff rates low enough to foster the outward flow of staples and the inward flow of manufactured goods.

The major pre–Civil War protectionist was Henry C. Carey of the nascent industrial city of Philadelphia, who championed protective tariffs as part of a "National school" of political economy. A high tariff, he thought, would assure national prosperity and "harmony" among "the various portions of society." But what a critic called Carey's "more than German readiness to defer to the co-ordinating power of the state, as a specific for social or economic discords," had little resonance in the atomized, intensely antistatist—indeed, anti-institutional—culture of pre–Civil War America.[1]

1 Morton Keller, *Affairs of State: Public Life in Late Nineteenth Century America* (Cambridge, Mass., 1977), 162–63.

15

Protectionism gradually became an attractive policy option. Its origins lay in the interests of the producers of wool, cotton, and iron. But it gained political and ideological force from its broader appeal to American nationalism. Protection came to be seen not only as a policy serving particular interests but as a way—ultimately the most important way—by which a representative government could secure the economic well-being of its people. It is important to recognize that the protectionist attitude that characterized American tariff protection from the Civil War to the Great Depression was not just a jerry-built rationalization of particular economic interests, but one that tapped broad and deep beliefs in American political life. As we will see, that mix of interest and ideology gave protectionism extraordinary staying power from the 1860s to the 1930s.

This historical perspective raises certain major questions for an understanding of contemporary trade policy: Does a similar mix of interest and ideology underpin the antiprotectionist policies that have predominated since the 1930s? If so, is this underpinning now eroding, to be replaced by a new, and comparably durable, protectionism? Or have the integuments of trade policy making changed so fundamentally since the 1930s that the old model of policy formation, decomposition, and reformation no longer applies?

I

The Civil War was the turning point in nineteenth-century American trade policy. The theoretical and practical lessons in national power that came with the war made the idea of an active and purposeful national government viable for the first time since the 1790s. Perhaps the longest-lasting policy product of that experience, with a continuing impact far greater than the wartime income tax, railroad land grants, or the greenbacks and national banks, was the protective tariff's entrenchment as the keystone of national economic policy.[2]

Why did this happen? Economic historians have found considerable reason to doubt whether the ups and downs of tariff policy had major consequences for late nineteenth-century American industrial and agricultural growth. The American portion of world trade was in a far from dominant 9 to 11 percent range from 1870 to 1940. And exports and imports combined rarely exceeded 10 percent of the nation's gross na-

---

2 Keller, *Affairs of State*, ch. 5; Richard F. Bensel, *Yankee Leviathan: The Origins of Central State Authority in America, 1859–1877* (Cambridge, 1990).

tional product: hardly a commanding height of the economy. No less an authority than Andrew Carnegie thought that the tariff's impact on the iron and steel industry was "trifling." And while statistician-economist Carroll Wright was all for setting the tariff on a "scientific basis," he had to admit that its effect on manufacturing was "unclear."[3]

Of course there were particular economic interests, agricultural and industrial, for whom tariff rates were important. Louisiana beet growers, Pennsylvania iron and steel manufacturers, West Virginia coal miners, and Ohio and Texas wool growers feared foreign competition. There was another incentive for protectionism as well: the free-rider effect created by the nineteenth-century hegemony of British free trade, which allowed the United States to indulge in selective protectionism with little retaliatory cost. But New York City importers, iron manufacturers dependent on imported ore, railroads seeking lower prices for steel rails, Chicago meat-packers who wanted a reduction in salt duties, and farmers and cattlemen with large overseas markets had similarly solid stakes in rate reductions.

Indeed, a retrospective look at the long haul of the late nineteenth and early twentieth centuries, during which American agricultural and industrial production and productivity led the world, might suggest that big business–led international market–seeking would have been the keynote of the nation's trade policy. Instead, the half century from 1880 to 1930 (with a few exceptions, deriving from interludes of Democratic political ascendancy) saw a commitment to protectionism of varying degrees of intensity. This became evident despite the fact that the reigning belief in classical economic theory, which supposedly predisposed judges and legislators to a laissez-faire approach to government policy, hardly reinforced protectionism. What was there in the American system of politics and government that produced a result seemingly so at odds with the conventional view of American economic policy as the work of corporate elites and prevailing economic beliefs?[4]

3 Carnegie quoted in Edward C. Kirkland, *Industry Comes of Age: Business, Labor, and Public Policy, 1860–1897* (New York, 1961), 189; Carroll D. Wright, "The Scientific Basis of Tariff Legislation," *Journal of Social Science* 19 (1884): 11. See also G. R. Hawke, "The United States Tariff and Industrial Protection in the Late Nineteenth Century," *Journal of Economic History* 28 (1975): 84–99; Bennett P. Baack and Edward J. Ray, "Tariff Policy and Comparative Advantage in the Iron and Steel Industry," *Explorations in Entrepreneurial History* 11 (1973): 3–24; Baack and Ray, "The Political Economy of Tariff Policy: A Case Study of the United States," *Explorations* 20 (1983): 73–90.
4 On the predominance of classical economic theory in the courts, see Herbert Hovenkamp, *Enterprise and American Law, 1836–1937* (Cambridge, Mass., 1991). Judith Goldstein's *Ideas, Interests, and American Trade Policy* (Ithaca, 1993) takes note of the "discor-

The most striking characteristic of trade policy as a public issue during this period was its blend of particular interests and broad ideological cast. The typical tariff bill in the nineteenth and early twentieth centuries was a patchwork quilt of hundreds of adjustments to and for special interests. It was said of the 1883 tariff act: "Its general character cannot be easily described; in truth, it can hardly be said to have any general character." Democratic presidential candidate Winfield Scott Hancock was derided by his Republican opposition for declaring in 1880 that the tariff was a local issue. But that was a coldly accurate statement, as Hancock's Republican opponent James A. Garfield recognized some years before: "It is . . . manifest that the [tariff] question has assumed a local rather than a national aspect."[5]

At the same time, trade policy was becoming an important expression of the ideological differences between the parties. Low-tariff Republicans and high-tariff Democrats, not uncommon during the 1870s and early 1880s, became scarce (or at least less conspicuous). One measure of the change was the choice of free-trader John Carlisle over protectionist Samuel J. Randall to be Democratic speaker of the House in 1883. Another was President Grover Cleveland's December 1887 message to Congress, the first (and last) to be devoted solely to the issue of tariff reduction. Cleveland's message was said to have "crystallized tariff sentiment in both parties." But that process had been under way at least since the end of Reconstruction. Why did the tariff come to play so important a party-defining role?

The very nature of the tariff-making process enmeshed economic interests in a close (and often costly) dependence on the major political parties. Each tariff bill was preceded by detailed and lengthy committee hearings, before which a long procession of spokesmen for specific products and industries made their arguments. Extended congressional debates then ensued, in which enormous stores of rhetorical ammunition were expended. (The House was subjected to 151 speeches when it considered the abortive Democratic Mills tariff of 1888.) Complex interbranch congressional negotiations crafted the final law: the Senate added more than 600 amendments to the 1894 bill, more than 800 to the 1897 act. And then, in

---

dance" between protectionist policy and national self-interest. She ascribes it to the inertial impact of the institutionalization of protection in Congress and to the absence of a compelling alternative vision.

5 F. W. Taussig, *The Tariff History of the United States,* 8th rev. ed. (New York, 1930), 249; Robert G. Caldwell, *James A. Garfield* (Indianapolis, 1911), 196.

a few years, the whole convoluted process would start again. The parties thereby assured themselves of financial and other forms of support from the multitude of interests who had stakes in tariff making.[6]

The issue derived its power from its ideological content as well. Free trade helped to bind together the two great, disparate wings of the Democratic party: agrarian southern Protestants and the northern urban Irish. Champions of free trade such as John Q. Mills of Texas, William L. Wilson of West Virginia, and James B. Beck of Kentucky made it an evocative expression of the Jeffersonian, small-government ideology that so attracted post–Civil War Southerners. And because it held out the prospect of lessening American reliance on British exports to the United States and weakening English-dominated international commerce, free trade had a special attraction to Irish Democrats as well.[7]

At the same time, a number of intellectuals and publicists found in free trade a cause that embodied their unease over the rise of large industries and the supremacy of professional politicians who ignored the natural laws of political economy. The most vocal of this breed was the economist David Ames Wells, who thought that free trade exemplified the "economic maxim . . . that that government is best which governs least." E. L. Godkin, editor of *The Nation,* believed that protection eroded individual freedom and led workers to expect something for nothing. He warned: "if the protectionist policy is persisted in, the process of assimilating American society to that of Europe must go on."[8]

Protectionism had at least as much resonance in the late nineteenth-century Republican party and among policy intellectuals. The very word conjured up security in an unstable, rapidly changing economy—"the maintenance of the *status quo* during the period of transition"—and most of all, shielding American jobs, wage scales, and economic growth from the overseas threat of cheap products and sweated labor. Simon N. Patten, the author of a pioneering analysis of an economy of abundance rather than scarcity, saw protection in this larger view. Once "a temporary expe-

6 Statement on Cleveland message in Ida M. Tarbell, *The Tariff in Our Times* (New York, 1911), 154; Taussig, *Tariff History.*
7 Festus P. Summers, *William L. Wilson and Tariff Reform* (New Brunswick, N.S., 1953), 94; Geoffrey Blodgett, *The Gentle Reformers: Massachusetts Democrats in the Cleveland Era* (Cambridge, Mass., 1966), chap. 4.
8 David Ames Wells, "Free Trade," in John J. Lalor, ed., *Cyclopaedia of Political Science, Political Economy, and of the Political History of the United States* (New York, 1884, 1890), vol. 2, 289; Edwin L. Godkin, "Some Political and Social Aspects of the Tariff," *New Princeton Review* 3 (1887): 176.

dient to gain specific ends," it had evolved into "a consistent endeavor to keep society dynamic and progressive."[9]

Protection served the Republican party in much the same way that free trade served the Democrats: as a public policy position that spoke to major but potentially conflicting components of the party's electoral core. As the binding issues of Union and antislavery faded, economic security and Protestant morality—protection and piety—came to serve as replacements. It was in this way that the Republican party could appeal to manufacturers, workingmen, and the broad middle class alike.

The continuity of rhetoric from the great days of the 1860s was evident: "Protection, in the broadest sense of the term, is not only the sole function of government, but the primal object sought in establishing its authority"; protection was "essential to the life of the nation, for the production upon which depend vitality and strength, and for the wages and comforts and elevation of the citizens, upon which rest national sanity and growth, and the conditions of greatness and splendor." To the classic Republican ideological triad of free soil, free labor, and free men, was added now the precept of protected economic growth.[10]

II

In a large sense, trade policy from the Morrill Tariff of 1861 to the Smoot-Hawley Tariff of 1931 was a seamless web, an interconnected series of bills in which the same underlying conditions—the demands of particular interest groups, the needs of party ideology and organization—prevailed. But it is also true that around the turn of the century the terms and conditions defining tariff policy altered substantially. That change reflected not only the nation's (and the world's) evolving economic situation but also the entry of new ideas and interests into American politics and government. It is this dimension of Progressive tariff making—the rise of new policy determinants and their interplay with an existing political and governmental framework—that is of most significance in our search for contemporary meaning in past experience.

9 David Rothman, *Politics and Power: The United States Senate, 1869–1901* (Cambridge, Mass., 1966), chap. 7; Edward Stanwood, *Tariff Controversies in the Nineteenth Century* (Boston, 1903), vol. 2; 256; Simon Patten, *The Economic Basis of Protection* (Philadelphia, 1890), 7–8.

10 David H. Mason, "Protection in the United States," in Lalor, ed., *Cyclopaedia*, vol. 3, 423; Robert E. Thompson, "Benefits of the Tariff System," *North American Review* 139 (1884): 391; Ellis Roberts, "Moral Aspects of the Tariff," *New Princeton Review* 3 (1887): 331.

Around the turn of the century, tariff making became a truly multinational issue, when before it had been limited chiefly to free-trade Britain and protectionist America. An increasingly integrated world economy, and the spread of representative political systems in which economic interest groups had an ever-larger voice in policy, saw to that. France's mildly protectionist Méline Tariff of 1892 and Germany's comparable tariff of 1902 reflected the growing political importance of agricultural interests in those countries. The appearance of a significant British movement for "tariff reform" (that is, protection) was fed by fear of American and German imports, the concerns of farmers, and the need for more revenue to pay for armaments and social welfare. Western economic and political life was becoming more dense and complicated, and so was trade policy.[11]

Several possible economic models might have shaped American tariff policy after 1900. American industrial preeminence, the subject of much European concern during the pre–World War I years and an even more evident fact in the 1920s, might have led corporate America to take on a free-trade/Pax Americana stance like that of mid-nineteenth-century Britain (or the post–World War II United States). Car makers, movie makers, and the like might well have been expected to be great advocates of freer trade. But they weren't.

A second prospect was that the rise of a social science–bureaucratic mentality in government would sanitize tariff making, subject it to the dictates and constraints of administrative oversight, commissions, and the teachings of economists. It didn't.

A third option: the sheer size of the domestic market, along with the xenophobic nationalism fostered by the First World War, would contribute to the growth of an American autarky: a reformulation, in more pinched and narrow terms, of the protectionist creed that had flourished since the Civil War. The prevailing view is that this comes closest to what in fact happened during the first third of the twentieth century.

But the continuing triumph of protectionism was the product of a more complex and revealing history. That complexity is evident in the McKinley Tariff of 1890, usually regarded as the chef d'oeuvre of classic Republican protectionism. It was in fact a more ambivalent bill than its predecessors. It increased the free list as well as dutiable imports, lowered the

---

11 Frederic A. Ogg, "Europe's Tariff Laws and Policies," *American Monthly Review of Reviews* 39 (1909), 427–32; Norman Stone, *Europe Transformed, 1879–1919* (Cambridge, Mass., 1984), 104–105; Alan Sykes, *Tariff Reform in British Politics, 1903–1913* (Oxford, 1979).

annual duty rate to 23.7 percent (from 29.9 percent in 1883), and empowered the President to lower (or raise) rates in reciprocal trade negotiations with other countries. (It is important to recognize that reciprocity around the turn of the century was regarded more as a tool of retaliation than as a step to rate reduction. As an Illinois Republican congressman put it, "Reciprocity is scientific protection.")[12]

The Dingley Tariff of 1897 was even more responsive to new conditions: the growing interest of large corporations in European markets, and a greater readiness (particularly in the wake of the Spanish-American War) on the part of Congress to accept executive-administrative discretion. Nelson Aldrich's Senate Finance Committee initially proposed rates lower than those of the McKinley Tariff, as well as a reciprocity provision that substantially empowered the president to enter into bilateral tariff-reducing arrangements with foreign nations. McKinley himself underwent a conversion to this more sophisticated view of America as an exporting nation. His last speech on the day before he was shot, at the Pan-American Exposition in Buffalo, was on this theme: "Our capacity to produce has developed so enormously and our products have so multiplied that the problem of more markets requires our urgent and immediate attention."

But local-interest-minded Senators substantially raised the Dingley rates on the floor of that chamber. And Congress killed the seven treaties negotiated by McKinley's Reciprocity Commissioner John A. Kasson. American economic internationalism and the lure of rational expertise still were far from displacing the traditional predominance of local interests, party ideology, and congressional leadership.[13]

American tariff politics during the Progressive years produced two major laws: the Republican Payne-Aldrich Tariff of 1909 and the Democratic Underwood Tariff of 1913. In one sense these belonged to a continuum of trade policy that had deep nineteenth-century roots. The same interplay between Republican protectionist and Democratic free trade arguments, the same panoply of particular economic interests, prevailed. But new players, and new plays, now figured more conspicuously in

---

12 David A. Lake, *Power, Protection, and Free Trade: International Sources of U.S. Commercial Strategy, 1887–1939* (Ithaca, N.Y., 1988), 99–102; Goldstein, *American Trade Policy*, 93, 113.
13 McKinley in James D. Richardson, ed., *Messages and Papers of the Presidents* (Washington, D.C., 1897f.), vol. 14, 6620–1; Lake, *Power, Protection, and Free Trade*, 125–41.

the tariff-making game. These included corporate and financial interests by no means wedded to protectionism as an article of belief; a Progressive/reformist low-tariff sentiment that identified high tariffs with big business ("the trusts") and was solicitous of consumers; and a burgeoning belief that tariffs should be constructed not by politicians but by disinterested experts. An issue that once had been defined by the sectional passions of antebellum America, and then by the organizational politics of the late nineteenth century, now was being reshaped by the increasingly diverse public life of the Progressive period.[14]

Protection defined as a national policy serving the interests of producers and workingmen had the better of the ideological argument during the post–Civil War decades. In the early twentieth century, free trade, or at least tariff reduction, seemed to speak more meaningfully to national needs and fears. Opposition to protection now drew on a richer, wider range of supporters and rationales. William Jennings Bryan and others brought a new anti–big business edge to traditional Democratic low-tariff rhetoric. So too did Republican Senator Albert B. Cummins, whose "Iowa idea" was to end protection for trust-made products. Many Progressives argued that by giving employment to new immigrants, protected industries added to the nation's social problems. And the National Association of Manufacturers (NAM) looked at the issue from a perspective rarely seen among earlier business spokesmen: "It is as important now to protect the manufacturers by open doors as it was to build them up by a tariff which has . . . begun to be hurtful."[15]

The *Edinburgh Review* perceptively thought that the tariff conflict in the United States was primarily between the promoters of the turn-of-the-century corporate-merger movement, who wanted high duties to protect the prices charged by their watered combines, and manufacturers who still directly controlled their own plants and sought to export abroad. They "found themselves seriously hampered in buying their raw materials," and fueled a movement for downward tariff revision. Herbert E. Miles, a Racine, Wisconsin, farm-implements manufacturer who headed the NAM's Tariff Commission, condemned the 1897 Dingley Tariff as a tool of the trusts. His answer: a tariff commission similar to those in Britain,

---

14 Morton Keller, *Regulating a New Economy: Public Policy and Economic Change in America, 1900–1933* (Cambridge, Mass., 1990), chap. 9.
15 Quoted in W. L. Saunders, "American Tariff Policy Now Shutting the Open Door," *Engineering Magazine* 21 (1901): 28.

France, and especially Germany, which would gather relevant data and present it to Congress.[16]

Tariff reform thus was strengthened by the now-fashionable desire to replace policy-by-politics with policy-by-bureaucracy. Pre-1900 tariff making had become a fine art of combining vast numbers of schedules, each the product of a political deal between politicians and economic interest groups: the proudest achievement of the old party politics. This highly politicized tariff making was a standing rebuke to the Progressive ideal of rational and efficient public policy, and many set out to change it.

It was against this backdrop that early twentieth-century tariff policy unfolded. After a decade of relative quiescence—the product of Republican political supremacy and the demands of the vast new domestic consumer market—the tariff issue came alive again in the wake of the 1907 panic and the ensuing recession. By now the sentiment for rate reduction cut across party and ideology, big and small business, industry and agriculture. A Who's Who of Republican leaders—Theodore Roosevelt, Elihu Root, Albert Beveridge, Robert LaFollette, Nelson Aldrich—paid at least lip service to lower tariffs worked out through negotiations with other nations rather than through Congressional horsetrading: a sign of the growing interest in markets abroad for American manufactured products. William Howard Taft pledged rate revision—almost all assumed downward—in his 1908 presidential campaign.[17]

The resulting Payne-Aldrich Tariff prescribed rates lower than any since the Civil War. It also prescribed a Tariff Board to work with the president in securing reciprocal trade agreements with other nations. And Taft was sufficiently sensitive to the winds of political change to call for explicit consumer representation at the Ways and Means Committee's hearings. All very Progressive. But the bill was hardly the product of rational planning. Once tariff reform entered the congressional maw a familiar drama played itself out.

Thus House Ways and Means Committee chair Sereno Payne, a Republican politico of the old school, believed in "frying the fat" out of

---

16 "Tariff Revision in the United States," *Edinburgh Review* 209 (1909): 72; "Tariff Revision and the Consumer," *Independent* 66 (1909): 524–28; H. E. Miles, "Why Manufacturers Want Tariff Revision," *North American Review* 187 (1908): 34–45, "An Argument for a Permanent Expert Tariff Commission," *Annals* 32 (1908): 434–39.
17 Francis G. Newlands, "A Solution of the Tariff Question," *Independent* 70 (1911): 334–36; Albert J. Beveridge, "A Permanent Tariff Commission," *Independent* 70 (1911): 409–28; Paul Wolman, *Most Favored Nation: The Republican Revisionists and U.S. Tariff Policy, 1897–1912* (Chapel Hill, N.C., 1992).

manufacturers in return for protection. Aldrich conducted Senate Finance Committee hearings along traditional lines: in private, with full deference to special interests. The general impression was that the Payne-Aldrich Tariff spectacularly violated the spirit (if not the letter) of Taft's 1908 campaign rate-reduction promises. Certainly the bill was no triumph of free trade over protection, or of the administrative over the political state.[18]

It is not surprising that Woodrow Wilson made tariff reduction an important part of his 1912 campaign. Long enjoying a secure place in Democratic party ideology, free trade now had additional appeal as a sop to agrarian–small business hostility to the trusts, and consumer concern over the rising cost of living. In the wake of his 1912 victory, Wilson and a Democratic Congress put through the rate-cutting Underwood Tariff of 1913 with relative dispatch. Many large manufacturers did not even bother to voice their concerns at the hearings. Their protectionist sensitivities appeared to be diminished by the fact that they already dominated the domestic market and owned plants abroad to service overseas markets.[19]

Raw materials producers, too, had more complex positions on the issue than in the past. Take sugar, for example. In the early 1890s the American Sugar Refining Company controlled more than 90 percent of its industry's output and thus was able to live with high sugar duties. But by 1913 its share had shrunk to less than 40 percent. Major figures in the industry such as Claus Spreckels (who had extensive interests in Cuban sugar) advocated lower sugar rates. So did many canners, who were increasingly important players in a consumer economy.[20]

The Underwood Tariff seemed to mark a sea change in trade policy. The *New York Evening Post* saw the end of the protectionism that had dominated industrial nations (except for Britain) since the 1870s. The United States now had a surplus of manufactured goods to export, and a vastly expanded urban population to consume its manufactures and agricultural products. The access to duty-free raw materials provided by Un-

18 "The Revision of the United States Tariff," *Edinburgh Review* 210 (1909): 269–302; F. W. Taussig, "The Tariff Debate of 1909 and the New Tariff Act," *Quarterly Journal of Economics* 24 (1909–10): 1–38; George M. Fisk, "The Payne-Aldrich Tariff," *Political Science Quarterly* 25 (1910): 35–68.

19 James D. Whelpley, "The Tariff Out of Politics," *Century Magazine* 66 (1914): 308.

20 Roy G. Blakey, "The Proposed Sugar Tariff," *Political Science Quarterly* 28 (1913), 230–48; "Tariff Rebellion in the Sugar and Wool States," *Literary Digest* 46 (1913): 931–33.

derwood would, it was thought, increase the efficiency of American industry.[21]

Underwood appeared to bring the advent of a new style as well as new substance to tariff-policy making. Leadership had passed from Congress to the president. Wilson far more than his predecessors galvanized Congress to act, in part by coming before that body to argue for a lower tariff, the first such appearance since Thomas Jefferson. Portentous, too, was his call for an independent Tariff Commission to oversee the rate-setting process in the future. Congress in 1916 duly created this analogue to the Interstate Commerce Commission, the Federal Trade Commission, and the Federal Reserve Board. Bipartisan in makeup, the Tariff Commission was charged to help Congress enact scientific, objectively constructed schedules. The tariff, thought one observer, was no longer a political or party issue.[22]

Another straw in the wind suggesting a profound shift in trade policy was the growing call from large industrial companies for government assistance in securing foreign markets for their products. By 1914 manufactured goods made up almost half of American exports. A look ahead in 1914 concluded that the tariff "has become . . . a force of third-rate importance in our industrial development," and predicted that after the war the United States would be as influential a voice for free trade as Britain had been in the nineteenth century.[23]

The First World War strengthened the impression that the old days of tariff making by deals between politicos and a multitude of special interests were over, replaced by a process dominated by technical experts devoted more to opening markets abroad than protecting them at home. Overseas sales of manufactured goods required more specific and intensive market-seeking than did wheat or cotton. As exports rose sharply during World War I, closer cooperation developed between large manufacturers and the government's National Foreign Trade Council and War Trade Board. The Webb-Pomerene Act of 1918 exempted exporters from

---

21 "The Long Struggle with the Tariff Comes to an End," *Current Opinion* 55 (1913): 221–22; Henry R. Mussey, "The New Freedom in Commerce," *Political Science Quarterly* 29 (1914): 600–25; "A New Era of Industrial Efficiency," *World's Work* 26 (1913): 380–81.
22 E. Pendleton Herring, "The Political Context of the Tariff Commission," *Political Science Quarterly* 49 (1934): 421–25; Whelpley, "Tariff Out of Politics," 303.
23 Henry R. Mussey, "The New Freedom in Commerce," *Political Science Quarterly* 29 (1914): 624.

the cartel and trust restrictions of the Sherman (1890) and Clayton (1914) Antitrust Acts.[24]

Nevertheless it became clear after the war that there was to be no New Era of depoliticized tariff making. In part this was due to the economic facts of American and international life. Rapidly expanding domestic consumer purchasing power, managerial rigidities such as Henry Ford's refusal to adapt the Model T to foreign markets, and European tariff and other barriers lowered the American trade potential abroad. Autarky and protectionism had a commanding place not only in American but in postwar Western economic thought. Even in traditionally free-trading Great Britain, Prime Minister Stanley Baldwin resurrected the prewar flirtation with higher duties, and trade unionists and younger Socialists were drawn to protectionism.[25]

Beyond this, there were institutional and political constraints on the establishment of a new trade order. The most concerned government agencies and departments—the War Trade Board, the Commerce and State Departments—fell to bureaucratic quarreling, and firms doing business abroad relied increasingly on their own arrangements.[26]

The Fordney-McCumber Act of 1922 and the Smoot-Hawley Tariff of 1931, the major tariff laws of the postwar years, bore witness to the recuperative power of traditional tariff politics and the persisting appeal of the protectionist mindset. Indeed, the tone and character of American public life in the twenties—the reaction against Progressivism and reform, the more xenophobic American nationalism stoked by wartime propaganda, and the postwar Red Scare—if anything strengthened the protectionist creed and politicized ratemaking. The National Tariff Institute spoke of "America First" and linked a high tariff with the exclusion of undesirable immigrants. Farmers and union workers continued to believe that lower tariffs threatened their price and wage scales. And after the wartime boom, exported manufactured goods became once again a small proportion of the national product.

24 William H. Becker, *The Dynamics of Business-Government Relations: Industry and Exports, 1893–1921* (Chicago, 1982).
25 George Crompton, *The Tariff* (New York, 1927); H. N. Brailsford, "Free Trade Ebbs in England," *New Republic* 63 (1930): 359–61. See also R. W. D. Boyce, "America, Europe, and the Triumph of Imperial Protectionism in Britain, 1929–30," *Millennium* 3 (Spring 1974): 53–70.
26 Democritus, "The Future Tariff Policy of the United States," *Annals of the American Academy of Political and Social Science* 141 (1929): 257n; Becker, *Dynamics*, 158.

Fordney-McCumber substantially raised the average of existing rates: from 26.8 to 38.3 percent. Republican senators and congressmen representing western farmers hard hit by the postwar drop in agricultural prices and the shrinkage of overseas markets joined the party's traditional protectionist majority. The Tariff Commission tried to lend an objective note to rate setting by proposing a cost-of-production standard. But Fordney-McCumber's schedules emerged instead from the traditional, intensely political process of give-and-take between legislators and economic interests.

William Starr Myers, close to then–Commerce Secretary Herbert Hoover, said of the result: "It is one of the most ill-drawn legislative acts of recent political history." No new corporatism, no organizational or associative state here, only old politics. Insofar as the fight over Fordney-McCumber had a larger context, it was the hoary confrontation between Republican protectionism and Democratic free trade.[27]

Fordney-McCumber did have a flexible tariff provision authorizing the president to change specific rates on the recommendation of the Tariff Commission—introduced, it may be noted, by that doubtful champion of scientific tariff making Senator Reed Smoot of Utah. But in practice neither the commission nor the flexible tariff proposal fostered a more rapid or "scientific" adjustment of rates. The Tariff Commission stayed firmly in the hands of Republican protectionists, and capture was effectively reinforced by dilatoriness. It spent four years investigating the cotton hosiery business. Its report went to the president in 1927, and half a year later no action had yet been taken. Only three schedules were reduced between 1922 and 1927, and these—for live bobwhite quail, paintbrush handles, and millfeed—were hardly of major importance.[28]

Far from evoking a new trade policy, the coming of the Great Depression initially stoked the fires of the old one. The Smoot-Hawley tariff of 1931 was the crowning achievement of traditional, protectionist policy making. What began as an attempt at "limited revision" in 1929 degenerated into an orgy of special-interest protectionism surpassing the worst

27 William S. Myers, "The Republican Party and the Tariff," *Annals* 141 (1929): 246; William R. Allen, "Issues in Congressional Tariff Debates, 1890–1930," *Southern Economic Journal* 20 (1953–54): 354; F. W. Taussig, "The Tariff Act of 1922," *Quarterly Journal of Economics* 37 (1922–23): 1028; Stephen Bell, "Our New Tariff Law," *Outlook* 132 (1922): 180–81. On the limits of the Tariff Commission, see T. W. Page, *Making the Tariff in the United States* (New York, 1924), and Herring, "Political Context," 426.

28 Catherine Hackett, "The Failure of the Flexible Tariff: 1922–1927," *New Republic* 51 (1927): 244–47; Herring, "Political Context," 427–32.

of the bad old days. The Committee on Ways and Means hearings, stretching through 1929 and into 1930, produced seven thousand pages of testimony from more than eleven hundred witnesses. Smoot-Hawley was debated longer and amended more often (fifteen hundred times in the Senate) than any tariff bill in American history. The result: the highest rates ever (though for a relatively small number of items; the overall duty level was lower than in the four previous tariffs).[29]

Informed economic opinion and sophisticated big business and government leaders were appalled by what had happened. Leading economists, major newspapers, Wall Street, and the American Bankers' Association protested, and President Herbert Hoover also disapproved (although, more interested in preserving the flexible tariff provision than in the specific rate levels, he reluctantly signed the act).[30]

But these voices were as nothing in the face of the pressures for special-interest protection. Smoot, the bill's Senate sponsor, watched out for Utah's beet sugar interests; David Reed of Pennsylvania spoke for the Eastern iron and steel manufacturers' bloc. Connecticut's Hiram Bingham boldly went beyond the traditional "infant industries" rationale to speak with pathos of "aged industries" no less in need of protection. Southern Democrats sacrificed their low-tariff tradition to the needs of hard-pressed agricultural constituents; California's Imperial Valley was a strong new voice for cotton protection; the American Federation of Labor's Matthew Woll wanted higher duties on books to protect the printing trades; fruit packers wanted higher duties designed to erode the preference of Italian Americans for tomatoes from their homeland. The result was a monument of sorts to the ability of pluralist particularism to override the administrative state.[31]

The Great Depression and the New Deal opened a "policy window" for trade as it did for other major components of American public policy. Economic catastrophe and a changing political order led to new controlling assumptions and procedural modes, which appeared to end the protectionist policy and tariff making system that dated from the Civil War.

29 "The New Tariff Crime Complete," *The Nation* (Great Britain) 130, 72; "The American Tariff," *New Statesman* 33 (1929): 462–3; J. N. Aiken, "National Realignments on the Tariff Issue," *Current History* 23 (1925–26): 49–55.

30 "The Tariff Crime Complete," *The Nation* (Great Britain) 130 (1930): 72; on poll, William O. Scruggs, "Revolt against the Tariff," *North American Review* 230 (1930): 18–24; Lake, *Power, Protection, and Free Trade*, 184–85, 193–201.

31 F. W. Taussig, "What the Tariff Has Done to Us," *Atlantic Monthly* 148 (1931): 669–75, "The Tariff, 1929–30," *Quarterly Journal of Economics* 44 (1929–30): 175–204, "The Tariff Act of 1930," *Quarterly Journal of Economics* 45 (1930–31): 1–21.

The Reciprocal Trade Agreements Act of 1934 empowered the president to raise or lower rates up to 50 percent in trade negotiations with other countries, and enter into most-favored-nation agreements with them. But the act's accompanying constraints made it anything but a revolution in trade policy. Congress put a three-year (renewable) limit on the president's negotiating authority and required that public hearings and consultations with the Tariff Commission and the Agriculture, Commerce, and State departments precede the implementation of any agreement. Reciprocity, most-favored-nation, and executive discretion had been parts of previous tariff bills, and free trade was no more an explicit part of the act (which in fact took the form of an amendment to Smoot-Hawley) than was protection.[32]

Yet in historical retrospect the Reciprocal Trade Agreements Act of 1934 *did* mark the beginning of a new era in tariff policy: new in the executive's role in rate setting, new in the sense that it initiated a long-term commitment to freer trade. Just as trade policy from the Morrill Tariff of 1861 to Smoot-Hawley in 1931 could be characterized as generally protectionist, congressional-led, intensely partisan tariff making, so can it be said that generally liberalizing, executive-led, nonpartisan tariff making has flourished from 1934 to the present.

Why did so dramatic—so almost suspiciously apposite—a change occur? Did it signify a paradigm shift to a free-trade policy mindset representing internationally competitive, high-value-added industry and agribusiness, in alliance with an increasingly assertive administrative state? Surely so—in part. But just as the previous protectionist era had deep roots in political culture and ideology, so the new era of open trade had more profound sources than service to particular economic interests.[33]

III

On first impression, the conditions that have shaped American trade policy since World War Two seem not to be essentially different from those that operated in the past. Particular economic interests—manufacturing, agricultural, commercial, labor—have a voice beyond their numbers precisely because they are so "interested." Technical experts, economists,

32 Lake, *Power, Protection, and Free Trade*, 204–209.
33 Thomas Ferguson, "From Normalcy to New Deal: Industrial Structure, Party Competition, and American Public Policy in the Great Depression," *International Organization* 38 (1984): 41–94.

journalists, and public policy savants seek to make trade policy something more than the product of competing economic interests. Congress delegates its authority to the bureaucracy only piecemeal, and for limited periods of time. The pressure continues—even grows—to give the issue a partisan cast (though, as has been the case with so many other policy issues, the parties have reversed their positions: the Democrats are more protectionist, the Republicans more inclined to freer trade).

What, then, has changed? Most obviously, the altered status of the American economy vis-à-vis the rest of the world. The worldwide economic predominance of the United States from 1945 to 1970 was not unlike that of Great Britain in the 1840s and the 1850s, and readily explains why this country turned to free trade as Britain had a century before. But in recent years neither American economic hegemony nor the autarky of the 1920s has prevailed. Rather, the last quarter of the twentieth century has seen the rise of a world economy with no single nation dominant. The United States, no less than major competitors such as Japan and Germany, has been swept up in a rapidly changing new world disorder, in which the only sure things about financial, currency, industrial, and market factors are their instability and flux.

Given these destabilizing facts of economic life, and the buffetings that American industry and agriculture have experienced in recent decades, one might reasonably expect to see a resurgence of protectionism: either the broadly defined, ideologically evocative sort that the GOP purveyed during the late nineteenth and early twentieth centuries, or the *sauve qui peut* sort that gave shape (if that is the word) to Smoot-Hawley in 1930–31.

If President Clinton had failed to win congressional approval of NAFTA, explanations would have come easily. Here was an issue well designed to catch up both economic and social (anti-immigrant) discontent. Given the decline of party discipline, Ross Perot's animadversions on the subject, the organized opposition of organized labor, the populist protectionism to which so many Democratic leaders had succumbed, and the anti-immigrant sentiments to which Republicans might be expected to appeal, it had no real prospect of passing. Except, of course, that it did.

Why? One hypothesis: the protectionist bent of the late nineteenth and early twentieth centuries coincided with the rise of an agricultural-industrial infrastructure that serviced an American population growth massively bolstered by immigration. Aside from agricultural exports, the national interest *did* lie ultimately more in closing the door to imports than in opening markets abroad. The half century since World War II has been dominated by a massive domestic consumer market, buying ever larger quantities of imported goods. That consumer market became as powerful a force for open trade as the producer-dominated political society of the past was for protection. At the same time, American business has become more international than ever before. Its political weight has shifted decisively from a protectionist to an open market preference.

Another view: as the slackness of our political parties grows, and their institutional and ideological autonomy declines, trade policy becomes an essentially nonpartisan issue. Congress, by large bipartisan votes, has passed a series of trade acts every four or five years since 1974. Clinton's NAFTA won more Republican than Democratic House votes. As the party-ideology dimension of trade policy declined, the capacity of well-financed, well-organized interests to get their way commensurately increased. So while there may well be a developing preference for protectionism in the populace at large, the parties are no longer effective conduits of those yearnings. In this political world, corporate interests with a stake in NAFTA can readily outgun their organized labor opponents.

Yet another, related supposition: as the Manichean high tariff–low tariff/protectionist–free trader division of the past gave way to the more complex, nuanced, and ambiguous creation of "trade policy," so has the influence of experts grown. The transformation of trade policymaking into a profoundly technical issue has meant, in a sense, its depoliticization. Detailed tariff schedules—the classic, congressionally mandated weapon of trade policy in the past—have been superseded by other, more administratively defined devices: import quotas, variable levies, export subsidies, import equalization fees, border taxes, government procurement practices, and antidumping regulations. True, Congress created (and changes) these provisions. But in practical terms, trade policy is crafted by administrative agencies—the International Trade Commission (ITC), the Office of the U.S. Trade Representative (USTR), the Department of Commerce's International Trade Administration (ITA), and the Court of International Trade (CIT)—and not, as in the past, through massive tariff acts.

From this perspective NAFTA's passage might be seen as the triumph of the chattering classes, who through their command of the media defined the debate as one between constructively enlightened and destructively self-serving trade policies. The Gore-Perot confrontation during that debate emerges as a symbolic (and one-sided) clash between a cosmopolitan and a parochial political subculture, reminiscent of the Clarence Darrow–William Jennings Bryan confrontation in the Scopes trial.

Taken together, these explanations might seem to support the view that American politics and government, and the character of the trade issue, have been so transformed in recent decades that the historical perspective has little more than antiquarian interest. Certainly no one would deny that the vastly expanded administrative/regulatory capacities of the American government and the slackened hold of the major parties are major facts of contemporary public life. But it is important, as Pietro Nivola has observed, to keep in mind the degree to which the new regulatory bottle is filled with old wine. The rules and instrumentalities of trade-policy making may have changed. But the demands of particular interests—autos, steel, footwear, textiles, lumber—make themselves heard in the world of the escape clause and the ITC as much as they did in the world of the protective tariff and the Ways and Means Committee.[34]

Nivola does draw a distinction: "Unlike the tariff policies of an earlier era, our modern regulatory apparatus administers redress to an aggrieved constituency of victims." But is it a distinction with a difference? One statistical measure of the protectionism that creeps in under this altered mode of governance is that protectionist policies affected a tenth of the volume of imports in 1975, more than a fifth in 1985.[35]

Nor is it clear that Congress has been thoroughly subordinated to an autonomous bureaucracy or an imperial presidency (or judiciary), as is suggested by those who see a profound disjuncture between the American governmental past and present. The powers that be in our polity still are in balance, though the powers they exercise have greatly expanded. And if the parties are hardly what they were, ours is still overwhelmingly a two-party system; the rules of the Constitution see—and will see—to that. So the institutional preconditions for trade policy driven by particular interests are still with us.

Through mind-boggling economic, social, and cultural change, America's governmental and political structures have displayed quite stunning staying power. The passage of NAFTA is testimony to the prevailing belief in open trade—but that is reminiscent of nothing so much as the dominant protectionist mindset of the late nineteenth and early twentieth cen-

---

34 Pietro Nivola, *Regulating Unfair Trade* (Washington, D.C., 1993).
35 Nivola, *Regulating Unfair Trade*, xiii, 1.

turies. If the reigning paradigm should change—if this nation should see a new birth of xenophobia, or the world economy see a new birth of autarky—the political potential of go-it-alone is still very much in place.

Here the early twentieth-century experience is instructive. The flow of attitudes, policies, and interests during those years seemed at first to suggest that the era of particular-interest protectionism, red in tooth and claw, was coming to an end. But Fordney-McCumber and above all Smoot-Hawley made it clear how weak were the political and governmental underpinnings of "rational," expert-driven trade policymaking. It would be rash indeed to assume that a combination of economic crisis, xenophobic public opinion, and slack leadership could not once again unleash the dogs of (trade) war.

3

The Triumph of Liberal Trade: American Trade
Policy in the Postwar Period

DAVID VOGEL

The post–World War II period marks the longest sustained period of
steady, if uneven, trade liberalization in the history of the United States.
The Reciprocal Trade Agreements Act of 1934, along with the American
ratification of the General Agreement on Tariffs and Trade the following
decade, fundamentally transformed American trade policy and the way it
was made. The former reduced the role of Congress in setting tariff rates,
while the latter marked America's assumption of a leadership role in
promoting economic interdependence. These developments remain the
cornerstone of the liberal trade regime of the last half century. Notwithstanding the periodic difficulties experienced by the American economy in
general and important industries in particular over the last two decades,
American trade policy has exhibited a high degree of continuity. Since the
1940s, trade barriers have progressively declined, and the American market has become more open than that of other major industrial nations.
Although the pace of future trade liberalization is unclear, barring a major
economic crisis the United States is unlikely to return to the high-tariff
policy that characterized the nation's first 150 years.

A HISTORICAL PERSPECTIVE

During the United States' first 150 years, trade issues were among the
most visible and divisive issues in American national politics. On two
occasions during the first half of the nineteenth century trade policies led
to major challenges to the authority of the federal government. The
Hartford Convention was precipitated by President Jefferson's trade embargo against England and France, while South Carolina's attempt to
nullify a federal statute a generation later was provoked by the so-called

35

"Tariff of Abominations." The tariff played a central role in the fierce sectional conflicts that defined much of American national politics during this period and that climaxed in the Civil War. The South's rebellion, in part, reflected the magnitude of the differences between it and the rest of the country regarding tariffs on manufactured goods. Southern planters favored lower tariffs both because it made European manufactured goods less expensive and because it encouraged those nations to whom they exported their crops to keep their tariffs low as well.

During the next seventy-five years, a period when partisan rivalries were especially pronounced, the tariff became a highly partisan issue.[1] The Democratic party supported lower tariffs, reflecting both the historical preferences of its southern electoral base and its effort to increase its support in the farm states and the northeast by representing the interests of the "common man." Republican party platforms, in turn, reflected the protectionist preferences of northern industry. Through the 1930s, tariff rates divided the Democratic and Republican parties in Congress more than almost any other issue.[2] And the two parties' presidential candidates frequently offered sharply contrasting views on trade policy.[3]

Due to close linkages between partisan identification and views toward trade, the broad contours of American trade policy during this period closely reflected the shifting political fortunes of the Democratic and Republican parties. The protectionist Payne-Aldrich Act of 1909 was passed during the Taft administration, while the election of Woodrow Wilson in 1912 was followed by the lower-tariff Underwood Act of 1913. The Republican ascendancy of the next decade led to the Fordney-McCumber Act of 1922, followed by the even more protectionist Smoot-Hawley Tariff of 1931. Nonetheless, the post–Civil War trade regime was, on balance, highly protectionist. Few Democrats supported general tariff rates below 30 percent, and it was only when they exceeded 40 percent for particular commodities that Democrats challenged them.[4]

CONTEMPORARY TRADE POLICY AND POLITICS

Trade policy during the last half century has differed markedly. It has come to assume a much lower political profile, only intermittently oc-

1 Judith Goldstein, *Ideas, Interests and American Trade Policy* (Ithaca, N.Y.: Cornell University Press, 1993), 81–136.
2 Pietro S. Nivola, "The New Protectionism: U.S. Trade Policy in Historical Perspective," *Political Science Quarterly* 101, no. 4 (1986): 587.
3 Goldstein, *Ideas, Interests and American Trade Policy*, 94, 164–165.
4 Ibid., 92.

cupying a prominent place on the national political agenda. In fact, one could write an acceptable political history of the United States in the postwar period that all but ignored trade policy—a feat that would not have been possible during any previous period in American history. Public interest in American trade policy has been episodic rather than sustained, despite the fact that Congress has either debated or enacted trade legislation in virtually every legislative session since World War II.

The reduced salience of trade issues on the agenda of contemporary American politics in part reflects the substantial expansion of the size and scope of the national government since the Great Depression. Prior to the 1930s, the tariff was among the most important sources of federal revenue. Hence, tariff policy was an integral component of federal taxing and spending policies. As the income tax became a major source of government revenue in the 1930s and 1940s, trade policy lost its fiscal importance. Accordingly, debate over the size and purpose of the federal budget now proceeds with little reference to the tariff, and vice versa.

The lower political salience of American trade policy is also linked to its decline as a partisan issue. The Republican Party is no longer committed to protectionism, while the Democratic Party no longer consistently favors free trade. Both parties contain both proponents and opponents of trade liberalization. Congressional voting on trade policy now more closely reflects the economic interests of firms and their employees in each district and state than it does the partisan affiliation of representatives and senators.[5] No Democratic or Republican presidential nominee during the last half century has sought to sharply distinguish his views on trade policy from those of his opponent. Nor has trade policy figured prominently in the presidential or Congressional platforms of either party. While a number of presidential candidates have made challenges to liberal trade policies a central focus of their campaigns—John Connally in 1980, Richard Gephart in 1988, Ross Perot and Jerry Brown in 1992, and Pat Buchanan in 1992 and 1996—their candidacies have been unsuccessful. In sharp contrast to the half-century prior to World War II, voter preferences on trade policy have had no discernible effect on the outcome of recent congressional and presidential elections. Consequently, trade policy in the postwar period has not mirrored the shifting electoral fortunes of the Democratic and Republican Parties. Like foreign policy in general,

---

5 Roger Baldwin, "The Changing Nature of U.S. Trade Policy since World War II," in *The Structure and Evolution of Recent U.S. Trade Policy*, Robert Baldwin and Anne Krueger, eds. (Chicago: University of Chicago Press, 1984), 15.

it has more frequently reflected a bipartisan consensus. Thus, compared to the previous century, it has become depoliticized.

The declining electoral significance of trade policy is reflected in the debates surrounding congressional approval of both the North American Free Trade Agreement (NAFTA) and the Uruguay Round General Agreement on Tariffs and Trade (GATT). At first glance, the debate over NAFTA appears to mark a return to the pattern of trade policymaking prior to the New Deal: it was both highly visible and divisive and it took place within Congress. It also had a partisan dimension: congressional Democrats were more opposed to the agreement than were Republicans. Opponents of NAFTA, including Ross Perot and organized labor, vowed to make supporters of the trade agreement pay a price at the polls. In a parallel development, the anti-GATT Citizens Trade Campaign, composed primarily of public interest groups and organizations representing small farmers, sought to force candidates to take a public position on American approval of the Uruguay Round GATT agreement. But public preferences with respect to either NAFTA or the GATT played no role in the outcome of the 1994 midyear elections.[6] In fact, the Republican Party's 1994 congressional "platform," while radical and innovative in many policy areas, did not even mention trade policy.

The relative political importance of trade policy to business has also declined. Trade policy was a major focus of business pressure-group activity at the federal level between the Civil War and the Great Depression. Yet the contrast between the level of business lobbying described in E. E. Schattschneider's historic account of congressional debate over the tariff in 1929–30 and the virtual indifference of business to the Trade Expansion Act of 1962, documented in *American Business and Public Policy,* demonstrates that the tariff's political importance to American business has notably diminished.[7]

The amount of resources that business devoted to political activity did dramatically increase during the 1970s, but heightened business interest in trade policy played no role in this development. Rather, the increase in business political mobilization was primarily motivated by opposition to the expansion of government social regulation and the power of trade

6 Adam Murray, "Global Trade Fizzles as an Election Issue," *Wall Street Journal,* November 7, 1994, 1.
7 E. E. Schattschneider, *Politics, Pressure and the Tariff* (Englewood Cliffs, N.J.: Prentice-Hall, 1935); Raymond Bauer, Ithiel De Sola Pool, and Lewis Dexter, *American Business and Public Policy* (Chicago: Aldine Atherton, 1963).

unions.[8] During the 1980s and 1990s, far more corporate political resources were committed to influencing economic deregulation and tax policy than trade policy. Significantly, recent studies of business-government relations or of business political influence devote little or no attention to the politics of trade policy; other issues, most notably government regulation and taxation, loom far more important, both as a focus of business interest and as a measure of business influence.[9]

Liberal trade has also triumphed intellectually.[10] According to mainstream economic thinking, it was the unilateral imposition of substantially higher tariff rates by the United States in 1932 that turned what would have been a "normal" economic downturn into the Great Depression. While the casual connection between the two events has since been disputed by a number of economic historians, the relationship between a major unilateral increase in trade barriers by the United States and global political and economic chaos remains an important article of faith among policy makers and the economists who advise them. In this sense, the legacy of Smoot-Hawley persists.

When Joseph Wharton endowed the nation's first business school in 1881, he explicitly stipulated that one of the school's basic missions was to teach students about the importance of high tariffs on manufactured goods for American prosperity. Indeed, throughout the second half of the nineteenth century few persuasive arguments were advanced for a low-tariff policy: the case for free trade made by the English economist David Ricardo had little resonance on this side of the Atlantic. But it is hard to conceive of a similar stipulation being attached to a university endowment or any intellectually respectable research institution today.

This stands in marked contrast with American policy discourse a century ago, even though on virtually every dimension the world economy was then more integrated and interdependent than today. Between 1870 and 1913, there was a single world currency standard, uniform global interest rates, and substantial cross-border movements of goods, capital,

---

8 David Vogel, *Fluctuating Fortunes: The Political Power of Business in America* (Basic Books, 1989).

9 See, for example, Kim McQuaid, *Big Business and Presidential Power* (New York: William Morrow and Co., 1982): Sar Levitan and Martha Cooper, *Business Lobbies* (Baltimore, Md.: John Hopkins University Press, 1984); David Vogel, *Fluctuating Fortunes* (New York: Basic Books, 1989); Dan Clawson, Alan Neustadt, and Denise Scott, *Money Talks* (New York: Basic Books, 1992).

10 For the role of ideas in shaping American trade policy, see Goldstein, *Ideas, Interests, and American Trade Policy.*

and people. "The world was so tied together by trade and investment in the late nineteenth century that, despite the glorious years of growth in trade and GNP from 1950 to 1973, it took most countries nearly 70 years for merchandise trade as a proportion of their GNP to overtake the levels it had achieved in the years before the first world war."[11] Trade as a portion of global production totaled 33 percent in 1913; by contrast it amounted to only 15 percent in 1980. Yet, as Keller's essay suggests, informed opinion still considered America as somehow uniquely isolated from the rest of the world. Indeed, as recently as 1930, "the philosophy of autarky seemed firmly in the saddle."[12]

LIBERALIZATION THREATENED

Nonetheless, the story of American trade policy during the last three decades does read like the Perils of Pauline: America's commitment to trade liberalization invariably appears to be in mortal peril, yet somehow it survives, its virtue tarnished, but still intact.

Thus at the conclusion of the Kennedy Round in 1962, one commentator observed that "the lowering of tariffs has, in effect, been like draining a swamp. The lower water level has revealed all the snags and stumps of non-tariff barriers that still have to be cleared."[13] In 1985, the *New York Times* reported that "industry by industry, the battle to maintain open markets is being lost."[14] A year later, Pietro Nivola wrote that "upbeat descriptions [of the postwar liberalization of American international policy] appear increasingly inappropriate today, considering the extent to which orderly marketing agreements, voluntary export restraints, selective procurement, product standards, and buy America requirements, to name a few, have replaced the old tariffs."[15] He added, "the present atmosphere in Congress is one of virtually unanimous alarm about the widening trade gap and of bipartisan movement toward protective countermeasures."[16]

I. M. Destler's 1986 book on American trade policy began: "In the mid-1980s, American foreign trade policies came under unprecedented

11 "The Nation State," *Economist,* September 22, 1990, 45.
12 Bauer, Pool, and Dexter, 25.
13 Quoted in Nivola, "The New Protectionism," 596.
14 Quoted in I. M. Destler, *American Trade Politics: System under Stress* (Washington, D.C.: Institute for International Economics, 1986), xiii.
15 Nivola, "The New Protectionism" 577.
16 Ibid, 589.

pressure from embattled domestic industries."[17] He argued that "industries beset by import competition were hurting as never before; exporters were demoralized." Accordingly, "Congress found itself under enormous pressure to 'do something' about trade."[18] Three years later Jagdish Bhagwati suggested that "United States trade policy . . . may have taken a turn for the worse." He cited in particular "the weakened commitment of the United States to multilateralism."[19]

In 1992, Laura Tyson's appointment as chair of the President's Council of Economic Advisors was greeted with dismay by supporters of trade liberalization. In her recently published book, *Who's Bashing Whom?* Tyson had described herself as a "cautious activist."[20] She urged that "the nation's trade laws be used to deter or compensate for foreign practices that are not adequately regulated by existing multilateral rules."[21] The *Financial Times* worried that "one consequence of her views would be to give *carte blanche* to US politicians and lobbyists, who are itching to have a go at perfidious foreigners, particularly the Japanese . . . [The most important result] could well be still more trade friction as the US adopts a narrowly sectoral and bilateral focus."[22]

Two years later, William Lash III concluded that "the Clinton tango in trade policy is actually moving the country away from free trade and free markets." He wrote that "the administration has liberalized trade while simultaneously encumbering markets with new agencies, development banks and market-distorting moves."[23] Among the latter, Lash specifically noted the administration's support for linking trade liberalization with the strengthening of environmental regulation by America's trading partners.

Yet in each case these fears have proven to be exaggerated. Protectionist pressures have been episodic rather than sustained. America has continued to play a leadership role in creating and sustaining an increasingly open global economy.

---

17 I. M. Destler, *American Trade Politics*, xi.
18 Ibid.
19 Jagdish Bhagwati, "United States Trade Policy at the Crossroads," *World Economy* 12, no. 4 (December 1989): 439.
20 Laura D'Andrea Tyson, *Who's Bashing Whom? Trade Conflict in High-Technology Industries* (Washington, D.C.: Institute for International Economics, 1992), 9–14 and passim.
21 Ibid, 13.
22 Martin Wolf, "The View from Silicon Valley," *Financial Times*, January 28, 1993.
23 William Lash III, "The Clinton Trade Tango: One Step Forward, Two Steps Back," Contemporary Issue Series 64, Center for the Study of American Business, May 1994, 1.

THE POLITICS OF ECONOMIC DECLINE

Clearly, American trade policy could hardly help being affected by the significant erosion in the market share of a large number of domestic industries since the initial establishment of the postwar multilateral trade regime. The United States emerged from the Second World War with a more dominant economic position than any nation in the history of modern capitalism. Like Britain in the previous century, its support for trade liberalization reflected its economic hegemony.

During the 1960s, America's economic dominance began to erode. The United States' share of merchandise exports of the fifteen largest industrial nations declined from 25.2 percent in 1960 to 20.5 percent in 1970 and 18.3 percent in 1979. America's share of the combined GNP of these countries stood at 57.1 percent in 1960, but it had declined to 50.2 percent by 1970 and to 38.1 percent by the end of the 1970s.[24] Not surprisingly, the American Federation of Labor and Congress of Industrial Organizations (AFL-CIO), which had previously supported liberal trade policies, responded to the rise in imports of manufactured goods such as textiles, footwear, automobiles, steel, and electrical consumer goods during the late 1960s by supporting import quotas.

Between 1980 and 1982, the American economy experienced its most severe economic downturn since the Great Depression. For the first time since the end of World War II, the number of manufacturing jobs declined for three consecutive years. Imports, which traditionally fall during recessions, actually increased: while U.S. manufactured exports declined by 17.5 percent, imports grew by 8.3 percent. Steel imports represented 25 percent of domestic consumption, leading to a nearly 50 percent decline in domestic employment in this historically important industrial sector.[25]

During the remainder of the 1980s, while the American economy grew relatively rapidly, America's trade deficit grew more rapidly still. Buttressed by an overvalued dollar, imports of foreign goods increased by 24 percent between 1983 and 1984 and, by the middle of the decade, totaled more than 300 billion dollars. Meanwhile, exports either stagnated or declined. Consequently, the United States' current account balance, the broadest measure of the difference between U.S. imports and exports of goods, investments, and services, reached a deficit of ten billion dollars in 1984. (The last time the ratio of imports and exports had been as negative

24 Baldwin, "The Changing Nature of U.S. Trade Policy since World War II," 22.
25 Nivola, "The New Protectionism," 580–81.

was in 1864, in the midst of the Civil War.[26]) America's current account deficit peaked in 1987 at 160 billion dollars, but remained at 100 billion dollars or more for six years.

Throughout the 1980s, one country, Japan, accounted for a persistently large share of America's trade imbalance. Its percentage of America's total trade imbalance averaged nearly 40 percent between 1983 and 1989. Even as America's overall trade deficit declined from its 1987 peak, the absolute size of its trade imbalance with Japan remained stable. Many Americans associated this trade deficit with the loss of American high-wage jobs and feared that Japan was replacing the United States as the world's dominant economic power. Worse still, they claimed that Japan was somehow "cheating" as it gained market share in the United States while continuing to restrict American imports.

THE STRUCTURE OF TRADE POLICY

Each of these developments increased domestic support for trade restrictions. But in sharp contrast to the half century prior to the Second World War, when protectionist forces rarely encountered effective political opposition in Congress or from the executive branch, during the postwar period they have more often been frustrated. Congress continues to endorse the broad principle of tariff reductions: every trade agreement submitted to the Congress, from the Tokyo Round GATT agreement in 1962 through NAFTA in 1993 and the Uruguay Round GATT agreement in 1994, has been approved, usually by large margins. Moreover, all of these agreements have been approved under "fast-track" procedures. This prevents them from being amended either in committee or on the floor of Congress, and thus maintains the ability of the executive branch to shape and negotiate trade agreements.

Nonetheless, Congress has faced powerful pressures from protectionist interest groups. During the last two decades Congress has been flooded with literally hundreds of pieces of protectionist legislation. Yet only a small number have managed to win approval. For example, when in 1970 the House of Representatives approved legislation that mandated statutory quotas for textiles, footwear, and oil and made it easier for other industries to secure similar redress, the legislation was defeated by a Sen-

26 Destler, *American Trade Politics*, xi.

ate filibuster.[27] During the 1970s, domestic content legislation—which would have severely curtailed Japanese automobile imports—was twice passed by the House of Representatives, but each time failed to secure Senate approval. Congress also refused to approve the Burke-Hartke Bill, which would have frozen the 1967–69 ratio of imported goods to the production of "similar" domestic goods.[28] In 1985, both houses of Congress approved legislation to curtail severely textile and shoe imports, but the bill was vetoed by the president. The only industries that have benefited from direct legislative action during the last twenty-five years have been the fishing industry in 1976 and frozen concentrated orange juice producers in 1984.[29]

Although Congress has approved protection for only a handful of industries, it has repeatedly made it easier for a number of industries to seek protection from the executive branch. Between 1962 and 1986, Congress enacted trade legislation that permitted and, in some cases required, the executive branch to impose quotas or tariffs on foreign producers when imports "cause or threaten to cause substantial injury . . . threaten to impair national security . . . [or] . . . are priced below 'fair market values.' " Congress also expanded the scope of the administration's ability to respond to industry complaints by permitting the executive branch to impose trade restrictions when exports to the United States are unfairly subsidized or when other nations treat U.S. firms in an "unjustifiable, unreasonable or discriminatory fashion."[30]

These legislative provisions have acted as a political "escape valve." They have provided a way for politically powerful private interests to demand and sometimes receive either protection or assistance in securing access to foreign markets, without permitting the kind of logrolling among producers that occurred when tariff schedules were set by Congress. By establishing various administrative procedures for addressing complaints by business firms and displaced workers, Congress has managed to combine redress or assistance for particular sectors without undermining the overall commitment of the United States to trade liberaliza-

---

27 Victor A. Canto, "U.S. Trade Policy: History and Evidence," *Cato Journal* 3, no. 3 (Winter 1984): 683.
28 Ibid., 684.
29 Pietro Nivola, *Regulating Unfair Trade* (Washington, D.C.: Brookings Institution, 1993), 111.
30 1974 Free Trade Act, Section 301, quoted in "Section 301 Law Offers a Big Stick," *Washington Post*, September 22, 1985, F2.

tion.[31] Still, during the 1970s and early 1980s the United States imposed restrictions on imports of footwear, television sets, textiles and apparel, sugar, specialty steel, motorcycles, and automobiles.[32] All told, between 1974 and 1990 the International Trade Commission (ITC) granted some form of protection for fifty-two major (greater than $100 million) industries.[33] The number of imports subject to "special restrictions" increased from $0.6 billion in 1955 to $28.9 billion in 1980 and $67.1 billion in 1984.[34] If automobiles, which were subject to a "voluntary" import quota, are included, then during the 1980s approximately one-quarter of imports into the United States were subject to some form of protection.

But this retreat from trade liberalization must be placed in perspective. The executive branch has consistently given industries less assistance than they have requested. For example, more than half of industry petitions to the ITC have been rejected.[35] Accordingly, American tariff rates have continued to decline. Between 1962 and 1974, the average tariff rate stood at 10 percent; by 1991 it had been reduced to 5.2 percent.[36] The United States currently has the lowest average tariff rates in the world, averaging approximately 4.5 percent weighted by trade, excepting oil.[37] "The most obvious indicator of the limited impact of American trade barriers is that from 1980 to 1986, the growth in U.S. imports outstripped the growth of world imports seven to one . . . Clearly, American protectionism has not been as severe or damaging as some have claimed."[38] In addition, "the scope of today's defense against imports is narrower than the all-embracing tariff in effect a half-century ago."[39] Even the expanded use of nontariff barriers by the United States during the 1970s and 1980s had a limited effect on trade: both global and American trade have continued to expand more rapidly than domestic production.[40]

31 I. M. Destler, *American Trade Politics*, 12–15.
32 Nivola, *Regulating Unfair Trade*, 111.
33 Ibid.
34 Quoted in David Yoffie, "American Trade Policy: An Obsolete Bargain," in *Can the Government Govern?* John Chubb and Paul Paterson, eds. (Washington, D.C.: Brookings Institution, 1989), 116.
35 Baldwin, "The Changing Nature of U.S. Trade Policy since World War II," 19.
36 Goldstein, *Ideas, Interests, and American Trade Policy.*
37 Richard Steinberg, "The Uruguay Round: A Legal Analysis of the Final Act," A Berkeley Roundtable on the International Economy Working Paper, 1994, 8.
38 David Yoffie, "American Trade Policy," 117–8.
39 Nivola, "The New Protectionism," 577.
40 Helen Milner, *Resisting Protectionism: Global Industries and the Politics of International Trade* (Princeton, N.J.: Princeton University Press, 1988), 11.

The United States has also continued to take a leadership role in negotiating new trade agreements. These include, most recently, the Free Trade
Agreement (with Canada) in 1989, the North American Free Trade Agreement in 1993, and the Uruguay Round GATT agreement in 1994. While
the latter was more limited than many of its proponents had hoped—it
only gradually reduced trade restrictions on textiles and did not extend the
GATT to services—it reduced both tariff and nontariff barriers in both the
United States and the world as a whole. Thanks to the Uruguay Round,
worldwide tariffs will fall by approximately 40 percent, and the United
States will cut industrial tariffs by 34 percent.[41] This country has also lent
support for initiatives to create a free-trade zone in Asia and the Americas.

DIFFUSING TRADE CONFLICTS

Equally importantly, the United States has managed to prevent its periodic
quarrels with its various trading partners from seriously disrupting trade
with them. In spite of the persistent complaints from American firms
about their inability to gain access to the Japanese market, only in the case
of semiconductors has the United States insisted on a sector-specific agreement establishing a numerical measure of Japanese market openness.
America has restricted imports of a number of Japanese products, most
notably automobiles, steel, and motorcycles. But, given the high political
visibility of America's trade deficit with Japan and widespread criticism of
Japanese trade practices, what is striking is the weakness of American
pressures to force Japan to open up its markets.[42] The American economy
has remained relatively open to Japanese imports, even as the access of
American producers to Japan's has remained restricted.

The fears expressed by numerous commentators that the Clinton
administration would aggressively seek to pry open Japan's domestic
market to American goods and services, creating a trade war between
the world's two largest economies, have proven groundless. American-
Japanese trade negotiations have frequently been extremely tense and
often on the verge of collapse. But each time the Clinton administration—
like the Bush and Reagan administrations before it—has backed away
from imposing serious trade sanctions. U.S.–European Union (E.U.) trade
relations have also been frequently strained, and there have been an

41 Steinberg, "The Uruguay Round," 8.
42 See Clyde V. Prestowitz, Jr., *Trading Places: How We Allowed Japan to Take the Lead*
(New York: Basic Books, 1988).

endless series of "trade wars," mostly over agricultural products.[43] Nonetheless, both parties were able to complete the Uruguay Round negotiations, bringing agriculture—a highly protected and subsidized sector in both regions—within the scope of the newly established World Trade Organization.

The United States has periodically threatened to invoke the provisions of "super 301," which permit the President to restrict imports from an entire country, not just a particular industry, if that nation unfairly restricts American commerce. But such sanctions have never been applied. Since 1962, in response to pressures from environmentalists and some American producers, the United States has enacted thirteen statutes that authorize the unilateral use of trade sanctions to advance environmental or conservation goals.[44] But with the notable exception of a ban on imports of tuna from nations whose fishing practices violated American standards for dolphin protection, they have rarely been imposed.[45] The same pattern holds true for American threats to restrict imports from countries that mistreat or exploit workers.

Many observers feared that the end of America's political, military, and ideological conflict with the Soviet Union would threaten the future of liberal trade policies, since America had frequently kept its markets open to imports from nations whose support it needed for geopolitical reasons. But while the Cold War had helped keep America's markets open, its linkages between trade and national security also served to promote trade restrictions. The United States made frequent use of restrictions on trade as a weapon against the Soviet Union and other Communist nations, often in ways that antagonized its allies. American restrictions on trade with South Africa can also be viewed in this context.

The ending of the Cold War has severely curtailed the use of trade restrictions as a political weapon. The United States now permits trade with more nations than at any time since the 1930s. Restrictions on trade with China, Vietnam, the nations of central Europe, the republics of the former Soviet Union, and South Africa have all been lifted. Domestic political pressures to link trade policy to human rights, working conditions, or environmental protection, while important and persistent, have

---

43 David Vogel, *Barriers or Benefits; Regulation in Transatlantic Trade* (Washington, D.C.: Brookings Institution, 1998).

44 Elizabeth DeSombre, "Baptists and Bootleggers for the Environment," *Journal of Environment and Development* 4, no. 1 (Winter 1995): 56–59.

45 David Vogel, *Trading Up: Consumer and Environmental Regulation in a Global Economy* (Cambridge, Mass.: Harvard University Press, 1995), 125–28.

proven weaker than those that linked trade policy with national security during the Cold War.

EXPLAINING THE PERSISTENCE OF LIBERAL TRADE

How can we account for the persistence of the American commitment to trade liberalization even though America's position in the world economy is so radically different than it was in the 1940s and 1950s? Why have those interests in favor of more protectionist policies not been more influential? Or, to put this question in historical perspective, why did the serious economic distress experienced by the United States during the 1970s not lead to the kind of protectionist spiral that characterized the 1920s, even though the global position of the United States was nearly identical in both decades?[46]

Three factors have been critical: the role of international norms and institutions, the structure of domestic trade policymaking, and the preferences and power of American business. An important role has been played by the institutional and normative legacy of the postwar period.[47] In sharp contrast to the first third of the twentieth century, after its victory in the Second World War the United States took the lead in creating a wide network of international economic, military, and political treaties, agreements, and institutions. These arrangements were based on the assumption that international cooperation in a number of policy areas, including trade policy, was in the long-term interests both of the United States and the noncommunist world.

America's international economic position has changed significantly since the GATT's formation in the late 1940s. And its relationship to the GATT has frequently been a stormy one. But its membership in this institution has both reflected and reinforced its commitment to the norms and practices of international economic cooperation and trade liberalization. In this sense, America's continued participation in the GATT (now the World Trade Organization), like its support for regional initiatives to liberalize trade, such as the European Community, the Caribbean Basin Initiative, and NAFTA, reflects national values as well as interests.

America's continued commitment to trade liberalization has also been

---

46 Milner, *Resisting Protectionism*, 7.
47 John Ruggie, "International Regimes, Transactions, and Change: Embedded Liberalism in the Postwar Economic Order," in *International Regimes*, Stephen Krasner, ed. (Ithaca, N.Y.: Cornell University Press, 1983).

sustained by the institutional changes in the way trade policy is made. Protectionist pressures in Congress have been diffused by strengthening the role of the executive branch both in negotiating trade agreements and in responding to pressures from industries for assistance. Without these two complementary developments, liberal trade policies would be far more politically threatened.

The third factor has been a significant change in the preferences of important segments of American business. The most important political actors affecting American trade policies have been, and remain, business firms. The protectionist policies of the late nineteenth century reflected the preferences of politically influential American manufacturers, who were for the most part uncompetitive, especially vis-à-vis British firms. Many American industries did become more competitive during the first third of the twentieth century, when America emerged as the world's largest industrial economy. But if much of heavy industry no longer needed high tariffs, neither did it have any incentive to reduce them, as their market orientation remained primarily domestic. The Smoot-Hawley Tariff led to retaliation by twenty-five nations and reduced American exports by two-thirds in two years. But its domestic impact was modest because American exports were so small to begin with.

The contrast with the participation of American firms in the global economy in the postwar period is marked. Even as the relative size of the American economy has declined, American exports have grown in relative importance. U.S. exports as a percentage of Gross Domestic Product stood at only 4 percent in 1959; by the early 1990s they had increased to 11 percent. During the 1980s, one-third of American farm production and nearly 20 percent of domestic manufacturing output was exported.

A significant portion of American businesses are highly competitive globally. These include firms in the rapidly growing service sector—which now constitutes 70 percent of the American economy and includes financial services, construction, entertainment, transportation, communications, insurance, software, and telecommunications—as well as a number of high-technology manufacturers and, as in the past, much of American agriculture. For these firms, an increase in American trade barriers would be extremely costly, since it would make their access to foreign markets vulnerable to retaliation by other countries. These firms have formed the political backbone of domestic support for trade liberalization.

The growth of American investment overseas constitutes another critical difference between the political economy of the pre- and postwar periods. While only 2.6 percent of the assets of American firms were held overseas in 1922, by the 1970s this figure had grown to 20 percent.[48] During the 1980s, one-third of American exports were bought by American-owned companies abroad while the subsidiaries of American-based multinational firms accounted for a fifth of total American imports.[49] Clearly, these large and politically influential firms have a major stake in the continued openness of the American economy, since trade barriers interfere with their ability to manage their international operations.

Another important postwar development has been the growth of foreign direct investment in the United States. (While foreign capital was much more important during the nineteenth century, it primarily took the form of portfolio investment.)[50] Foreign-owned firms now control 9 percent of domestic assets and employ 4 percent of the labor force, including 10 percent of workers employed in manufacturing; they account for 10 percent of domestic sales. Equally significantly, they are responsible for about one-third of American imports.[51] These firms and their employees constitute another important political constituency for maintaining trade liberalization, one that did not exist before the Second World War. In addition, many domestic manufacturers are dependent on components produced by foreign suppliers. And of course many domestic retailers, most notably automobile dealers, have a strong economic interest in liberal trade policies.

In short, the oft-cited confusion over "who is us?" has not only made the task of organizing a protectionist business coalition more difficult, but has also created a set of powerful business interests that oppose the classical protectionist position and favor strategic trade policies and market opening measures.[52] The growth of economic interdependence has also made it more difficult to restrict imports without also injuring firms and workers in America.

In part for this reason, many recent American trade initiatives have been directed less at protecting domestic producers than in seeking to open up foreign markets to American exports of goods, services, and

48 Ibid, 27.
49 "The Myth of Economic Sovereignty," *Economist,* June 23, 1990, 67.
50 See Robert Gilpin, *U.S. Power and the Multinational Corporation* (New York: Basic Books, 1975).
51 "The Myth of Economic Sovereignty"; see also Robert Reich, "Who Is Us?" *Harvard Business Review* (January/February, 1990): 55.
52 See Reich, "Who Is Us?" 53–64.

agricultural products. Indeed, for many American companies the best strategy for protecting their domestic markets is to liberalize foreign ones. Consequently, a major source of trade friction between the United States and its trading partners has been American efforts to use the threat of retaliation against imports to demand a more open market for American exports.[53]

These efforts, of course, can be highly disruptive of world trade.[54] They can easily degenerate into neomercantilist disputes over "mutual" market access. But it is important not to confuse "strategic trade policy" or "managed trade" with traditional protectionism. There is an important difference between attempting to use the power of the American government to demand that other countries reduce their trade barriers and in pressuring one's own government to restrict imports. While both may violate the orthodoxy of liberal trade, the former reflects economic strength; the latter, economic weakness. The former represents an embrace of international competition; the latter, a retreat from it.

Changes in the American economy have also weakened the effectiveness of labor opposition to free trade. While the AFL-CIO strongly supported the Kennedy administration's Trade Expansion Act, more recently, "organized labor has become a driving force in a wide assortment of anti-import campaigns."[55] Yet its efforts have had only limited success, in part because, unlike in the nineteenth century, the interests of American manufacturing firms and their employees are no longer identical. The political strength of American unions has also steadily diminished during the last two decades, thus further weakening the strength of proprotectionist political forces in Congress.

When placed in a historical context, what is especially important is the geographic dispersion of globally oriented firms. During the nineteenth century, both protectionist and export-oriented producers tended to be geographically concentrated. Hence trade policies and partisan politics were tightly linked. But this is no longer the case: even those states with significant concentrations of producers and employees who favor trade restrictions—such as the textile-producing states in the south or manufacturing firms in the northeast and the industrial heartland—now also contain large numbers of firms who have a stake in either keeping the Ameri-

---

53 See David Yoffie and Helen Milner, "Why Corporations Seek Strategic Trade Policy," *California Management Review* (Summer 1989): 113–31.
54 See Marc Levinson, "Kantor's Cant," *Foreign Affairs* (March/April 1996): 2–7.
55 Nivola, "The New Protectionism," 583.

can economy open or increasing access to foreign markets, or both. In sharp contrast to the past, the politics of trade policy no longer divide along geographical or regional lines. All but a handful of senators and representatives are now exposed to pressures from business interests who stand to benefit from more liberal trade policies.

The geographic diffusion of business supporters of open markets also helps account for the relative decline in partisan conflict over trade policy. As both the extent of Democratic opposition to NAFTA in 1993–95 and Republican support for the Buchanan candidacy in 1996 illustrate, each party contains vocal constituencies who are opposed to trade liberalization. They have blamed the growth of international trade for reducing the number of high-wage jobs, increasing economic insecurity, exacerbating economic inequality, threatening American living standards, and undermining strict health, safety, and environmental standards.[56] Within the Democratic Party, trade unions have emerged as a major focus of opposition to further trade liberalization, leading the successful opposition to fast-track renewal in the fall of 1997.

But both parties also include a number of important business constituencies who are strongly opposed to increasing trade barriers. And the latter are sufficiently powerful in both parties to resist populist pressures that would result in a significant shift in the broad postwar direction of American trade policies. Significantly, Ross Perot, the most prominent contemporary political proponent of protectionism who led the opposition to NAFTA, has operated outside the two-party system. In short, due to the shift of the locus of trade policy to the executive branch, the geographic dispersion of the "winners" and "losers" of trade policy, and the political strength of globally oriented producers, the role of the contemporary American party system as a vehicle for promoting protectionist policies has been reduced.

This does not mean that we can expect a continued reduction in trade barriers. In fact, progress toward further trade liberalization may well prove difficult. Cutting tariffs on manufactured goods, which has been the historic focus of trade policy for the last two centuries, is relatively straightforward, if often politically painful. But reducing barriers to trade in services, which now constitutes approximately one-quarter of world trade, is much more complex. Negotiations to liberalize trade in such sectors as telecommunications and financial services, as well as the reduc-

56 Gary Burtless, "Worsening American Inequality," *Brookings Review* (Spring 1996): 26–31.

tion of national restrictions on foreign investment, are likely to be protracted.

Moreover, a significant proportion of trade barriers in the United States and other countries are nontariff ones, ranging from government procurement policies to product standards and environmental regulations.[57] Reducing them will require nations to coordinate more closely a wide variety of politically sensitive national and regional public policies. Many of these efforts to reduce national regulatory autonomy are likely to prove highly controversial, especially if they are viewed as undermining politically popular health, safety, and environmental regulation. In addition, to the extent that American trade negotiators demand "reciprocity" as a condition for future trade liberalization, the scope of future American trade reductions will be significantly affected by the preferences and priorities of other countries. Finally, the growth of public concern about the impact of economic globalization on domestic wages, employment security, and environmental quality is also likely to slow the pace of future trade liberalization.

Nonetheless, it took the Depression and American participation in the Second World War to reverse a century of protectionism. It would take a series of domestic and international events of similar magnitude to reverse the liberal trade policies of the last half century.

---

57 See, e.g., Vogel, *Trading Up: Consumer and Environmental Regulation in a Global Economy* and Alan Sykes, *Product Standards for Internationally Integrated Goods Markets* (Washington, D.C.: Brookings Institution), 1995.

II

Immigrants and Aliens

4

The Progressive State and the Legacy of
Collective Immigrant Identities

REED UEDA

In the Progressive era, public policies to control immigration were designed to reflect concepts of collective ethnic identity. The American system of immigration and nationality established in the early 1920s hinged
on the classification of immigrants in a hierarchy of group types, each
with distinctive and fixed characteristics. Lawmakers and bureaucrats
who constructed the official identity of each immigrant group in public
policy were influenced by a grid of preconceived dualisms for evaluating
and defining collective identity: binary oppositions between assimilable
and perdurable cultures, the Nordic and the non-Nordic races, Americanism and foreign heritage, and Western and non-Western civilizations.

The ethnocultural dualisms that informed Progressive immigration
policy lacked the capacity to represent the dynamic and mutable character
of immigrant communities. Instead, these dichotomies turned the variegated parts of the complex immigrant pattern into absolute values that
became "unavailable" to each other. The application of these overaggre-
gated abstractions made the relations of group life less free, voluntary,
open, and democratic. Anglo-Saxon restrictionists asserted that their history, culture, and identity were unavailable to the new immigrants from
southern and eastern Europe and Asia, in a way that prevented the successful assimilation of these new arrivals.

Official ethnic categories were useful instruments in the hands of restrictionists. Applying these in legislation, restrictionists established the
first public policy keyed to proportional representation according to ethnoracial identity, a system of quotas based on group preference for northern and western Europeans, group discrimination against southern and
eastern Europeans, and the total exclusion of Asians. By officially nor-
malizing ethnoracial identities, Progressive-era immigration policy adum-

57

brated public policies based on ethnoracial categorization and preferences that would develop in the late twentieth century.

Juxtaposed against admissions controls keyed to group categorization and preference, however, were another set of Progressive-era public policies that pointed toward incorporation according to nonethnic principles. Federal lawmakers established categories of immigrant admissions based on nonethnic factors of familial relationship and occupation that were prototypes for selective admissions under the worldwide system of immigration controls administered after 1965. In addition, Progressive reformers created programs to assimilate immigrants and their children that built a strong consciousness of national identity and citizenship. By supporting Americanization through education and naturalization, social reformers expressed a belief in the practical possibilities for civic acculturation irrespective of ethnoracial background.

THE CHANGING RELATION BETWEEN IMMIGRATION AND THE STATE

African Americans and American Indians had been classed as racial categories in public policies since the founding of the United States, but in the Progressive era, immigrants were subjected for the first time to systematic ethnoracial categorization. In the national debate over admissions and naturalization procedures, federal lawmakers constructed new classifications of collective ethnic identity for immigrant groups and gave them official validation.

In the face of the greatest wave of mass immigration in the nation's history, nativists searched for admissions policies to stabilize the lines of nationality. They sought to constrict and protect the boundaries of the Anglo-Saxon core group by establishing entry criteria based on ratings of group assimilability. Nativists grew increasingly interested in the possibilities offered for control of nationality through the admission of "assimilable" immigrants and the exclusion of the "unassimilable," who would be identified by official classification.[1]

The legal foundation for the innovations in immigration policy of the Progressive era was laid by an 1875 U.S. Supreme Court decision. The case of *Henderson v. Mayor of New York* invalidated the historic immigration controls of individual state governments as an infringement on the

---

1 Quote from testimony by Representative John J. McSwain, Sixty-Eighth Congress, House, First Session, *Congressional Record—House*, April 5, 1924, Part 3, 5685.

federal power over commerce. The constitutional pathway was thereby cleared for a federal regulatory apparatus. In 1882, Congress passed the Chinese Exclusion Act, which prohibited the immigration of Chinese laborers, setting a precedent for restricted admissions based on nationality. It was not until 1891, however, that Congress passed a law instituting full-scale federal administrative supervision over immigration. This act provided that a superintendent of immigration be appointed in the Treasury Department. In 1895, Congress established the office of Commissioner-General of Immigration to oversee the Bureau of Immigration under the Secretary of the Treasury.[2]

The bureaucratic framework for federal management of immigration was thus installed and in the subsequent years it became a permanent fixture of the executive branch. Congress transferred the Bureau of Immigration to the newly created Department of Commerce and Labor in 1903. The Immigration Act of 1906 enlarged the Bureau of Immigration into the Bureau of Immigration and Naturalization. In 1913, Congress moved this office to the Department of Labor and subdivided it into a Bureau of Immigration and Bureau of Naturalization, each headed by its own commissioner. The federal authority over immigration and naturalization would reside there until 1940, when it was moved to the Immigration and Naturalization Service under the Department of Justice.[3]

Congress established a federal regulatory bureaucracy to administer a set of standards for immigrant admissions that was constructed in an ad hoc fashion. These criteria evolved according to changing public opinion about who could be assimilated into the host society and who should be excluded as difficult to assimilate or dangerous to the nation's welfare and security. Federal legislators found that this basis for regulating admissions warranted the exclusion of criminal, immoral, or diseased classes of applicants in 1891, political subversives in 1903, and illiterates in 1917.[4]

The discussions in Congress on admissions legislation in the half century after Reconstruction evolved into an ongoing public discourse on the character of ethnicity and the role of pluralism in industrial society.

2 *Henderson v. Mayor of New York* (92 U.S. 259); Chinese Exclusion Act of May 6, 1882 (22 Stat. 58); Immigration Act of March 3, 1891 (32 Stat. 825); Immigration Act of February 14, 1903 (32 Stat. 825).
3 Immigration Act of February 14, 1903 (32 Stat. 1213); Immigration Act of June 29, 1906 (34 Stat. 596); Immigration Act of March 4, 1913 (37 Stat. 737); Immigration Act of June 14, 1940 (54 Stat. 230).
4 Immigration Act of March 3, 1891 (26 Stat. 1084); Immigration Act of March 3, 1903 (32 Stat. 1213); Immigration Act of February 5, 1917 (39 Stat. 874).

Through these debates a set of labels for the collective ethnic identities of immigrants was officially recognized. Federal bureaucrats and expert consultants designed a scheme for classifying immigrants according to ethnic groupings. Lawmakers employed these as a guide to patterns of assimilability. Beginning in the 1890s, the Bureau of Immigration provided a specific listing of immigrant "races or peoples" to be enumerated in its annual statistical reports, a more precise determination of the ethnic character of immigrants than country of birth.[5]

Federal immigration officials and lawmakers rated as particularly problematic two general categories of newcomers. The first was composed of immigrants from southern and eastern Europe and the Near East, the so-called new immigrants, who formed the largest and most expansive wave after 1890. The Italians, Jews, Slavs, Greeks, Armenians, and Lebanese, who began to outnumber arrivals from northern and western Europe, were seen as a culturally and racially alien element who posed unprecedented problems of assimilation. The second problematic category consisted of immigrants from east Asia and south Asia—Chinese, Japanese, Koreans, Indians, and Filipinos. They were a tiny fraction of total immigration from 1850 to 1920, less than 2 percent. But Asian immigration was localized in the far west in such a way as to arouse powerful anti-Asian nativistic movements. Furthermore, as a racially and culturally distant non-European populace they were subjected to special restrictive treatment. As such, they were important beyond their numbers in the development of immigration and naturalization policy and in the conception of membership in the American nation.

Public policies rested on the assumption that these groups, like the Irish Catholic immigrants before the Civil War, existed apart from other Americans. Their ethnic ancestry submerged their identity based on individual behavior and achievement. In contrast, lawmakers regarded immigrants from northern and western Europe as capable of blending into an American society rooted in an Anglo-Saxon individualist political culture. Collective ethnic categorization was a convenient way for policymakers to perceive the unfamiliar new foreigners during a time of rapidly shifting social and cultural boundaries, the high tide of industrialization.[6]

---

5 See the ethnic labels used for statistical tabulation in U.S. Commissioner-General of Immigration, *Annual Reports* (Washington, D.C.: U.S. Government Printing Office, 1899); Oscar Handlin, *Race and Nationality in American Life* (Boston: Little, Brown, 1957), 83–86.
6 Samuel P. Hays, *The Response to Industrialism, 1885–1914* (Chicago: University of

Educated elites became receptive to the premise that predetermined ethnic factors governed human behavior in a way that set people apart. The school of social thought influenced by the English philosopher Herbert Spencer provided theoretical support for this understanding of group life. Its members were inaccurately labeled "social Darwinists"; their Spencerian views more appropriately made them "social Spencerists." William Graham Sumner and other followers of Spencer were convinced that human behavior was governed by inexorable cultural and biological forces. These scholars argued that social institutions and political behavior derived from an inertial structure of customs and mores. Culture was a prior formation that made law and government subordinate.[7]

Influential social scientists expounded a monolithic and abstract view of the culture of collective groups. They dwelt on the perdurably retrograde character of particular ancestral cultures. Henry Adams observed in his famous autobiography: "The Russian people could never have changed—could they ever be changed? Could inertia of race, on such a scale, be broken up, or take new form? Even in America, on an infinitely smaller scale, the question was old and unanswered. All the so-called primitive races, and some nearer survivals, had raised doubts which persisted against the most obstinate convictions of evolution."[8] The eminent geologist Nathaniel Shaler surveyed the European peasantry and decided that "the inheritances of a thousand years or more" in the Old World could not be counteracted by American influences: "The truth is that a man is what his ancestral experience has made him."[9] Henry Cabot Lodge believed that when it came to Slavs, Jews, and Italians, it was well to question "the theory that opportunity was equivalent to capacity."[10] He denied "that a people . . . to whom freedom and self-government were

Chicago Press, 1967), chaps. 2, 4, 5; Robert Wiebe, *The Search for Order, 1877–1920* (New York: Hill and Wang, 1967), chap. 2; John Higham, "The Reorientation of American Culture in the 1890s," in John Higham, *Writing American History: Essays on Modern Scholarship* (Bloomington: Indiana University Press, 1970), 73–102.

7 Morton White, "Prologue: Coherence and Correspondence in American Thought," in Arthur M. Schlesinger, Jr. and Morton White, *Paths of American Thought* (Boston: Houghton Mifflin, 1963), 5; Donald Fleming, "Social Darwinism," in Schlesinger and White, *Paths of American Thought*, 123–130; Herbert Spencer, *The Principles of Sociology*, vol. 2 (New York: D. Appleton and Co., 1899), 3–14; William Graham Sumner, *Folkways: A Study of the Sociological Importance of Usages, Manners, Customs, Mores, and Morals* (Boston: Ginn and Co., 1911; 1906), 53–57.

8 Henry Adams, *The Education of Henry Adams* (Boston: Houghton, Mifflin, 1918), 409.

9 Barbara Miller Solomon, *Ancestors and Immigrants: A Changing New England Tradition* (Cambridge, Mass.: Harvard University Press, 1956), 93.

10 Ibid., 115.

unknown could carry on successfully the complex machinery of constitutional and representative government." Prescott F. Hall, a founder of the Immigration Restriction League, summed up the dolorous situation. The immigration issue, he explained, was whether Americans wanted their country "to be peopled by British, German and Scandinavian stock, historically free, energetic and progressive, or by Slav, Latin and Asiatic races, historically down-trodden, atavistic, and stagnant."[11] Ellwood P. Cubberley, the leading historian of American education, lamented in 1909 that the newcomers from southern and eastern Europe were "illiterate, docile, often lacking in initiative, and almost wholly without the Anglo-Saxon conceptions of righteousness, liberty, law, order, public decency, and government."[12]

The most radical views of collective culture surfaced in the treatment of Asian immigrants. The conception of culturally archaic and unassimilable Asians sprang from the nativist reaction to the coming of Chinese immigrants. Nativists deplored the Chinese as fixed in orientation toward an ancient, despotic past, looking backward to kinsmen, village, headman, and emperor. These critics complained that the Chinese could not learn the "sanctity of an oath," and thus could not adapt to an American citizenship that depended on ideological allegiance.

Californians presented a petition to Congress in 1876 assailing the unchanging and stagnant culture of the Chinese. It alleged that because the Chinese were "impregnable" to "all the influences of Anglo-Saxon life," they "remain the same stolid Asiatics that have floated on the rivers and slaved in the fields of China for thirty centuries of time."[13] The petition noted that the unyielding servility and despotism of the Chinese derived from "the unalterable structure of their intellectual being." A special joint committee of Congress reported on the Chinese in 1876 "that they did not assimilate with the whites, and never could become an integral and homogeneous part of the population."[14]

During a debate over legislation to control immigration from China, Senator John Sherman averred that the Chinese were so completely and permanently alien that they could never be incorporated into the Ameri-

---

11 Ibid., 111.
12 Quote by Cubberley cited by David B. Tyack, *The One Best System: A History of American Urban Education* (Cambridge, Mass.: Harvard University Press, 1974), 132, from Ellwood P. Cubberley, *Changing Conceptions of Education* (Boston: Houghton Mifflin, 1909), 15.
13 Mary Roberts Coolidge, *Chinese Immigration* (New York: Henry Holt, 1909), 83.
14 Roy L. Garis, *Immigration Restriction: A Study of the Opposition to and Regulation of Immigration into the United States* (New York: Macmillan, 1927), 291.

can nation: "I am inclined to think . . . that the admission of a foreign race, so entirely inconsistent with ours, so different from ours in modes and habits of thought, a people that are entirely of a distinct race kind, quality and religion so different in everything from us [ought] not to be allowed to the extent of our trying to absorb that population with the other elements we have got already, some of which are bad enough."[15] American nativists who could not see beyond the alien appearances of the Chinese newcomers surrendered to the fatalistic belief that they were uniquely unadaptable to a modern democratic culture.[16]

When the perception of a permanently alien Chinese culture was coupled to the economic argument that they represented a threat to American workers, the presence of the Chinese became an incendiary matter posing great public danger. Senator Henry Teller of Colorado announced the need "to protect the American citizen and the American laborer against what is the more than pauperized labor of Asia."[17] Teller and other opponents of the Chinese charged that they had a degraded living and working standard. "By many hundreds of years of training and of discipline," pointed out Teller, " 'the survival of the fittest' being applied to them, they are a people who, starved for centuries, can live upon that which every American citizen would go to the grave upon; they can live upon less food and with less clothing; they have neither houses nor homes, nor families."[18] This way of life could become the norm for native Americans, if the Chinese masses flooded the labor market. Teller charged that the settler generation of Chinese communities lacked the social, cultural, and behavioral prerequisites to be acceptable to native Americans as fellow workers and fellow citizens. Perceived as dehumanized labor and servants of foreign despotism, these Asians could not be granted a place in the social and political life of American democracy. Indeed they were regarded as an obstacle to nation-building.[19]

Some influential nativist thinkers similarly concluded that the assimilation of the "new immigrants" into the national culture was not possible.

15 Forty-Ninth Congress, First Session, *Congressional Record—Senate*, May 26, 1886, 4958–59.
16 Milton R. Konvitz, *The Alien and the Asiatic in American Law* (Ithaca, N.Y.: Cornell University Press, 1946), 5–6, 8; *Chew Heong v. United States* (112 U.S. 536; 1884).
17 Forty-Ninth Congress, First Session, *Congressional Record—Senate*, May 26, 1886, 4961–62.
18 Ibid.
19 Charles A. Price, *The Great White Walls Are Built: Restrictive Immigration to North America and Australasia, 1836–1888* (Canberra: Australian National University Press, 1974), 257, 269–70.

The anthropologist Madison Grant derided the naive environmentalism of those who believed that the country could absorb them. "With a pathetic and fatuous belief in the efficacy of American institutions and environment to reverse or obliterate immemorial hereditary tendencies," Grant observed, "these newcomers were welcomed and given a share in our land and prosperity." The optimists failed to see that the new immigrants were a permanently degraded element.[20]

Another scholar, Jacob Gould Schurman of Columbia University, who was also cited in congressional debates over limiting immigration through discriminatory national-origins quotas, explained clearly how the new immigrants introduced balkanization into American life:

The public has awakened from the delusion created by the shibboleth of the "melting pot." It is disquieted and disturbed by the spectacle of immense alien communities . . . more or less self-contained speaking many foreign languages, containing an influential foreign-language press, with their own banks, markets, and insurance companies and sometimes with separate schools—unleavened lumps of many European nationalities, unchanged masses of foreigners intrenched in America, yet not of it, owing in many cases foreign allegiance, and, in general, tied to foreign countries by their language, their sympathies, their culture, their interests, and their aspirations.[21]

The crusade for restriction attracted a diverse constituency. Social reformers, including many academics and progressives, who worried that immigration increased social disorder and national decline, favored restriction. Fearing foreign cultural and racial influences, southern and western xenophobes supported both Asian exclusion and restrictive quotas against the new immigrants from southern and eastern Europe. The American Federation of Labor urged restriction on the ground that the flow of immigration obstructed the organization of unions and undercut working conditions and wages.

The forces in favor of maintaining immigration were also varied. They included the growing ranks of naturalized immigrants and their adult descendants and spokesmen for immigrant associations. Progressive assimilationists and internationalists such as Jane Addams, Randolph Bourne, Woodrow Wilson, and Theodore Roosevelt advocated immigra-

20 Madison Grant, *The Passing of the Great Race: Or The Racial Basis of European History* (New York: Charles Scribner's and Sons, 1916), 89–90.
21 Quote from testimony by Representative John J. McSwain, Sixty-Eighth Congress, House, First Session, *Congressional Record—House*, April 5, 1924, Part 3, 5685.

tion by citing its cultural contributions and benefits. Corporate interests seeking cheap labor lobbied against exclusions and restrictions.[22]

The opposed coalitions of proimmigration and restrictionist partisans cut across the Democratic and Republican political parties. The forces of restriction were never able to gain enough power in Congress to pass a radically restrictive measure until after World War I. Congressional majorities seeking to enact a literacy-test act to limit immigration were thwarted by vetoes by presidents Grover Cleveland, William Howard Taft, and Woodrow Wilson. The drive for Americanization and national unity generated in the wake of World War I tipped the balance in favor of the forces advocating restriction. They vanquished the supporters of open immigration with claims that the need for racial and cultural consolidation made intolerable the difficulties of assimilating non-Protestant and non-Nordic newcomers. John Higham concluded that the war years "virtually swept from the American consciousness the old belief in unrestricted immigration . . . by creating an urgent demand for national unity and homogeneity that practically destroyed what the travail of preceding decades had already fatally weakened: the historic confidence in the capacity of American society to assimilate all men automatically."[23]

By the early 1920s large majorities among both Democrats and Republicans in Congress agreed that continuing immigration would bring people who could not be assimilated. Support for restriction was sectionally balanced to an impressive degree. In his analysis of the "sweeping majorities" in the House and Senate that passed the Second Quota Act of 1924, the historian Robert A. Divine concluded that "the legislation met with the approval of all elements in the United States except minority groups from southeastern Europe." Only 71 out of 323 Representatives and 6 out of 62 Senators voted against the bill. Most of the opponents in the House came from urban areas where the new immigrants were concentrated.[24]

Citing expert assessments of what were now widely viewed as fixed national and ethnic subcultures, Congress installed in the 1920s the first

---

22 Aristide R. Zolberg, "Reforming the Back Door: The Immigration Reform and Control Act of 1986 in Historical Perspective," in Virginia Yans-McLaughlin, *Immigration Reconsidered: History, Sociology, and Politics* (New York: Oxford University Press, 1990).
23 Higham, *Strangers in the Land*, 301.
24 Thomas Muller, *Immigrants and the American City* (New York: New York University Press, 1993), 36–47; Higham, *Strangers in the Land*, 301–324; Robert A. Divine, *American Immigration Policy, 1924–1952* (New Haven, Conn.: Yale University Press, 1957), 17.

program of group preference in regulatory public policy. Federal law-makers attempted to control admissions in such a way as to shape the ethnic structure of the American population. They completed the total exclusion of immigrants from Asia that had begun with the Chinese Exclusion Act of 1882 and the Gentlemen's Agreement with Japan in 1907–08. Legislators prohibited laborers from the Asiatic Barred Zone in 1917 and in 1924 excluded all Asian immigrants as "aliens ineligible for citizenship." The immigration acts of 1921 and 1924, the first and second Quota Acts, installed a system of annual quotas for immigrants from Europe. These were calibrated to reinforce the ethnic ratios in the population that favored the dominance of the Anglo-Saxon core. They provided Great Britain and countries of northern and western Europe with much larger quotas than those received by nations in southern and eastern Europe.[25]

These quotas mirrored the proportions of the foreign-born nationalities recorded first in the federal census of 1910 (as mandated in the 1921 act) and then in the census of 1890 (as mandated in the 1924 act). Congress included in the 1924 law a provision for a new quota program based on an assessment of total ethnic representation in the population. Congress appointed a Quota Board, whose charge was statistically to estimate the "National Origins" of the American population as of 1790. The country's population was broken down into collective ethnic ancestry groups—for example, all persons of German descent or all persons of Italian descent. Once established, these ethnic shares of the American population set the percentage of admissions visas that were assigned annually to each country sending immigrants.[26]

The new admissions program pivoted on a more ambitious conception of the possibilities for establishing collective identities. The resulting National Origins quota system employed from 1929 to 1965 was based on several interlocked assumptions: fixed ethnic categories existed in the population; distinctive collective qualities marked these ethnic categories; it was possible to determine the demographic size of these categories and to map their distribution as proportional shares in the population; and quotas allocating opportunities or representation should be

25 Chinese Exclusion Act of May 6, 1882 (22 Stat. 58); Quota Law of May 19, 1921 (42 Stat. 5); Immigration Act of May 26, 1924 (43 Stat. 153).
26 Robert A. Divine, *American Immigration Policy, 1924–1952* (New Haven, Conn.: Yale University Press, 1957), 28; William S. Bernard, ed., *American Immigration Policy* (New York: Harper and Brothers, 1950), 26–31.

assigned to ethnic categories according to their numerical proportion in the population.

The casting of admissions policies in the mold of a quota system heightened tensions between immigrant minorities. It triggered a round of competition and rivalry by ethnic pressure groups for their claimed shares. In particular, representatives of German, Scandinavian, and Irish constituencies alleged that the National Origins system, based as it was on the 1790 distribution of nationality groups, produced an unfair apportionment of quotas. The German-American Citizens League, the Danish Brotherhood of America, the Sons of Norway, the [Swedish] Vasa Order of America, and the representatives of Irish American organizations complained that the National Origins system estimates of the proportion of German, Scandinavian, and Irish ethnic populations in the United States would decrease the annual quotas of their home countries and enlarge the visa quota for Great Britain. The Irish and German critics of the National Origins quota plan alleged that it was the creation of Anglo-chauvinists and warned that its adoption would produce the "Anglicization of these United States . . . at a feverish pace." A congressman from Massachusetts with a large constituency of Irish Americans feared that the new quota system would be racially divisive rather than producing the national unity its supporters sought. German, Irish, and Scandinavian pressure groups argued that the new discriminatory quotas would inflame resentment and hostility among their constituents.[27]

Leaders of native American patriotic and ancestral societies countermobilized and jointly petitioned Congress in favor of National Origins quotas. The "battle of petitions" for group immigration rights drew in the Junior Order of United American Mechanics, the Sons of the American Revolution, the Patriotic Order Sons of America, and the Daughters of America.[28]

The presidential candidates in 1928 were pulled into the political crossfire between the ethnic and nativist pressure groups. Republican nominee Herbert Hoover spoke out against the National Origins plan in his nomination acceptance speech in an effort to court Irish and German voters. The Democratic candidate, Al Smith, vaguely opposed both the foreign nationality quotas under the 1921 and 1924 immigration acts and

27 Divine, *American Immigration Policy*, 33–35, 37.
28 Ibid., 38.

the National Origins system, allowing his critics to charge that he was against the restriction of immigration.[29]

On one level of regulatory policy, Congress managed admissions by group preference and quotas; on another level it experimented with non-ethnic selective criteria for admission. The Immigration Act of 1917 excluded illiterate adults but made an exception for family relationships. According to this statute, any admissible alien could bring in or send for "his father or grandfather over fifty-five years of age, his wife, his mother, his grandmother, or his unmarried or widowed daughter, if otherwise admissible, whether such relative can read or not." This provision assured that illiteracy would not be an obstruction to family reunification.[30]

Furthermore, the immigration acts of 1921 and 1924, whose restrictive measures have dominated the attention of historians, actually created a new category of unrestricted immigration, the "nonquota" class. For a number of admitted nationalities, the arriving aliens in this category exceeded the alloted numbers of quota immigrants. The nonquota category expressed the principle of encouraging family reunion. It included the wives of American citizens and their unmarried children under twenty-one. The nonquota category also included professors, students, and natives of western hemisphere nations.[31]

The Immigration Act of 1917 and the Quota Acts of 1921 and 1924 introduced new selective criteria for admissions that promoted permanent residency, family reunion, and social stability. The loopholes inherent in restrictive policy represented new rules for admissions that would be as consequential for future policy as the discriminatory quotas based on national origins. They added up to a new selective control system over immigration that was more responsive to social and economic conditions.

In the 1920s, return migration dwindled sharply among immigrants from southern and eastern Europe. The quota reductions stanched the flow of transient labor migrants from that region. At the same time, the nonquota admissions class for relatives furthered permanent settlement by facilitating family migration. These policies helped to reduce the volatility of the southern and eastern European population.

29 Ibid., 40–41.
30 First proviso, section 3 of the Immigration Act of February 5, 1917 (39 Stat. 874); continued by section 212b of the Immigration and Nationality Act of June 27, 1952 (66 Stat. 163).
31 Reed Ueda, *Postwar Immigrant America* (Boston: Bedford Books of St. Martin's Press, 1994), 24–25.

Unlike admissions policies that drew distinctions on the basis of ethnicity, naturalization policy erased the dividing line between "old immigrants" and "new immigrants." Buttressed by court decisions interpreting the meaning of the statutory requirement that an applicant be a "free white person," Jews, Armenians, Turks, and Arabs were officially considered "white" with respect to naturalization policy, equally qualified by race for naturalization as aliens from northern and western Europe. Just after World War I, the federal government made an exception to the rule excluding Asian aliens from naturalized citizenship by giving special recognition to the military service of inhabitants of the Philippines. Filipinos who served in the United States armed forces during World War I were permitted to apply for naturalized citizenship under laws passed in 1918 and 1919, although technically they were American nationals of a United States territory.[32]

The important provision of birthright citizenship continued to be made available to the children of immigrants from Asia. The United States Supreme Court decided in the case of *U.S. v. Wong Kim Ark* in 1898 that a child of Chinese immigrants was entitled to American citizenship under the clause of the Fourteenth Amendment providing citizenship to a person through birth in the United States (the principle of jus soli). This decision set a crucial precedent. Even in Asian ethnic communities where the immigrant generation was deprived of citizenship on grounds of race, their descendants would be incorporated into the political community. The Supreme Court's decision found that the constitutional prescription for jus soli citizenship trumped the racial exclusion of the Chinese Exclusion Act that implies the jus sanguinis principle of citizenship according to ancestry. The right to citizenship according to birth in the United States assured that no immigrant group could be compartmentalized as a permanent alien subpopulation. It meant that as immigrant communities evolved into multigenerational communities they would be assured of eventual incorporation into the political community.[33]

As immigration and industrialization combined to produce a complex society of ethnic and class subgroups, government officials began to ex-

---

32 Paul S. Rundquist, "A Uniform Rule: The Congress and the Courts in American Naturalization, 1865–1952," Ph.D. dissertation, University of Chicago, 1975, 194–204; Konvitz, *Alien and Asiatic in American Law,* 93–94.
33 *U.S. v. Wong Kim Ark* (169 U.S. 649; 1898); Peter H. Schuck and Rogers M. Smith, *Citizenship Without Consent: Illegal Aliens in the American Polity* (New Haven, Conn.: Yale University Press, 1985), 75–79.

plore ways in which citizenship could be strengthened and turned into a vehicle of national identity. Progressive reformers like John Dewey, Walter Lippmann, Charles E. Merriam, and Herbert Croly endeavored to invigorate American citizenship in such a way as to promote the integration of a more functionalist social order. In their eyes, citizenship would overcome the divisive effects of ethnicity and class in the mature stages of urban-industrial society. Progressive reformers explored the potential of citizenship as a social nexus. They promoted the overriding civic duties to the community, the public interest, and the nation as a means to heal social and economic divisions. As the historian Yehoshua Arieli noted, "Visualizing an immense enlargement of the functions of government in the service of social democracy," the Progressive movement "hoped to create a new center of loyalty and identification in the state." Progressives realized that a vigorous citizenship hinged upon the capacity of society to provide decent living and working conditions. Moreover, they sought to organize "socializing" agencies and experiences—the family, the school, voluntary organizations, and political parties—into tools for "making" citizens with practical knowledge and a civic sense.[34]

The movement toward stronger national citizenship entailed that the value of citizenship would rise. The heightening status of citizenship conversely meant the deepening legal derogation of alienage. A wave of laws spread in various states and municipalities limiting the rights of aliens to employment in professions, in civil service, public works, and to property ownership. The state of Arizona in 1915 passed an unprecedented law based on the use of discriminatory quotas for group protection. Citizens as a protected class had to constitute no less than 80 percent of employees in businesses employing at least five persons. Although the Supreme Court invalidated this initiative, it represented a policy of social engineering

---

34 Yehoshua Arieli, *Individualism and Nationalism in American Ideology* (Cambridge, Mass.: Harvard University Press, 1964), 346–47; Richard L. McCormick, "A Reappraisal of the Origins of Progressivism," *The American Historical Review* 86 (1981): 264–265; David P. Thelen, *The New Citizenship: Origins of Progressivism in Wisconsin, 1885–1900* (Columbia: University of Missouri Press, 1972), 55–56, 82–85; Seba Eldridge, *The New Citizenship: A Study of American Politics* (New York: Thomas Y. Crowell, 1929), chap. 2; Charles E. Merriam, *Civic Education in the United States* (New York: Charles Scribner's and Sons, 1934), 54ff; "Address of Samuel Gompers" and "Address of J. M. Berkey" in *Proceedings of the First Citizenship Convention* (Washington, D.C.: U.S. Government Printing Office, 1917), 28–31, 35–43; Richard Hofstadter, *The Age of Reform: From Bryan to F.D.R.* (New York: Alfred A. Knopf, 1955), 257–71.

based on proportional group representation that was acceptable in federal admissions policies toward immigrants.[35]

The adoption by immigrants of American citizenship became the key to their incorporation into the nation. Policy makers and opinion makers argued over the variable capacity for citizenship of different nationalities. In his lectures on citizenship at Yale, Supreme Court Justice David J. Brewer warned that the United States faced "the dangers which come from an heterogeneous population, a not inconsiderable fraction of which is of peoples with no conception of that which is the only true liberty— liberty regulated by law—peoples who look upon every policeman as an enemy, every sheriff as a tyrant, and all forms of law as so many processes of despotism." The Commissioner General of the Bureau of Immigration warned against the "fallacy" of believing that "all aliens not barred from the United States will make good citizens" and called for "an aroused national consciousness in matters relating to citizenship." Nevertheless, a consensus emerged that these aliens could be acculturated to democracy provided they were guided through naturalization and progressive education, and by their participation in reformed electoral politics.[36]

Congress passed the Naturalization Act of 1906 to replace the nineteenth-century tradition of lax local naturalization with a uniform national procedure. It reaffirmed that transference of allegiance remained based on individual qualification and voluntary initiative. Naturalized citizenship, as in the past, would not be tied to class or religion. The new law installed procedures for stricter verification of the minimum five-year residency. It raised the qualifications for naturalization by requiring a rudimentary knowledge of American history and civics. Furthermore, the

35 *Truax v. Raich* (239 U.S. 33; 1915); Konvitz, *Alien and Asiatic in American Law,* 174– 75; Morton Keller, *Regulating a New Society: Public Policy and Social Change in America* (Cambridge, Mass.: Harvard University Press, 1994), 237–38.
36 David J. Brewer, *American Citizenship* (New York: Charles Scribner's and Sons, 1902), 25–27; U.S. Commissioner General of Immigration, *Annual Report* (Washington, D.C.: U.S. Government Printing Office, 1927), 21; Nathaniel Shaler, *The Citizen: A Study of the Individual and the Government* (New York: A. S. Barnes and Company, 1904), 200– 206; James Bryce, *Hindrances to Good Citizenship* (New Haven, Conn.: Yale University Press, 1909), 106–107; Robert E. Park and Herbert A. Miller, *Old World Traits Transplanted* (New York: Harper and Brothers, 1921), 267–73; Philip Davis, ed., *Immigration and Americanization: Selected Readings* (Boston: Ginn and Company, 1920), 600– 606; Julius Drachsler, *Democracy and Assimilation: The Blending of Immigrant Heritages in America* (New York: Macmillan, 1920), chaps. 8, 9; Kate H. Claghorn, *The Immigrant's Day in Court* (New York: Harper and Brothers, 1923), 5–24, 300–304; Gino Speranza, *Race or Nation: A Conflict of Divided Loyalties* (Indianapolis: Bobbs-Merrill, 1923), 57–58.

law mandated a basic ability to speak and understand English. The United States Commission on Naturalization in 1905 explained the rationale for requiring knowledge of English: "[If the immigrant] does not know our language he does in effect remain a foreigner, although he may be able to satisfy the naturalization laws sufficiently to serve our citizenship."[37]

The five-year minimum residency period still stood, at least in the eyes of policymakers, as an adequate probationary period for applicants to establish the civic knowledge and linguistic qualifications for naturalization. Immigrants required time to fulfill the knowledge and English requirements, especially since so many were poorly educated, spoke a non-English mother tongue, and came from undemocratic states.

From the point of view of "anxious Americanizers," it was important that immigrants, who came increasingly after 1890 from countries with political and cultural traditions distant from the United States, be given a proper foundation in English, American history, and civics. Public schools in areas with high concentrations of immigrants began offering night classes in these subjects for persons applying for naturalization. Cambridge, Massachusetts, typified American communities where public-school leaders perceived the importance of this task, especially in a time when natives worried about the potential for disloyalty or radicalism among immigrants. The School Committee of Cambridge explained in 1913:

In a city like Cambridge, the instruction of the immigrant is the most important educational work that devolves upon the evening school. Cambridge is no longer a native city. . . . It is no longer necessary to argue that these men and women must somehow be given an acquaintance with our language and our institutions. The menacing shadow of the I. W. W. hovering over the manufacturing cities of New England has brought this fact home all too clearly. . . . If nothing is done to assimilate these new arrivals, we cannot complain if they follow the smooth-tongued demagogue. On the other hand, if the community recognizes its responsibility both to itself and to them, there is little to fear and every reason to be optimistic regarding the influence of this influx of new and strange blood from over-seas.[38]

Americanizers expressed impatience with immigrants who did not efficiently move toward adoption of American citizenship and sought ways to

37 *Report to the President of the Commission on Naturalization* (Washington, D.C.: U.S. Government Printing Office, 1905), 10.
38 City of Cambridge, *Annual Reports,* 1913 (Cambridge, Mass.: City of Cambridge, 1913), 482–83.

prompt them in the public media. To their critics, they conveyed the appearance of coercing alien newcomers into becoming "good Americans." Many Americanizers, however, shrewdly knew that they must coax immigrants to join the country in a voluntary spirit. Otherwise, immigrants would become citizens in name only and not possess the proper willingness to belong to the nation. Americanizers such as Frances Kellor and organizations such as the New York branch of the North American Civic League generally understood that new Americans with the desired civic and patriotic disposition emerged through a diplomatic educational outreach that made the decision to become a citizen an attractive and rational choice.[39] They endorsed the capacity of the immigrant to exchange inherited traditions for new customs and loyalties, to internalize an Americanism based on individual consent.

Naturalization was a safety valve for the European alien, distrusted and suspected by anxious natives, to establish a claim to American national identity. As they prepared in evening school classes for the naturalization exam they learned how to use the vocabulary of official Americanism to exhibit the knowledge and attitudes for good citizenship. Participation in the naturalization process was a symbolic act for dramatizing and proclaiming their Americanism. Immigrants could lay claim to the tradition of republican opportunities through ritualized patriotic consent. Speaking of the "privilege of naturalization," the British immigrant Horace J. Bridges noted that it conferred "participation in American sovereignty," the "moral and civic equality" with "fellow citizens," and opportunities to the "enormous wealth of the country."[40]

Progressive education proved to be a useful vehicle for civic and social integration. Although at the philosophical level progressive education aimed at turning the school into a tool for social reform and democratiza-

---

39 Drachsler, *Democracy and Assimilation*, 192–93; Edwin Holt, *The Teaching of Citizenship* (Boston: W. A. Wilde Co., c. 1909), chap. 1; Howard C. Hill, "The Americanization Movement," *American Journal of Sociology* 24 (1919), 613–16; John T. Buchanan, "How to Assimilate the Foreign Element in Our Population," *Forum* 32 (1902), 691; Frances A. Kellor, "Who is Responsible for the Immigrant?" *Outlook* 106 (1914), 912–17, "What Is Americanization," *Yale Review*, n.s. 8 (January 1919), 282–99; Edward G. Hartmann, *The Movement to Americanize the Immigrant* (New York: Columbia University Press, 1948), 56–63; Royal Dixon, *Americanization* (New York: Macmillan, 1916); City of Boston, Committee for Americanism, *A Little Book for Immigrants in Boston* (Boston: City of Boston, 1921).
40 John Palmer Gavit, *Americans by Choice* (New York: Harper and Brothers, 1922), 7–14; Percy MacKaye, *The New Citizenship: A Civic Ritual Devised for Places of Public Meeting in America* (New York: Macmillan, 1915), 14–22; Horace J. Bridges, *On Becoming an American: Some Meditations of a Newly Naturalized Immigrant* (Boston: Marshall Jones Co., 1919), 5–8, 13–23.

tion, at the practical level educators managed schooling to prepare the individual for a role in an efficient and regulated society constituted of functional groups and organizations.[41] However different, the philosophy and practice of progressive education both aimed at enlarging the civic identity and making it socially functional.[42] Progressive education lifted the teaching of national identity out of the moralistic realm of formal iconographic patriotism into the arena of civic problem solving for the modern age. It culturally united the children of immigrants by inculcating in them a shared awareness of their rights and their duties to the general society and the public interest.[43] Collective categories of ethnic culture were irrelevant to the progressive model of educationally guided social reconstruction because progressive citizenship subsumed and transcended subgroup identity. Citizenship learned in the school would function as a supraidentity that would act as a building block for integrating social experiences.[44]

Liberal progressives interpreted the American social milieu as a melting pot that would transform or "amalgamate" the immigrant.[45] While Theodore Roosevelt endorsed a homogeneous national identity and inveighed against "hyphenated Americanism," he uncompromisingly declared his faith in the capacity of all immigrants to become American by stating, "Americanism is a matter of spirit and of the soul."[46] History

41 Diane Ravitch, *The Troubled Crusade: American Education, 1945–1980* (New York: Basic Books, 1983), 47–48; Roscoe Lewis Ashley, *The Practice of Citizenship: In Home, School, Business, and Community* (New York: Macmillan, 1922), chap. 2.

42 David Snedden, *Civic Education: Sociological Foundations and Courses* (Yonkers-on-Hudson, N.Y.: World Book Company, 1923), 121–26.

43 Reed Ueda, "American National Identity and Race in Immigrant Generations," *Journal of Interdisciplinary History* 22 (Winter 1992): 483–91.

44 See Carl C. Taylor, *Human Relations: A College Textbook in Citizenship* (New York: Harper and Brothers, 1926); Earle U. Rugg, *Curriculum Studies in the Social Sciences and Citizenship* (Greeley: Colorado State Teachers College, 1928); Thomas J. Mahan, *An Analysis of the Characteristics of Citizenship* (New York: Teachers College, 1928); Howard C. Hill, *Community and Vocational Civics* (Boston: Ginn and Co., 1928); Edith Emma Beechel, *A Citizenship Program for Elementary Schools* (New York: Teachers College, 1929); Frederick E. Lumley, *Ourselves and the World: The Making of an American Citizen* (New York: McGraw-Hill, 1931); John C. Jones, *Readings in Citizenship* (New York: Macmillan, 1932); Vernon A. Jones, *Character and Citizenship Training in the Public School: An Experimental Study of Three Specific Methods* (Chicago: University of Chicago Press, 1936).

45 Arthur Mann, *The One and the Many: Reflections on the American Identity* (Chicago: University of Chicago Press, 1979), 112.

46 Theodore Roosevelt, "Americanism," address to the Knights of Columbus, New York City, 1915, in Arthur Mann, *Immigrants in American Life*, rev. ed. (Boston: Houghton Mifflin, 1974), 180.

textbooks written by historians such as Charles Garret Vannest, Henry Lester Smith, and Harold Rugg indicated that immigrant newcomers were changing and adapting positively to conditions in the United States.[47] These scholars believed in the capacity of immigrants to assimilate under an inclusive civic Anglo-Saxonism. Those espousing this integrationist nationalism believed that the transference of culture and of its proprietary possession could effectively occur.[48] Others, such as Hull House reformer Jane Addams and her followers, were willing to accept ethnic differences to provide public respect to newcomers but they expected that ethnic qualities would properly fade with the passage of generations.[49]

The champions of liberal nationalism—such as Theodore Roosesvelt, Jane Addams, Frances Kellor, and Woodrow Wilson—stood against dogmas holding that communication and sharing across boundaries could not form the basis of nationhood. They rejected doctrines that deprived individuals of the power to determine their rights on the basis of a rational and civic identity that only the liberal state could provide and safeguard. They opposed limiting the subjects of rights by membership in the naturalistic racial community. In the area of immigration policy, the adherents of liberal nationalism presupposed the political role of philosophy: the creation of a national identity based on reason, a philosophical politics, that preserved the individual's right to consent and change and, concomitantly, the individual's citizenship in a community with open boundaries. The application of these principles in a society receiving mass immigration meant that the collective self-concept of immigrant nationhood would centrally shape the idea of American nationhood.[50]

The liberal nationalists in the nineteenth and early twentieth centuries contended against immigration restrictionists. In the debates over the admission of Chinese immigrants in the last quarter of the nineteenth century, federal lawmakers who adhered to universalist principles defended the rights to admission of the Chinese. During the debate over the legislation that became the Chinese Exclusion Act of 1882, Senator

---

47 Frances FitzGerald, *America Revised: History Schoolbooks in the Twentieth Century* (Boston: Little, Brown, 1979), 79–81.
48 Hans Kohn, *American Nationalism: An Interpretive Essay* (New York: Macmillan, 1957), 150; Solomon, *Ancestors and Immigrants*, 3–6; Mann, *The One and the Many*, 127–28; Arieli, *Individualism and Nationalism*, 87–89.
49 Ruth Shpak Lissak, *Pluralism and Progressives: Hull House and the New Immigrants, 1880–1919* (Chicago: University of Chicago Press, 1990), 60–61.
50 Kohn, *American Nationalism*, 150; Solomon, *Ancestors and Immigrants*, 3–6; Mann, *The One and the Many*, 127–28; Arieli, *Individualism and Nationalism*, 87–89.

Joseph Hawley of Connecticut criticized the arbitrary use of race to dis-
qualify immigrants from China from admission and naturalization.
Hawley assailed the provision that the Chinese were ineligible for citizenship as making "no distinction upon the ground of merit or education or
intelligence or patriotism." Hawley continued, "An exclusion based
purely upon race or color is unphilosophical, unjust, and undemocratic."
He pointed out that such a ruling was "not only contrary to our fifteenth
amendment, but contrary to our whole tradition and policy."[51] In 1886,
as the Senate considered more proposals to limit Chinese immigration,
Senator George Frisbie Hoar invoked the inclusive and individualist principles of liberal nationhood to attack racial restriction. Hoar explained to
his colleagues, "Here is legislation aimed at men, not on account of any
individual crime or inferiority or fault, but simply because they are laborers and because they belong to a certain race; and that in defiance of
the two great foundation principles of this republic: that labor is honor-
able and that there ought to be no distinction between human beings in
their privilege on account of race."[52] The liberal nationalist ideal of individual and rational identity to which Hoar subscribed was most elo-
quently expressed in his last speech attacking Chinese exclusion in 1902.
He inveighed against "the principle of striking at any class of human
beings merely because of race, without regard to the personal and individual worth of the man struck at." Hoar declared, "I hold that every human
soul has its rights, dependent upon its individual personal worth and not
dependent upon color or race, and that all races, all colors, all nationalities contain persons entitled to be recognized everywhere they go on the
face of the earth as the equals of every other man."[53]

Notwithstanding eloquent invocations of founding values, a generation of xenophobic restrictionists in the Progressive era eschewed the
liberal nationalist ideals of immigrant nationhood. A succeeding generation of lawmakers in the mid-twentieth century, however, resurrected
these fundamental principles of American nationalism. They abolished
Asian exclusion from 1943 to 1952 and the National Origins admissions

51 Forty-Seventh Congress, First Session, *Congressional Record—Appendix,* 1882, 183.
   These statements and the context of debate in Congress are examined in Henry Cohn,
   "No, No, No, No!—Three Sons of Connecticut Oppose the Chinese Exclusion Acts,"
   unpublished manuscript, 1995.
52 Forty-Ninth Congress, First Session, *Congressional Record—Senate,* May 26, 1886,
   4958.
53 Fifty-Seventh Congress, First Session, *Congressional Record—Senate,* April 16, 1902,
   4252.

system that restricted immigration from southern and eastern Europe in 1965.[54]

THE RETURN OF COLLECTIVE IDENTITIES IN NATIONAL POLICIES

In the era after the Great Society, lawmakers still grappled with the legacies of the Progressive era and their internal tensions. They abolished the discriminatory admissions system in 1965, instituting the sphere of universalist, individual identity in immigration and naturalization policy, returning this area of policy to original founding values of cosmopolitan national membership. The result was the opening of an era of global immigration. Lawmakers resubscribed, however, to the Progressive-era principles of group preference and proportionality by transferring them to social policy to create a form of state-empowered pluralism. They espoused the "mosaic" to replace the Progressive integrationist model for nationalizing identity and consciousness. Thus, the installation of separate spheres of collective identity for Hispanics, Asians, and Pacific Islanders occurred without the retooling of the Progressive balance wheel of civic assimilation that once brought newcomers and natives together.

In the twentieth century, as assimilative patterns reached ever higher degrees of inclusiveness through the potent forces of social mobility and acculturation, collective identities paradoxically attained an ever greater salience in the politics and public policies of the nation. In the 1970s and 1980s, when racial minorities crossed intergroup and interclass boundaries with unprecedented frequency, new public policies supporting group interests intensified the differences between natives and immigrants. The binary oppositions of the Progressive era reemerged in a modified format pitting assimilation against diversity, whites against people of color, Eurocentrism against multiculturalism, and the West against the third world. Activist leaders of Hispanics and Asians contended that their history, culture, and identity were "unavailable" to Eurocentric whites in a basic and important way. A voluntary and consensual ethnic life was crowded by the abstract formulas for collective identities constructed by social engineers and power brokers. Historian Arthur Mann noted the distorting and overshadowing effects of group identity in the political arena: "A statute penalizing congressmen for failing to do their homework [on the

54 Act of December 17, 1943 (57 Stat. 600); Immigration and Nationality Act Amendments of October 3, 1965.

irreducible complexity of ethnicity] would fall very short of spurring them to accomplish the task at hand. For even if they learned to distinguish among heritages, they would go on legislating for groups without concern for the individuals who are said to belong to them. Lawmakers cannot bother with individuals, because the business of lawmaking bodies is with groups, farmers and manufacturers, exporters and importers, trade unionists and bankers, and on and on."[55] The instrumentalities of state engineering that proliferated with the growth of centralized government raised the potential for the political reorganization of ethnic life. Other forces furthered this end result. The commercial and journalistic mass media marketed ethnic issues. A consultancy and poll-driven political culture constructed collective issues for targeted constituency groups. The political scientists Susanne and Lloyd Rudolph have warned about the subtle workings of this process:

[President] Clinton and others too easily invoke 'ancient hatreds' to explain what are really contemporary conflicts [in India and in former Yugoslavia]. The question, in other words, is not why old conflicts are flaring up anew, but rather why traditionally harmonious mosaics have been shattered. . . . Before democracy, modernization and the nation-state, Hinduism [for example] was loose, open and diverse. . . . As political ideology recedes with the collapse of communism, the politics of identity and community . . . have begun to occupy the space vacated by political ideology. . . . Which identities become relevant for politics is not predetermined by some primordial ancientness. They are crafted in benign and malignant ways in print and the electronic media, in textbooks and advertising, in India's T.V. megaseries and America's talk shows, in campaign strategies, in all the places and all the ways that self and other, us and them, are represented in an expanding public culture.[56]

The pursuit of power and recognition by ethnic groups produced a new philosophy of ethnic relations that was called multiculturalism by the early 1970s. It consisted of two variations. One resembled the voluntary ethnicity of democratic pluralism. "Much of this soft multiculturalism is not new," historian Gordon S. Wood has noted, "[and] we used to call it pluralism, which assumed a process of assimilation. Celebrating the distinctiveness of one's group or ethnicity always has been part of the process of becoming American. Nineteenth- and twentieth-century immigrants, as historian John Higham has pointed out, often 'constructed an ethnic

55 Mann, *The One and the Many*, 168.
56 Susanne Hoeber Rudolph and Lloyd I. Rudolph, "Modern Hate," *The New Republic* (March 22, 1993): 24–29.

identity and a new American identity concurrently.' " But there emerged simultaneously a harder variant based on the tenets of particularistic ideology and the principle of government subsidized ethnicity. This political multiculturalism assumed the need for a continuous set of spheres for corporate ethnic identity enacted by public policy in such a way that marginalized or precluded assimilation. Gordon S. Wood noted, "What is new and alarming is the use of 'identity politics' and what might be called hard multiculturalism to break up the nation into antagonistic and irreconcilable fragments. Such hard multiculturalism denies the possibility of assimilation and erodes our national sense of ourselves as Americans."[57] The advocates of hard multiculturalism urged that particularistic collective solidarity should replace civic, consensual, and achieved qualities as the basis of personality.[58]

These excesses of multicultural politics eventually provoked a reaction on the right that revived early twentieth-century xenophobic ideologies of restrictive American nationhood. The new nativists were as anxious as their Progressive-era predecessors that the newest minorities could not be absorbed as the immigrants of the past had been. They grew more willing to accept American society as a closed society and counseled retreat into a new restrictive nationalism. The opposite parties of particularistic ideology mirrored each other's logic for organizing the American ethnic pattern into homogeneous and permanent blocs. In the 1990s, xenophobic restrictionists sought to divide the population into "European Americans" and "third-world immigrants" and urged that the subgroups of the former unite in solidarity to keep out those of the latter. Radical multiculturalists likewise bisected the population into a "Eurocentric" white majority and "people of color," while directing the latter to unite in solidarity against the former.[59]

In a subtle yet basic way, the opposed parties of particularistic ideology made each other's existence possible. Each summoned up monotonic and timeless compartments of race that could be set in opposition against another, thereby confirming each other's perception that society was divided into "they" and "we." Once the social situation was defined in terms of opposition between incommensurate entities, the potential arose

57 Gordon S. Wood, "The Losable Past," *The New Republic* (November 7, 1994), 48–49; Diane Ravitch, "Multiculturalism: E Pluribus Plures," *American Scholar* 59 (1990): 337–54.
58 Mann, *The One and the Many*, 125–34.
59 Peter Brimelow, *Alien Nation: Common Sense About America's Immigration Disaster* (New York: Random House, 1995).

for group relations to take the form of mutual rivalry, conflict, and aggression. Furthermore the reification of exclusive groups in the United States resonated with patterns of nationalism in the post–Cold War world. A *New York Times* European correspondent described the view of ethnic groups held by right-wing nationalists of the 1990s in Germany, France, Italy, and Austria. "Like Louis Farrakhan, whom they cite approvingly," wrote Mark Hunter, "they believe that different races and ethnicities cannot mix without losing their cultures and identities."[60]

In the 1990s, the opposed parties of hard multiculturalism and xenophobic Eurocentrism combined to obscure the popular vision of a hybridized and transformative pluralism. As in the Progressive era, in the 1990s, overconstructed collective identities often enfeebled the capacity for developing proper controls over immigration in an era of renascent nativism and advocacy of multiculturalism. Popular opinion could overlook the possibilities for future reception of immigrants by rational regulation of admissions. Influenced by politicized images of unassimilable and unassimilating immigrants, the public could be tempted to support calls for unnecessary and radical cutbacks of annual admissions.

The anxious nationalists who sought restriction to protect an ethnoracial core culture represented only one wing of the advocacy movement seeking to reduce immigration. Other proponents of restriction included liberals who worried that immigrants took away economic opportunities from the native lower class and environmentalists who were concerned about overcrowding and the destruction of natural resources. In the mid-1990s, lawmakers became increasingly sensitive to restrictionist sentiments from all parts of the political spectrum and appeared more receptive to proposals for moderate reductions in yearly admissions. Many commentators anticipated that if the flow of immigrants continued into the next century, it was not improbable that new laws would reduce it to a significantly smaller scale.

60 Mark Hunter, "Europe's Reborn Right," *The New York Times Magazine*, April 21, 1996, 39.

5

The Racialization of Immigration Policy

PETER SKERRY

"We are a nation of immigrants." This has become a familiar antiphon in the liturgy of our civil religion. Invoked whenever immigration is under discussion, this truism underscores our need to make sense of the current influx by placing it in the broader context of who and what have come before.

In the current debate, we are told that immigrants today are (or are not) fundamentally different from those who arrived in the last great influx at the turn of the century. We are reminded that the American economy can no longer absorb the unskilled newcomers it once did. And we are warned that welfare state programs unavailable to earlier immigrants now foster dependency among increasing numbers of today's immigrants and their families. At the same time, we hear that contemporary means of communication and transportation make it difficult, if not impossible, to control immigrant flows—compared to earlier this century when as many as three-fourths of all immigrants to the United States arrived by ship at Ellis Island.[1] And perhaps most frequently, we are told that precisely because in the past this nation successfully absorbed large numbers of immigrants, it can and should do so again.

Yet despite such attempts to put contemporary immigration dilemmas in historical perspective, one obvious dimension of the issue is habitually overlooked. I refer to the profound changes in our political institutions since the last great wave of newcomers. At the turn of the century, immigrants encountered locally based institutions that provided a variety of incentives facilitating their participation in the political process. For sev-

---

[1] Philip Taylor, *The Distant Magnet: European Emigration to the U.S.A.* (New York: Harper Torchbooks, 1971), 126.

eral reasons, not the least of which were problems and abuses involving the foreign born, this regime was gradually transformed into a more nationalized and professionalized polity with many fewer access points and opportunities.[2]

Confronting this political-institutional vacuum in their neighborhoods and communities, contemporary immigrant leaders have adapted to an array of post–civil rights institutions that were originally established in response to the political mobilization of black Americans during the 1960s. The result is that immigrants today imitate the political posture of black Americans and define themselves as a discriminated-against racial minority. Embraced by some immigrants more than others, this racial minority stance has nevertheless led Americans to liken the problems of immigrants generally to those of black Americans. Many believe racial discrimination to be a major impediment to immigrant progress but nevertheless continue to support high levels of immigration. Others have come to the opposite conclusion: that immigrants present us with another daunting race problem, and that therefore their numbers should be drastically curtailed.[3]

In both instances immigration policy has been racialized.[4] This reflects a more general tendency in our political culture: we now have one dominant way of discussing and analyzing disadvantage—in terms of race. This profound change in the context in which immigration policy gets made, and in which immigrants learn to define their goals and interests, has gone largely unexamined. The present colloquy among historians and political scientists in search of continuities and discontinuities in American politics and governance over the last century offers an ideal opportunity to correct this oversight.

My purpose is to argue that the racial lens we have adopted distorts our

---

2 See William M. Lunch, *The Nationalization of American Politics* (Berkeley, Calif.: University of California Press, 1987).

3 See Peter Brimelow, *Alien Nation: Common Sense about America's Immigration Disaster* (New York: Random House, 1995).

4 In this article I avoid the distinction sometimes drawn between *immigrant* policy (how governments deal with immigrants once they are here) and *immigration* policy (how governments decide who and how many to let in). I have never found this distinction very useful. On occasion it is downright misleading. In any event, I find it of no help in the present context. But for those interested, see Michael Fix and Wendy Zimmerman, "After Arrival: An Overview of Federal Immigrant Policy in the United States," in Barry Edmonston and Jeffrey S. Passel, eds., *Immigration and Ethnicity: The Integration of America's Newest Arrivals* (Washington, D.C.: Urban Institute Press, 1994), 251–85.

understanding not only of the past but also of the present. It distorts contemporary policies toward immigrants to the point where some problems are exacerbated, others ignored. And it stymies efforts to achieve the kind of control of the immigrant stream that the American public has been demanding.

Why this tendency to overlook the impact of contemporary political institutions on immigration politics and policy?[5] I cannot offer an exhaustive explanation here, but a few points are worth highlighting. In part, this oversight reflects the bias of social scientists, who often reduce politics to an epiphenomenon of economic and social forces over which political actors are then assumed to have no independent or unique influence. Arguably less pronounced now than a generation ago, this bias has nevertheless been sustained by the populist strain in our political culture that refuses to see politics as anything other than a straightforward matter of administration. In recent years this tendency has been reinforced by the affirmative-action ethos that expects social, economic, and political outcomes to mirror demographic trends.

Affirmative action is of course another reason why the racialization of immigration has not been more closely examined. As Hugh Graham points out elsewhere in this volume, pluralist politics have spread affirmative-action benefits beyond the original black beneficiaries to include women, the handicapped, and Hispanics.[6] Indeed, Hispanic beneficiaries of affirmative action include recently arrived immigrants and even illegal immigrants.[7] Consequently, scrutiny of the racialization of immigration leads to scrutiny of established political interests and institutions. To be sure, immigrant interests and institutions are recently organized and remain relatively weak. But having little political power is not the same as having none. Particularly when it comes to race, "the powerless," their spokesmen, and their benefactors have considerable veto power to keep certain subjects off the agenda. Until the mid 1990s, this was clearly the case with immigration.

But to return to my theoretical point, I am not going to argue here that

5 One recent exception to this tendency is Michael Jones-Correa, *Between Two Nations: The Political Predicament of Latinos in New York City* (Ithaca, N.Y.: Cornell University Press, 1998).

6 Hugh Davis Graham, "Since 1964: The Paradox of American Civil Rights Regulation," in this volume.

7 In this article, I will follow the lead of the Washington-based advocacy group, the National Council of La Raza, and use the terms Hispanic and Latino interchangeably.

politics is *more* important than social, economic, and cultural forces. Such is the political determinism of the ancients and their contemporary expositors, who maintain that the regime defines and gives shape to society—not the other way around.[8] Instead, I strive for a balance between the political determinism of the ancients and the reductionism of the moderns. My perspective is that politics is critical and can in important ways shape social, economic, and cultural processes, not to mention how we perceive them.[9]

Immigration policy is definitely a case in point. There has for some time now been clear evidence of a discernible though not large measure of labor market competition between immigrants and low-skilled American workers. There has been some debate over how much competition there is and why the sophisticated methodologies of economics have not been able to find what many laymen, and even a few economists, believe to be there. Yet the important question is not how much competition there is between immigrants and native-born Americans, but how much is too much? How much makes immigration a salient issue among groups that feel threatened? How much competition arouses active opposition? While I cannot answer these questions here, I can offer some insights into the political context within which they will be decided.

Consider another example. There is substantial evidence that in many respects, though not all, immigrants today are assimilating—socially, economically, and culturally—into the mainstream of American life, much as immigrants at the turn of the century did. Yet it is not clear how much comfort we should derive from such findings. For the intellectually interesting and politically relevant question is whether the progress of immigrants will be fast enough to satisfy them, not to mention the American public, in a political culture characterized by considerable impatience. More generally, instead of asking (as we typically do) *whether* immigrants will assimilate, we should be asking *how*—on what terms—they will assimilate. In any event, these too are questions that will get answered in the crucible of politics.

8 See, e.g., Thomas Pangle, "Commentary," in Robert A. Goldwin et al., *Forging Unity Out of Diversity* (Washington, D.C.: American Enterprise Institute for Public Policy Research, 1989), 85–100.

9 For a similar perspective see Benjamin Ginsberg and Martin Shefter, *Politics by Other Means: The Declining Importance of Elections in America* (New York: Basic Books, 1990), 108, 114; and Theda Skocpol, "The Origins of Social Policy in the United States: A Polity-Centered Analysis," in Lawrence C. Dodd and Calvin Jillson, eds., *The Dynamics of American Politics* (Boulder, Colo.: Westview Press, 1994), 191–92.

WHAT DOES IT MEAN THAT WE ARE A NATION OF IMMIGRANTS?

Whenever it is asserted that "we are a nation of immigrants," the intended meaning is usually that we are the *quintessential* nation of immigrants. And though it is true that the populations of several other nations have had higher proportions of immigrants, the United States has without a doubt been the primary destination for most of the world's migrants.[10] Of the approximately sixty-two million individuals who moved from one country to another during the period from the end of the Napoleonic Wars to the beginning of the Great Depression, the United States received by far the greatest share: 60 percent. Canada was our closest competitor, receiving 12 percent. Argentina was the destination for 10 percent, Brazil about 7 percent, Australia 5 percent, New Zealand 3 percent, and South Africa slightly more than 2 percent.[11]

But how does today's so-called "Fourth Wave" of immigration compare with what came before?[12] During the decade leading up to World War I, approximately ten million immigrants arrived here. At the time this was the largest immigrant influx in our history. Approximately 15 percent of the nation's population was foreign-born. About the same number of immigrants—ten million—arrived here over the decade between 1980 and 1990.[13] But with a much larger population base, these translate into only about 9 percent of the annual population being foreign-born.[14] This

10 For some interesting crossnational data on this point, see John Higham, "The Immigrant in American History," in John Higham, ed., *Send These to Me: Jews and Other Immigrants in Urban America* (New York: Atheneum, 1975), 13–14.

11 Arthur Mann, *The One and the Many: Reflections on the American Identity* (Chicago: The University of Chicago Press, 1979), 76.

12 This term for the present influx was popularized by a major study by that name issued by the Urban Institute. See Thomas Muller et al., *The Fourth Wave: California's Newest Immigrants* (Washington, D.C.: Urban Institute Press, 1985).

13 Jeffrey S. Passel and Barry Edmonston, "Immigration and Race: Recent Trends in Immigration to the United States," in Edmonston and Passel, eds., *Immigration and Ethnicity*, 35. Based on census data, this figure includes illegal as well as legal immigrants. But because we know that the census misses a substantial proportion of illegal aliens, this figure necessarily underestimates total immigration over the decade. The INS currently estimates that five million illegal aliens reside in the United States, with the number growing by 275,000 each year. It is also worth pointing out that there was an undetermined but apparently less significant amount of illegal immigration earlier this century. See Jeffrey S. Passel, "Undocumented Immigration," *The Annals of the American Academy of Political and Social Science*, volume 487 (September 1986), 181–200.

14 Kristin A. Hansen and Carol S. Faber, *The Foreign-Born Population: 1996*, Current Population Reports, P20–494 (Washington, D.C.: U.S. Bureau of the Census, March 1997).

figure has led many observers to conclude that today's influx prima facie
poses less of a strain than the last one.

Yet a few caveats are in order. First, because fertility in the United States
has decreased significantly since the beginning of this century, contemporary immigrants, who have high fertility rates relative to native-born
Americans, contribute more to our total population growth than did their
predecessors. Thus, net immigration contributed 37 percent to U.S. population growth from 1980 to 1990, compared to 28 percent from 1900 to
1910.[15]

Second, *emigration* rates are important. At the beginning of this century, fully one-third of all those who arrived here wound up returning
home.[16] Among some groups, such as the Italians, the proportion was
even higher.[17] Today, emigration rates are much lower. For example, during the decade ending in 1910, there were 8.0 million immigrants and 3.1
million emigrants, resulting in a net immigration of 4.9 million. For the
decade ending in 1990, there were about 10 million immigrants but only
1.8 million emigrants, resulting in a net immigration of 8.2 million. As
demographers Barry Edmonston and Jeffrey Passel, who derived these
figures, conclude, "compared with a century ago, immigration levels are
slightly higher; emigration is considerably lower; and net immigration is
substantially greater."[18]

Why emigration rates have diminished is not clear. Some trace the
decline to increased numbers of female migrants and the emphasis on
family unification in our immigration policy since 1965. Others point to
welfare state benefits as inducing immigrants to remain here.[19] This is not
the place to sort out these arguments. But regardless of the fragmentary
evidence on this specific point, it is undeniable that the welfare state—its

15 Barry Edmonston and Jeffrey S. Passel, "Ethnic Demography: U.S. Immigration and
   Ethnic Variations," in Edmonston and Passel, eds., *Immigration and Ethnicity*, 15.
16 Robert Warren and Ellen Percy Kraly, *The Elusive Exodus: Emigration from the United
   States* (Washington, D.C.: Population Reference Bureau, March 1985), 4–5.
17 Michael J. Piore, *Birds of Passage: Migrant Labor and Industrial Societies* (Cambridge:
   Cambridge University Press, 1979), 149–51.
18 Jeffrey S. Passel and Barry Edmonston, "Immigration and Race," 34. Again, Passel and
   Edmonston do not take into account those illegal aliens missed by the census. But the
   thrust of their conclusion nevertheless stands.
19 Journalist Peter Brimelow has made this argument in his recent polemic, *Alien Nation*.
   But so have some academics. See for example James F. Hollifield and Gary Zuk, *The
   Political Economy of Immigration: Electoral, Labor, and Business Cycle Effects on
   Legal Immigration in the United States*, paper presented at the Annual Meeting of the
   American Political Science Association, September 1995. It is worth pointing out that
   welfare utilization rates among immigrants have been rising in recent years. See George J.
   Borjas, *Immigration and Welfare, 1970–1990*, Working Paper No. 4872 (Cambridge,
   Mass.: National Bureau of Economic Research, September 1994).

benefits and the broader ethos of rights and entitlements that it institutionalizes—is another big difference between the contemporary context and that at the turn of the century.[20] Some researchers have even argued that such rights and entitlements explain why immigration to the United States in the post-1945 period no longer tracks the business cycle.[21]

Ethnicity and race are other dimensions of change. While the overwhelming majority of immigrants to the United States from its colonial origins through the 1950s were of European stock, today Asians and Latinos account for about 85 percent of legal immigrants.[22] Over these demographic facts there is no dispute. What is disputed are the social, economic, and political implications of this shift.

Policy advocates, restrictionists and nonrestrictionists alike, make much of the non-European origins of today's immigrants. Unfortunately, so do serious scholars. Consider this observation by sociologists Alejandro Portes and Min Zhou: "Descendants of European immigrants who confronted the dilemmas of conflicting cultures were uniformly white. Even if of a somewhat darker hue than the natives, their skin color reduced a major barrier to entry into the American mainstream. For this reason, the process of assimilation depended largely on individual decisions to leave the immigrant culture behind and embrace American ways. Such an advantage obviously does not exist for the black, Asian, and mestizo children of today's immigrants."[23]

Particularly troublesome here is a kind of presentism that takes the successful assimilation of immigrants earlier in our history and ignores how different things looked to many contemporaries.[24] The result is to downplay or ignore the barriers that earlier immigrants to the United

20 For an extremely thoughtful treatment of this topic, see Gary Freeman, "Migration and the Political Economy of the Welfare State," *Annals of the American Academy of Political and Social Science* 485 (May 1986): 51–63. For an analysis of this point in the context of contemporary Europe, see James F. Hollifield, *Immigrants, Markets, and States: The Political Economy of Postwar Europe* (Cambridge, Mass.: Harvard University Press, 1992).

21 Hollifield and Zuk, *The Political Economy of Immigration*, 15–18. For a contrary perspective that emphasizes the importance of economic factors to explain the specific dynamics of illegal immigration into California, see Hans Johnson, *Undocumented Immigration to California, 1980–1993* (San Francisco: Public Policy Institute of California, September 1996).

22 Passel and Edmonston, "Immigration and Race," 33, 40–41.

23 Alejandro Portes and Min Zhou, "The New Second Generation: Segmented Assimilation and Its Variants," *The Annals of the American Academy of Political and Social Science*, 530 (November 1993): 76.

24 For an insightful discussion of the problem of "presentism" in the study of ethnic and racial groups, see Michael Banton, *Racial and Ethnic Competition* (Cambridge: Cambridge University Press, 1983), 33–34, 76–77.

States did in fact encounter. To be sure, many of these barriers were religiously based, but others were based on what were then presumed to be innate racial differences among various national-origin groups that today we lump together as "Europeans."[25] And while such immigrants never experienced the systematic oppression and degradation visited upon African-origin slaves, or even black freedmen, they were subjected to discrimination, mob violence, and even lynchings.[26] Finally, Portes and Zhou ignore what Reed Ueda reminds us of elsewhere in this volume: that many such "uniformly white" immigrants were eventually excluded from this nation by restrictive policies based on explicitly racialist theories.[27]

The Portes and Zhou perspective exemplifies what Donald Horowitz refers to as "the figment of the pigment" by greatly exaggerating barriers based on the distinctive phenotypical characteristics of today's immigrants.[28] For example, Portes and Zhou ignore the remarkably high rates of intermarriage between native-born whites and Asians or "mestizos" (an infrequently used term that the authors use here to refer to Latinos, apparently in order to emphasize their Indian origins). I will highlight intermarriage below; here I merely emphasize how race distorts historical understanding of our immigrant past, and how those distortions are driven by contemporary political dynamics.

THE POLITICAL ASSIMILATION OF CONTEMPORARY IMMIGRANTS

Discussions of the integration of immigrants into contemporary America typically focus on the economic, social, or cultural dimensions of assimilation. Yet there is a critical political dimension. As I have already suggested,

25 On the religious sources of tensions and conflicts surrounding immigration earlier this century, see Philip Gleason, *Speaking of Diversity: Language and Ethnicity in Twentieth-Century America* (Baltimore: Johns Hopkins University Press, 1992), 231–300.

26 The standard historical treatment of these events in the pre–Civil War era is Ray Allen Billington, *The Protestant Crusade, 1800–1860: A Study of the Origins of American Nativism* (New York: Rinehart and Company, 1952). For the post–Civil War era, see John Higham, *Strangers in the Land: Patterns of American Nativism, 1860–1925* (New York: Atheneum, 1975). For a more analytic treatment of anti-immigrant activities throughout American history, see Seymour Martin Lipset and Earl Raab, *The Politics of Unreason: Right-Wing Extremism in America, 1790–1970* (New York: Harper Torchbooks, 1973).

27 Reed Ueda, in this volume.

28 Donald L. Horowitz, "Conflict and Accommodation: Mexican Americans in the Cosmopolis," in Walker Connor, ed., *Mexican-Americans in Comparative Perspective* (Washington, D.C.: Urban Institute Press, 1985), 58.

American politics has undergone an enormous transformation since the last great influx of immigrants. Understanding and evaluating this transformation, especially since the turbulent 1960s, has become a staple of political science. Yet its implications for today's immigrants have been generally ignored.

This transformation is nowhere more evident than in our political parties. As Gerald Pomper has written, formerly parochial, geographically based political parties have since the 1960s been "torn from their local roots and transformed into national bureaucratic competitors."[29] National party organizations are wealthier and better staffed than ever before, but they lack firm organizational bases in the communities where people actually live and work.[30] As Benjamin Ginsberg and Martin Shefter observe in their recent critique of contemporary politics, the parties "have essentially become coalitions of public officials, office seekers, and political activists; they lack the direct organizational ties to rank-and-file voters that had formerly permitted parties to shape all aspects of politics and government in the United States.[31] Concomitant with this deracination of the parties is their increasingly consistent ideological orientation.[32] Yet such ideologies do not seem to bind individual voters to the parties very tightly. Or, as Hugh Heclo observes, "It is the parties' inability to carry forward meaning-endowed practices that makes us feel our own era is one of dying party institutions."[33]

These developments have been accompanied by the professionalization of politics. While local party organizations have atrophied, there has been tremendous growth in the roles, incomes, and power of campaign finance experts, pollsters, and campaign consultants.[34] And of course any such

---

29 Gerald Pomper, "An American Epilogue" in Vernon Bogdanor, ed., *Parties and Democracy in Britain and America* (New York: Praeger, 1984), 271.

30 On the growth of national party bureaucracies, see A. James Reichley, "The Rise of National Parties" in John E. Chubb and Paul E. Peterson, eds., *The New Direction in American Politics* (Washington, D.C.: Brookings Institution, 1985), 175–202.

31 Ginsberg and Shefter, *Politics by Other Means*, 10.

32 See Reichley, "The Rise of National Parties," 195–200; and Pomper, "An American Epilogue," 259–62.

33 Hugh Heclo, "Ideas, Interests, and Institutions," in Lawrence C. Dodd and Calvin Jillson, eds., *The Dynamics of American Politics: Approaches and Interpretations* (Boulder, Colo.: Westview Press, 1994), 378.

34 For an analysis of how campaign finance laws have contributed to the increased influence of campaign finance specialists and to the bureaucratization of party organizations more generally, see Timothy J. Conlan, "Politics and Governance: Conflicting Trends in the 1990s," *Annals of the American Academy of Political and Social Science* 509 (May 1990): 128–38. For an insightful critique of the impact of campaign consultants on American politics, see Marshall Ganz, "Voters in the Crosshairs: How Technology and

list of ascendant political elites under the current regime should include the electronic media.[35]

The causes of these developments cannot be explored in any depth here. But it is worth noting that while analysts such as Robert Putnam emphasize social, economic, and especially technological explanations, distinctly political factors can also be identified.[36] Indeed, such political factors can in part be traced back to the last influx of immigrants. For example, the origins of today's partially demobilized electorate can be found in the efforts of Progressive reformers to curb the electoral participation of immigrants by means of voter registration requirements.[37]

Yet as Ginsberg and Shefter point out, the fingerprints of the New Deal can also be found on today's regime. For although Roosevelt mobilized the immigrant, working-class voters disdained by the Progressives and included them in an unlikely coalition with elite reformers, blacks, and Southern Bourbons, he accomplished this feat by establishing direct ties between emergent interest groups and federal agencies such as the Social Security Administration and the National Labor Relations Board— thereby circumventing geographically based conservative party bosses, whether in the urban North or the rural South. Ginsberg and Shefter conclude: "New Deal liberals thus began the process through which the Democrats became a party grounded in governmental bureaucracies rather than local organization."[38] Similarly, Sidney Milkis writes in his compendious *The President and the Parties:* "The decline of parties . . . is not the result of ineluctable constitutional forces. It is rather a partisan

the Market Are Destroying Politics," *The American Prospect* (Winter 1994, no. 16), 100–109. A similar critique of advocacy groups is presented in John B. Judis, "The Pressure Elite: Inside the Narrow World of Advocacy Group Politics," *American Prospect* (Spring 1992): 15–29.

35 See, e.g., Austin Ranney, "Broadcasting, Narrowcasting, and Politics," in Anthony King, ed., *The New American Political System,* Second Version (Washington, D.C.: American Enterprise Institute Press, 1990), 175–201.

36 Robert D. Putnam, "Bowling Alone: America's Declining Social Capital," *Journal of Democracy* 6 (January 1995): 74–77. A revealing example of how distinctly political forces can both sustain and undermine voluntary organizations emerges from my field research on Mexican-American politics in San Antonio, Tex. On that city's heavily Mexican south side, local politicians have long financially underwritten Little League teams as a means of maintaining neighborhood-based political ties. But in recent years such efforts have been curtailed in the wake of criticism from ascendant Anglo Republicans, who have characterized them as the corrupt use of children for political purposes.

37 Gary R. Orren, "Registration Reform," in *Voting for Democracy* (Cambridge, Mass.: Kennedy School of Government, Harvard University, 1983), 1–2.

38 Ginsberg and Shefter, *Politics by Other Means,* 81.

project, one sponsored by the Democratic party and built on the foundation of the New Deal realignment."[39]

To be sure, the lore about those local party organizations has often exaggerated the benefits accruing to immigrants. Historian Steven Erie reminds us that local party leaders scarcely reached out to every newcomer appearing in their precincts.[40] Yet neither did they spurn all of them. Decades of wholesale distribution of citizenship papers on the eve of elections, which ended in 1906 when the federal government stepped in to supervise naturalization proceedings, suggest that in many cases local political operatives literally met newcomers as they disembarked.[41] However tainted, such ties between immigrants and the political process have considerably more heft than anything experienced by newcomers today. Indeed, to anyone who has spent time in contemporary immigrant communities, the almost total absence of any political organizational life presents a glaring contrast.[42]

Despite the difficulty of mobilizing their communities under these conditions, contemporary immigrant leaders aspire to recognition and political power. This is understandable, given the enormous role the contemporary welfare state plays in the lives of immigrants. Whether recently arrived or long settled, illegal or legal, noncitizen or citizen, immigrants have interests to be represented. And especially since the political upheavals of the 1960s, Americans have heightened, if modest, expectations that disadvantaged groups will be represented in the political process.

39 Sidney M. Milkis, *The President and the Parties: The Transformation of the American Party System Since the New Deal* (New York: Oxford University Press, 1993), 300.

40 Steven P. Erie, *Rainbow's End: Irish-Americans and the Dilemmas of Urban Machine Politics, 1840–1985* (Berkeley: University of California Press, 1988), 64–66. For similar findings specific to New York City, see Martin Shefter, *Political Parties and the State: The American Historical Experience* (Princeton, N.J.: Princeton University Press, 1994), 200–201. An extremely useful survey of the evidence on this point is presented in Dennis R. Judd and Todd Swanstrom, *City Politics: Private Power and Public Policy* (New York: HarperCollins College Publishers, 1994), 53–74.

41 Higham, *Strangers in the Land*, 97–98, 118. See also Shefter, *Political Parties and the State*, 236–38. And for a retelling of these events in the service of an intriguing new interpretation of immigrant politics, see John C. Harles, *Politics in the Lifeboat: Immigrants and the American Democratic Order* (Boulder, Colo.: Westview, 1993), 102–116.

42 For an informative historical analysis of the atrophying of our popular political institutions, see Michael E. McGerr, *The Decline of Popular Politics: The American North, 1865–1928* (New York: Oxford University Press, 1986). From my own field research in Los Angeles, I offer the example of an independent film crew I encountered attempting to make a documentary of neighborhood politics during the 1993 mayoral election. These filmmakers eventually had to abandon their project because they could find almost no evidence of such political activity.

But an irony now confronts us. As needs and expectations for political mobilization have increased, the institutional capacities to realize them have diminished or even disappeared. Faced with an enormous gap between means and ends, immigrant leaders and their allies have done what any rational-choice theorist might have predicted (though, to my knowledge, none did): they established organizations with drastically reduced membership costs. Indeed, in some instances those costs have been reduced to zero.

The quintessential example is the Mexican American Legal Defense and Educational Fund (MALDEF), which claims to represent all Mexican Americans—indeed all Latinos. In this capacity MALDEF's role is widely and routinely accepted. The organization has been an important and visible participant in numerous policy debates, including the controversy over California's Proposition 187 and immigration policy generally.

Yet MALDEF is not a membership organization. It has no members whatsoever in the communities it represents, and therefore no real bonds of accountability to those communities. The organization gets most of its funding from a few corporations and large foundations—in particular the Ford Foundation, which played the critical role in establishing the organization in the late 1960s.[43]

PUBLIC INTEREST POLITICS AND IMMIGRANTS

Without any membership base, MALDEF is admittedly an extreme example. But it differs more in degree than in kind from other organizations representing immigrant interests.[44] More to the point, MALDEF and other such efforts are examples of a more generic type of organization that has emerged since the 1960s: the public interest organization. Intended to represent interests and constituencies previously left out of the political process, public interest organizations are characterized by their heavy reliance on third-party funding (from wealthy individuals, corporations, and especially foundations) and relatively modest reliance on membership

43 Karen O'Connor and Lee Epstein, "A Legal Voice for the Chicano Community: The Activities of the Mexican American Legal Defense and Educational Fund, 1968–1982," *Social Science Quarterly* 65 (1984): 245–56.
44 Two other prominent organizations representing immigrant interests are the National Council of La Raza and the League of United Latin American Citizens. While they have either individual or organizational members, both are basically staff-driven operations heavily dependent on third-party funding sources.

dues.[45] Indeed, in his meticulous survey of Washington interest groups, Jack Walker reports that public interest groups receive less than one-third of their revenues from membership dues, substantially less than more conventional organizations.[46]

But even when public interest organizations have members, they tend to be widely dispersed, with direct but not very strong ties to the organization and very weak or nonexistent ties to one another. In Jeffrey Berry's formulation, membership in such organizations is "cheap."[47] Common Cause is perhaps the quintessential public interest organization, and as Berry explains: "For the busy individual who worries about the problem of campaign finance, but has neither the time nor true commitment to work personally on the issue, mailing a $20 check to Common Cause can fulfill a need to do something."[48] Such "checkbook organizations" are low on what Robert Putnam calls "social connectedness."[49] As Putnam notes, "The bond between any two members of the Sierra Club is less like the bond between any two members of a gardening club and more like the bond between any two Red Sox fans (or perhaps any two devoted Honda owners): they root for the same team and they share some of the same interests, but they are unaware of each other's existence. Their ties, in short, are to common symbols, common leaders, and perhaps common

---

45 For an insightful and cogent analysis of the public interest movement that places it in the broader context of the post-1960s administrative state, see Sidney M. Milkis, "The Presidency, Policy Reform, and the Rise of Administrative Politics," in Richard A. Harris and Sidney M. Milkis, eds. *Remaking American Politics* (Boulder, Colo.: Westview Press, 1989), 146–87.

46 Jack L. Walker, Jr., *Mobilizing Interest Groups in America: Patrons, Professions, and Social Movements* (Ann Arbor: University of Michigan Press, 1991), 81–85. A more recent but less ambitious study of Washington-based public interest groups comes up with a similar finding. See Allan J. Cigler and Anthony J. Nownes, "Public Interest Entrepreneurs and Group Patrons," in Allan J. Cigler and Burdett A. Loomis, eds., *Interest Group Politics,* fourth ed. (Washington, D.C.: Congressional Quarterly Press, 1995), 77–99.

47 Jeffrey M. Berry, *The Interest Group Society,* second ed. (Glenview, Ill.: Scott, Foresman, and Company, 1989), 55. In their survey of organized interests in Washington, D.C., Schlozman and Tierney confirm that members of public interest groups are "the least intensely involved organization members" among the types of organizations they examined. See Kay Lehman Schlozman and John T. Tierney, *Organized Interests and American Democracy* (New York: HarperCollins Publishers, 1986), 140–41.

48 Berry, *The Interest Group Society,* 55. The standard and near-classic study of Common Cause is Andrew S. McFarland, *Common Cause: Lobbying in the Public Interest* (Chatham, N.J.: Chatham House Publishers, 1984). A more recent work is Lawrence S. Rothenberg, *Linking Citizens to Government: Interest Group Politics at Common Cause* (Cambridge: Cambridge University Press, 1992).

49 Putnam, "Bowling Alone," 71.

ideals, but not to one another."[50] Strikingly, the structure of public interest organizations resembles the disturbing image social theorists used to paint of mass society: as an agglomeration of uprooted and isolated individuals prone to manipulation by elites.[51]

Yet MALDEF is more than just another public interest organization. It also represents the institutionalization of the post–civil rights view that Mexican Americans ought to emulate the political posture of black Americans. Thus, when the Ford Foundation launched MALDEF in 1968, its model was the NAACP Legal Defense and Educational Fund.[52] As Ford president McGeorge Bundy opined at that time, "in terms of legal enforcement of civil rights, American citizens of Mexican descent are now where the Negro community was a quarter-century ago."[53] Accordingly, Mexican Americans have come to present themselves not as an immigrant ethnic group like Italians or Poles but as a discriminated against racial minority with longstanding grievances that can now be rectified only by extraordinary measures. Those measures include affirmative action programs as well as the Voting Rights Act (VRA). The Mexican American Legal Defense and Education Fund has played a key role in securing the benefits of both measures for Mexican Americans—broadly construed to include both citizens and noncitizens, including illegal aliens.[54]

In essence, the VRA and affirmative action programs, along with organizations like MALDEF, have filled the institutional void left by the atrophied state and local political institutions described above. To be sure, these developments have affected Hispanics more than Asians, but the consequences have been profound for immigrant politics generally and for our overall immigration policy.

Ironically, these changes in our political system have had the effect of advantaging resources that immigrant communities typically lack, such as money and technical-professional expertise, while disadvantaging resources these communities have in relative abundance, such as social capital.[55] One of the most persistent findings from the research literature on

---

50 Ibid.
51 For the classic, still informative, and extremely subtle explication of this perspective, see William Kornhauser, *The Politics of Mass Society* (Glencoe, Ill.: Free Press, 1959).
52 O'Connor and Epstein, "A Legal Voice for the Chicano Community," 248, 252.
53 Ibid., 248.
54 For example, MALDEF initiated the suit that culminated in the now-controversial Supreme Court ruling that illegal alien children be provided free public education. See *Plyler v. Doe,* 457 U.S. 202 (1982).
55 I emphasize "relative" here, since immigrant communities are typically characterized by high geographic mobility, even transience, which can of course diminish social capital.

migration is that in order to minimize the costs and risks of long-distance migration, immigrants rely on dense networks of face-to-face relationships built up over the years among family and neighbors.[56] The source of critical information and help at the point of origin, such networks continue to be vital at the destination, where they provide social support and in particular help immigrants find jobs. Such networks also help immigrants to hold onto jobs by fostering cooperative arrangements for childcare, transportation, and other such needs. Moreover, employers come to rely on these networks to help them select and discipline employees.[57]

In the past, such face-to-face networks were directly incorporated into local political organizations. Immigrants and their families were drawn into politics not only by patronage jobs and the fabled Christmas turkeys but also by the fellowship at neighborhood political clubs, where precinct captains and other familiar faces offered camaraderie along with an array of personalized services. In this fashion, unsophisticated and, very likely, indifferent peasants were coaxed into the political process of a modern nation.

Today face-to-face, primary group relationships among immigrants are bypassed by a depersonalized and professionalized politics of campaign consultants, media buys, and computerized direct mail.[58] This is not to say that politics is completely beside the point in today's immigrant communities. A few hardy souls are attempting to knit together political organizations from these dense social networks.[59] Party officials and com-

---

For more on immigrant transience, see Peter Skerry, *Mexican Americans: The Ambivalent Minority* (Cambridge, Mass.: Harvard University Press, 1995), 65–66. For evidence on the adverse effects of such mobility on the educational performance of immigrant children, see Lorraine M. McDonnell and Paul T. Hill, *Newcomers in American Schools: Meeting the Educational Needs of Immigrant Youth* (Santa Monica, Calif.: RAND, 1993), 75–77.

56 See Douglas Massey et al., *Return to Aztlan: The Social Process of International Migration from Western Mexico* (Berkeley: University of California Press, 1987), 139–71.

57 On the personalistic nature of employment ties among immigrants, see Piore, *Birds of Passage*, 17. For a comparison of black and immigrant networks, see William Julius Wilson, *When Work Disappears* (New York: Alfred A. Knopf, 1996), 65–66; and Philip Kasinitz and Jan Rosenberg, "Missing the Connection: Social Isolation and Employment on the Brooklyn Waterfront," *Social Problems*, vol. 43, no. 2 (May 1996), 511–12.

58 Here again, Marshall Ganz's work is particularly helpful. In fact, Ganz specifically cites how the effort to mobilize California Latinos for Robert Kennedy's 1968 Presidential campaign would not likely be undertaken in today's world of rationalized, consultant-dominated politics. See Ganz, "Voters in the Crosshairs," *The American Prospect*.

59 Community organizations working across the nation under the aegis of the Industrial Areas Foundation (IAF) come to mind. For more on the IAF, see Skerry, *Mexican Americans*, 144–74. See also Dennis Shirley, *Community Organizing for Urban School Reform* (Austin, Tex.: University of Texas Press, 1997).

munity activists do mount periodic voter registration campaigns, but these are episodic, often built around the campaigns of individual candidates and almost by definition lack much, if any, organizational longevity.

Quite aside from the practical problems of mobilizing immigrant communities under such conditions, there are less apparent but more important drawbacks to the "public interest model" of politics. The lack of social connectedness in Common Cause may be compensated for by the convenience and gratification afforded those committed and affluent enough to send in their membership dues. But such checkbook organizations deprive the politically unsophisticated of important lessons that are probably best learned in face-to-face settings. To rely on Albert Hirschman's formulation, organizations like Common Cause provide easy "exit" but little opportunity for "voice."[60] Uprooted and politically unconnected immigrants already know a good deal about exit; what they need to learn about are the possibilities of voice. In our past, political machines, along with unions, taught such lessons. Today, school's out; there are few, if any, substitute teachers; and such political education is almost nonexistent.[61]

Still, organizations like MALDEF and tools like the VRA have produced some real gains. From 1973 to 1994 the number of Mexican-origin and other Hispanic elected officials in six key states increased 229 percent.[62] And while population growth accounts for some of this increase, most of it is attributable to the VRA, under whose coverage Hispanics were first included in 1975.[63] Without enduring political organizations, however, rooted in the day-to-day life of local communities, it is not clear how much staying power and clout underlie such electoral gains. It is

---

60 See McFarland, *Common Cause*, 97.
61 A possible exception to my point here would be those unions attempting to organize immigrants, though it remains to be seen how effective such efforts will be. See Chris Erickson et al., "Helots No More: A Case Study of the Justice for Janitors Campaign in Los Angeles," Department of Sociology, University of California, Los Angeles (March 1996); Immanuel Ness, "Organizing in Immigrant Communities: UNITE's Workers' Center Strategy," Brooklyn College, City University of New York, n.d.; and Hector L. Delgado, *New Immigrants, Old Unions: Organizing Undocumented Workers in Los Angeles* (Philadelphia: Temple University Press, 1993).
62 The six states are: Arizona, California, Florida, New Mexico, New York, and Texas. My figures are derived from Table 14 in 1992 *National Roster of Hispanic Elected Officials* (Washington, D.C.: National Association of Latino Elected Officials, 1992), x; and from Table 18 in 1994 *National Roster of Hispanic Elected Officials* (Los Angeles: National Association of Latino Elected Officials, 1994), xii.
63 On Hispanic coverage under the VRA, see Abigail M. Thernstrom, *Whose Votes Count? Affirmative Action and Minority Voting Rights* (Cambridge, Mass.: Harvard University Press, 1987), 43–62.

certainly arguable that this VRA-generated increase in office holding has not resulted in a commensurate sense of empowerment among Latinos.[64]

Clearly, as a society we have become much more concerned with *who* gets represented than with *how* they are represented. On this point, Lani Guinier's critique of the Voting Rights Act is on target. One need not agree with her controversial notion of racial authenticity or her proposal for proportional representation to acknowledge the validity of Guinier's concerns that the VRA has narrowed our focus to the technocratic counting of black and minority elected officials and oriented us away from a more fundamental set of questions about what happens between elections. Specifically, Guinier demands that we look beyond minority "tokens" and "role models" and scrutinize minority political participation and community organizations that would hold officials accountable once elected to office. Indeed, her more strenuous point is that the effect of such VRA-induced outcomes has often been to demoralize and depoliticize minority communities.[65]

Certainly as applied to Hispanics, the VRA smacks of a legalistic quick fix that refuses to acknowledge the real obstacles to the group's political advancement: lack of economic resources, low educational attainments, limited English skills, a high proportion of non-voting-age youth, and a high incidence of noncitizenship, including illegal status.[66] As such, the VRA satisfies the demands of an impatient society whose elites, in particular, seem more concerned that the disadvantaged be formally represented than that their actual influence or power be enhanced.[67] Such impatience is understandable, even laudable, on behalf of black Americans. But when transposed to immigrants, it overlooks the necessarily long and arduous process by which they become full participants in American life. We forget our own history—not just that of Mexicans in the Southwest but of

---

64 For more on this point, see Peter Skerry, "Why the Voting Rights Act Is Not Empowering Mexican Americans," *The Brookings Review* (Summer 1993), 43–45.

65 Lani Guinier, *The Tyranny of the Majority: Fundamental Fairness in Representative Democracy* (New York: Free Press, 1994), 55, 59, 67, 83, 85–86.

66 In theory, the VRA also applies to Asians, but in practice, their residential dispersion is such that few VRA districts have been drawn or litigated for them. This point has been made in Bruce E. Cain and D. Roderick Kiewet, *Minorities in California* (Pasadena: California Institute of Technology, Division of Humanities and Social Sciences; March 5, 1986), 1-27.

67 For an analysis of affirmative action that similarly emphasizes the incentives elites have in supporting such controversial programs, see John David Skrentny, *The Ironies of Affirmative Action: Politics, Culture, and Justice in America* (Chicago: University of Chicago Press, 1996).

immigrant groups back East. We seem unable to wait for today's immigrants to settle in and adapt to their new home before declaring them to be victims of a regime that fails to include them. The danger is that by trying to jump-start the process, we end up short-circuiting it.

To be sure, the November 1996 elections apparently brought a surge of Hispanic voting. Some statewide polls in California indicated that whereas in 1992 Hispanics were about 7–8 percent of the electorate, in 1996 they were about 10–11 percent.[68] In Texas, Hispanics went from 10 percent of electorate in 1992 to 16 percent in 1996.[69]

But such results merely prove my point. Lacking the material and solidary incentives available to their counterparts earlier this century, contemporary immigrant leaders must resort to more emotional or ideological incentives.[70] The real and perceived threats of recent restrictionist proposals in Sacramento, Calif., and in Washington, D.C., have provided the grist for just such appeals. Yet it remains to be seen whether the response will result in enduring gains.

COURTING REACTION

The effectiveness of the VRA in developing Hispanic political power can be debated. Much less debatable is that the VRA has contributed to the racialization of immigrant politics. Moreover, this racialization has in turn contributed to the anti-immigrant backlash we have been experiencing.

Consider the recent controversy over Proposition 187, the ballot initiative prohibiting the provision of various public services to illegal aliens that was approved by a majority of California voters in November 1994. Proponents typically argued that Prop 187 was necessary to stop the flood

---

68 Lou Cannon, "California's Sleeping Giant Awakens," *San Diego Union-Tribune* (November 18, 1996). I say "apparently" because the respected Field Poll indicates a much more modest increase in Hispanic voting, from 10 percent of California voters in 1992 to 11 percent in 1996. Not only are these shifts within the margin of error, but poll results for Hispanics are notoriously imprecise. On this latter point, see Skerry, *Mexican Americans,* 308–12; and Rodolfo O. de la Garza, ed., *Ignored Voices: Public Opinion Polls and the Latino Community* (Austin, Tex.: The Center for Mexican American Studies, 1987).

69 Patrick J. McDonnell and George Ramos, "Latinos Make Strong Showing at the Polls," *Los Angeles Times* (November 18, 1996).

70 Charles Hamilton makes this point about black politicians working in the postmachine environment of New York City. See his important article, "The Patron-Recipient Relationship and Minority Politics in New York City," *Political Science Quarterly* 94 (1979): 211–27.

of immigrants—who, in the proponents' view, refuse to learn English, reject mainstream American culture, and threaten to become an underclass.[71] Though only imperfectly supported by the available evidence, such claims no doubt rang true because they echoed what immigrant, especially Latino, leaders had been arguing for two decades: specifically, that because racism has prevented Latinos and Asians from entering the mainstream of American life, they now reject assimilation and at the same time require the same extraordinary benefits afforded blacks. No wonder voters responded with fear, anxiety, and resentment.

This racial-minority posturing may be expected of protest leaders and community activists. But it has been more pervasive than that. Indeed, such posturing reflects the influence of public interest dynamics on immigrant politics. As Jack Walker has pointed out, the third-party benefactors that public interest organizations rely on "often show a pronounced affinity toward broad efforts to reshape public attitudes or values."[72] With members who are typically anonymous to one another, public interest organizations tend to rely on "outside strategies" that seek out public attention, especially in the media. In this way they keep patrons and members alike informed of what's going on and thereby reinforce the loyalties of both. Although Walker doesn't put it this way, such organizations practice a kind of revivalism that, like the explicitly religious version, requires continuous—and public—rededication to their highly charged goals.[73]

Burton Weisbrod and his colleagues at the University of Wisconsin's Institute for Research on Poverty come to a similar conclusion from the perspective of economics. In their study of public interest law firms, Weisbrod and company point out that such organizations operate in a nonmarket environment where their effectiveness is difficult to assess. So, instead of maximizing profit, such firms maximize publicity—which attracts funding.[74]

---

71 Virtually all of the evidence we have is that immigrants, especially their children, do—over time—learn to speak English. See Gillian Stevens, "Immigration, Emigration, Language Acquisition, and the English Language Proficiency of Immigrants in the United States," in Edmonston and Passel, *Immigration and Ethnicity*, 163–85. Of course, whether and how well immigrants learn to *write* English is a different and rather neglected issue. For some troubling evidence on this point, see McDonnell and Hill, *Newcomers in American Schools*, 68–69.
72 Walker, *Mobilizing Interest Groups in America*, 107.
73 For more on "outside strategies" see Ibid., 103–21.
74 Burton A. Weisbrod et al., *Public Interest Law: An Economic and Institutional Analysis* (Berkeley: University of California Press, 1979), 88–89.

This does not mean that public interest organizations eschew the quiet inside maneuvering favored by traditional interest groups.[75] But to the extent that they are not constrained by members to whom they must deliver concrete benefits in the near term, public interest groups may prove less than eager to engage in pluralist bargaining and compromise. This has certainly been evident with MALDEF, whose posture in various legislative battles has been criticized by allies and opponents alike as intransigent, even obstructionist.[76]

These regrettable dynamics are exacerbated by the racial minority agenda embraced by immigrant leaders. For the VRA and other forms of affirmative action draw immigrants benefiting from such programs into a political calculus very different from that engaged in by earlier immigrants. Under the logic of affirmative action, steadily increasing numbers of Mexican immigrants translate into demands for steadily increasing numbers of Hispanic employees in the public sector, Hispanic students in colleges and universities, and Hispanic-majority electoral districts. By contrast, immigrant leaders earlier in this century had no such entitlement claims at the ready. They consequently had to weigh the advantages of increased numbers of their countrymen against the destabilizing effects of such newcomers on established organizations such as political machines and trade unions. Today, immigrant leaders less situated in community-based or membership organizations are less threatened by the challenges newcomers pose for organizational maintenance. (It is certainly striking that the one Latino group that has visibly wrestled with its stance on immigration is the United Farmworkers Union, a conventional membership organization.)[77] Whereas immigrant leaders used to operate in a political system where raw numbers had to be translated into organizational muscle at the polls or factories, the leaders of today's protected immigrant groups have relatively few reasons not to press for ever increasing levels of immigration. To state the case bluntly, contemporary immi-

75 On the origins of the public interest movement's establishment-antiestablishment schizophrenia, see Richard A. Harris and Sidney M. Milkis, *The Politics of Regulatory Change: A Tale of Two Agencies,* second ed. (New York: Oxford University Press, 1996), 81–92.
76 Christine Marie Sierra, "Mexican Americans and Immigration Reform: Consensus and Fragmentation," paper presented to the annual meeting of the Western Political Science Association, March 1989, Salt Lake City, (1989), 24–27.
77 See Philip L. Martin, "Collective Bargaining in Agriculture," in Paula B. Voos, *Contemporary Collective Bargaining in the Private Sector* (Madison, Wisc.: Industrial Relations Research Association, 1994), 515.

grant leaders don't necessarily need members, voters, or even protesters—just warm bodies to be counted by the census.[78]

But there's more going on here than a mere numbers game. For the proliferation of overcrowded barrios and other such immigrant enclaves where not a word of English is spoken serves to mask the assimilation that is in fact occurring. More to the point, the continuous arrival of poor, uneducated newcomers and the inevitable difficulties they encounter reinforce the perception that immigrants experience racial discrimination. Immigrant leaders may not consciously think in such calculating terms, but the incentives of contemporary politics result in their acting as if they did.

All of this implies a competition with the racial minority group whose claims originally brought the affirmative action regime into being: black Americans. As I will illustrate below, a numerical competition has already arisen in specific contexts. But the competition is even more insidious and alarming. This was impressed upon me when I was in Los Angeles a couple of weeks after the 1992 riots. As the Latino leaders and officeholders I met with said with alarm: "Blacks are getting all the attention. It's the sixties all over again."[79] I was then urged to communicate to my fellow Anglos that Latinos felt strongly that "This was our riot, too!"

Subsequent research proved these leaders right. A study by researchers at RAND found that more than half those arrested during the riots were Latinos.[80] Yet this datum is hardly reassuring. When seasoned leaders, not youthful activists, are preoccupied with gaining public attention by such means, it is not irrational—or racist—for other Americans to worry about the continued influx of newcomers.

To be sure, such tendencies do not go unchallenged. Understanding that the racial minority stance has its drawbacks, Latino leaders seek to moderate it with the more positive image of their people as aspiring immigrants in the American tradition. For example, during the spring of

78 My argument here draws on Charles Hamilton's insightful comparative analysis of patron-client and patron-recipient politics in his "The Patron-Recipient Relationship and Minority Politics in New York City." For a fuller elaboration of my analysis, see Skerry, *Mexican Americans,* 336–41.

79 For more evidence on perceived political competition between blacks and Latinos see Rufus P. Browning et al., *Protest Is Not Enough: The Struggle of Blacks and Hispanics for Equality in Urban Politics* (Berkeley: University of California Press, 1984), 194–95.

80 Joan Petersilia and Allan Abrahamse, "A Profile of Those Arrested," in Mark Baldassare, ed., *The Los Angeles Riots: Lessons for the Urban Future* (Boulder, Colo.: Westview Press, 1994), 135–47.

1998 MALDEF sponsored a television ad directed at non-Latinos that was intended, according to the organization's president, "to show what we have in common with other Americans."[81]

This immigrant-group posture does not of course jibe with racial minority claims. No matter. Both get asserted, which is why I have dubbed Mexican Americans "the ambivalent minority."[82] Indeed, these are the two poles of a political dialectic that must be addressed by any disadvantaged group seeking help from the contemporary welfare state. On the one hand, the disadvantaged need to establish the seriousness of their claims on the public sector. On the other, claimants must provide evidence that they are not so disadvantaged as to be beyond hope. For Latinos, racial minority status speaks to the first concern; immigrant group status to the second. In light of the emphasis Latino leaders place on their racial minority status, it may be tempting to disregard their immigrant claims as posturing. Yet these are critical to establishing the group's worthiness. At the same time, the aspirations and careers of too many Latinos depend on the racial minority paradigm, without doubt the more powerful of the two poles.[83]

IMMIGRANT ETHNIC GROUPS OR RACIAL MINORITY GROUPS?

So far, I have either implied or simply asserted that contemporary immigrants, Hispanics in particular, are not accurately or prudently viewed as racial minorities. This is because my primary concern has been the political and institutional context of these racial minority claims, not their factual validity. But now I would like to pause and examine some of the pertinent evidence.

The most straightforward but overlooked indicator that Hispanics do not easily fit the racial minority mold is census data on racial self-identification. In 1980, 56 percent of Hispanics told the census that they considered themselves to be racially "white." To be sure, 40 percent assigned themselves to an ambiguous "other race" category, while about 4 percent identified themselves as black, American Indian, or Asian/Pacific Islander.

---

81 See Denise Gellene, "In Their Own Images: TV Ad Seeks to Broaden the Public's View of Latinos," *Los Angeles Times* (April 2, 1998).
82 Hence, the title of my book, *Mexican Americans: The Ambivalent Minority*.
83 I elaborate on this argument in Peter Skerry, "E Pluribus Hispanic?" in F. Chris Garcia, ed., *Pursuing Power: Latinos and the Political System* (Notre Dame, Ind.: University of Notre Dame Press, 1997), 16–30.

In 1990 52 percent of Hispanics identified themselves as white, a slight downward trend that may itself reflect the racialized politics I'm highlighting.[84] In any event, one seldom hears from any of the participants in the ongoing debates over immigration and multiculturalism that the majority of this growing "minority group" actually identify themselves as white.[85]

Another revealing but neglected indicator pertains to residential segregation. Here the data are unambiguous. Hispanics and to a lesser extent Asians initially experience the kind of segregation that occurs when immigrants first arrive and settle in densely populated, low-rent neighborhoods. But over time these immigrants, and certainly their children, move up and out of such enclaves. As a result the residential segregation of Hispanics and Asians, as quantified in standard indices, is comparable to that experienced by European-origin immigrants earlier in our history.[86]

This pattern is fundamentally different from that of black Americans, whose socioeconomic mobility still fails to translate into diminished residential segregation. Thus, black families earning $50,000 or more annually are just as segregated as those earning less than $2,500. In fact, such black families are more segregated than Hispanic or Asian families earning under $2,500.[87] Such data have led Douglas Massey and Nancy Denton, the leading students of residential segregation, to develop the concept of "hypersegregation" to depict the unique plight of black Americans in this regard.[88]

84 U.S. Census, unpublished data tabulated by the Census Bureau. I present similar data for Mexican-Americans in Skerry, *Mexican Americans,* 16–17. I present and analyze similar but more recent data from a special 1995 supplement to the monthly Current Population Survey on the racial identification of various Hispanic subgroups, in Peter Skerry, "Many American Dilemmas: The Statistical Politics of Counting by Race and Ethnicity," *The Brookings Review* (Summer 1996), 36–39.

85 It is further interesting to note that when the Current Population Survey asks Hispanics to identify themselves racially, respondents must choose among black, white, American Indian, and Asian/Pacific Islander. The "other race" option is not offered. Under these conditions, 96 percent of Hispanics say they are white. See Jorge H. del Pinal, *Exploring Alternative Race-Ethnic Comparison Groups in Current Population Surveys.* Current Population Reports, P23 Document # 182 (Washington, D.C.: Bureau of the Census, December 1992).

86 This point is made in Douglas S. Massey, "Racial and Ethnic Residential Segregation: The Hypersegregation of Blacks," in Gerald David Jaynes, ed., *Immigration and Race: New Challenges for American Democracy* (New Haven, Conn.: Yale University Press, forthcoming). See also Joan Moore and Harry Pachon in *Hispanics in the United States* (Englewood Cliffs, N.J.: Prentice-Hall, Inc., 1985), 60.

87 Massey, "Racial and Ethnic Residential Segregation."

88 Douglas S. Massey and Nancy A. Denton, *American Apartheid: Segregation and the Making of the Underclass* (Cambridge, Mass.: Harvard University Press, 1993), 74–78.

Similarly divergent patterns for Latinos and Asians on the one hand and for blacks on the other emerge from the data on intermarriage, which analysts typically regard as the most revealing indicator of intergroup barriers. National Academy of Sciences demographer Barry Edmonston reports that as of 1990, 19 percent of all married Hispanics had non-Hispanic spouses and 12 percent of all married Asians had non-Asian spouses. The comparable figure for blacks was only 6 percent. Moreover, if foreign-born individuals are excluded from the analysis, the "intermarriage gap" between native-born Hispanics and black Americans and between native-born Asians and black Americans is even more dramatic.[89] Once again, the pattern for Asians and Latinos today is comparable to that for European immigrants earlier this century.[90]

Yet despite such trends many immigrants still face significant challenges. For example, a small but steadily growing number of immigrants participate in cash welfare programs, which is consistent with the evidence that the education and skill levels of immigrants (relative to native-born Americans) have been declining.[91] In the same vein, a recent study by the RAND Corporation reveals that while some immigrants fare quite well in the labor market, others do not. Thus, Japanese, Korean, and Chinese immigrants enter with wages much lower than those of native-born workers, but within 10 to 15 years they have reached parity with the native-born. On the other hand, Mexican immigrants enter with very low wages and experience a persistent wage gap relative to the native-born, even after differences in education are taken into account.[92]

Of course, citing such trends is one thing, explaining them another. I certainly do not set that task for myself here. But it is worth pointing out

Indeed, for this very reason I have elsewhere argued that the term "residential segregation" is misleading when applied to today's Asian and Latino immigrants and have therefore argued that the term "residential concentration" be used instead. See Skerry, *Mexican Americans*, 69–70.

89 James P. Smith and Barry Edmonston, eds., *The New Americans: Economic, Demographic, and Fiscal Effects of Immigration* (Washington, D.C.: National Academy Press, 1997), 11–12, 45.

90 This specific comparison has been made in John N. Tinker and Gerald Horiuchi, *Mexican-American Marriage Patterns: Evidence for Ethnic Assimilation,* unpublished paper, California State University, Fresno, n.d.; 16–19. See also Edward Murguia, *Chicano Intermarriage: A Theoretical and Empirical Study* (San Antonio: Trinity University Press, 1982), 40–42.

91 On immigrants' reliance on welfare, see Borjas, *Immigration and Welfare, 1970–1990.* On declining education and skill levels, see George J. Borjas, *Friends or Strangers: The Impact of Immigrants on the U.S. Economy* (New York: Basic Books, 1990).

92 Robert F. Schoeni et al., *The Mixed Economic Progress of Immigrants* (Santa Monica, Calif.: RAND, 1996), xiv–xv.

that the authors of the RAND study are themselves agnostic as to the causes of this immigrant wage gap. Possibilities they cite include quality of education, English language skills, time of arrival (during periods of greater or lesser economic growth), wage penalties experienced by illegal aliens, cultural differences in attitudes toward work, and finally, discrimination.[93]

Latino advocates and their allies are far less precise. "Discrimination" is virtually the first and only explanation they offer for this or any other problem experienced by Mexican immigrants, Mexican Americans, and Latinos generally. How such pervasive discrimination can coexist with the levels of residential integration and intermarriage cited above is never explained, or even posed as a question.

To be sure, Latinos have experienced discrimination. Yet in the small agricultural towns of South Texas, where as recently as the 1950s and 1960s Mexican-origin individuals suffered the harshest treatment, discrimination, according to one widely cited study, "revolved at least as much around questions of class and culture as of race."[94] More to the point, whatever discrimination Mexicans faced was never as thorough-going or as systematic as what blacks endured. Mexicans in Texas, for example, were never subjected to the infamous regime of "white primaries" struck down by the Supreme Court in 1944.[95] The segregation of Mexican from Anglo school children was a matter of local policy in Texas, whereas separate schools for whites and blacks was actually written into the state constitution. Indeed, according to the prevailing jurisprudence, Mexicans were "Caucasian."[96] For Mexicans in the Southwest, conditions from place to place typically varied enough so that there were opportunities to get out from under locally oppressive situations. Such possibilities can be traced back to the steady influx of pliant immigrant labor from Mexico, which obviated the need for the kinds of labor and social controls imposed on blacks in the South.[97]

A serious reading of the historical record highlights the enormous difference between the past and the present for Mexicans in the United

93 Ibid., 52–58.
94 John Staples Shockley, *Chicano Revolt in a Texas Town* (Notre Dame, Ind.: University of Notre Dame Press, 1974), 13.
95 Clifton McCleskey and Bruce Merrill, "Mexican American Political Behavior in Texas," *Social Science Quarterly* 53 (1973), 786.
96 See David Montejano, *Anglos and Mexicans in the Making of Texas, 1836–1986* (Austin: University of Texas Press, 1987), 262.
97 For a fuller analysis of the evidence on this important issue, see Skerry, *Mexican Americans*, 291–97.

States. Whatever problems and challenges Mexicans faced in the past, they are fundamentally different from those facing Mexicans today, whose life chances are shaped less by the history of the American Southwest than by their experiences as recent immigrants to the United States. Yet such important distinctions get lost in the contemporary scramble for political recognition and rewards. The incentives facing immigrant political entrepreneurs, especially Latinos, certainly point to one simple response: "This was our riot, too."

Social scientists are apparently not immune to these incentives. For example, numerous studies document a disturbing trend: the school performance of immigrant adolescents has a tendency to deteriorate with assimilation into the mainstream. In the words of one veteran high school teacher, "As the Latino students become more American, they lose interest in their school work . . . They become like the others, their attitudes change."[98] Other teachers describe students born in Mexico and recently arrived in the United States as "cheerful," "shy but unfailingly courteous," and "grateful for what you can do for them."[99] To be sure, such students often experience significant adjustment problems attributable to their rural background, inadequate schooling, and poor English-language skills. But these problems do not typically include negative attitudes or antisocial behaviors.

Among many Mexican-descent students born in the United States, the opposite is more nearly the case. Despite fluency in English and familiarity with American schools, such students often adopt an adversarial stance toward school and school personnel. Cultivating a cynical antiachievement ethic, such students dismiss as "wannabes" (as in "want to be white") those among their peers who strive for academic success.[100] In a

98 Carola Suarez-Orozco and Marcelo Suarez-Orozco, *Transformations: Immigration, Family Life, and Achievement Motivation Among Latino Adolescents* (Stanford, Calif.: Stanford University Press, 1995), 6.

99 Maria Eugenia Matute-Bianchi, "Ethnic Identities and Patterns of School Success and Failure among Mexican-Descent and Japanese-American Students in a California High School: An Ethnographic Analysis," *American Journal of Education,* vol. 95, no. 1 (November 1986), 241. See also Maria Eugenia Matute-Bianchi, "Situational Ethnicity and Patterns of School Performance among Immigrant and Nonimmigrant Mexican-Descent Students," in Margaret A. Gibson and John U. Ogbu, eds., *Minority Status and Schooling: A Comparative Study of Immigrant and Involuntary Minorities* (New York: Garland Publishing, Inc., 1991), 205–47; and McDonnell and Hill, *Newcomers in American Schools,* 56–57.

100 Matute-Bianchi, "Situational Ethnicity and Patterns of School Performance among Immigrant and Nonimmigrant Mexican-Descent Students," 219. For more on this antiachievement, antimainstream response on the part of second-generation Mexican and other immigrant youths, see Portes and Zhou, "The New Second Generation."

similar vein, a RAND study reveals that while 61 percent of new immigrant students in the Los Angeles Unified School District are considered well motivated by their teachers, only 35 percent of their more settled immigrant classmates are so rated.[101]

How are such disturbing outcomes to be explained? The prevailing tendency among social scientists who focus on these matters is to interpret such oppositional, antiachievement values among immigrant children as rational responses to a history of group oppression and racial discrimination by the dominant society. Anthropologist Maria Eugenia Matute-Bianchi, whose study of a central California high school was just cited, argues as follows: "The observed pattern of school failure among many Mexican-descent students at Field High School suggests a reactive process and an intensive intragroup reliance in developing a collective identity as a disadvantaged, disparaged minority group. The construction of this identity is the product of historical and structural forces of exclusion and subordination by the dominant group, as well as the vehicle of resistance that the group has made to structured inequality."[102] One problem here is that the "historical and structural forces of exclusion and subordination" that Matute-Bianchi emphasizes are shared, according to her own analysis, by Mexican-descent students who succeed in school as well as by those who fail. Indeed, one of the interesting findings in Matute-Bianchi's work is that students of Mexican descent have very different responses to school and the future. To be sure, many such students adopt an oppositional, minority group identity. But many others do not. While a good number assert that "people like us face a lot of prejudice because there are a lot of people who don't like Mexicans," many others observe "some people are just lazy, and before they realize it, they have messed up too much to start going right."[103]

It is of course not surprising that different individuals of Mexican descent would respond differently to a common past. But surely the intellectually interesting and policy relevant question here is why. Why do some of these adolescents believe they can get ahead if they apply themselves, while others believe the system is rigged against them? But on this point Matute-Bianchi is of no help, because she has only one explanation in her repertoire: a history of exclusion and racial oppression. In essence, Matute-Bianchi is left trying to explain a variable with a constant.

101 McDonnell and Hill, *Newcomers in American Schools*, 56–57.
102 Matute-Bianchi, "Ethnic Identities and Patterns of School Success and Failure," 255.
103 Ibid., 251.

For that matter, Matute-Bianchi is not very precise as to the nature of the "historical and structural forces of exclusion and subordination" that she places at the center of her analysis. Nevertheless, her meaning does emerge. Drawing on the work of anthropologist John Ogbu, Matute-Bianchi classifies Mexican-origin individuals in the United States as members of an "involuntary minority" whose experiences have been fundamentally shaped by their forced incorporation into American society. And while Ogbu is not much more specific than Bianchi as to the precise nature of this experience for Mexicans in the United States, he does make it clear that the paradigmatic example of the "involuntary minority" is black Americans.[104]

Working within Ogbu's perspective, Matute-Bianchi characterizes Mexican-origin students as experiencing "discrimination" and "prejudice," but she gives these terms no analytic content or even definitions.[105] She never clarifies the meaning of such terms in light of the evidence on intermarriage and residential patterns cited above.

Locked in this monocausal perspective, Matute-Bianchi also neglects to explore alternative hypotheses to explain the emergence of antiachievement values among Mexican-descent youth. For example, she presents clear evidence that the efforts of some of the successful female students in her study had not been supported by their parents and that in fact their parents had discouraged them from going to college out of fear that they would then live away from home.[106] Similar evidence of such intrafamilial, cultural dynamics negatively affecting educational achievement among Mexican-origin youth has in fact been presented in other studies.[107] But, again, Matute-Bianchi is silent on this point.

Even more surprising is Matute-Bianchi's silence about the possible effects of social class on the educational success of Mexican-descent students. To be sure, she does allude to class differences among the students in her study. But she simply ignores such factors when trying to explain

---

104 See John U. Ogbu, "Immigrant and Involuntary Minorities in Comparative Perspective," in Gibson and Ogbu, eds., *Minority Status and Schooling,* 3–35.

105 See Matute-Bianchi, "Situational Ethnicity and Patterns of School Performance," 208, 215, 239. I would contrast Matute-Bianchi's use of these terms with the much more precise and analytic usage in Christopher Jencks, *Rethinking Social Policy* (Cambridge, Mass.: Harvard University Press, 1992), 40–46.

106 Matute-Bianchi, "Situational Ethnicity and Patterns of School Performance," 231.

107 See McDonnell and Hill, *Newcomers in American Schools,* 73–76; also Rubén G. Rumbaut, "Ties That Bind: Immigration and Immigrant Families in the United States," paper presented to the National Symposium on International Migration and Family Change, Pennsylvania State University, University Park, Pa., November 2–3, 1995.

the antiachievement values among some Mexican-descent individuals. Once again, her emphasis is single-mindedly on racial oppression as the explanatory variable.

In all these respects, Matute-Bianchi's work resembles that of other researchers in this area.[108] After reviewing the body of research represented by her, Ogbu, and others, sociologist Rubén Rumbaut registers a dissent similar to mine: "The development of 'oppositional' subcultures . . . need not hinge on a history of racial oppression and the formation of reactive ethnicities."[109] Rumbaut then goes on to cite a study of an inner-city housing project where white youths have adopted an oppositional, antiachievement ethic, while their black counterparts have taken the opposite tack. Summing up what can be learned from this research, Rumbaut concludes, "although nearly all immigrant children confront substantial social adjustment and academic learning problems initially, these problems seem to diminish over time for some but seem to persist and to become aggravated over time for others. Why this is so remains an unanswered question."[110]

Again, I am not suggesting that Mexican Americans, Hispanics, or other immigrants do not experience obstacles and discrimination in contemporary America. Nor I am denying that at various times and places in our past Mexican-origin individuals (or, for that matter, Asians) have experienced racial oppression and exclusion from the dominant society. I *am* suggesting that such experiences, past or present, are not accurately or prudently equated with the racial discrimination and isolation that has been and continues to be experienced by black Americans.

It is certainly evident that many immigrants, especially Latinos, believe that in order to succeed they must overcome discriminatory barriers. Yet Matute-Bianchi and like-minded researchers fail to point out that such views are hardly unprecedented. Earlier this century, the children and grandchildren of European-origin immigrants similarly felt mistreated by

---

108 See Marcelo M. Suarez-Orozco, "Immigrant Adaptation to Schooling: A Hispanic Case," in Gibson and Ogbu, eds., *Minority Status and Schooling*, 56; Suarez-Orozco and Suarez-Orozco, *Transformations*, 188–190; Portes and Zhou, "The New Second Generation;" and Harriet Romo, "The Mexican Origin Population's Differing Perceptions of Their Children's Schooling," *Social Science Quarterly* vol. 65, no. 2 (June 1984), 635–50.

109 Rubén G. Rumbaut, "The New Californians: Comparative Research Findings on the Educational Progress of Immigrant Children," in Rubén G. Rumbaut and Wayne A. Cornelius, eds., *California's Immigrant Children* (San Diego: Center for U.S.-Mexican Studies, 1995), 65.

110 Ibid., 64.

American society. Lacking "the dual frame of reference"[111] that allows immigrants to compare their travails in their new home with what they left behind, the second and third generations have typically expressed frustration and discontent. Many such children of the previous wave of immigrants dropped out of school, joined street gangs, or engaged in political protest.[112]

Failing to put their findings into historical context, Matute-Bianchi and her colleagues also ignore how contemporary political institutions encourage the children and grandchildren of today's immigrants to define their problems in racial terms. Encountering many obstacles and hostilities, these young people see them as caused by racial discrimination and prejudice in part because that is the repertoire of explanations now offered by the broader political culture. Indeed, it is their very assimilation into this political culture that helps to explain why the longer individuals of Mexican descent live in the United States, the more they are likely to feel discriminated against.[113]

CONSEQUENCES FOR IMMIGRATION POLICY

The racialization of immigration has had unfortunate effects not just on politics but on policy as well. This has doubtless contributed to the reluctance of our political and policy elites to address immigration. Immigration is the kind of issue that such elites would just as soon avoid. It is an immensely complex topic affecting myriad interests in complicated, often unforeseeable ways. As Gary Freeman has pointed out, immigration politics does not fit neatly into the familiar fourfold typology of concentrated/dispersed costs and benefits.[114] To the extent that the costs and benefits of

111 The phrase is John Ogbu's. See Ogbu, "Immigrant and Involuntary Minorities," 10–11.
112 For example, Michael Piore links both New Deal electoral mobilization and union organizing efforts during the 1930s to the resentments of second-generation immigrant workers. See his *Birds of Passage,* 156–57.
113 For example, one panel study of Mexican immigrants reports that the percentage claiming discrimination against their ethnic group nearly doubles after three years in the United States. See Alejandro Portes and Robert L. Bach, *Latin Journey: Cuban and Mexican Immigrants in the United States* (Berkeley: University of California Press, 1985), 277–82. I present and analyze other such findings in Skerry, *Mexican Americans,* 358–60.
114 Gary P. Freeman, "Mass Politics and the Immigration Agenda in Liberal Democracies," paper prepared for delivery at the Annual Convention of the American Political Science Association, Chicago, August 31–September 3, 1995; 8–10. In another paper, as if to illustrate the point, Freeman takes a somewhat different position. See Gary P. Freeman, "Modes of Immigration Politics in Liberal Democratic States," *International Migration Review* vol. 29 (Winter 1995), 881–902.

immigration can be pinpointed, they frequently cut across prevailing political loyalties—for example, allying socially conservative Republicans
with protectionist Democrats against free-marketeers and civil libertarians. And to the extent that its impacts cannot be readily specified,
immigration as an issue is in the highly volatile, and therefore hazardous,
realm of symbolic politics.[115]

Elites have also been reluctant to deal with this issue because they tend
to be supportive of relatively high levels of immigration—a stance that
reflects both their cosmopolitan values and their interests as affluent consumers of the goods and services produced by immigrants.[116] In sum, it is
no surprise that elites in this and other liberal democratic states have been
eager to keep immigration off the political agenda.[117]

This unfortunate elite tendency has been exacerbated by the racialization of immigration. As Robert Reinhold of the *New York Times* has
noted, during the 1980s when California's population increased by a
"staggering" 6.1 million, "the subject of controlling population was
taboo in polite circles, where people feared being accused of racism."[118]
As recently as 1995, Gary Freeman could write "The boundaries of legitimate discussion of immigration policy are narrow, precluding, for example, argument over the ethnic composition of migrant streams, and
subjecting those who criticize liberal policies to abusive charges of
racism."[119] Such observations are easy to overlook now that immigration
is on the agenda. But it is critical to recall what it took to get it there: the

115 Jack Citrin et al., *American Identity and the Politics of Ethnic Change*, Working Paper
    89-1 (Berkeley: Institute of Governmental Studies, University of California, March
    1989), 3.
116 See, for example, the Gallup survey data presented in John E. Rielly, *American Public
    Opinion and U.S. Foreign Policy 1995* (Chicago, Chicago Council on Foreign Relations, 1995), 13–21, 39; also Stephen Moore, "Social Scientists' Views on Immigrants
    and U.S. Immigration Policy: A Postscript," *The Annals of the American Academy of
    Political and Social Science*, vol. 487 (September 1986), 213–217.
117 The implications of the proimmigration views of elites in liberal democracies generally
    are explored in Freeman, "Modes of Immigration Politics in Liberal Democratic
    States." See also Gary P. Freeman and Katharine Betts, "The Politics of Interests in
    Immigration Policymaking in Australia and the United States," in Gary P. Freeman and
    James Jupp, eds., *Nations of Immigrants: Australia, the United States, and International Migration* (Melbourne: Oxford University Press, 1992).
118 Robert Reinhold, "In California, New Talk of Limits on Immigrants," *New York
    Times*, December 3, 1991, A20. I personally witnessed a revealing episode in 1991,
    when a senior vice president of the University of California vehemently dismissed
    as "racist and unfounded" an innocent question from an undergraduate whose
    premise was that there is a connection between population growth in California and
    immigration.
119 Freeman, "Modes of Immigration Politics in Liberal Democratic States," 884.

pent-up frustration of rank-and-file voters who supported California's harsh and ill-considered Proposition 187, and the bold desperation of a politician, Governor Pete Wilson, who seized the immigration issue as he prepared for a tough reelection battle in 1994.

If the inaction of elites contributed to the immigration backlash we are now experiencing, so too have the actions of immigrant leaders. The logic of affirmative action arguably encourages leaders to maximize the numbers of newcomers—not because they seek to control their people by keeping them isolated in barrio enclaves with bilingual ballots and bilingual education but because they understand the powerful forces drawing immigrants into the American mainstream. The goal of today's immigrant leaders is to dominate not their constituents but the political agenda. And one means of dominating, or at least getting on, the agenda is to have a steady stream of struggling newcomers arriving in our nation's already overburdened cities.

The strongest indication of Hispanic leaders' lack of interest in controlling immigration has been their stance on employer sanctions. The imposition of penalties and fines on those who hire illegal aliens was discussed as far back as 1951. The idea surfaced again during the 1970s and was subsequently included in the reform package put forward by the Select Commission on Immigration and Refugee Policy in 1981.[120] After much controversy, sanctions were enacted into law as part of the Immigration Reform and Control Act of 1986 (IRCA). More recently, sanctions have been embraced by the bipartisan U.S. Commission on Immigration Reform, formerly chaired by the late Barbara Jordan.

But if employer sanctions are generally viewed as critical to any serious policy of curtailing illegal immigration, the 1986 IRCA sanctions, which are still on the books, have proved completely ineffective: the flow of illegal immigrants into the United States now approximates what it was when Congress was debating IRCA in the early 1980s.[121] The problem under present law is that employers have no reliable means of determining who is a legal resident of the United States. The documents that workers

---

120 *U.S. Immigration Policy: Restoring Credibility* (Washington, D.C.: U.S. Commission on Immigration Reform, September 1994), 88–89.
121 Data on illegal immigration are notoriously difficult to pin down. I base this judgment on Joyce C. Vialet, *Illegal Immigration: Facts and Issues* (Washington, D.C.: Congressional Research Service, The Library of Congress; September 23, 1993), 93-836 EPW; for a much more detailed treatment, see *Illegal Aliens: Despite Data Limitations, Current Methods Provide Better Population Estimates* (Washington, D.C.: General Accounting Office, August 1993), GAO/PEMD-93-25.

may use to verify their status to employers—drivers' licenses, birth certificates, social security cards—are all easily counterfeited.[122] Accordingly, the Commission on Immigration Reform has recommended that sanctions be bolstered with a computerized registry that would provide employers a secure means of verifying the legal status of workers.[123]

Of course, any such proposal immediately arouses fears of national identity cards and invasions of privacy, which is precisely why more secure means of employee verification were not created in 1986. Then, as now, civil libertarians collaborated with business interests, which fought sanctions as still another unfair regulatory burden, and were joined by Hispanic advocacy organizations, including MALDEF.

There are two things to note about Hispanic opposition to sanctions. First, it has rarely been accompanied by any serious alternative proposals to curb illegal immigration. As I have already indicated, this is because the political incentives of our post-1960s regime encourage immigrant leaders to maximize their numbers.[124]

Second and perhaps more important is the stated rationale for Hispanic opposition to sanctions. During the period leading up to the passage of IRCA, Hispanic organizations, with MALDEF in the lead, argued that sanctions would lead to employment discrimination—not just against illegal aliens, but against "all brown-skinned people." Their reasoning was that employers, faced with penalties if they hired illegal aliens, would play it safe by not hiring anyone who looks foreign.

I have argued elsewhere that, at the time they were advanced, such arguments were not supported by much evidence.[125] Even after IRCA's watered-down sanctions became law, Hispanic leaders insisted that they were causing discrimination against Hispanics and other foreign-looking individuals. Yet congressionally mandated evaluations of the IRCA sanc-

122 Michael Fix, "Toward an Uncertain Future: The Repeal or Reform of Sanctions in the 1990s," in Michael Fix, ed., *The Paper Curtain: Employer Sanctions' Implementation, Impact, and Reform* (Washington, D.C.: The Urban Institute Press, 1991), 306.

123 *U.S. Immigration Policy: Restoring Credibility* (Washington, D.C.: U.S. Commission on Immigration Reform, September 1994), 92–114.

124 To be sure, proimmigration advocates have recently been voicing support for efforts to clamp down on illegal immigration that a few years ago they would have—and did—denounce as racist. Yet the bright line between legal and illegal immigration now being drawn by such advocates is misleading and dubious. The two migration streams are in fact closely intertwined. Proimmigration advocates understand this and are merely engaged in a tactical retreat until the current restrictionist tide subsides. For more on the false distinction between legal and illegal immigration, see Peter Skerry, "Why Separate Legal, Illegal Immigrants?" *Los Angeles Times* (August 4, 1996), M1.

125 See Skerry, *Mexican Americans,* 326.

tions by the General Accounting Office (GAO) proved to be less than conclusive. At best, a relatively small number of technical violations of the antidiscrimination provisions of IRCA were uncovered.[126]

There is other evidence indicating that Hispanic leaders have seriously exaggerated the level of discrimination caused by employer sanctions. Throughout the 1980s, when the sanctions debate was raging, opinion polls consistently revealed substantial, if not always majority, support for sanctions among Hispanics.[127] More recently, the debate has died down, undoubtedly because it is evident that employers have continued to hire a large number of foreign-looking individuals, including illegal aliens, regardless of what the law requires.

Here again, I am not arguing that Hispanics and other foreigners never experience discrimination in the labor market. I am suggesting that there is a lot of daylight between the position taken by Hispanic leaders and the evidence. More to the point, I am suggesting that these leaders did not have to oppose IRCA on the grounds they did. Like all political actors, they had choices. They could have adopted the perspective that sanctions unfairly burdened business. Or they could have argued, as even Patrick Buchanan did during the 1980s,[128] that such restrictions on immigration violated fundamental American values.

A similar point is made by David North, a long-time analyst of labor and employment issues. In his evaluation of the labor-market impacts of IRCA, North observes: "While the number of ill-paid and illegally paid workers is legion, and while a disproportionately large number of these workers are immigrants, the immigrant-rights groups pay relatively little attention to such matters. Instead they pay a great deal of attention to a public policy problem that touches what I am sure is a much smaller population, the problem of employer-sanction-caused discrimination against foreign-looking job applicants."[129] Explaining why immigrant-rights groups make the political choices they do, North emphasizes the

126 See Peter Skerry, "Hispanic Job Discrimination Exaggerated," *Wall Street Journal*, April 27, 1990, A12; also *Immigration Reform: Employer Sanctions and the Question of Discrimination* GAO/GGD-90-62 (Washington, D.C.: General Accounting Office, March 1990). See especially the internal critique of this GAO report by the Assistant Comptroller General for Program Evaluation and Methodology, Eleanor Chelimsky, "Memorandum to Comptroller General: Requested Methodological Review of a GAO Draft Report," (Washington, D.C.: General Accounting Office, March 12, 1990).
127 Skerry, *Mexican Americans*, 302–304.
128 Sceptics are referred to Patrick Buchanan, "Reagan Should Veto the Mean-Spirited Simpson-Mazzoli Bill," *Los Angeles Herald-Examiner*, June 27, 1984, A9.
129 David S. North, "Enforcing the Minimum Wage and Employer Sanctions," *The Annals of the American Academy of Political and Social Science*, vol. 534 (July 1994), 64.

peculiar dynamics of public interest law, much as I have.[130] What he overlooks, and what I emphasize, is that the choices made by Hispanic organizations such as MALDEF are fundamentally shaped by our racialized post–civil rights political culture.

Employer sanctions highlight another way in which racialization has affected immigration policy: It is now very difficult to deal with the tensions between immigrants and black Americans, much less arrive at an honest assessment of the impacts of immigration on native-born blacks.

The Immigration Reform and Control Act's sanctions have clearly contributed to serious strains between blacks and Hispanics. These came to a head in the spring of 1990, when Hispanic organizations demanded that Congress repeal sanctions but then realized that their black allies in the Leadership Conference on Civil Rights would not support them. The dispute broke into public view when Hispanics picketed the Coalition's fortieth anniversary banquet amidst threats that MALDEF and the National Council of La Raza would quit the Coalition.[131]

This dispute was soon quieted—and brought back behind closed doors. Black and Hispanic leaders really had no alternative, for their differences over sanctions challenged one of the basic tenets of the post–civil rights regime: namely, that as "people of color" Hispanics as well as Asians have interests that are fundamentally congruent with those of black Americans. This perspective is to some extent sustained by a misreading of our racial history, one that assumes a rigid social divide between white Europeans and all others. In fact, while such a line has been and continues to be drawn between whites and blacks (the "one-drop rule"), there have been no similarly rigid boundaries between white Europeans and Mexicans, or even between whites and Asians. While Mexicans and Asians have undeniably experienced discrimination, they have also been absorbed into the dominant group. I have already noted that Mexican-origin individuals in Texas used to be regarded as "Caucasian." As one student of our variegated race relations concludes, "Racially mixed persons in the United States, except for those with black ancestry, generally have been treated as assimilating Americans after the first generation of miscegenation."[132]

---

130 Ibid., 65.
131 Dick Kirschten, "Hispanics Seek More Recognition . . . Within the Civil Rights Lobby," *National Journal* 19 May 1990, 1210–11; Sam Fullwood III, "Rights Group Avoids Split With Latino Organizations," *Los Angeles Times,* May 9, 1990, A14.
132 F. James Davis, *Who Is Black? One Nation's Definition* (University Park: Pennsylvania State University Press, 1991), 118.

The "people of color" perspective is further sustained by the contemporary concern to avoid invidious comparisons between successful immigrants and marginalized blacks. For some, this "people of color" perspective is a desideratum; for others, it is merely a research hypothesis. But for the elites whose interests and careers are tied to the affirmative-action regime, the congruence of interests among Hispanics, Asians, and blacks emerges as a full-blown ideology.

On the ground, this ideology is continually being contradicted. The tensions and outright conflicts between Asian immigrants and blacks are perhaps most glaring.[133] Yet because of their relatively small numbers and often substantial human, economic, and social capital, Asians, though often the targets of black frustration and rage, tend not to be in direct competition with blacks. The same cannot be said of Hispanics, whose large numbers and similar position at the low end of the labor market translate into a greater threat to black Americans.[134]

The very size of this threat seems to increase the need to deny its existence. Among those who would sustain the "people of color" ideology, there is active avoidance of what common sense and social science reveal.[135] During the latter half of the 1980s, for example, economists typically reported that there were no, or only marginally, negative labor market impacts of immigrants on black Americans.[136] Such findings were widely and uncritically embraced, especially by those sympathetic to high levels of immigration. Yet there was a certain whistling-past-the-grave-

---

133 See, for example, Claire Jean Kim, "The Politics of Black-Korean Conflict: Black Power Protest and the Mobilization of Racial Communities in New York City," in Jaynes, *Immigration and Race* (forthcoming). Analyzing the widely reported 1990 Red Apple Boycott in the Flatbush section of Brooklyn, Kim presents the intriguing but not completely convincing view that such a reaction by blacks to Asian merchants is not to be dismissed as irrational scapegoating but as "a purposive protest campaign designed to mobilize the black community against racial domination."

134 As of 1995, blacks constituted 12 percent of the U.S. population, Hispanics 10 percent, and Asians a mere 3 percent. See Carol J. DeVita, "The United States at Mid-Decade," *Population Bulletin* vol. 50, no. 4 (March 1996), 19–23. Even in the huge Los Angeles Consolidated Metropolitan Statistical Area, which includes Los Angeles, Orange, and Riverside counties, Asians constitute only 9 percent of the population, blacks an additional 9 percent, and Hispanics fully 33 percent. See *Statistical Abstract of the United States: 1994*, 114th ed. (Washington, D.C.: U.S. Bureau of the Census, 1994), 42.

135 In the common-sense category, I would point to the apparent (and not entirely unjustified) effort by the *Los Angeles Times* to downplay possible tensions between blacks and Hispanics over the beating of black motorist Rodney King by Los Angeles police officers. One of the four officers charged in that case, Theodore Briseno, was a Latino. Yet the *Times* repeatedly and routinely referred to the four officers as "white."

136 Muller, *The Fourth Wave*, 95–123; Robert D. Reischauer, "Immigration and the Underclass," *The Annals of the American Academy of Political and Social Science*, vol. 501 (January 1989), 120–31.

yard quality to this embrace. If pressed, social scientists would admit that important immigration effects might not be picked up in metropolitan-level, cross-sectional data sets that, for example, did not take into account how many low-skilled workers (black and white) might be moving from one metropolitan area to another in order to cope with the competition from immigrants. But the matter was seldom pursued.

There was a similarly studied lack of curiosity about the fact that, whatever economists were finding in labor markets, there were other highly visible arenas in which blacks and Hispanics did compete. For example, in Los Angeles County during the 1980s, Latinos began aggressively competing with blacks for public-sector jobs. Based on their steadily increasing population numbers, Latinos argued—correctly, according to the logic of affirmative action—that they were underrepresented in the county workforce.[137] More recently, Hispanics in the U.S. Postal Service have been arguing not only that they are underrepresented but that blacks are overrepresented, which according to the same logic is also indisputable.[138] With the Hispanic share of the total population steadily increasing and the black share decreasing, such zero-sum competition continues apace.

Throughout the 1980s and into the 1990s, economists were allowed to dominate whatever discussion there was about black-immigrant competition. This meant that the topic was narrowly and artificially construed to be a question of labor-market competition when it was evident that in cities across the nation blacks were competing with Hispanic immigrants for public services as well as for political resources and media attention.[139] As I frequently heard from both Latino and black politicos in Los

137 For more on this point, see Peter Skerry, "Borders and Quotas: Immigration and the Affirmative Action State," *The Public Interest* (Summer 1989, no. 96), 93–94. For evidence of black-Latino competition in ten California cities for public-sector jobs and for political resources generally, see Rufus P. Browning et al., *Protest Is Not Enough: The Struggle of Blacks and Hispanics for Equality in Urban Politics* (Berkeley: University of California Press, 1984), 194, 260–61.

138 On the postal service dispute, see *Hispanic Employment at USPS* (Washington, D.C.: GAO; September 3, 1993; GAO-GGD-93-58R). See also Bill McAllister, "Postal Service Record in Recruiting Hispanics 'Disappointing,' Report Says," *Washington Post* November 27, 1996, A13.

139 For the competition between blacks and Latinos over public services, see Melvin L. Oliver and James H. Johnson, Jr., "Inter-Ethnic Conflict in an Urban Ghetto: The Case of Blacks and Latinos in Los Angeles," *Research in Social Movements, Conflict and Change* 6 (1984): 57–94. One study of 49 U.S. cities reported political—but no socioeconomic—competition between blacks and Hispanics. See Paula D. McClain and Albert K. Karnig, "Black and Hispanic Socioeconomic and Political Outcomes: Is There Competition?" paper delivered at the annual meeting of the American Political

Angeles during this period, "There is only room for one minority in this town."[140]

Subsequent research has made it increasingly difficult to ignore Hispanic-black competition. Demographer William Frey has documented how low-skilled blacks—and whites—have been pushed out of metropolitan areas heavily impacted by immigrants.[141] Sociologists focusing on neighborhood-level effects have demonstrated how Hispanic social networks help them get established in various employment sectors at the expense of blacks, whose networks tend to be weaker and less supportive. Indeed, these issues have been most prominently documented and discussed in the work of William Julius Wilson.[142]

CONCLUSION

The evidence for black-Hispanic competition has a hard row to hoe in a polity dominated by the post–civil rights ideology analyzed here. More to the point, this is no garden-variety ideology. Rather than defend and rationalize any ordinary set of interests, it serves what its defenders (and even some of its detractors) regard as a moral imperative: the protection of beleaguered racial minorities. Challenging this worldview can earn one the charge of racism, and pointing out the divergent interests of blacks and Hispanics can earn one the accusation of fomenting racial discord.

Racialization thus makes everything about immigration more intractable. Not only will we continue to have difficulties squarely addressing the effects of what may prove to be the largest influx in our history, we will also be hampered in our efforts to control or regulate that influx.

I have argued that the origins of this unfortunate development are to be found in the structures and institutions of contemporary American poli-

Science Association September 1995, Chicago. For more recent evidence of continued political competition between blacks and immigrants generally, see Paula D. McClain and Steven C. Tauber, "We Win! You Lose! Implications of Black, Latino, and Asian Socioeconomic and Political Resources for the Other Groups' Electoral Success in Urban Politics," paper delivered at the annual meeting of the American Political Science Association September 1995, Chicago.

140 See Skerry, *Mexican Americans*, 83–86.

141 William H. Frey, *College Grad, Poverty Blacks Take Different Migration Paths*, Research Report No. 94-303 (Ann Arbor: Population Studies Center, University of Michigan, March 1994); and William H. Frey, "Immigration and Internal Migration 'Flight': A California Case Study," *Population and Environment* vol. 16, no. 4 (March 1995), 353–75.

142 See Wilson, *When Work Disappears*, 140–45. See also Kasinitz and Rosenberg, "Missing the Connection," 501–19.

tics. I cannot therefore anticipate any easy answers. Nevertheless, it is possible to suggest a perspective toward which we might want to move.

I have in mind the work of the renowned student of group relations, University of Chicago sociologist Robert Park. Writing to a former associate in the wake of the 1943 Detroit race riot, Park commented: "I am not quite clear in my mind that I am opposed to race riots. The thing that I am opposed to is that the Negro should always lose."[143] Here are the basic elements of Park's "race relations cycle," which took competition, conflict, accommodation, and eventually assimilation as the inevitable outcomes of group contact.[144] For all the sound criticisms that have been directed against Park's perspective, it retains the singular virtue of realism—which is greatly lacking in contemporary analyses and discussions of immigration.[145]

Today's post–civil rights ideology allows us high-mindedly to rule group competition and conflict out of bounds, to the point where they are not topics quite suitable for serious inquiry. Our middle-class sensibilities are perhaps thereby spared offense, but our understanding of immigration's impact on us, and what we may need to do about it, is greatly diminished.

143 Quoted in Fred H. Matthews, *Quest for an American Sociology: Robert Park and the Chicago School* (Montreal and London: McGill-Queen's University Press, 1977), 189. On Park and his legacy of realism to social research on race, see Gleason, *Speaking of Diversity,* 158–62.
144 For Park's terse exposition of his race-relations cycle, see Robert Ezra Park, *Race and Culture* (Glencoe, Ill.: Free Press, 1950), 149–51.
145 John Stone criticizes Park's failure to take into account power relations in his analysis of race relations, which reflects Park's more general tendency to ignore politics. Michael Banton focuses on the problems with the ecological basis of Park's race relations cycle. See John Stone, *Racial Conflict in Contemporary Society* (Cambridge, Mass.: Harvard University Press, 1985), 48–56; and Banton, *Racial and Ethnic Competition,* 78–81. For an insightful analysis of one source of the moralism that has displaced realism in our public discourse on race see Walter A. Jackson, *Gunnar Myrdal and America's Conscience* (Chapel Hill: University of North Carolina Press, 1990).

III

Conservation and Environmentalism

6

The Many Faces of Conservation: Natural Resources and the American State, 1900–1940

DONALD J. PISANI

"Conservation" is a slippery, elusive term. In the four decades prior to World War II it was many things to many people. It stood for the denial of monopoly, democratic control over the allocation of natural resources, the prevention of waste, the protection of natural beauty, and the affirmation of the rights of future generations. Conservation was a set of disparate responses to the growth of urban-industrial America rather than a coherent "reform movement." Try as they might to march under one banner, the champions of conservation never united. Their objectives were inconsistent and some rested on a shaky scientific foundation. Moreover, there were deep divisions within and among natural resource bureaus, and American federalism gave far greater power to the states and local interest groups than to the central government.

In the twentieth century, the persistence of the term "conservation" suggests an ability to change with the times. During the Progressive Era, conservation reflected the interests of elites in and out of government and narrow interest groups. In the 1930s, the New Deal broadened conservation's appeal by extending benefits to a much larger number of Americans, particularly the jobless. From the 1960s on, it embraced new concerns, including human health, and attracted new champions from an expanding middle class. This essay looks at conservation from several angles: the natural resource issues and policies, the "science" upon which they were based, and the obstacles bureaucratic turf wars and federalism posed to political reform. It concludes with a discussion of how conservation prior to World War II relates to the environmental movement of the 1960s and after.

123

NATIONAL CONSERVATION POLICIES

Conservation had many roots. In the late nineteenth and early twentieth centuries, many Americans believed that the nation's identity depended upon maintaining a remnant of the United States "as it was." National parks showcased the natural gifts and wonders of the United States, but they were also permanent "frontiers"—monuments to the Euro-Americans who conquered the West. Others supported conservation for more practical reasons. It appealed to those who thought that the United States was running out of natural resources, especially farmland and forests. It appealed to those who opposed the monopolization of natural resources by giant corporations, including cattle, mining, and railroad companies. It appealed to stockgrowers' associations and timber companies that hoped to limit the access of competitors to the public domain. It appealed to westerners who feared that the depression of the 1890s had permanently stalled the region's economic development—which had been robust during the 1870s and 1880s. Finally, it appealed to bureaucrats in Washington who wanted, simultaneously, to promote the efficient use of resources and to expand the size and responsibilities of their bureaus.[1]

Since conservation served many masters, the policies it produced were inconsistent. The reclamation of arable arid lands is a case in point. At the dawn of the twentieth century, the remaining public domain consisted of mountains, grasslands, and desert—land incapable of producing high-value crops without irrigation. The Reclamation Act of 1902 used the proceeds from public land sales to construct dams and canals to render the deserts productive. Government farmers paid nothing for their land but they were required to repay the cost of watering it in ten—later twenty and forty—installments, without interest. The Reclamation Act tacitly acknowledged that agriculture in the West was not profitable enough to

---

1 The most important surveys of conservation in the Progressive and New Deal eras include Samuel P. Hays, *Conservation and the Gospel of Efficiency: The Progressive Conservation Movement, 1890–1920* (Cambridge, Mass.: Harvard University Press, 1959); Elmo Richardson, *The Politics of Conservation: Crusades and Controversies, 1897–1913* (Berkeley: University of California Press, 1962); John F. Reiger, *American Sportsmen and the Origins of Conservation* (Norman: University of Oklahoma Press, 1986); Lee Clark Mitchell, *Witnesses to a Vanishing America: The Nineteenth-Century Response* (Princeton, N.J.: Princeton University Press, 1981); James L. Penick, *Progressive Politics and Conservation: The Ballinger-Pinchot Affair* (Chicago: Loyola University Press, 1968); Donald C. Swain, *Federal Conservation Policy, 1921–1933* (Berkeley: University of California Press, 1963); and A. L. Riesch Owen, *Conservation under F.D.R.* (New York: Praeger Publishers, 1983).

pay for itself and that the family farm could not flourish there without a substantial subsidy from the federal government.

In 1902, the memory of the severe depression of the 1890s was still fresh. The proponents of reclamation profited from the fear of unassimilated immigrants, unemployment, and class conflict. In the future, they argued, urban discontent could be averted by moving the poor to vacant land in the West. As much as seventy-five to one hundred million acres could be watered, providing homes and a subsistence to ten or twenty million people. Social critics were joined by manufacturers and railroads, which longed for new markets, and by labor unions, which hoped to improve wages in eastern factories by exporting "surplus" workers to the West.

In the West, land prices had fallen sharply during the depression, and established farmers and ranchers hoped that federal reclamation would trigger a new land rush to the benefit of private as well as public land. Federal reclamation was sold to the nation through sentimentalism as well as fear: irrigation could reverse the tide of people moving from the countryside to the city and restore order to the streets of strike-plagued eastern cities. There were, however, few unbroken blocks of public land left near water, even in the arid West. Farmers and ranchers—who often controlled the rivers that served public land—threatened to block government projects unless they could secure a more reliable water supply and sell land to new settlers unable to find arable public land.

The split personality of federal reclamation—its attempt to serve established farmers and their families while simultaneously encouraging new settlement—doomed the program from the start. In many ways the federal reclamation program was a throwback to the Homestead Act (1862) rather than an experiment in scientific agriculture or social planning. The Reclamation Service (later Reclamation Bureau) made no attempt to plan settlement, lay out model towns, or even instruct project farmers in desert agriculture. It was a construction agency and it did nothing to provide western farmers with the capital needed to clear land, grade it, fence it, purchase livestock, and build houses and barns. The cost of building dams and canals soared in the first decade of the twentieth century, and revenue from land sales proved to be hopelessly inadequate. By the 1920s, the U.S. Reclamation Service provided water to less than 10 percent of the irrigated land in the West and farmers on most of its nearly thirty projects had trouble repaying their debt to the government. The agricultural depression of the 1920s demonstrated that the family farm had little future in most parts of the West.[2]

Inconsistent objectives and competing constituencies plagued many progressive-era conservation policies. In 1891, at the request of the secretary of the interior, Congress authorized the president to designate "forest reserves"—they were not labeled "national forests" until 1907. By 1900, about forty-two million acres had been set aside. Theodore Roosevelt added three times that amount—138 new national forests in twenty-one states—along with over fifty wildlife refuges. He also protected seventy-five million acres of mineral lands, hundreds of potential hydroelectric power sites, and five new national parks. Nevertheless, the government did not harvest trees from its forests, nor did it pump oil from its petroleum reserves or generate power at hydroelectric sites on the public domain. In the Progressive Era the choice policymakers faced was not public versus private enterprise but, rather, how much regulatory authority the central government should exercise over private corporations.[3]

At the beginning of the twentieth century, most national forests were far removed from railroads and markets. Therefore, they generated little revenue from timber sales. Stockmen benefited most from the new reserves. From 1891 to 1898, both the secretary of the interior and the commissioner of the General Land Office opposed opening the government forests to grazing, and from 1898 to 1905 these officials limited the privilege of running stock to those who lived in or near the forest.[4] Yet in 1905, when administrative control over the land passed to Gifford Pinchot's Forestry Bureau in the Department of Agriculture, he instituted a permit system and increased the number of cattle permitted access to the forests. This was done to win political support in the West for his agency and for Theodore Roosevelt. (Roosevelt depended heavily on Senate Re-

---

2 On the background to federal reclamation see Donald J. Pisani, *To Reclaim a Divided West: Water, Law, and Public Policy, 1848–1902* (Albuquerque: University of New Mexico Press, 1992). On the federal reclamation program itself see Paul W. Gates and Robert W. Swenson, *History of Public Land Law Development* (Washington, D.C.: Government Printing Office, 1968), 635–98; Michael C. Robinson, *Water for the West: The Bureau of Reclamation, 1902–1977* (Chicago: Public Works Historical Society, 1979); and Donald Worster, *Rivers of Empire: Water, Aridity & the Growth of the American West* (New York: Pantheon Books, 1985).

3 Samuel Trask Dana, *Forest and Range Policy: Its Development in the United States* (New York: McGraw-Hill, 1980); Harold K. Steen, *The U.S. Forest Service: A History* (Seattle: University of Washington Press, 1977).

4 William D. Rowley, *U.S. Forest Service Grazing and Rangelands: A History* (College Station: Texas A&M University Press, 1985), 32, 36–37.

publicans such as Francis E. Warren of Wyoming, who was often referred to as "the greatest shepherd since Abraham.")

The Forest Service did not adopt uniform grazing regulations for all national forests. Instead, it encouraged local stockmen to form livestock associations, which, in negotiations with the government, helped to draft regulations specific to the individual forests. As historian James L. Penick has noted, "Pinchot shamelessly courted the leading grazing interests." The Forest Service allowed large stockmen to purchase the grazing rights of small operators, which made the administration of permits and rights simpler. Forest Service policies encouraged cooperation among some livestock owners and reduced the number of range wars, but they also favored cattlemen at the expense of sheepmen and large operators at the expense of small.[5]

Local interests repeatedly thwarted national conservation policies in the Progressive Era, as the history of the Public Lands Commission (1903–1905) and Inland Waterways Commission (1907) demonstrates. The Reclamation Act contained serious flaws. It did not modify or supplant nineteenth-century land policies, and the success of federal reclamation depended on a comprehensive reform of American land laws. The public domain had to be closed to private development. Twenty million acres of government land had been claimed in fiscal year 1902 alone, which suggested that within a few years most of the West's irrigable government land would be lost in spite of the Reclamation Act. The friends of reclamation and reform wanted to repeal the existing laws and then charge a presidential commission with the job of drafting new legislation to regulate grazing and other uses of government land. Obviously, years might elapse between the repeal of the old laws and the adoption of new ones. Initially, Theodore Roosevelt showed great enthusiasm for reform, but only until he discovered that there was substantial opposition in the West, led by Warren and other powerful Republican U.S. senators. Roosevelt then backtracked and thought about the 1904 elections. Subsequently, he signed the Kinkaid Act (1904), the Forest Homestead Act (1906), and the Enlarged Homestead Act (1909), which resulted in the

---

5 Rowley, *U.S. Forest Service Grazing and Rangelands,* 33, 47, 63, 81; James L. Penick, "The Progressives and the Environment: Three Themes from the First Conservation Movement," in Lewis L. Gould, ed., *The Progressive Era* (Syracuse, N.Y.: Syracuse University Press, 1974), 120–21; Penick, *Progressive Politics and Conservation,* 4; Donald J. Pisani, "Forests and Reclamation, 1891–1911," *Forest & Conservation History,* 37 (April 1993), 73–74.

transfer to private ownership of the last great bloc of public domain. Stockmen and land speculators profited much more than actual settlers.[6]

The most far-reaching conservation legislation considered during the Progressive Era was Senator Francis G. Newlands' inland waterways bill. The only legislation that involved comprehensive planning, in some ways it anticipated the Tennessee Valley Authority (TVA) launched during the 1930s. Roosevelt created the Inland Waterways Commission in 1907 and asked it to coordinate the different uses of water, along with rail and waterway transportation, treating watersheds as discrete units rather than as parts of streams tributary to politically powerful towns or cities. Relieving the nation's overburdened railroads of bulky cargo, he hoped, would reduce both the cost of transportation and the cost of living. By permitting an executive commission to design a national transportation system, irregular and wasteful rivers and harbors bills would become a thing of the past. Experts in transportation and water would decide where to build projects. If various uses of the streams were properly coordinated, Newlands promised, proceeds from the sale of water power would pay for the improvements. This anticipated the New Deal's emphasis on "multiple use" water policies.[7]

Such was the ideal, and Newlands introduced the legislation many times before an emasculated version finally passed Congress in 1917. Eventually he bowed to local pressure and curbed the autonomy of his proposed commission by stipulating that expenditures would be spread evenly throughout the country and shared among the various federal agencies interested in waterways, including the Bureau of Reclamation, the Corps of Engineers, and the U.S. Geological Survey. But local commercial and booster groups preferred to deal directly with congressional committees. They feared that such a commission would favor some river basins over others and delay the construction of existing navigation projects. Wasteful or not, the existing system served the needs of a democratic, pluralistic nation.[8]

---

6 Donald J. Pisani, "George Maxwell, the Railroads, and American Land Policy, 1899–1904," *Pacific Historical Review*, 63 (May 1994), 14–17; Gates and Swenson, *History of Public Land Law Development*, 498–529.
7 Francis G. Newlands, "The Inland Waterways Commission," a speech delivered to the Irrigation Congress on September 3, 1907, in *Official Proceedings of the Fifteenth National Irrigation Congress* (Sacramento, Calif.: News Publishing Co., 1907), 53–58.
8 The most perceptive discussion of the Inland Waterways Commission is still Hays, *Conservation and the Gospel of Efficiency*, 91–121 and 199–218.

Conservation at the national level continued during the decades that separated the two Roosevelts, with the creation of the National Park Service (1916), water power legislation (1920), and the first attempts at flood control (1920s). But these efforts paled in comparison to the vast conservation programs of the 1930s.

By 1933, the "context" of conservation had changed dramatically. The Great Depression undermined public faith in business and "free" markets, and it dealt a serious—though hardly fatal—blow to the congressional supporters of states' rights. Urbanization altered the nation in countless ways. Six million people moved from farms to cities in the 1920s alone. The Model T and paved roads all but obliterated the line between rural and urban. The automobile, combined with greater leisure time and the advent of paid vacations for factory workers, expanded the horizons of city dwellers. During the Progressive Era, conservation focused on rural land, most located within the public domain. It appealed entirely to urban elites. But many conservation programs of the 1930s—from hydroelectric power projects to flood control dams to wildlife preservation—attracted a far larger constituency. So did the jobs provided by New Deal public works.

Nature contributed to the changing political and economic climate. The most severe flood of the century hit the Mississippi Valley in 1927, and in 1929 the most serious drought since the late 1880s and early 1890s descended on many parts of the West. It lingered with varying severity until the mid-1930s, followed by severe flooding in New England and other parts of the United States in 1936 and 1937. The drought contributed to the Dust Bowl on the Great Plains and dried up marshlands and breeding grounds vital to migratory birds. (The expansion of wheat cultivation during and after World War I also reduced the wetlands.) Most important, these natural disasters challenged the Progressive Era faith that there were no limits to human control over nature.

Nevertheless, without the depression, Franklin D. Roosevelt's conservation policies could never have been enacted; Congress would not have appropriated the money. For example, the Weeks Act (1911) had authorized the Forest Service to create national forests in the eastern United States by purchasing private land, much of which had been stripped of trees and abandoned. In no single year before 1933 did Congress give the Forest Service funds to buy more than 500,000 acres. But in fiscal year 1933–34, over four million acres were added to the eastern national forests and another 12.5 million acres were purchased by 1941. The federal government also secured millions of acres of "marginal" land on the Great Plains and elsewhere damaged by wind or water erosion. These acquisitions could be justified for any number of reasons including watershed protection, navigation improvement, and flood control. But the most compelling reason was jobs, and many new conservation agencies— including the Soil Conservation Service and the Civilian Conservation Corps (CCC)—owed their existence to the need for work. Land was desperately needed for CCC camps near large centers of population in the East.

Much of the money spent on conservation came from the Public Works Administration (PWA) or Works Progress Administration (WPA). For the first eight years of F.D.R.'s administration, Harold Ickes—one of conservation's strongest friends in government—served simultaneously as secretary of the interior and head of the PWA. The Park Service's annual budget increased only modestly during the 1930s, and the agency received twice as much in emergency money than in regular allocations. Water projects also depended heavily on appropriations for relief. In fiscal year 1934 alone, the PWA provided the Reclamation Bureau with $103 million— about half the amount spent on federal reclamation during all the years from 1902 to 1933.[9]

Not all conservation programs benefitted from relief money. Congress required the WPA to spend at least 90 percent of the money it received on wages. No more than 10 percent of relief appropriations could be spent on the administration and equipment vital to conservation programs dependent on research or laboratory science. Nor did the relief money always go where it was most needed. It was parcelled out to the states for all sorts of reasons that had little to do with the efficient use of natural resources.[10]

The Civilian Conservation Corps was a case in point. Like the Tennessee Valley Authority, the CCC combined relief and conservation. Unlike the TVA, it was a national rather than a regional institution. It performed labor-intensive jobs—building roads, fighting forest fires, planting trees—jobs that went well beyond the scope of conservation in

---

9 Donald C. Swain, "The National Park Service and the New Deal," *Pacific Historical Review,* 41 (Aug. 1972), 324; Richard Lowitt, *The New Deal and the West* (Norman: University of Oklahoma Press, 1993), 75–77, 81.

10 R. Douglas Hurt, *The Dust Bowl: An Agricultural and Social History* (Chicago: Nelson-Hall, 1981), 130.

the Progressive Era and would not have been funded without the Depression. The Soil Conservation Service and the National Park Service employed far more workers from the CCC than from their own staffs.[11]

Champions of the CCC hoped it would become a permanent public works agency dedicated to building roads, public buildings, dams, and other structures. Some even wanted to extend its work to private lands, especially those adjoining the national forests. (Roosevelt balked at the idea, though he did permit the CCC to help states and counties lay out parks, campgrounds, and other recreational facilities.) The vexing question was whether the CCC should perform the routine work of conservation or only emergency work, such as fire fighting and drought abatement.[12] Moreover, the agency's objectives—relief, education, and, after the late 1930s, military training and preparation—were not compatible. As a relief program it was expensive, and F.D.R. resisted opening the CCC to any but those whose immediate families were on welfare. Congress required CCC workers to send most of the $30 monthly salary home to dependents. But it cost the federal government nearly $1,200 per year to maintain each "soldier." It was far cheaper to promote conservation and jobs through other programs, such as dam-building, than through the CCC. Once World War II began, there were plenty of civilian and military jobs, and the agency was abolished.[13]

Even though the CCC did not survive, it broadened the constituency of conservation during the 1930s, as did wildlife conservation. Theodore Roosevelt designated the first wildlife refuges, and there were fifty-one by the close of his first term. Most were sponsored by genteel wildlife or sportsmen's organizations, such as the Boone & Crockett Club and Izaak Walton League. Franklin D. Roosevelt was no less interested in wildlife than Theodore Roosevelt. During the New Deal years, the Resettlement Administration, Works Progress Administration, and Civilian Conservation Corps expanded the federal land devoted to refuges from 1.8 to 13.6

11 For example, by 1933 every major white pine region in the U.S. had been invaded by blister rust, which threatened to destroy entire forests. Civilian Conservation Corps workers scoured the woods and by hand pulled out currants, gooseberry bushes, and other plants that served as alternate hosts and by which the disease spread from tree to tree. By 1942, the blight had been controlled within most forests on public lands. See John A. Salmond, *The Civilian Conservation Corps, 1933–1942: A New Deal Case Study* (Durham, N.C.: Duke University Press, 1967), 122–23.

12 Franklin D. Roosevelt to Robert Fechner, July 28, 1937; Fechner to Roosevelt, Aug. 21, 1937; and Henry A. Wallace to Roosevelt, March 15, 1938, in Edgar B. Nixon, ed., *Franklin D. Roosevelt and Conservation, 1911–1945* (Hyde Park, N.Y.: Franklin D. Roosevelt Library, 1957), vol. 2, 90–91, 107–109, 195.

13 Riesch Owen, *Conservation Under F.D.R.*, 83–84.

million acres. "It is pertinent to remind you here," F.D.R. observed in a 1936 speech in West Virginia, "that seven million of our citizens take out fishing licenses each year and that six million more take out annual hunting licenses, a total of thirteen million—a veritable army to uphold the banner of conservation." The automobile, a shorter work week in many industries, and paid vacations helped destroy the image of hunting as a hobby of the wealthy. By the 1920s and 1930s, the appeal of sportsmen's organizations extended far beyond the "leisure class."[14]

The CCC and wildlife conservation shattered the image of conservation as elitist or "upper class," but federal reclamation had a far greater impact on society, particularly in the West. From its inception the Reclamation Bureau had grappled with a profound question: Was its primary job to build up the West economically or to perpetuate the family farm? It found the answer during the 1930s, when the need for jobs and electrical power transformed reclamation. In a decade dominated by crop surpluses and burgeoning cities, the appeal of the family farm faded. Hoover Dam on the Colorado River, and other large reservoirs—such as Shasta in California and Grand Coulee in Washington—served primarily urban rather than rural water users. True, turning arid lands into new farms remained one of the Reclamation Bureau's nominal goals, and the sale of power from "high dams" subsidized agriculture in the Imperial Valley, Central Valley, and many other parts of the West. But by providing an immense new supply of cheap power, the bureau increased the migration of small farmers into the West's cities, particularly during and after World War II, when hydroelectric power created well-paying jobs in the defense industry. The Great Depression allowed the Reclamation Bureau to "recreate itself."[15]

In the "High Dam Era," the Reclamation Bureau drifted away from the Jeffersonian ideals of the nineteenth century. In the West, most hydraulic works were still constructed under terms of the Reclamation Act of 1902. But home-making now took a back seat to flood control, recreation, and power. Between 1933 and 1943, the electricity generated in the West by federal agencies increased by over twenty times. Prior to 1933, expenditures for federal reclamation averaged about nine million dollars per year; from 1933 to 1940 the annual average was over five hundred million.

14 Speech by Franklin D. Roosevelt at the Mountain State Forest Festival, Elkins, Va., Oct. 1, 1936, in Nixon, *Franklin D. Roosevelt and Conservation, 1911–1945*, 1, 586.
15 For an excellent overview of federal reclamation in the 1930s, see Lowitt, *The New Deal and the West*, 81–99.

Hydroelectric power allowed the Reclamation Bureau to build dams and canals that would have been financially infeasible in 1902. More important, it gave the bureau a source of revenue independent from Congress and it permitted the farmers who received benefits from such works to evade their responsibility to repay the cost of construction.[16]

When the Bureau of Reclamation took over construction of California's Central Valley Project in 1935, it tacitly abandoned the small farm ideal. Large corporations owned many farms within the project, and many growers did not reside on the land. In 1938 Congress exempted the Colorado Big-Thompson Project from the 160-acre limitation on cheap water contained in the 1902 Reclamation Act. World War II completed the transformation of the Bureau of Reclamation. "Grand Coulee began producing prodigious quantities of electricity in October, 1941, just in time for use in the burgeoning defense industries of the Northwest," historian Donald Swain has observed. "The War Production Board authorized a crash program to complete Shasta Dam [at the headwaters of the Sacramento River] and to enlarge the generating capacity of a number of other reclamation projects. During the war the expansion of reclamation power accounted for 84 percent of the total expansion of electrical power in the eleven far-western states." By the end of the war, the Bureau of Reclamation was the largest single producer of power in the world.[17]

Time and again F.D.R. called for a unified national water policy, but powerful interest groups, allied to competing committees in Congress, separated flood control and navigation from arid land reclamation. Between the flood of 1936 and the beginning of World War II, federal appropriations to manage the nation's rivers increased from thirty-nine million dollars to 173 million. By the end of the 1930s, Army Corps of Engineers expenditures for this purpose rivalled those of the Bureau of Reclamation for irrigation and power on the Colorado, Columbia, and Sacramento rivers.[18]

The CCC, wildlife protection, and federal dam-building reflected a sea-change in policy. Pressed to provide jobs that did not worsen unemployment by competing with private enterprise, F.D.R. and Congress found conservation ideal. The Great Depression expanded and democratized

16 Jordan A. Schwarz, *The New Dealers: Power Politics in the Age of Roosevelt* (New York: Knopf, 1993), 202–16, 297–308; Linda Lear, "Boulder Dam: A Crossroads in Natural Resource Policy," *Journal of the West*, 24 (Oct. 1985), 90.
17 Donald C. Swain, "The Bureau of Reclamation and the New Deal, 1933–1940," *Pacific Northwest Quarterly*, 61 (July 1970), 146.
18 Riesch Owen, *Conservation under F.D.R.*, 114.

conservation and gave it a hard-headed, practical image. Conservation's value could be seen everywhere, from national parks rendered accessible to the masses by the automobile, to flood control structures on the Mississippi River and its tributaries, to reforestation projects carried on by the Forest Service and CCC. Conservation had a new set of concerns and a new constituency.

MORALISM, SCIENCE, AND REFORM

Science is not just a "body of knowledge" or a collection of disciplines; it is a set of ideas that characterize a culture and an age. Historians too often forget that science and politics are close allies; scientific ideas are not simply "timeless truths" discovered by a class of uniquely "objective" human beings. As the environmental historian Donald Worster has observed, most histories of science disregard "the fact that science is always, in some measure, involved in matters of value and moral perception."[19]

Much of what passed for science in the nineteenth century consisted of observation, fact gathering, and the compilation of statistics rather than laboratory experimentation: the line between "pure" and "applied" science was blurry. Indeed, the technology of the time had a limited capacity to test and verify hypotheses. Nature was not studied as something independent of human beings; mankind was at the center of the scientific universe. In an 1883 address on evolution, John Wesley Powell—head of the U.S. Geological Survey and the most prominent government scientist of the late nineteenth century—urged physical scientists to maintain a proper perspective: "When a man loses faith in himself, and worships nature, and subjects himself to the government of the laws of physical nature, he lapses into stagnation, where mental and moral miasma is bred." Science's goal was not to describe nature in some disinterested, impartial way, but to use the lessons of nature to benefit human beings. Scholarly detachment posed great danger if it distracted scientists from that basic goal.[20]

Powell dismissed many pseudoscientific ideas, including the notion that forests increased rainfall.[21] But he embraced others as articles of faith

19 Donald Worster, *Nature's Economy: A History of Ecological Ideas* (New York: Cambridge University Press, 1985), xii (quote), 221–53.
20 The Powell quote is as reprinted in Arthur Ekirch, *Man and Nature in America* (New York: Columbia University Press, 1963), 85.
21 As reputable a scientist as Bernhard E. Fernow, head of the Forest Bureau in the Interior

or received truths. He was convinced, for example, that water itself was a fertilizer, claiming that "the water comes down from the mountains and plateaus freighted with fertilizing materials derived from the decaying vegetation and soils of the upper regions, which are spread by the flowing water over the cultivated lands. It is probable that the benefits derived from this source alone will be full compensation for the cost of the process [of irrigation]."[22] When Powell wrote those words in 1878, the soils of the West had not been classified or tested, nor had its streams been measured, and desert agriculture had not been studied in any depth. Logic, not empirical observation or laboratory tests, convinced him that water flowing through forests absorbed nitrogen from decaying vegetable matter. That assumption became a dangerous delusion among government officials who favored arid land reclamation. Much of the land irrigated by the federal government after 1902 eventually had to be abandoned, in part because Powell and his followers assumed that all desert soil was fertile given sufficient water. One historian has fairly observed that "Powell was a politician first, and a scientist second (if at all) and . . . his testimony on this point, as on so many others, was tuned in each case to what he believed would bring about the most favorable reaction among his audience."[23]

A similar question may be raised about the scientific foundation of Progressive Era wildlife conservation. The most famous attempt to manage nature in the early decades of the twentieth century took place under the direction of C. Hart Merriam, head of the Agriculture Department's Bureau of Biological Survey. In the 1,200 square mile Kaibab Plateau on the North Rim of the Grand Canyon—land set aside in 1893 as part of the Grand Canyon Forest Reserve—the Forest Service encouraged the Biological Survey to eliminate predators that threatened big game and livestock. Merriam cooperated fully, hoping to convince the public that his bureau's work was practical rather than experimental; the ethics of science had little to do with his decision. From 1906 to 1931, the Biological

Department, observed in 1891: "Once let woods spread over the now arid plains of the West and there would be rain in plenty there." See "Forests," *Scientific American*, 65 (Sept. 19, 1891), 181. Fernow also believed that forests once covered virtually all of North America, "and had rendered the climate equable to a degree now unknown." "A Forest 3,000 Miles Long by 1,700 Miles Wide," *Scientific American*, 72 (March 2, 1895), 139.

22 John Wesley Powell, *Report on the Lands of the Arid Region of the United States* (Washington, D.C.: Government Printing Office, 1878), 20.

23 Stanley Roland Davison, *The Leadership of the Reclamation Movement, 1875–1902* (New York: Arno Press, 1982), 127.

Survey's hunters killed and poisoned 781 mountain lions, 30 wolves, 4,849 coyotes, and 554 bobcats. This, it was hoped, would increase the number of deer available to hunters. It did. Freed of predators, the deer population multiplied tenfold from 1906 to 1920, far outstripping the food supply and causing great damage to the forest—until the severe winter of 1924–25 killed off much of the herd.[24]

The scientific foundations of the policies espoused by Gifford Pinchot, perhaps the most famous conservationist of the Progressive Era, were equally shaky. A professional forester trained in Germany and France, Pinchot was deeply committed to sustained-yield forestry but he was also strongly moralistic and politically ambitious. He predicted that the timber supply of the United States would be exhausted in 20 to 25 years, that the supply of anthracite coal would be gone in less than 50 years and bituminous reserves in a century, that the nation's cache of iron ore was being rapidly depleted, and that soil erosion threatened to drive up the price of food. He offered little evidence to support these warnings; it was easier to win public attention through fear than through scientific truth.[25]

Pinchot argued that forests had two major effects on streamflow: they maintained a more consistent year-round flow, even during the irrigation season when the volume was most likely to fall off, and they prevented destructive floods.[26] Following a deluge on the Ohio River in 1907, he insisted that the damage was "due fundamentally to the cutting away of the forests of the watersheds of the Allegheny and Monongahela rivers." Once "a heavy undergrowth and thick cover of leaves on the ground, and the intertwining roots of trees and shrubs so held back the water from rains and melting snow that dangerous floods seldom occurred." Over-cutting and fires had eliminated the sponge-like ground deposits, and by 1907 water cascaded down the mountain sides, in Pinchot's words, "as from a house roof." He used the 1907 flood as an excuse to seek legisla-

---

24 Thomas R. Dunlap, *Saving America's Wildlife* (Princeton, N.J.: Princeton University Press, 1988), 38, 65–70, 79–81; James B. Trefethen, *An American Crusade for Wildlife* (New York: Winchester Press, 1975), 195–201.

25 The supply of timber depended on what forests were considered accessible, what species of trees were considered desirable for different purposes, and what units of measurement were used. An honest scientist would have admitted that his or her predictions rested on certain variables. Pinchot did not. For examples of Pinchot's warnings on timber famine see *Washington Post*, Nov. 5, 1907; *Boston Herald*, March 20, 1908; *New York Herald*, March 22, 1908. Also see Sherry Olson, *The Depletion Myth* (Cambridge, Mass.: Harvard University Press, 1971).

26 Gifford Pinchot, "Report of the Forest Reserves," in S. Doc. 189, 55 Cong., 2 sess., Serial 3600 (Washington, D.C.: Government Printing Office, 1898), 37.

tion to preserve the Southern Appalachian and White Mountain watersheds, promising that the protection of this land would prevent floods on the Potomac, James, Roanoke, Savannah, Chattahoochee, Coosa, Tennessee, New, Cumberland, Kentucky, Monongahela, and many other rivers.[27]

Pinchot shrugged off strenuous objections from William B. Greeley of the Forest Service, Hiram Martin Chittenden of the Army Corps of Engineers, and many others who argued that flooding was primarily a function of heavy rainfall rather than deforestation. In 1908, Bernhard Fernow, one of the oldest advocates of the theory of deforestation and floods, candidly admitted: "To tell the truth, while we know much of the general philosophy of the influence of the forest cover on water flow, we are not so fully informed as to details of this influence as we might wish. . . . [A]ll the general assertions that are found in literature on forest influences, except perhaps those on soil erosion, need more careful investigations."[28] Despite the well-reasoned protests of critics, Pinchot clung to his theory, even in testimony before Congress.[29]

Fernow understood that science could not sell conservation to the public or to Congress. It took a mixture of history, science, fear, faith, myth, and publicity to prompt legislative action. "In the case of Mr. Pinchot before a Congressional Committee," Fernow observed, "it is to be understood that at such meetings considerable buncombe needs to be performed, if you want to handle the half-informed legislators. It is sad that it is still the expert's position in court & legislative committees to have to accentuate one side to the detriment of the exact truth, but that seems needful in this mundas [sic] qui vult decipi [world that wants to be deceived]!"[30]

Pinchot was heir to a generation of nineteenth-century conservationists who regarded the gospel of wise use as a religious mission. He detested the emotionalism of aesthetes who wanted to protect nature for nature's sake, and he thought of himself as a hard-headed realist. But his practical bent often took the form of a jeremiad. Cutting down forests was more than

---

27 *Washington Post*, March 17, 1907; Gifford Pinchot, "The Upper Ohio Flood," *Forestry and Irrigation*, 13 (April 1907), 169.

28 Andrew Denny Rodgers II, *Bernhard Eduard Fernow: A Story of North American Forestry* (Princeton, N.J.: Princeton University Press, 1951), 128–29.

29 See, e.g., the frequent articles in *American Forestry*, particularly in 1910, including 16 (March, April, and June 1910), 156–73; 209–40; and 349–51.

30 Fernow's comment is as reprinted in Gordon B. Dodds, *Hiram Martin Chittenden: His Public Career* (Lexington: University Press of Kentucky, 1973), 183–84.

improvident; if Americans refused to respect the laws that governed nature, they would pay a terrible price for their greed and profligacy.[31] Theodore Roosevelt's last annual message to Congress in 1908 included Pinchot's warning. The President pointed to stark photographs of denuded, sterile land in northern China, land that had been heavily damaged by floods, land beyond redemption. "The lesson of deforestation in China is a lesson which mankind should have learned many times already from what has occured in other places. . . . What has thus happened in central Asia, in Palestine, in North Africa, in parts of the Mediterranean . . . will surely happen in our country if we do not exercise that wise foresight which should be one of the chief marks of any people calling itself civilized."[32] Those who pushed for the protection of American forests were not so much scientists as evangelists. As one historian has written, "Their commitment was to a cause, not to scientific evidence, if the evidence contravened the cause."[33]

For scientists, bureaucrats, popular writers, and the public alike, the conservation movement rested as much on passion and emotion as science and more on history and observation than experimentation. It consisted of "received knowledge" more than discovered truths. Scientific arguments were political weapons used to structure discourse and to define the opposition. Dressing in the cloak of science allowed conservationists to ennoble their cause while they demonized opponents as monopolists, apologists for business, or crooks.

The Great Depression both helped and hindered science. Many blamed

---

31 Donald J. Pisani, "Forests and Conservation, 1865–1890," *Journal of American History*, 72 (September 1985), 340–59.

32 As reprinted in Paul Russell Cutright, *Theodore Roosevelt: The Making of a Conservationist* (Urbana: University of Illinois Press, 1985), 219. Two years after Theodore Roosevelt's speech, Gifford Pinchot showed the same photographs to the New York Legislature's Forests, Fish, and Game Committee, headed by Franklin D. Roosevelt. F.D.R. never forgot the lesson of desertification and frequently repeated Pinchot's message in the 1930s.

33 Dodds, *Hiram Martin Chittenden*, 183. Many conservationists argued that experience was a more reliable guide to nature's laws than laboratory science. For example, U.S. Senator Francis G. Newlands, one of the architects of the 1902 Reclamation Act, observed: "It is hardly possible to take seriously the gentlemen who argue that forests do not impede run-off. The experience of other nations, no less than our own, proves that they do. Every man who has lived in a wooded country knows by his own observation how the dead leaves, branches and undergrowth hold the water in check, causing it to soak into the soil and forming a spongy blanket over the earth, from which the water oozes slowly into the rills." Those who argued for a strong correlation between forests and run-off insisted that since the best forests had been stripped away—those with the most controlling influence—there was no practical way to test or disprove their hypothesis. See Newlands, "The Control of Waterways," *Independent*, 74 (April 10, 1913), 809–814.

science for creating the agricultural and industrial overproduction responsible for the economic collapse, and hard times deeply cut funds for research. "Research programs could wait," one historian of science has written, "in a period of closed banks when the hungry unemployed trod the streets."[34] Nevertheless, during the darkest years of the 1930s the federal bureaucracy was one of the few places where recent university science graduates could find a job, and they entered government service in large numbers. The hallmark of the New Deal was planning, and planning required specialists in both the physical and social sciences.[35]

Meanwhile a revolution was underway. During the 1920s, the process of dividing science into specialized departments within the nation's universities accelerated, the number of graduate programs increased, and the Rockefeller and Guggenheim foundations began to award research grants.[36] Human beings slowly receded from the center of science during the first third of the twentieth century. In 1929 Aldo Leopold began lecturing on wildlife management at the University of Wisconsin, and his book *Game Management* (1933) became a classic.[37] Leopold made enormous contributions to the fledgling science of ecology. They included the understanding that animals had different requirements for food, water, space, and cover that varied according to the seasons; that the "carrying capacity" of a particular environment differed dramatically from year to year; that all species, particularly the short-lived ones, produced surplus young to ensure that an adequate number reached the age of reproduction; that the surplus population of any species was taken by disease, predators, climatic extremes, and starvation; that if one factor—such as predation—were eliminated the impact of the others would increase; and that hunting was an important way to maintain an optimum-sized population.[38]

34 A. Hunter Dupree, *Science in the Federal Government: A History of Policies and Activities to 1940* (Cambridge, Mass.: Harvard University Press, 1957), 347. The social sciences, not the physical sciences, received the greatest government support during the 1930s. Although some agencies, such as the Soil Conservation Service, conducted limited research, the New Deal emphasized practical science.

35 Philip W. Warken, *A History of the National Resources Planning Board, 1933–1943* (New York: Garland Publishing Co., 1979), 84–85.

36 Stanley Coben, "American Foundations as Patrons of Science: The Commitment to Individual Research," in Nathan Reingold, ed., *The Sciences in the American Context: New Perspectives* (Washington, D.C.: Smithsonian Institution Press, 1979), 229, 232–33.

37 Aldo Leopold, *Game Management* (New York: Charles Scribners' Sons, 1933).

38 Curt Meine, *Aldo Leopold: His Life and Work* (Madison: University of Wisconsin Press, 1988); Susan Flader, *Thinking Like a Mountain: Aldo Leopold and the Evolution of an Ecological Attitude toward Deer, Wolves, and Forests* (Columbia: University of Missouri Press, 1974); James B. Trefethen, "Wildlife Regulation and Restoration," in Henry

During the Progressive Era, conservation focused on the needs of human beings, not the "environment." Wildlife refuges were created largely to curb the slaughter of animals by market hunters and trappers. This began to change during the 1930s as more and more scientists studied nature apart from human beings. In 1935, Jay N. "Ding" Darling of the Biological Survey launched the Cooperative Wildlife Research Program, a system of research stations for graduate students in wildlife management at the nation's land-grant colleges. These research units were funded by the survey, state fish and game agencies, the colleges, and the American Wildlife Institute. They studied the optimum amount of land needed by various species, including bison, antelope, mountain sheep, grizzly bear, Kodiak bear, elk, moose, caribou, sage grouse, wild turkey, prairie chicken, beaver, marten, fisher, deer, ruffled grouse, and migratory waterfowl. This work was still utilitarian—designed to serve the needs of hunters and fishers—but it also exhibited a greater interest in the animals themselves.[39]

So did the creation of national parks and monuments. Secretary of the Interior Harold Ickes urged the Park Service to set aside wilderness areas in existing parks, and some parks created during the 1930s—especially Olympic, Kings' Canyon, Everglades, and Isle Royale—contained large, roadless primitive areas. This represented a sharp break with the assumption that the primary purpose of national parks was the preservation of spectacular scenery, such as the geysers and sulfur springs at Yellowstone or the glacier-carved valleys of Yosemite. The Everglades owed its importance to the large variety of wildlife it contained and to the swamp's role in the ecology of southern Florida.

There were many inconsistencies in New Deal policies. Franklin Roosevelt created the Quetico-Superior Reserve in 1934 by executive order and then appointed a commission to study how it ought to be managed. The committee's report proposed the administration of the forests "under modern forestry practices for a sustained yield" and that wildlife be managed for "maximum natural production." But it also proposed to "keep all lakes and streams, with their islands, rapids, water-falls, beaches, wooded shores, and other natural features undisturbed in a state of na-

Clepper, ed., *Origins of American Conservation* (New York: The Ronald Press Co., 1966), 32. Also see Dunlap, "Values for Varmints: Predator Control and Environmental Ideas, 1920–1939," *Pacific Historical Review,* 53 (May 1984), 141–61, and *Saving America's Wildlife,* 73–74.
39 Trefethen, "Wildlife Regulation and Restoration," 34.

ture." In short, the New Deal combined Progressive Era goals of running nature like a factory with the new faith that parts of nature deserved respect in their own right.[40]

Popular perceptions of nature began to change. By the 1930s, few Americans saw drought or flood as retribution for human sin and improvidence, as they had in the late nineteenth century. Nor were they as likely to exhibit the Progressive Era faith that they could or should treat nature as a factory. Nevertheless, laboratories, experiment stations, and research institutes did not completely displace the moralism and received truths that had guided scientists in the past. Some New Deal conservation policies rested on thin evidence. One of Roosevelt's favorites, the shelterbelt, assumed that bands of trees planted no more than a mile apart on the Great Plains would reduce wind velocity and wind erosion and permit the soil to store more moisture. Roosevelt wanted to plant a one-hundred mile wide forest from Bismarck to Amarillo at the cost of $60 million. Forest Service employees grumbled that the money would be better spent on soil erosion and retiring marginal land from cultivation than on tree planting. Ultimately, Congress approved a much more modest scheme than that favored by Roosevelt. It demonstrated what most silviculturists already knew: trees would not grow on much of the Great Plains and the Dust Bowl had little to do with their absence.[41]

BUREAUCRACY

Science was not just a body of knowledge but a political tool to increase the power of some bureaus at the expense of others. This was evident in the famous Ballinger-Pinchot controversy between the Secretary of Interior and the Chief Forester in 1909–10.[42] Pinchot noted that at the end of Theodore Roosevelt's administration,

every separate Government agency having to do with natural resources was riding its own hobby in its own direction. Instead of being, as we should have been, like a squadron of cavalry, all acting together for a single purpose, we were like loose horses in a field, each one following his own nose. Every bureau chief was for himself and his own work, and the devil take all the others. Everyone operated inside his own fence, and few were big enough to see over it. They were all fighting

40 Swain, "The National Park Service and the New Deal," 330; Ernest C. Oberholtzer to Franklin D. Roosevelt, Feb. 25, 1938, in Nixon, *Franklin D. Roosevelt and Conservation, 1911–1945*, vol. 2, 183–84.
41 Hurt, *The Dust Bowl*, 121–37.
42 Penick, *Progressive Politics and Conservation*.

each other for place and credit and funds and jurisdiction. What little co-operation there was between them was an accidental, voluntary, and personal matter between men who happened to be friends.[43]

Little changed during the New Deal. Ding Darling, head of the Biological Survey during the mid-1930s, remarked: "Conservation as a national principle has no substance or co-ordination. . . . Fourteen agencies in the Federal Government and forty-eight states with some semblance of an official organization in charge of conservation! But they are like so many trains running on single-track roads, often in opposite directions and without any train dispatcher or block system. Collisions are frequent, wrecks are a daily occurrence, and the destruction is greater than the freight delivered at the specified destination."[44]

The rivalries most important to national conservation policies first emerged in the late 1880s and 1890s. The U.S. Geological Survey (USGS), established in 1879 and led after 1881 by John Wesley Powell, assumed many new jobs during the 1880s, from gathering statistics on mining to locating and mapping the West's major reservoir sites (the "Irrigation Survey," launched in 1888). But Powell's attempts to monopolize government science, combined with chronic complaints from western politicians that the USGS did little work of "practical" value and the depression of the 1890s, persuaded Congress to slash the agency's appropriation from $875,000 in 1890 to $500,000 in 1895. Powell was fired and the new director, Charles D. Walcott, set out to rebuild the USGS by emphasizing topography (mapping) rather than scientific work. His office assumed new responsibilities, such as the measurement of stream flow, the location of pools of underground water, and the inventory of timber within the new forest reserves. Finally, in 1902, the USGS won the right to build irrigation projects in the West. The agency went on to determine the value of coal deposits on the public domain, classify the public lands according to their best uses, and recommend land to be purchased under the Weeks Act (1911), which authorized the purchase of forested or cutover lands in the East to protect watersheds and navigation.[45]

Powell fought hard to protect his turf from potential rivals in the Department of the Interior. He feared that the creation of national forests

43 Gifford Pinchot, *Breaking New Ground* (New York: Harcourt, Brace and Company, 1947), 321.
44 Jay N. Darling, "Desert Makers," *Country Gentleman*, 105 (Oct. 1935), 5.
45 Thomas G. Manning, *Government in Science: The U.S. Geological Survey, 1867–1894* (Lexington: University of Kentucky Press, 1967).

under the General Land Office would reduce USGS appropriations; some conservationists assumed that forests were nature's reservoirs and that placing forested public land off-limits would eliminate the need to construct expensive reservoirs and canals.[46] But the conflict between the Interior Department and the Agriculture Department was even more important. In the 1880s and 1890s, officials in the United States Department of Agriculture (USDA) opposed direct aid to irrigation for fear that any expansion of agriculture in the West would compete with established farms in the East and upper Midwest and further depress crop prices. In the late 1880s and early 1890s, a prolonged drought threatened to depopulate large parts of the western Great Plains settled during an unusually wet string of years in the 1870s and 1880s. Great Plains politicians helped to kill Powell's Irrigation Survey in 1890. They succeeded in getting an Artesian Well Survey created in the USDA to rescue their section from drought without benefiting other parts of the West—particularly the Rocky Mountain region, which competed with the Great Plains for settlers. By the early 1890s the West had been divided between the two departments. Interior focused on the far West and the public domain; Agriculture dominated the Great Plains and won the support of private landowners. This division continued into the 1930s.[47]

The Agriculture Department's Artesian Well Survey gave way to an Office of Irrigation Inquiry in 1892. Secretaries of Agriculture J. Sterling Morton (1893–97) and James Wilson (1897–1913) feared alienating the support of Eastern farmers, so they limited the Office of Irrigation Inquiry to gathering information about irrigation and prohibited its small staff from lobbying for bills pertaining to land or water and from public participation in any organization that favored arid land reclamation. Its leaders felt a powerful hostility toward the USGS. In 1894 the head of the Office of Irrigation Inquiry noted in private correspondence:

You speak of the half million, or more, dollars wasted by the Geological Survey. I have seen this waste going on from year to year . . . and I am satisfied that it will be found hereafter, that all which they have done in the field [of irrigation] will be worthless, perfectly useless, but then, the Geological Survey has such a character for *scientific work* that they can obtain any amount, whatever they ask, while this department, making an effort to bring out practical matters on the subject of irrigation, and place in the hands of those most needing the information thus obtained, is barely allowed an existence.

46 Pisani, "Forests and Reclamation, 1891–1911," 70.
47 Pisani, *To Reclaim a Divided West*, 304; Lowitt, *New Deal and the West*, 80.

In 1895 Congress feebly attempted to coordinate the activities of the federal agencies interested in arid land reclamation by creating a Board of Irrigation. Half its members came from the USGS and the Office of Irrigation Inquiry. The others represented the General Land Office, Indian Office, Weather Bureau, Forestry Office, Division of Soils, and Division of Physiology and Pathology. The board met frequently but accomplished little, especially after Congress abolished the Office of Irrigation Inquiry and reallocated the money saved to a new Hydrographic Department in the Geological Survey.

Western politicians feared that if the USGS won the right to build dams and canals, that victory would come at the expense of state control over water rights, which would profoundly affect land values. Therefore, when the depression of the 1890s lifted in 1898, Senator Francis E. Warren persuaded Congress to create a new Irrigation Office within the Office of Experiment Stations in the Agriculture Department. Elwood Mead, a Wyoming State Engineer who had once proposed transferring the Geological Survey to the Agriculture Department, became its head. He declared publicly and privately that the Hydrographic Department in the USGS (led by Frederick H. Newell) had no practical knowledge of irrigation. Both men wanted to direct a federal reclamation program, which promised to be the largest public works program ever undertaken in the United States. The dispute between Mead and Newell turned into one of the bitterest bureaucratic battles in American history. Mead had strong support in the Rocky Mountain states. But Newell, as a result of his friendship with Gifford Pinchot, became one of Theodore Roosevelt's conservation advisers while Roosevelt was still governor of New York, and in 1902 the new reclamation program went to the Geological Survey.[48]

Each side feared that the other wanted to take over its work and each used every political weapon to prevent it. Newell charged that too many bureaus in Agriculture had an interest in irrigation.[49] Mead savagely criticized the Interior Department's ignorance of agriculture. In 1905 he noted that "[t]his tendency to magnify the construction side of irrigation is still manifest. While we may not give too much attention to problems connected with dam and canal building, we fail to give enough to those connected with the agricultural and economic sides. It is the work of the

---

48 Pisani, *To Reclaim a Divided West*, 305–12.
49 F. H. Newell to Gifford Pinchot, July 2, 1903, Box 602, Gifford Pinchot Collection, Library of Congress.

farmer which, after all, determines the value of irrigation properties."[50] Seven years later, in a letter to California's U.S. Senator John D. Works, Mead remarked that the Reclamation Act should have made the west "the land of opportunity." "It has not done so," he continued, "because the forces in control are so narrowly selfish. They have studied how to extend and strengthen their own power rather than how to get the best results." The Reclamation Bureau, according to Mead, had done nothing to bring irrigated farms within the reach of poor families.[51]

Interagency rivalries increased after 1933. The growth of old programs and the advent of new ones, the personal ambitions of strong bureau chiefs, and the tension between conservation and work relief intensified traditional fears and suspicions. The New Deal institutionalized fragmentation. For example, the Civilian Conservation Corps was the creature of the Labor, War, Interior, and Agriculture departments. The program operated through a twenty-five-member advisory council composed of the CCC's director and representatives from each department. The Labor Department selected enrollees and emphasized vocational training. The War Department laid out the camps and provided transportation, food, clothing, housing, and medical care; it urged the CCC to give preference to unemployed military veterans. Virtually all bureaus and offices in Interior proposed work projects, as did the Forest Service, the Soil Conservation Service, the Bureau of Entomology, the Bureau of Plant Industry, and the Bureau of Animal Husbandry in Agriculture. There were over 2,900 camps by the end of the first year. About 2,100 were assigned to Agriculture, another 700 to Interior, and little more than 100 to War. Harold Ickes regularly complained that the Interior Department had been shortchanged. Such complaints reduced the chances that Congress would make the agency permanent, and it was abolished in 1943.[52]

Interior and Agriculture differed over most conservation policies, from grazing to irrigation. When Ickes took over the Department of the Interior, its image suffered from Teapot Dome and other scandals of the 1920s. In the minds of many conservationists, the Agriculture Department represented conservation and wise use; Interior, disposal and waste. Gifford Pinchot and others wanted Agriculture to administer *all* renew-

---

50 Elwood Mead, "Irrigation in the United States," *Transactions of the American Society of Civil Engineers,* 54 (1905), 84.
51 Elwood Mead to John D. Works, Dec. 24, 1912, Mead File, John D. Works Collection, Bancroft Library, University of California, Berkeley.
52 Riesch Owen, Conservation under F.D.R., p. 128; Salmond, *The Civilian Conservation Corps, 1933–1942,* 31–32, 36, 59, 72, 82–84, 146, 171–72.

able resources—whether trees or mountain sheep—with inorganic, non-renewable resources left to Interior. But F.D.R. believed that the division of responsibilities should focus on public and private lands. The Department of the Interior should manage the public domain and all it contained; the Department of Agriculture should confine its work to privately owned land.

Ickes wanted the National Park Service to administer wilderness areas within the national forests. He believed that the TVA and any other river basin authorities should be located in the Department of the Interior. He also blocked the Department of Agriculture's attempt to build water projects on the Great Plains and criticized the Biological Survey's efforts to designate the Okeefinokee Swamp as a wildlife refuge. (Ickes thought that a national monument would provide greater protection to wildlife.) Secretary of Agriculture Henry Wallace had plans of his own. He proposed that the Soil Conservation Service should be located in Agriculture rather than Interior and that Agriculture should have exclusive control over all public grazing land.[53]

Grazing prompted the most bitter dispute between the two departments.[54] The Taylor Grazing Act (1934) increased the Secretary of the Interior's control over the public domain by granting that department jurisdiction over forested lands used principally for grazing—lands designated by the president. The legislation also permitted the secretary to consolidate national grazing lands by exchanging private land within a proposed district for public land outside it.[55] A two-year truce followed passage of the act. But in 1936 the Forest Service published a report entitled *The Western Range,* which recommended that it administer the

---

53 On the famous Ickes-Wallace disputes see T. H. Watkins, *Righteous Pilgrim: The Life and Times of Harold L. Ickes, 1874–1952* (New York: Henry Holt and Co., 1990), 445–591; Graham White and John Maze, *Harold Ickes of the New Deal: His Private Life and Public Career* (Cambridge, Mass.: Harvard University Press, 1985), 160–66, 181, 184–87, 190–93, 207; and Richard Polenberg, "The Great Conservation Contest," *Forest History,* 10 (Jan. 1967), 13–23. On reorganization in general see Polenberg, *Reorganizing Roosevelt's Government: The Controversy Over Executive Reorganization, 1936–1939* (Cambridge, Mass.: Harvard University Press, 1966); Barry Karl, *Executive Reorganization and Reform in the New Deal* (Cambridge, Mass.: Harvard University Press, 1963); and Clayton B. Koppes, "Environmental Policy and American Liberalism: The Department of the Interior, 1933–1953," *Environmental Review,* 7 (Spring 1983), 17–41.

54 Allan J. Soffar, "Differing Views on the Gospel of Efficiency: Conservation Controversies Between Agriculture and Interior, 1898–1938" (Ph.D. diss., Texas Tech University, 1974), 211–289; Harold Ickes, *The Secret Diary of Harold L. Ickes: The Inside Struggle, 1936–1939* (New York: Simon and Schuster, 1954), 43–44, 101, 624–26.

55 Lowitt, *The New Deal and the West,* 65–66.

Taylor Act rather than the Grazing Office in the Department of the Interior. Wallace charged—with justification—that Interior had permitted a small number of livestock owners to monopolize the grazing districts. The report suggested that the Forest Service could enlist the help of bureaus that studied land, plants, and animals; Agriculture had "the largest group of men with training and experience in range management."[56] Ickes responded that only 25 percent of the grazing land covered by the Taylor Act was forested and that only one in four users of the public domain depended on the national forests. The Forest Service, Ickes charged, sacrificed timber and watershed protection to court grazing interests. He again urged the transfer of all grazing lands within the national forests to the Department of the Interior.[57]

These rivalries created discord within departments, not just between them. Although both agencies were in the Department of the Interior, the National Park Service repeatedly clashed with the Forest Service. The creation of new parks and the expansion of old ones frequently involved moving lands from one agency to the other. And in the Agriculture Department, the Biological Survey, Forest Service, and Soil Erosion Service each sought to expand the land they administered.[58]

Franklin Roosevelt has been criticized for not consolidating the conservation agencies into one executive department. But simply creating a Department of Conservation would not have ended the infighting. Not just the bureaus, but the committees in Congress to which they reported, resisted change. Bureau chiefs and committee members developed an atmosphere of mutual trust and accommodation. Bureau personnel resisted change because moving to a new department undermined morale and threatened their future. No employee could be certain to retain his or her job in a new department, or that the mission of the bureau would remain the same. Finally, the "clients" served by bureaus resisted change. Most bureaus served well-organized interest groups with a clear stake in maintaining the administrative status quo.[59]

The goals of reorganization were clear: to integrate government services into a unified administrative machine; to clarify the lines of admin-

56 Harold Ickes to Henry A. Wallace, Aug. 19, 1936, and Wallace to Ickes, Nov. 13, 1936, in Nixon, *Franklin D. Roosevelt and Conservation, 1911–1945*, 1, 554, 602.
57 Harold Ickes to Franklin D. Roosevelt, March 7, 1940, in Nixon, *Franklin D. Roosevelt and Conservation, 1911–1945*, 2, 429–32.
58 Swain, "The National Park Service and the New Deal," 319, 321–22.
59 Frederic A. Delano, "Shifting Bureaus at Washington," *Review of Reviews and World's Work*, 87 (May 1933), 33.

istrative authority and responsibility; to eliminate redundant personnel
and duplication of efforts; to encourage cooperation between agencies
operating in the same field; to centralize business operations such as the
procurement of supplies and the recruitment of new employees; and to
contribute to an efficient federal budget system. But there were no agreed-
upon principles or uniform standards to follow. Franklin Roosevelt faced
the same dilemma as Theodore Roosevelt: would the creation of independent agencies such as the TVA and CCC be more efficient than those
lodged in the traditional departments? Critics of wholesale reorganization
argued that the way to attack inefficient resource management was not to
reshuffle federal agencies and their responsibilities but, rather, to place
greater emphasis on interagency cooperation through bodies like the National Resources Planning Board. Franklin Roosevelt's leadership style
may have contributed to the bureaucratic quagmire, but no president has
been successful in reorganizing the federal bureaucracy.

FEDERALISM

Some New Dealers wanted to centralize power in Washington, some
sought to create regional governments, and some tried to work through
state and local agencies. The expansion of national responsibility for the
administration of natural resources resulted in power flowing simultaneously in two directions, to Washington and to the states. Bureaucratic
competition worked against the concentration of power in Washington.
Federalism also limited the authority of natural resource agencies by encouraging the states to implement their own policies. The federal government found it convenient, therefore, to enter a multitude of partnerships
with state and local governments.

Besides reining in federal agencies that threatened to become too independent, Congress encouraged the states to plan and administer a variety
of conservation programs in cooperation with federal authorities. In the
nineteenth century Congress granted huge amounts of land to the states to
support education, improve transportation, drain swamps, and undertake
other useful public works. The advent of the national income tax in 1913
gave the central government a new source of revenue that permitted
federal grant-in-aid expenditures to rise from less than $3,000,000 in
1901 to $220,000,000 in 1931. Federal subventions increased from one
or two percent of total state revenue receipts before World War I, to an

average of seven or eight percent during the 1920s, to eleven percent in 1932.[60]

The Weeks (1911) and Clark-McNary (1924) acts encouraged federal-state protection of private land within the watersheds of navigable streams and the suppression of fires on private as well as public land. The Forest Service established guidelines, but conditions varied too much from state to state to impose uniform standards. The Weeks Act permitted the central government to buy forested or cutover land in the East but it also laid the foundation for federal-state programs to control floods, reduce soil erosion, and eradicate insects and diseases that preyed on trees. The Clark-McNary Act focused on reforestation and fire fighting and permitted the federal government to purchase land for timber production as well as watershed protection. Both statutes encouraged the states to create or expand forestry departments and enact new restrictions on logging and burning, much as federal highway programs stimulated the growth of state highway bureaucracies.

The 1920s saw a rapid expansion of cooperative forestry programs. Participating states increased from eleven under the first Weeks Act allotment to thirty-eight by the end of 1927. Federal expenditures on cooperative programs rose from $37,000 to $710,000 during this period, but state and private spending grew from $220,000 to $3,450,000. By 1933, half the forested land in the United States came under some form of organized protection, and the line between federal, state, and private policy was extremely blurred.[61]

Although the Hundred Days gave F.D.R. an unprecedented opportunity to centralize power in Washington, federal-state cooperation increased rather than diminished. The national government purchased 400,000

60 Henry J. Bitterman, *State and Federal Grants-In-Aid* (New York: Mentzer, Bush, and Co., 1938), 126, 141, 146; Leonard D. White, *The States and the Nation* (Baton Rouge: Louisiana State University Press, 1953), 18; *Historical Statistics of the United States: Colonial Times to 1957* (Washington, D.C.: Government Printing Office, 1961), 712–13.

61 William G. Robbins, *American Forestry: A History of National, State & Private Cooperation* (Lincoln: University of Nebraska Press, 1985), 50–104; Steen, *The U.S. Forest Service,* 129–31, 173, 189–90, 193; Dana, *Forest and Range Policy,* 237; Gulick, *American Forest Policy,* 146; Clepper, *Professional Forestry in the United States,* 89. Both the states and the federal government had a strong interest in regulating the use of private forests, particularly where they adjoined public lands. There was no way to protect against fire or disease unless the forests were treated as a whole. Not until 1949 did the courts rule on the police power of individual states to dictate forest policies on private land. U.S. Supreme Court rulings in the 1930s suggested that the high court would uphold a federal regulatory power under the commerce or general welfare clauses, but the Forest Service was reluctant to follow this course.

acres of submarginal land—most within fifty miles of large cities—
improved it for recreation purposes, and transferred it to the states for
parks. This was particularly important in the East, where forested land was
limited. Harold Ickes strongly favored assigning CCC workers to state
parks. In 1933, thirteen states—most in the South—lacked state park
systems and a few had no parks at all. By 1939, with CCC aid, ten of the
thirteen had established at least rudimentary systems.[62]

Although the Taylor Grazing Act (1934) involved public rather than
private land, it too promoted federal-state cooperation. As F.D.R. noted
in a 1936 letter to Harold Ickes, the "most noteworthy feature of the
program . . . is the unique coordination of local and Federal effort
whereby fifteen thousand stockmen have participated successfully in the
policy of the Department of the Interior to give local autonomy in the
administration of the new law."[63] No grazing district could be created
without the consent of those who used the land, and the district's board of
directors served as de facto federal officials with the job of limiting the
number of animals grazed by each district member. Since a quarter of the
fees collected went to improve the land and half went to the state for
distribution to the counties in which the district was located, the people of
the nation—the real owners of the public domain—received little from
the Taylor Act except higher beef and mutton prices.[64]

When the initial eighty million acres designated by the Taylor Grazing
Act proved to be inadequate, Congress added an additional sixty-two
million acres to the districts in June 1936, and CCC workers and Soil
Conservation Service money was used to "rehabilitate" the land. Harold
Ickes often worried about the "little fellow," but the district advisory
boards—representing 15,000 grazers—confirmed the status quo. Seven
percent of the permit holders owned 44 percent of the allotted cattle, and
4 percent held 22 percent of the allotted sheep. The Secretary of the
Interior specified the number of animals pastured within each district and
the seasons of use. But the law required him to favor those already using

---

62 Perry H. Merrill, *Roosevelt's Forest Army: A History of the Civilian Conservation Corps*
   (Montpelier, Vt.: Perry H. Merrill, 1981), 29–30.
63 Franklin D. Roosevelt to Harold Ickes, Jan. 3, 1936, in Nixon, *Franklin D. Roosevelt
   and Conservation, 1911–1945*, 1, 463.
64 The political power of the West in Congress increased dramatically after the Omnibus
   States entered the Union in 1889–90. Thereafter, the region became more and more
   successful in securing revenue generated by the public domain. For example, the mineral
   leasing bill of 1920 granted 50 percent of all fees collected to the reclamation fund, 37.5
   percent to the states, and only 12.5 percent to the federal treasury. Frank Smith, *The
   Politics of Conservation* (New York: Pantheon Books, 1966), 142.

the land and to renew permits at the end of their ten-year term if failure to do so would reduce the value of livestock pledged as security for loans.[65] Nowhere was deference to local interests more apparent than in dam-building and soil erosion. Federal water projects did not sell water and power directly to urban consumers. This job was left to private utility companies and public districts, which stimulated the growth of new institutions—such as the gigantic Metropolitan Water District in Southern California. This is not to suggest that the relationship between the states and central government did not involve tension. Some federal officials favored the creation of river basin authorities with regulatory powers comparable to those exercised by the Tennessee Valley Authority, and there was also a plan for a "Dust Bowl Authority" on the Great Plains. Westerners strongly opposed both ideas. Congress rejected all soil conservation legislation that did not include farmer-run districts. In 1937, F.D.R. submitted a model soil-conservation district law to the states, and twenty-two enacted it in that year alone. By June 1939, nineteen million acres in the Dust Bowl states were included in thirty-seven districts. Only Texas refused to adopt the legislation.[66]

CONCLUSION

National conservation policies have assumed many forms in the twentieth century. They have responded to sweeping changes in American society, including urbanization, the decline of the family farm, a rising American standard of living in the years from 1945 to the early 1970s, and the emergence of a "New West," whose economy is characterized increasingly by manufacturing, electronics, service, and tourist industries rather than by mining, lumbering, and stock-raising. The line between city and countryside has faded, and the middle class has expanded its conception of "home" and "neighborhood" to include national parks, wilderness areas, and other outdoor attractions. Scenic beauty and recreation became part of the post–World War II consumer culture. In the 1960s and since, preservation—a small part of conservation in 1900—has taken on increasing importance while conservation for use has come under fire.

65 Lowitt, *The New Deal and the West*, 67; Clayton R. Koppes, "Efficiency, Equity, Esthetics: Shifting Themes in American Conservation," in Donald Worster, ed., *The Ends of the Earth: Perspectives on Modern Environmental History* (New York: Cambridge University Press, 1988), 245.
66 Hurt, *Dust Bowl*, 73, 74, 83–84; H. Wayne Pritchard, "Soil Conservation," in Henry Clepper, ed., *Origins of American Conservation* (New York: The Ronald Press Co., 1966), 97.

From 1891 to 1933 conservation emphasized the management of nature, both to increase the nation's wealth and to distribute it more equitably. During the 1930s, with the market for most natural resources glutted, the emphasis shifted to jobs. An even more important change took place after World War II. Recreation and human health played a negligible role in Progressive Era conservation, but in the 1960s and after they took center stage. Human health became more important than access to natural resources.

Americans had always been interested in public health, but during the first third of this century they defined "health" as the absence of disease rather than an optimum physical condition. Typhoid and cholera killed in days and weeks, but environmental pollutants took their toll over a much longer period of time. How could the public be protected from invisible chemicals that *might* cause diseases like cancer after decades of exposure? Science provided few answers to the question of how much was too much. It could identify potentially toxic substances and it could measure them, but only politicians could set acceptable limits.[67]

Shep Melnick's discussion of environmental policies and politics since the 1960s suggests both continuity and discontinuity with the earlier years of the century. At first glance the differences appear to be greater than the similarities. The dangers to nature and human beings from oil spills, pesticides, food additives, global warming, the depleted ozone layer, disappearing species, and a host of other hazards seem to be unprecedented. The sheer mass of environmental legislation, the emergence of environmental law, and the proliferation of agencies concerned with the environment—in the states as well as in Washington—testify to a new public awareness, if not a revolution in thinking and values. The issues of the 1960s and 1970s had an immediacy and urgency not present in earlier decades.

Both the beauty and the abuse of nature lent themselves to television, and technology profoundly affected environmental politics. Pristine wilderness, polluted streams, and the plight of endangered mammals found their way into the living rooms of the people. The "media" nationalized local problems; environmental issues became everybody's business. From 1900 to 1940, the executive branch of government administered con-

---

67 Samuel P. Hays, *Beauty, Health, and Permanence: Environmental Politics in the United States, 1955–1985* (New York: Cambridge University Press, 1987), and "Three Decades of Environmental Politics: The Historical Context," in Michael J. Lacey, ed., *Government and Environmental Politics: Essays on Historical Developments Since World War II* (Baltimore: Johns Hopkins University Press, 1989), 19–79.

servation. Policies originated in the resource agencies, or among presidential advisers, or within conservation organizations. Congress and the courts were seen as impediments to natural-resource planning and administration.

In recent decades, as Melnick shows so well, presidents and executive agencies have exercised less leadership than Congress and the courts, both of which were regarded as unsympathetic to conservation during the decades before World War II. The growth of subcommittees and their staffs allowed Congress to enact increasingly complicated laws and to monitor their implementation and administration. It was no accident that the U.S. Senator who led the fight against air pollution produced by automobiles was Edmund Muskie of Maine, who chaired the Senate Subcommittee on Air and Water Pollution. Maine, whose automobile production was nil, was a safe state from which to pursue an environmental agenda. It was far easier to make major policy changes at the national level than in fifty state legislatures.

At the same time, resource agencies such as the Reclamation Bureau and the Forest Service came under the increasing scrutiny and suspicion of environmental interest groups. In the Progressive Era, conservation flowed from the top down. Progressive conservationists lauded these bureaus as guardians of the "public interest." But the agencies made little effort to include the public or any significant part of it in policy formulation or review. Long before the 1960s, they had become captives of powerful groups of resource users.

As the role of Congress and the courts expanded, so did the power of environmental groups. Once the Sierra Club had been an elite group of professionals—mainly academics—devoted to organizing outings in the Sierra Nevada Mountains, and the Audubon Society was a collection of bird lovers. From the 1960s on, these and many other environmental groups broadened their agendas. Transformed from tax-exempt educational foundations run by volunteers to professional advocacy groups staffed by large numbers of skilled lobbyists, lawyers, and scientists, they exercised far greater influence in congressional committees than conservation organizations did in earlier eras.

They also exercised far greater influence in the courts. Traditionally, the courts refused to hear damage suits unless the plaintiff could show direct physical or economic injury. Since environmental organizations seldom suffered direct injury, their ability to litigate was limited. But in the late 1960s and 1970s, the courts transformed environmental law in two ways:

they increased the number of people eligible to bring suit, and they expanded the concept of injury to include "nature" and not just people.

The new leadership exercised by Congress, the courts, and environmental organizations represented a significant break with the past. But many aspects of environmental policy have been remarkably consistent throughout the twentieth century. Neither natural resource nor environmental policies have played a large part in presidential or congressional elections, and many changes in values are more apparent than real. Some environmentalists claim that the root cause of the environmental crisis is the ethic of unlimited economic growth. That message is too pessimistic for most Americans, who in the 1960s and 1970s believed in cleaning up the environment but not in closing factories that polluted or in taxing automobiles with poor fuel economy. The environmental movement arose in a prosperous time, when the United States seemed wealthy enough to protect the environment and guarantee continued economic growth simultaneously. Most Americans still assume that they can have it all—a clean environment and a robust economy.

As in the Progressive Era, fear and moralism remain powerful tools. In 1900, Americans fretted that corporate control over the nation's forests would lead to shortages of wood, a soaring cost of living, and perhaps the destruction of American civilization (as deforestation seemed to have destroyed civilizations in the ancient world). By the 1960s and 1970s, human health rather than the health of American civilization became the paramount concern. Environmentalists exhibited an ambivalent attitude toward science, as they had in the earlier period. They used it to give their cause respectability, as Powell and Pinchot had before them, and they hoped that science would provide norms or at least guidance in formulating policy. But they also realized—as Rachel Carson so brilliantly argued in *Silent Spring* (1962)—that all too often science was the slave of those with long purses who subsidized organized research in the nation's universities.

As Melnick notes, while federal natural resource bureaus have assumed many new responsibilities in recent years, they have not been able to achieve autonomy. In the 1930s and after, the efforts of bureaus to sell their policies to the public built up "pressure groups" and "iron triangles" that made centralized planning and coordination all but impossible.[68] The

68 During the presidency of Theodore Roosevelt, the number of publications issued by the Forest Service increased from three in 1901 to sixty-one in 1907. Simultaneously, Gifford Pinchot compiled a mailing list of more than 800,000 civic and commercial

historian Ellis Hawley has wisely observed, "what the New Deal really had at hand, then, was not only a set of prescriptions for giving America an administrative state, but also formulations for using government in ways that were supposed to allow us to continue without such a state. . . . The state that emerged had a 'hollow core' where the state managers were supposed to be." Central government can grow even in a society that is hostile to bureaucracy and planning.[69]

The national government assumed more and more responsibility for protecting the public health, as in setting air and water pollution standards. Yet as federal power increased, so did state power. For example, because the Environmental Protection Agency was never funded at a level that permitted it to live up to its mandate, it has relied heavily on state and local environmental agencies to monitor compliance. The Cold War and the civil rights revolution contributed more to the growth of federal power than the environmental movement. No professional ruling class or set of disinterested bureaucrats emerged in the 1960s and 1970s to provide independent leadership; indeed, many natural resource agencies lost rather than gained power.

Conservation has never lost its chameleon nature. It remains a tool of economic and social reform as well as a method of allocating natural resources. In the Progressive Era, federal reclamation promised to defuse urban tensions by turning landless immigrants into property owners and good citizens. It also sought to prevent fledgling hydroelectric companies from monopolizing the best power plant sites on the public domain. In the 1930s, New Dealers used conservation not just to create jobs but as the foundation for a planned economy. In recent decades, "environmentalism" has come to represent a "lifestyle" as well as a public policy. Virtually all environmentalists question the Progressive Era assumption that human beings exist beyond or outside nature, and many question capitalism's obsession with economic growth, if not capitalism itself. They deny that the nation can be run like General Motors and distrust the materialism at the heart of American values. In 2000 as in 1900, natural resource policies say as much about American culture as about natural resources.

organizations, newspaper editors, and politicians to enlist their support for legislation favored by the forestry office. See Cutright, *Theodore Roosevelt*, 217–18, and Stephen Fox, *The American Conservation Movement: John Muir and His Legacy* (Madison: University of Wisconsin Press, 1981), 129.

69 Ellis W. Hawley, "The New Deal State and the Anti-Bureaucratic Tradition," in Robert Eden, ed., *The New Deal and Its Legacy: Critique and Reappraisal* (New York: Greenwood Press, 1989), 81, 89.

7

Risky Business: Government and the Environment after Earth Day

R. SHEP MELNICK

In 1972, two years after the first Earth Day, Anthony Downs wrote a short, influential article warning that "American public attention rarely remains sharply focused upon any one domestic issue for very long." Typically an issue "suddenly leaps into prominence, remains there for a short time, and then—though still largely unresolved—gradually fades from the center of public attention."[1] Political news has a short shelf-life; newspaper reporters and readers quickly grow sated, jaded, and just plain bored. Organized interests and the public begin to recognize the cost of change. Meanwhile other issues become the talk of Washington and the nation. Existing programs grind on, but with markedly reduced public support, aggressiveness, and success.

Part of the appeal of Downs's "issue-attention cycle" was that it seemed to fit so well with what historians and political scientists had told us about regulation in the Progressive and New Deal eras. Marver Bernstein, for example, claimed that the typical commission starts off "in an aggressive crusading spirit" but inevitably "becomes part of the status quo and thinks in terms of the protection of its own system and its own existence and power against substantial change." This administrative "life-cycle" ends with "the commission's surrender to the regulated."[2] Organized interests inevitably dominate policymaking once public attention dwindles. This generalization was about as close to an "iron law" as political science could muster.

---

1 Anthony Downs, "Up and Down with Ecology—The 'Issue-Attention Cycle,'" *The Public Interest* 28 (1972), 38.
2 *Regulating Business by Independent Commission* (Princeton University Press, 1955), 75–76.

In retrospect, it is remarkable just how poorly the seemingly sensible models of Downs and Bernstein fit environmental regulation. Environmental issues have hardly faded from view. If anything they are more prominent in the news today than they were in the watershed years of 1969–70. The Exxon Valdez oil spill, spotted owls and snail darters, radon, acid rain, greenhouse gasses, Alar, dioxin, asbestos, toxic waste dumps, destruction of the rain forests, recycling—just to mention a few key terms—remind us how ubiquitous environmental issues have become.

Just as importantly, federal environmental programs have grown steadily since the late 1960s. Pollution control regulations have expanded in both scope and stringency. A variety of new initiatives—to clean up hazardous waste sites, to provide "cradle to grave" monitoring of new chemicals, to enhance the quality of drinking water, to combat ozone depletion and global warming—have been added to the duties of the federal government. By 1990 pollution abatement cost the United States about $100 billion per year, a little more than 2 percent of the Gross National Product (GNP). This is expected to rise to $160 billion or 2.8 percent of GNP by the year 2000.[3] In 1960 the federal government had reserved about seventy-five million acres for national parks, wilderness areas, and wildlife refuges. By 1990 that figure had grown to nearly three hundred million acres. In many parts of the country, logging on public lands, construction of water projects, and highway building was substantially curtailed by the threat of lawsuits under the National Environmental Policy Act of 1969 and the Endangered Species Act of 1973.

The vitality of environmental policy appears all the more surprising when one considers the central political and economic events of the past three decades. The first Earth Day took place toward the end of an era of unprecedented economic growth. By 1973 economic growth had stalled, and the United States entered a prolonged period of "stagflation." The energy crises of 1973 and 1978 created enormous pressures for encouraging more exploration and use of fossil fuels. Our huge foreign trade deficit gave political force to business's argument that promoting competitiveness in international markets requires relaxing environmental regulation. Plummeting confidence in government helped to revitalize a Republican

---

3 Daniel Fiorino, *Making Environmental Policy* (University of California Press, 1995), 121–22, citing figures produced by the Environmental Protection Agency; Paul Portney, Katherine Probst, and Adam Finkel, "EPA at Thirtysomething," *Environmental Law* 21 (1991), 1462; and Council on Environmental Quality, *Environmental Quality, Twenty-Second Annual Report* (Washington, D.C., 1992), 220.

Party highly critical of regulatory programs. If environmental protection had been scaled back in 1973, 1981, or 1995, political scientists and journalists would have no shortage of convincing explanations.

The persistence of divided government and the conflicting demands of the "three Es"—environment, energy, and the economy—help explain why environmental policy never became the politically insulated preserve of bureaucrats and organized interests that was predicted by Bernstein and others. In comparative perspective American environmental politics is notable for its contentiousness.[4] Virtually every important Environmental Protection Agency (EPA) rule is condemned by vocal interest groups, reviewed, delayed, and amended by the Office of Management and Budget (OMB), criticized and modified by congressional subcommittees, and challenged in court by both industry and environmentalists.

This chapter contends that the political staying power of environmentalism, the expansion of federal regulation, and the adversarial nature of environmental policy making are best understood as the result of broader changes in the American polity since the mid-1960s. The public now expects the federal government to protect it from a wide variety of hazards. Not only have hundreds of new groups sprung up to demand, defend, and contest government regulations, but institutional change has made it easier for them to gain access to government. Both the demands and the constraints on regulatory agencies have steadily increased, making governing the environment a devilishly difficult task.

CULTURE SHIFT?

Many students of environmental politics attribute the resilience of these issues and programs to an emerging environmental consciousness. The public, they claim, now recognizes the damage done to the planet by uncontrolled development and places greater value on such collective goods as clean air and water, wilderness preservation, and biodiversity. This alleged "paradigm shift" from the material values of an industrial era

---

4 Ronald Brickman, Sheila Jasanoff, and Thomas Ilgen, *Controlling Chemicals: The Politics of Regulation in Europe and the United States* (Cornell University Press, 1985). Other works that come to similar conclusions include David Vogel, *National Styles of Regulation: Environmental Policy in Great Britain and the United States* (Cornell University Press, 1986); John Mendelloff, *The Dilemma of Toxic Substances Regulation: How Over Regulation Causes Under Regulation at OSHA* (Massachusetts Institute of Technology, 1988); and Robert Kagan, "Adversarial Legalism and American Government," *Journal of Policy Analysis and Management* 10 (1991), 369.

to the "postmaterial values" of our "postindustrial age" has produced a quantum leap in environmental politics.[5]

Polling data on environmental issues tells a less dramatic, more equivocal story. On the one hand, the public strongly supports programs to protect and improve the environment. For years large majorities of those polled agreed with the statement that "protecting the environment is *so* important that requirements and standards cannot be too high, and continuing environmental improvement must be made *regardless* of cost." In fact, by 1989, 80 percent agreed and fewer than 20 percent disagreed. In 1990–91 about 60 percent of the public believed there was "too little" environmental regulation; only 15 percent answered "too much." Even in 1994, the year the Republicans gained control of Congress, almost half those polled thought that current laws "don't go far enough in protecting the environment," and fewer than one-fifth stated these laws "have gone too far." In early 1996 Republican pollsters warned that congressional attacks on environmental programs were seriously wounding the party.[6]

On the other hand, few voters consider environmental issues as important as drugs, crime, or the state of the economy. Only about 10 percent of the public list the environment as the most important issue facing the nation. High popularity but low salience—that is the paradox of public opinion on the environment.[7] One indication of the low salience of environmental issues is the fact that Ronald Reagan's opposition to environmental regulation did little to damage his approval ratings.

5 See, for example, Samuel Hayes, "Three Decades of Environmental Politics: The Historical Context," in Michael Lacey, ed., *Government and Environmental Politics: Essays on Historical Developments Since World War II* (Woodrow Wilson Center Press and Johns Hopkins University Press, 1989). This line of analysis often refers to Ronald Inglehart's *The Silent Revolution: Changing Values and Political Styles Among Western Publics* (Princeton University Press, 1977).

6 Riley Dunlap, "Public Opinion and Environmental Policy," in James Lester, ed., *Environmental Politics and Policy: Theories and Evidence* (Duke University Press, 1989), 87; Robert Cameron Mitchell, "Public Opinion and the Green Lobby: Poised for the 1990s?" in Norman Vig and Michael Kraft, eds., *Environmental Policy in the 1990s* (CQ Press, 1990), 81; Karlyn Bowman and Everett Carl Ladd, "Opinion Pulse: Environmental Protection," *The American Enterprise* (March/April 1995), 108; Bob Benenson, "GOP Sets the 104th Congress on New Regulatory Course," *Congressional Quarterly Weekly Report* (June 17, 1995), 1693–7; Margaret Kriz, "The Green Card," *National Journal* (September 16, 1995), 2262; Ben Wildavsky, "Carrying On," *National Journal* (May 4, 1996), 911; and *Environment Reporter—Current Developments* (February 2, 1996), 1870.

7 Robert Cameron Mitchell, "Public Opinion and Environmental Politics in the 1970s and 1980s," in Norman Vig and Michael Kraft, eds., *Environmental Policy in the 1980s: Reagan's New Agenda* (CQ Press, 1984). For recent figures on the saliency of environmental issues, see Benenson, "GOP Sets the 104th Congress on New Regulatory Course," 1697.

Twenty-five years of experience should lead us to question whether 80 percent of the public will really stand behind the claim that environmental improvements must be made "regardless of cost"—especially when these costs fall directly on them. As soon as costs become visible to consumers and taxpayers, opposition to environmental regulation surges. For example, compared to many pollution control requirements, requiring private citizens to keep their cars' pollution control equipment in good working order is quite cost-effective. But strict inspection and maintenance rules are inconvenient and costly for motorists, and consequently extremely unpopular. Proposals to raise gasoline taxes in order to discourage fuel use, to reduce automobile traffic in smog-choked cities, and to shut down particularly dirty facilities attract little support and heated opposition.[8] Public support for environmental programs often rests on the soothing belief that someone else—auto companies, the chemical industry, midnight haulers, upwind utilities—will pay the freight. Since politicians realize this, most environmental programs are designed to disguise costs and make them hard to trace.

To question the emergence of a new "environmental consciousness" is not to deny that there is a link between affluence and support for environmental protection. Economic growth creates both wealth and externalities. A richer population is likely to spend some of the former to eliminate some of the latter. Wealthier citizens are also more likely to spend more time and money on recreation. These changes are particularly apparent in the West, where extractive industries have declined in importance and outdoor recreation has boomed. In the post-War United States, growing affluence has gone hand-in-hand with suburbanization. Environmental protection can be thought of as a collective form of moving to the suburbs. Now that we are more economically comfortable and secure we can afford green grass, colorless air, and even vacations to Yellowstone and Aspen.

Far from creating a new consensus, heightened demand for what Samuel Hayes has called "environmental amenities" has intensified conflict over the use of natural resources. As the continuing battle between Oregon loggers and defenders of the spotted owl demonstrates, wilderness

---

8 On gasoline taxes, see Pietro Nivola, *The Politics of Energy Conservation* (Brookings Institution, 1986), chap. 5; on plant closings and automobile restrictions, see R. Shep Melnick, *Regulation and the Courts: The Case of the Clean Air Act* (Brookings Institution, 1983), chaps. 7 and 9; on inspection and maintenance, see Gary Bryner, *Blue Skies, Green Politics,* 2nd ed. (CQ Press, 1995), 189–99 and 249–50.

preservation can still run headlong into demands for jobs, cheaper housing, and more convenient transportation. Moreover, environmentalism has become a "big tent" that covers a variety of divergent interests. For example, members of the "hook and bullet set" hope to kill the very wildlife that "bird and bunny" groups are trying to protect.[9] Some people want to visit a silent Grand Canyon, others to fly over it in noisy planes. Some want to improve urban environments by dispersing pollution; others to prevent dispersion in order to preserve the quality of rural life and the visibility in wilderness areas. And everyone wants to be the last to move into a quiet suburb.

Some contemporary controversies over the use of natural resources will seem eerily familiar to students of the Progressive Era. Members of John Muir's Sierra Club continue to attack Gifford Pinchot's Forest Service for promoting logging and grazing rather than preservation. Western Senators still berate federal land managers for being insensitive to local concerns. Although the conflict between "conservation for use" and "conservation for preservation" endures, the potent combination of affluence, suburbanization, and increasing demand for outdoor recreation have swung the pendulum in the direction of the latter. It is hard to imagine, for example, that the Hetch Hetchy reservoir could have been built after 1970. John Muir would have quickly filed suit under the National Environmental Policy Act or Endangered Species Act. Pinchot would still be working on the environmental impact statement.

Another major difference between the conservationism of the early 1900s and environmentalism today is the contemporary emphasis on public health. Over the past three decades the United States has spent more and more money trying to eliminate smaller and smaller health risks. Efforts to control potential carcinogens have dominated the headlines and garnered the lion's share of the environmental protection budget. This "public health, anticancer emphasis," Daniel Fiorino writes, "was seen at the time as a necessary political adaptation to the antiregulatory pressures of the day."[10] According to a 1990 report by the EPA's Science Advisory Board, "The Agency has considered the protection of public health to be

---

9 These colorful terms come from an environmental lobbyist quoted in George Hager, "For Industry and Opponents. A Showdown Is in the Air," *Congressional Quarterly Weekly Report* (January 20, 1990), 147.
10 Fiorino, *Making Environmental Policy,* 39. Also see Marc Landy, Marc Roberts, and Stephen Thomas, *The Environmental Protection Agency: Asking the Wrong Questions,* expanded edition (Oxford University Press, 1993), chap. 11; and Melnick, *Regulation and the Courts,* 277–81.

its primary mission, and it has been less concerned about risks posed to ecosystems." "The imbalance," the board warned, "is a manifest, if inadvertent, part of current national environmental policy."[11]

Despite the shift from conservation of natural resources to protection of public health, contemporary environmentalists share a key trait with their Progressive forbearers: an uneasy combination of moralism and scientism. As Donald Pisani observes in his essay, nineteenth-century conservationists "preached the gospel of conservationism as redemption. Their moralizing about the abuse of nature took the jeremiad form: if Americans refuse to respect the laws that govern nature, they would pay a terrible price for their greed and profligacy."[12] Substitute "toxic chemicals" for clear-cutting and chemical companies for "the trusts," and the message remains the same. Just as Pinchot repeatedly argued that science demonstrated that clear-cutting causes flooding, today's environmentalists insist that science demonstrates that Alar causes cancer, acid rain destroys forests, and greenhouse gasses cause extensive climate change. Evidence to the contrary is quickly dismissed as propaganda produced by the lackeys of big business. Opponents of regulation are just as quick to claim that objective science supports their position. Each side in the debate accuses the other of using "bad science" and asserts that "good science" will produce good public policy.

UNLIMITED GOVERNMENT

When environmentalism burst upon the scene in 1970, pollution was not getting worse—indeed, in some respects the environment was getting cleaner. But it was getting easier to convince the public that a pressing problem required a corresponding federal program. Just five years before the first Earth Day the federal government entered the health-care field by establishing Medicare and Medicaid. 1965 was also the year that Congress broke new ground by providing federal funds for local school systems, asserting unprecedented federal control over state elections, and set about creating a "Great Society." Three years later, Congress established the National Highway Traffic Safety Administration. In the first half of the 1970s a variety of new federal laws prohibited discrimination on the basis of gender, handicap, and age. After waging a War on Poverty, attack-

---

11 Environmental Protection Agency, Science Advisory Board, EPA Document SAB-EC-90-021, "Reducing Risk: Setting Priorities and Strategies for Environmental Protection" (September 1990), 9.
12 Pisani, "The Many Faces of Conservation," in this volume.

ing "crime in the streets," and desegregating local schools, setting nationally uniform standards for air and water quality seemed less than revolutionary. The cumulative effect of presidentially led breakthroughs in the Progressive, New Deal, and Great Society years was to make subsequent expansion of the government's agenda seem commonplace.

Regulating pollution to protect the public health was hardly unprecedented in the United States. As early as 1906, New York City had banned the burning of bituminous coal to improve air quality.[13] What was unprecedented about the environmental legislation of the 1970s was the proliferation of nationally uniform standards issued and enforced by the federal government. Given the long-standing American commitment to decentralized government, this was a shift of great significance. Before 1970 the federal government provided a small amount of money and cautious scientific advice to state regulators.[14] State and local governments remain key players in environmental policymaking but the roles have been reversed: in earlier years state and local governments set standards and the federal government provided some of the resources needed to carry them out; now the federal government sets the standards and expects subnational governments to provide administrative resources to enforce them.

It is a paradox of no little importance that the responsibilities of the federal government were growing just as public confidence in government was plummeting. In 1964 only 22 percent of the public agreed with the statement "you cannot trust the government to do what is right most of the time." This rose to 36 percent in 1968, 44 percent in 1970, 73 percent in 1980, and 80 percent in 1995.[15] Not surprisingly, this period also witnessed the election of three Republican presidents and a Republican Congress promising to get the federal government "out of our pockets and off our backs." More surprising is the fact that by 1972 mistrust of

13 Morton Keller, *Regulating a New Society: Public Policy and Social Change in America, 1900–1933* (Harvard University Press, 1994), 194.
14 Although the most significant expansion of environmental regulation took place in the 1970s, the federal government began to take a more aggressive stance during the Johnson administration. In 1965, Congress authorized the Department of Health, Education, and Welfare to establish auto emission standards. In 1967, Congress required states to establish and enforce ambient air quality standards. This suggests that changing views on federalism were an important precursor of contemporary environmentalism.
15 S. M. Lipset and William Schneider, *The Confidence Gap: Business, Labor, and Government in the Public Mind*, revised edition (Johns Hopkins University Press, 1987), 17; Karlyn Bowman and Everett Carl Ladd, "Opinion Pulse," *The American Enterprise* (March/April 1995), 102–3.

government and bureaucracy was as common among liberals as among conservatives.[16]

Part of the explanation for the concomitant growth of government responsibilities and public distrust of government is that other institutions lost public support even faster than the federal government.[17] The civil rights movement destroyed the legitimacy of "states' rights." Just as important for the expansion of federal regulation was a rapid drop in public confidence in business firms. In 1968, 70 percent of those polled agreed with the statement that "business tries to strike a fair balance between profits and the interests of the public." That figure dropped to 30 percent in 1970 and 20 percent by 1974. Ironically, the Reagan years did more to rehabilitate government's image than that of business, which remained an inviting target for policy entrepreneurs.[18]

One way of describing the expansion of the responsibilities of the federal government is to list major laws enacted during the 1970s and 1980s (see Appendix). This impressive succession of enactments is only a starting place for understanding the expansion of regulation during the two decades. Not only does it fail to convey a sense of the specificity, cost, and intrusiveness of many of these new programs, but it also leaves the mistaken impression that change came primarily through the legislative process. A brief review of one of the programs, regulation of air pollution, will help fill out the picture.[19]

Before 1970 the federal government neither established nor enforced legally binding air pollution rules. The 1970 Clean Air Act contained specific, "technology-forcing" auto-emission standards. It required the EPA to set air-quality standards for major pollutants and nationally uniform emission limitations for newly constructed sources of pollution. The law ordered the states to formulate and enforce plans to meet all these standards by 1975. The sponsors of the legislation expected key industries—auto, steel, coal-burning utilities, smelters—to develop new technology to meet these standards quickly and cheaply. To a large extent this

16 Norman Nie, Sidney Verba, and John Petrocik, *The Changing American Voter* (Harvard University Press, 1976), 127. Also see Hugh Heclo, "The Sixties' False Dawn: Awakenings, Movements, and Postmodern Policy-making," *Journal of Policy History* 8 (1996), 34–63.
17 Lipset and Schneider, *The Confidence Gap*, chaps. 1, 2, and 13.
18 Ibid., 426. The polling data is reported on 183.
19 For more details, see Melnick, *Regulation and the Courts*; and Gary Bryner, *Blue Skies, Green Politics*, chaps. 3 and 4.

was an exercise in wishful thinking by politicians who dared not be branded weak on pollution.

Two years later the federal courts ordered the EPA to establish an additional program to prevent the "significant deterioration" of air quality in areas already meeting national standards—which meant most of the country. Despite vociferous complaints from western Senators, Congress accepted and even expanded this convoluted program.[20]

By the mid-1970s it was obvious than many cities would continue to violate air quality standards long into the future. The EPA was understandably hesitant either to place a moratorium on all development in "nonattainment" areas or to condone additional pollution in areas already out of compliance. Consequently it announced an innovative "offset" policy: in order to build a new facility in a nonattainment area, a firm must purchase pollution rights from an existing facility. In 1977 Congress accepted the outlines of this program but increased the restrictions on sources seeking to build or expand in nonattainment areas. Each time Congress extends a deadline, it spreads the regulatory net wider and tightens the screws on new development.

Meanwhile, environmental groups demanded that the EPA use its statutory authority to reduce emissions of hundreds of potential carcinogens released in relatively small amounts. The EPA resisted, but Congress and the courts ordered it to proceed. The Clean Air Act Amendments of 1990 require the EPA to establish the "maximum achievable control technology" for nearly two hundred hazardous pollutants. The 1990 Act also tightened standards for new cars and trucks, created new programs to curb acid rain and chlorofluorocarbons, established a complex system of national permits, and mandated use of alternative fuels in nonattainment areas. In 1972 the cost of air pollution abatement was about $5.5 billion per year. By 1988 it was $32 billion. By 2000 spending on air-pollution control may exceed $60 billion annually.[21]

Air-pollution control is a classic example of what Bardach and Kagan have called the "regulatory ratchet."[22] In the early days of the environmental era Congress set ambitious goals for pollution reduction without knowing what it was getting into. Although few of the original deadlines

---

20 Melnick, *Regulation and the Courts,* chap. 4.
21 Paul Portney, "Policy Watch: Economics and the Clean Air Act," *Journal of Economic Perspectives* 4 (1990), 173.
22 Eugene Bardach and Robert Kagan, *Going by the Book: The Problem of Regulatory Unreasonableness* (Temple University Press, 1987), chap. 7.

were met, the restrictions imposed on polluters became ever more extensive and costly. Business firms and labor unions subject to the most stringent requirements—usually those in urban areas—convinced Congress
and regulators to "level the playing field" by imposing more restrictions
on sources located in cleaner areas. Meanwhile, new problems—Love
Canal, acid rain, global warming, the hole in the ozone layer—produced
new programs. The government's reach and responsibility grew in ways
most citizens—and most politicians—could hardly fathom.

INSTITUTIONAL COMBAT

The conventional wisdom holds that the multiple veto points embedded
within the American political system give those who oppose action by the
federal government a powerful strategic advantage. The history of the
Clean Air Act shows that separation of powers creates not only "veto
points" but also "opportunity points" for those pushing new ventures.
The initial proposal for uniform national standards came from the Nixon
administration, the idea of "technology forcing" standards and deadlines
came from the Senate subcommittee, stricter controls on hazardous emissions from the House, prevention of significant deterioration from the
courts, and the "offset policy" from the agency.

Such policy innovation would not have been possible without the substantial institutional change that took place at the national level in the late
1960s and early 1970s. Congress successfully threw off the yoke of the
conservative southern "Committee Barons," replacing this oligarchy with
"subcommittee government" run by entrepreneurial Democrats from the
north and west. Congress also made a concerted effort to regain powers
previously ceded to the executive branch.[23] The Nixon administration
counterattacked by increasing White House control over spending and
agency rule making. The techniques of the "administrative presidency"
were refined and expanded by succeeding presidents.[24] Meanwhile, the
federal judiciary was shedding its New Deal deference and starting to take
a "hard look" at agency decisions. Many of the key elements of the
"reformation of American administrative law" were announced in en-

---

23 James Sundquist, *The Decline and Resurgence of Congress* (Brookings Institution,
   1991); and Thomas Mann and Norman Ornstein, eds., *The New Congress* (American
   Enterprise Institute, 1981).
24 Richard Nathan, *The Administrative President* (Wiley, 1983); and Sidney Milkis, *The
   Presidents and the Parties: The Transformation of the American Party System Since the
   New Deal* (Oxford University Press, 1993).

vironmental cases.[25] Conflict between the president and Congress often allowed judges to tip the balance in the direction of their preferred policies.

Just as importantly, divided government—usually accused of turning mere stalemate into "gridlock"—produced bidding wars as each party tried to show it was at least as "green" as the other. Democrats have seen environmentalism as an issue that can return to their party some of the lost elements of the New Deal coalition. Republicans have often realized that their ties with business and their skepticism about government intervention can become liabilities when the public focuses on environmental issues. Presidents Nixon and Bush were determined to deprive the Democrats of this issue. This encouraged Democrats to up the ante, hoping to expose the Republicans as fairweather environmentalists. Stringent environmental laws, congressional Democrats learned, could serve as convenient sticks for beating Republican administrations. The more unrealistic the deadline, the surer the opportunity for inquisitorial oversight hearings. In short, party competition in an age of weak party organization and divided government created a dynamic that has kept environmental issues before the public and produced rigid, demanding environmental statutes.

The clearest instance of a bidding war came in the 1970. Edmund Muskie, the front-runner for the Democratic presidential nomination, personified the congressional challenge to the Nixon White House. By virtue of his chairmanship of the Public Works Committee's subcommittee on air and water pollution, Muskie staked out his claim on the topic before it had became politically fashionable. Stung by criticism from public interest groups and in danger of being upstaged by Nixon, Muskie and his staff wrote particularly demanding laws, including a mandate for 90 percent emission reduction from new cars by 1975 and the requirement that all lakes and rivers to be "fishable and swimmable" by 1983.

President Nixon reluctantly signed the Clean Air Act. The 1972 water pollution law passed over his veto. Predictably, the administration pressured the EPA to show leniency in implementation of the acts. This led to congressional hearings attacking the administration for failing to comply with the "intent" of Congress, as well as a blizzard of law suits, many of which were won by environmental groups. The Administrator of the EPA, Russell Train, recalled that Muskie's staff "didn't let many days go by

---

25 Richard Stewart, "The Reformation of American Administrative Law," *Harvard Law Review* 88 (1975), 1667; and Martin Shapiro, *Who Guards the Guardians? Judicial Control of Administration* (University of Georgia Press, 1988).

without calling and telling you what you did wrong."[26] With Watergate weakening Nixon, the EPA's administrators openly allied themselves with Muskie rather than with the president. This led the Nixon and Ford administrations to intensify their efforts to "get control" over the agency. As one EPA official put it, Train survived only "because Richard Nixon did not."[27]

A strikingly similar pattern appeared twenty years later. During the 1988 campaign, George Bush proclaimed that he wanted to be the "Environmental President," and pledged to support strong air-pollution legislation. The Bush Administration subsequently proposed an innovative acid rain program. Democrats in Congress strengthened the Bush proposal and added a wide variety of other mandates. The White House threatened to veto the 314-page omnibus bill, but eventually backed down. House subcommittee chair Henry Waxman noted that "the specificity of the 1990 Amendments reflects the concern that without detailed directives, industry intervention might frustrate efforts to put pollution control steps in place. . . . History shows that even when the EPA seeks to take strong action, the White House will often intervene at industry's behest to block regulatory action."[28] Before long, Waxman's subcommittee was holding well-publicized hearings claiming that the Bush administration's Competitiveness Council had ordered the EPA to ignore provisions of the new law.[29]

From the dawn of "subcommittee government" in the early 1970s to the Republican takeover of Congress in 1994, self-selection in committee assignments produced committees, subcommittees, and staff dedicated to the cause of environmental protection. Members asked to sit on these panels because they considered environmental protection to be a particularly noble and popular cause. Subcommittee leaders tended to view the Clean Air Act, Superfund, the Toxic Substances Control Act, and other enactments as their laws and were not shy about explaining to administrators what they meant. Committees held regular oversight hearings, hired more staff to monitor agency activity, created elaborate reporting mecha-

---

26 Environmental Protection Agency, *Oral History Interview-2: Russell E. Train* (July 1993), 12.
27 Robert Sansom, *The New American Dream Machine* (Doubleday, 1976), 25. Deputy Administrator John Quarles tells a similar story in *Cleaning up America* (Houghton Mifflin, 1976). Also see Melnick, *Regulation and the Courts*, 122–38.
28 Henry Waxman, "An Overview of the Clean Air Act Amendments of 1990," *Environmental Law* 21 (1991), 1743–44.
29 Robert J. Duffy, "Divided Government and Institutional Combat: The Case of the Quayle Council on Competitiveness," *Polity* 18 (Spring 1996), 379.

nisms, and placed more than 250 legislative veto provisions in federal statutes. During the 1970s and 1980s EPA officials appeared before congressional committees between fifty and one hundred times per year.[30]

Congress also rewrote major laws on a regular basis. With each reauthorization the laws became more detailed and more demanding. The Clean Air Act increased in length from 62 pages in 1970 to 404 in 1990. The 1990 law included 90 specific emission limitations for motor vehicles alone. When Congress rewrote the 1976 Resources Conservation and Recovery Act in 1984, it added a long list of new substances to be controlled, sixty-seven deadlines for agency rule making, and eight "hammers" (a term used to describe the new practice of inserting into the statute a draconian rule that goes into effect unless the agency establishes a rule that meets numerous legal requirements). In 1986 Congress rewrote the Safe Drinking Water Law to require the EPA to establish forty new standards over the next two years and twenty-five additional standards every three years after that. The EPA was required to set all these standards "at the level at which no known or anticipated adverse effects on the health of persons occur and which allows an adequate margin of safety." The Water Quality Act of 1987 required the EPA to issue twenty-five rules, produce forty policy documents, prepare thirty-one reports to Congress, and meet ninety deadlines—all within three years.[31] According to an influential House subcommittee chair, "the traditional reliance on delegated responsibility has collapsed," requiring Congress to set "specific policy and implementation decisions traditionally in the domain of the agency."[32]

One consequence of this pattern was administrative overload. A 1985 study found the EPA to be subject to more than three hundred statutory deadlines—most of which it failed to meet.[33] Congress, Walter Rosenbaum has noted, "easily falls into a 'pollutant of the year' mentality," which produces "a multitude of new programs, hastily enacted without

---

30 Richard Lazarus, "The Neglected Question of Congressional Oversight of EPA: Quis Custodiet Ipsos Custodes (Who Shall Watch the Watchers Themselves)?" *Law and Contemporary Problems* 54 (1991), 211–13. In 1989 alone EPA officials testified on 142 occasions.

31 Fiorino, *Making Environmental Policy,* 57.

32 James Florio (D-N.J.), quoted in Alexis Halley, "Hazardous Waste Disposal: The Double-Edged Sword of the RCRA Land-Ban Hammer," in Robert Gilmour and Alexis Halley, eds., *Who Makes Public Policy?* (Chatham House, 1994), 89.

33 Environmental and Energy Study Institute, "Statutory Deadlines in Environmental Legislation: Necessary but Need Improvement" (September 1985), 11.

sufficient time or resources provided for the task."[34] This congressionally-induced administrative overload conveniently created new opportunities for subcommittees: they could hold hearings and press conferences berating the executive branch for failing to protect public health and the ecosystem.[35]

Of course not all members of Congress share committee members' zeal for environmental protection. Many of the four to five thousand letters members of Congress send to the EPA each year complain bitterly about the regulatory burdens placed on their constituents. But once a bill gets to the floor, opposition can be politically dangerous. Given the broad appeal and low salience of environmental issues, most members of Congress discover that "a pro-environmental voting record can only help, not hurt at reelection time."[36] Playing it safe—the strategy of most incumbents—means not appearing to favor dirty air, dirty water, or hazardous waste dumps.

Obviously the 1994 election disrupted the pattern of legislative-executive interaction that characterized the previous quarter-century. Not only were Republicans in control of both houses of Congress for the first time in more than forty years, but the party leadership and most of the new members were overtly hostile to environmental regulation. Tom DeLay, the new Majority Whip, accused the EPA of employing "gestapo tactics."[37] The incoming chair of the House Resources Committee described environmentalists as "a dangerous bunch," a "waffle-stomping, Harvard graduating, intellectual bunch of idiots." He warned that if they wouldn't accept change, "I'm just going to ram it down their throats."[38] Many Republican leaders and freshmen had close ties to small business and strong roots in the mountain West and South. This was one reason why they seriously misread public opinion on environmental programs.

Republicans in the 104th Congress launched an unprecedented assault on environmental programs. This effort quickly became a miserable failure. The Republicans' first setback came on generic regulatory reform

---

34 Walter Rosenbaum, *Environmental Politics and Policy*, 2nd ed. (CQ Press, 1991), 113.
35 For an example, see R. Shep Melnick, "Pollution Deadlines and the Coalition for Failure, *The Public Interest* 75 (1984), 125.
36 Robert Cameron Mitchell, "Public Opinion and Environmental Politics in the 1970s and 1980s," 68.
37 Allan Freedman, "Republicans Concede Missteps in Effort to Rewrite Rules," *Congressional Quarterly Weekly Report* (December 2, 1995), 1347.
38 Representative Don Young (R-Alaska), quoted in Margaret Kriz, "Out of the Wilderness," *National Journal* (April 8, 1995), 864, and Kriz, "Not-So-Silent Spring," *National Journal* (March 9, 1996), 522.

legislation. Early in 1995 the House passed a bill requiring the EPA and other agencies to use cost-benefit analysis and risk assessment when establishing new environmental standards. The legislation made it easier for industry to challenge regulations in court and required compensation for owners whose property value dropped more than 20 percent as a result of regulatory action. Senate leader Robert Dole sponsored legislation that went even further, applying these standards not just to future rules but to existing ones as well. Warning that the Dole bill would tie regulators up in knots, Senate Democrats filibustered. When a few Senate Republicans refused to sign a cloture petition, the legislation died.[39]

House Republicans also proposed slashing the EPA's budget by one-third. This appropriations bill came to the floor with seventeen riders attached. Among other things, these riders would halt enforcement of the Clean Water Act and several sections of the Clean Air Act and the Endangered Species Act. This ignited a revolt by moderate Republicans in the House.[40] The Senate rejected most of the riders, and President Clinton eventually vetoed the entire appropriations bill. Despite strenuous Republican efforts to cut EPA spending, the agency's appropriation remained only slightly below what it was in 1994. Republican efforts to revise the Clean Water Act, Clean Air Act, Endangered Species Act, and Superfund failed as well.

By the time the 104th Congress returned for its second session in January 1996, its leaders recognized that they had blundered on environmental issues. Not only had serious divisions appeared within the majority party, but Republican pollsters reported that the issue had done serious damage to its public image. Speaker Gingrich publicly acknowledged that, "we clearly are strategically out of position on the environment. . . . We approached it the wrong way, with the wrong language. . . . We have to go back and revisit the whole issue."[41]

The 104th Congress had its biggest effect on environmental policy not by rewriting laws but by scaring the EPA into discovering more "flexibility" under existing laws. Alarmed by the prospect of conservative Republicans tinkering with key statutes, the EPA's political executives searched for administrative methods to respond to the concerns of industry and state and local governments. After hearing a series of complaints

39 Allan Freedman, "Regulatory Overhaul Stymied by Internal Doubts, Divisions," *Congressional Quarterly Weekly Report* (March 9, 1996), 613, and "Republicans Concede Missteps in Effort to Rewrite Rules," 3645.
40 *Environment Reporter—Current Developments* (August 4, 1995), 657.
41 Quoted in *Environment Reporter—Current Developments* (November 10, 1995), 1176.

from the National Governor's Associations, the agency gave ground on several issues on which it had previously been implacable. For example, the EPA approved a California smog-control plan that had little chance of attaining air-quality standards and allowed several states to institute inspection and maintenance programs that it had previously rejected. The agency also instituted a pilot project to loosen emission requirements for firms claiming to know how to get more environmental "bang for the buck." The head of the White House Council on Environmental Quality described the initiative as an offer "to throw away the rule book."[42]

Once it was clear that the Republicans' environmental initiatives were dead and that the Democratic administration viewed environmental protection as a winning issue, regulatory flexibility received much less attention at the EPA. In 1997, the EPA adopted—with White House approval—new air quality standards for ozone and particulate matter, one of the most costly and controversial regulations ever issued by the agency. The agency's shifting emphasis demonstrates not just its responsiveness to public moods but also the continuing vitality of environmentalism.

The EPA's initial strategy of appeasing critics of regulation required environmental groups to refrain from challenging its new policies in court. For a while environmentalists cooperated. But as the threat of Republican legislation faded, environmental groups reverted to their previous practice of using litigation to push for stricter rules. Industry, too, continues to challenge in court most major agency rules. The EPA is not alone. The Forest Service, Bureau of Land Management, and Park Service also find themselves in court on a regular basis. A variety of studies have shown that in the United States, "resort to the courts by one or another interest group has become so commonplace that major regulatory issues are seldom settled without litigation."[43]

This pattern of "adversarial legalism" extends well beyond environmental protection and reflects a redefinition of the role of the judiciary.[44] No longer did judges see their primary role as protecting private property from unauthorized government intrusion. In 1971, Judge David Bazelon of the D.C. Circuit marked the arrival of what he called "a new era in the

---

42 *Environment Reporter—Current Developments* (September 22, 1995), 938; (May 19, 1995), 218; (January 27, 1995), 1827; (March 15, 1996), 2133; (December 23, 1994), 1658.
43 Brickman, Jasannoff, and Ilgen, *Controlling Chemicals,* 45–46.
44 Robert Kagan, "Adversarial Legalism and American Government," *Journal of Policy Analysis and Management* 10 (1991), 369.

long and fruitful collaboration of administrative agencies and reviewing courts" by ordering recalcitrant administrators to initiate proceedings to ban DDT. The court explained that henceforth judges would push environmental protection agencies to be more aggressive in protecting citizens' "fundamental personal interests in life, health, and liberty," which, according to Judge Bazelon's idiosyncratic reading of judicial history, "have always had a special claim to judicial protection, in comparison with the economic interests at stake in a ratemaking or licensing proceeding."[45] When in doubt, the courts have ruled, judges and administrators should err in the direction of protecting public health and the environment, not private property.[46]

Initially the courts focused on procedural matters. But by the mid-1970s the most important issues before the court involved interpretation of the substantive mandates of federal statutes. "Our duty," explained D.C. Circuit Judge Skelly Wright "is to see that the legislative purposes heralded in the halls of Congress are not lost in the vast halls of the federal bureaucracy."[47] The courts frequently ordered the EPA and other agencies to perform such "nondiscretionary duties" as issuing air-quality standards for lead, writing transportation control plans for Los Angeles, setting limits on the release of PCBs into the nation's rivers, and prohibiting timbering in potential wilderness areas. A symbiotic relationship developed between lower-court judges and some congressional subcommittees. The latter wrote liberal judicial review provisions, often allowing "any citizen" to challenge EPA rules. The former frequently relied on legislative histories written by subcommittee leaders and staff to establish legislative intent. Many judges suspected that without the courts looking over their shoulders, regulators would be too susceptible to the influence of regulated industries.

Court action has had a profound effect on environmental agencies, expanding their responsibilities, slowing decision making, and making enforcement more difficult.[48] That judges have placed conflicting demands on agencies is not all that surprising. Courts are good at respond-

---

45 Environmental Defense Fund v. Ruckelshaus 439 F.2d 584 (1971), 598.
46 For a review of these cases, see Melnick, *Regulation and the Courts*, chaps. 3 and 8.
47 Calvert Cliffs Coordinating Committee v. AEC 449 F.2d 1109 (D.C. Cir., 1971), 1111.
48 Kagan, "Adversarial Legalism"; and R. Shep Melnick, "Administrative Law and Bureaucratic Reality," *Administrative Law Review* 44 (1992), 245. For a more benign assessment, see Rosemary O'Leary, *Environmental Change: Federal Courts and the EPA* (Temple University Press, 1993).

ing to complaints, and people have lots of complaints about the operation of government bureaucracies. Forum shopping often allows complainants to make their arguments before a sympathetic judge. Judges are seldom forced to ask themselves if all these demands are compatible. That, they usually argue, is someone else's job.

THE ADVOCACY EXPLOSION

One of the most common themes in the political science literature on regulation is that it is much more difficult to mobilize diffuse interests (such as breathers or hikers) than business firms, trade associations, or labor unions. One reason why environmentalism has exhibited such staying power since 1970 is that environmental groups have found ways to cope with this "collective action" problem. They have developed experienced staff who skillfully publicize issues, mobilize members, sue administrators, and forge broad legislative coalitions.

Many of these organizations were a product of the movement politics of the 1960s and 1970s. Founders of the Natural Resources Defense Council, the Environmental Defense Fund, Friends of the Earth, Greenpeace, and Environmental Action learned valuable organizational lessons for the civil rights and antiwar movements.[49] Joining the effort were traditional conservation- and recreation-oriented groups with a large, middle-class membership base. Over the years, both sets of organizations have managed to maintain a high level of commitment among their barely paid staff. Asked how environmentalists could compete with highly paid industry lobbyists, a Sierra Club staffer replied, "The bottom line is they're mercenaries and we're true believers."[50]

Environmentalists were fortunate to be able to count on the support of such generous patrons as the Ford, Carnegie, Field, and Rockefeller Foundations. Environmental organizations also received substantial financial support from the government itself. Sometimes this took the form of direct grants and contracts. Just as important were the attorneys' fees collected in cases against polluters and the government. Environmental groups use funds generated in one set of cases to subsidize further litigation.

Money allowed environmental groups to survive but is hardly the basis of their influence. Their success in Congress and the administrative pro-

---

49 Richard A. Harris and Sidney M. Milkis, *The Politics of Regulatory Change: A Tale of Two Agencies* 2nd ed. (Oxford University Press, 1996), 62–81.
50 Quoted in Hager, "For Industry and Opponents, A Showdown Is in the Air," 147.

cess rests on their ability to mobilize—or threaten to mobilize—what Douglas Arnold calls "inattentive publics." Ralph Nader was one of the first to discover a way to tap this valuable political resource. As Arnold explains,

Nader's contribution was not to organize consumers—a nearly impossible task—but rather to label legislative votes as pro- or anticonsumer. The media then disseminated these messages, challengers helped citizens reach the proper political conclusions, and suddenly a formerly inattentive public was alive. Once Nader had demonstrated his ability to mobilize an otherwise inattentive public several times, he no longer had to do so regularly; simply labeling legislative votes as anticonsumer provided ammunition that others could use, and the mere existence of this ammunition was threatening enough to some legislators.

Environmental groups, Arnold notes, adopted Nader's strategy:

Here one of the finest tactical maneuvers was to label legislators who had the worst environmental records as "The Dirty Dozen," in order to generate media attention and make it easier for inattentive citizens to identify the obstacles to clean water and fresh air.[51]

"Members are deathly afraid of being labeled anti-environment," one House staffer told a CQ reporter. "They can dump 5,000 or 10,000 signatures on you in pretty short order," noted another.[52] The success of environmental groups reflects not just the organizational and political skills of their leaders, but also the new opportunities offered by the political system. Environmentalists found reliable allies among the large number of reporters looking for dramatic stories with "good visuals" and for evidence of misdeeds by industry and government. Environmentalism is clearly a cause with which most journalists can identify. Asked to identify sources to which they would turn to get reliable information on environmental issues, 69 percent of the journalists named environmental advocates, 68 percent listed federal environmental agencies, and only 24 percent said business.[53] Moreover, environmentalists' political strategies work best in an electoral system in which members run

51 R. Douglas Arnold, *The Logic of Congressional Action* (Yale University Press, 1990), 68–69.
52 Quoted in Hager, "For Industry and Opponents, A Showdown Is in the Air," 145.
53 Robert Lichter, Stanley Rothman, and Linda Lichter, *The Media Elite: America's New Powerbrokers* (Hastings House, 1986), 57. According to William Ruckelshaus, "environmental reporters are often as close to the environmental movement as the members of the movement itself." Environmental Protection Agency, *Oral History: U.S. Environmental Protection Agency Administrator William D. Ruckelshaus* (Washington, D.C.: EPA, 1995), 35.

as independent entrepreneurs rather than as members of a party. They have thus benefited from the steady decline of party organization and the erosion of party discipline.

Business leaders were initially caught off guard by the rise of environmentalism. They failed to understand the extent to which the public had lost confidence in them. David Vogel has convincingly argued that "business has tended to lose political influence when the economy was performing relatively well and has become more influential when the performance of the economy deteriorated." After the unprecedented growth of the 1950s and 1960s, "significant segments of the American middle class began to take both their own prosperity and the success of business for granted."[54] The economic downturn of 1973–74 threw this assumption into question. Meanwhile, business leaders became more politically active. More firms hired Washington representatives. Changes in election laws made it easier for corporations to form political action committees. New trade associations emerged, often in response to new regulatory demands. Corporations contributed to probusiness think tanks, sponsored "public information" campaigns, and experimented with new techniques for stimulating "grass roots" support for business positions.

Despite these efforts, business remained on the defensive on environmental issues. As regulation expands, it has became increasingly difficult for business to agree on policies or strategies. As Richard Leone has pointed out, "every act of government, no matter what its broader merits or demerits for society at large, creates winners and losers within the competitive section of the economy."[55] "Good apples" that have spent millions of dollars to comply with environmental laws have an interest in strict enforcement against those "bad apples" who have not. Similarly, firms that have already invested in compliance will not relish seeing new entrants freed from these requirements. Firms with low marginal pollution reduction costs will be more favorably disposed toward stringent regulation than those with high marginal costs. Firms in heavily polluted areas will seek to ensure that firms in cleaner areas face regulations that are at least as strict as those that apply to themselves. Big business is likely to prefer one set of federal rules to fifty sets of state rules; small business is

54 *Fluctuating Fortunes: The Political Power of Business in America* (Basic Books, 1988), 8.
55 Richard Leone, *Who Profits? Winners, Losers, and Government Regulation* (Basic Books, 1986), 3.

likely to oppose such centralization. High-sulfur coal producers bene-fited from the strict "scrubbing" requirements of the 1997 Clean Air Act Amendments.[56] Trial lawyers have provided substantial support for Superfund—a statute many deride as a full employment program for lawyers.[57]

Some environmental laws are consciously designed to pit one industry against another. Under the Clean Air Act, stationary sources face sharp emission reductions if auto makers do not produce cleaner cars. This provides environmental advocates with allies in their effort to squeeze Detroit. The auto makers, in response, have argued that the oil industry should produce cleaner fuel. Oil companies claim that they had already taken it on the chin—so other sources of pollution (such as dry cleaners and paint manufacturers) should do more. In 1989, ARCO announced that it would start selling cleaner "reformulated" gasoline. Senators from farm states (many of whom received sizable contributions from Archer Daniels Midland, the politically frenetic firm that produces 70 percent of all ethanol) thought this was a great idea—so long as the law mandated use of ethanol, a corn derivative.[58]

An additional feature of contemporary governance is the rise of the "intergovernmental lobby"—associations of governors, mayors, legisla-tors, administrators, and policy specialists. For example, western gover-nors, aided by the staff of the Western Governors Policy Office, have played an influential role in the development of federal land policy.[59] Northeastern governors and legislators were among the most vocal pro-ponents of acid rain control. In recent years few organizations have had as much influence on air pollution policy as the State and Territorial Air Pollution Program Administrators and the Association of Local Air Pollu-tion Control Officials. These professional associations employ full-time Washington lobbyists and are a repository of knowledge about how federal rules will affect particular areas of the country. For that reason they often receive a cordial reception in Congress.

56 Bruce Ackerman and William Hassler, *Clean Coal, Dirty Air* (Yale University Press, 1981).
57 Marc Landy and Mary Hague, "The Coalition for Waste: Private Interests and Super-fund," in Michael Greve and Fred Smith, Jr., eds., *Environmental Politics: Public Costs, Private Rewards* (Praeger, 1992).
58 Jonathan Adler, "Clean Fuels, Dirty Air," in Greve and Smith, *Environmental Politics;* Peter Stone, "The Big Harvest," *National Journal* (July 30, 1994), 1790; Bryner, *Blue Skies, Green Politics,* 140.
59 Frank Gregg, "Public Lands Policy: Controversial Beginnings for the Third Century," in Lacey, ed., *Government and Environmental Policy.*

THE HAZARDS OF GOVERNANCE

One might have predicted (as indeed many did) that rapid expansion of environmental protection programs would create powerful, centralized bureaucracies. Certainly the EPA, Park Service, Forest Service, Fish and Wildlife Service, and the Nuclear Regulatory Commission all have large responsibilities and substantial power. Yet one of the most notable features of these bureaucracies is their lack of autonomy. They are subject to a variety of conflicting demands from congressional subcommittees, the White House, the OMB, the courts, state and local governments, and the multiplicity of interest groups described above. In this they are hardly alone. Recent studies have shown that even those agencies previously noted for their success and autonomy—including the Social Security Administration, the Internal Revenue Service, and the Federal Bureau of Investigation—are now the target of attack and extensive outside supervision.[60]

Hardly any part of government has been left untouched by the rise of environmentalism. The Department of State negotiates environmental treaties. As major polluters, the Department of Defense, the Energy Department, and the TVA have clashed with the EPA and been sued by environmental groups. Environmental issues have been particularly important for three types of agencies. First are those development-oriented agencies long considered components of stable "iron triangles." Examples include the Corps of Engineers, the Federal Highway Administration, the Nuclear Regulatory Commission, and various components of the Department of Agriculture. These agencies were constantly attacked by environmental groups. Among the most potent weapons in the arsenal of environmentalists trying to dislodge these "subgovernments" are court suits and "cross-cutting" statutory mandates, most notably the National Environmental Policy Act's environmental impact statement (EIS) requirement and the dictates of the Endangered Species Act.

Litigation over impact statements and endangered species not only enhanced environmentalists' ability to block the projects of development-oriented agencies but also allowed them to make agency policy the subject

---

60 Martha Derthick, *Agency Under Stress: The Social Security Administration in American Government* (Brookings Institution, 1990); and James Q. Wilson, *Bureaucracy: What Government Agencies Do and Why They Do It* (Basic Books, 1989), chap. 10.

of public debate.[61] The federal courts—most notably the D.C. Circuit—demanded extensive changes in the AEC/NRC's licensing procedures, putting an end to the AEC's fabled autonomy and contributing to the rapid decline in operating permits issued to nuclear power.[62] Public utilities commissions experienced a similar reduction in autonomy.[63] National Environmental Policy Act suits forced the Corps of Engineers and other development agencies to hire new sets of professionals and to integrate them into the planning process.[64] Pesticide regulation was transformed from an agriculture subgovernment "dominated by a limited and relatively exclusive set of actors" to a policy arena characterized by "broad issue conflict among multiple competitors."[65]

Development-oriented agencies faced new demands from Congress as well. One of the principal characteristics of the post-1970 Congress is the vague and overlapping jurisdiction of its subcommittees. In 1974, the powerful Joint Committee on Atomic Energy was disbanded. Jurisdiction over nuclear power was parceled out to five committees. Each contained critics as well as supporters of nuclear power and offered its members an opportunity to express their opinions on the subject. The Senate Agriculture Committee must now share jurisdiction over pesticides with the Committee on Labor and Human Resources. Overlapping jurisdiction combined with decentralization enabled entrepreneurial Congressmen to destabilize previously resilient subgovernments.[66]

---

61 Kagan, "Adversarial Legalism"; Richard N. L. Andrews, *Environmental Policy and Administrative Change* (Lexington, 1976); Daniel Mazmanian and Jeanne Nienaber, *Can Organizations Change? Environmental Protection, Citizen Participation, and the Corps of Engineers* (Brookings Institution, 1979); and Eugene Bardach and Lucian Pugliaresi, "The Environmental-Impact Statement vs. the Real World," *The Public Interest* 49 (1977), 22.

62 Constance Ewing Cook, *Nuclear Power and Legal Advocacy* (Lexington, 1980); and Robert Duffy, "Remaking Nuclear Politics? The Dynamics of Subgovernment Change," (Ph.D dissertation, Brandeis University Politics Department, 1991).

63 Douglas Anderson, *Regulatory Politics and Electric Utilities: A Case Study in Political Economy* (Auburn House, 1981); and Nivola, *The Politics of Energy Conservation*, chap. 4.

64 Serge Taylor, *Making Bureaucracies Think: The Environmental Impact Statement Strategy of Administrative Reform* (Stanford University Press, 1984).

65 Christopher J. Bosso, *Pesticides and Politics: The Life Cycle of a Public Issue* (University of Pittsburgh Press, 1987), 13. Also see George Hoberg, "Reaganism, Pluralism, and the Politics of Pesticide Regulation," *Policy Sciences* 23 (1990), 263; and Angus MacIntyre, "A Court Quietly Rewrote the Federal Pesticide Statute: How Prevalent is Judicial Statutory Revision?" *Law and Policy* 7 (1985), 249.

66 See Martha Derthick and Paul Quirk, *The Politics of Deregulation* (Brookings Institution, 1988), chap. 4.

The second set of agencies, those charged with managing federal lands, has faced similar challenges to their authority and tranquility. The shifting political environment had its most dramatic effect on the Forest Service, the proud carrier of the progressive conservation ethos and a bureaucracy known for its professionalism and autonomy.[67] Environmentalists argued that behind the Forest Service's "multiple use" rhetoric lay a special attachment to producer interests, especially the timber industry and ranchers. They used litigation and legislation to block timber cutting and to create new wilderness areas. In the late 1970s, local interests mounted a counterattack. The "Sage Brush Rebellion" never really caught fire (so to speak) in the West. But Reagan administration officials, most notably Secretary of the Interior James Watt, sought to achieve a major shift in these agencies' policies. Administration proposals were invariably challenged—and in most instances blocked—by Congress and the courts. More recently, Secretary of the Interior Babbitt has tried to institute reforms favored by environmentalists. Most of these, too, have been stopped by Congress.[68]

Such controversy has not induced Congress to delegate control over federal lands to the executive branch. To the contrary, Congress has jealously guarded and extended its prerogatives. For example, the Wilderness Act of 1964 reasserted congressional authority to designate wilderness areas, a task previously left to the Forest Service. Over the next three decades Congress set aside millions of acres for preservation, most notably in the Alaska Lands Conservation Act of 1980. Between 1971 and 1980, Congress nearly tripled the acreage of the national parks, often purchasing more land than recommended by the administration. Congress wrote new authorizing statutes for both the Forest Service and the Bureau of Land Management (BLM), requiring both to conduct extensive studies and go through elaborate procedures to determine the proper use of federal lands.

According to Joseph Sax, in the 1960s and 1970s the Forest Service moved from "the old era of administrative discretion and expertise" to "the modern period of legislative skepticism toward the federal land-management bureaucracy." Once among "the most independent and self-

---

67 Herbert Kaufman, *The Forest Ranger* (Johns Hopkins University Press, 1960).
68 Margaret Kriz, "Land Wars," *National Journal* (September 2, 1995), 2146, "Shoot-Out in the West," *National Journal* (November 15, 1994), 2388, "The Wild Card," *National Journal* (January 13, 1996), 65; and Allan Freedman, "Clash of Interests and Ideology Threaten Grazing Overhaul," *Congressional Quarterly Weekly Report* (March 9, 1996), 609.

governing of federal bureaucracies," the Forest Service now finds itself "among the most challenged." Its forest management plans for Alaska, Colorado, Montana, and West Virginia were rejected in court as inconsistent with NEPA, the Multiple Use Sustained Yield Act, and a 1897 statute on timber harvesting. Having the federal courts play such a large role in timber and wilderness policies "seemed to undermine everything in which the Forest Service believed and on which it had been founded: expertise, scientific forestry, discretion, and professional independence."[69] Former BLM Director Frank Gregg offers a similar picture of the other land management agencies: "their leaders were simply too busy coping with the staccato series of new policy proposals from others to assert across-the-board leadership."[70]

Finally we come to the Environmental Protection Agency, the largest of the units charged with reducing environmental hazards. The central fact of life for EPA administrators is that they have been given far more duties than they could ever hope to perform. Moreover, the agency has never developed a stable, reliable clientele. The scope and stringency of its regulatory programs have produced an adversarial relationship with industry and the White House. Environmental activists and authorizing subcommittees in Congress have also adopted a critical stance, choosing to emphasize what has yet to be achieved rather than what has already been accomplished. The media, meanwhile, has attacked the agency for failing to protect public health and for hurting local economies, for failing to move quickly, and for acting before it has adequate information.

The administrative overload that is such a central part of the agency's performance is not a function just of the large number of tasks handed to the EPA but also of the inherent difficult of carrying out each one. For example, the EPA must set health standards for thousands of substances. In doing so, agency officials inevitably encounter a high degree of scientific uncertainty. Not only is the evidence produced by scientific research spotty and shifting, but there is substantial disagreement about how one extrapolates from what is known (for example, the effects of extraordinarily high doses of a potential carcinogen on a rodent) to what one needs to know to set a standard intelligently (the long-term effect of very low doses on humans). As one EPA scientist put it, "One of the nice things

69 Joseph L. Sax, "Parks, Wilderness, and Recreation," in Lacey, *Government and Environmental Politics*, 121–2 and 133.
70 "Public Lands Policy," in Lacey, *Government and Environmental Politics*, 164–65.

about the environmental standard-setting business is that you are always setting the standard at a level where the data is lousy."[71]

A second problem is that frequently no technology currently exists to achieve the desired environmental goal at a reasonable cost. Many statutory provisions are designed to be "technology forcing"—far enough beyond what can currently be accomplished to induce the development of innovative technologies. For technology forcing to work, of course, business firms must believe that the government will stand behind its strict standards and tight deadlines. That the government seldom does so is one reason why technology forcing has worked poorly. Yet hope—or at least political posturing—springs eternal.

Third, to achieve many of its statutory goals, the EPA must somehow induce thousands upon thousands of public and private parties to comply with complex regulations. Among those subject to EPA rules are 40,000 major sources of air pollution, 68,000 point sources of water pollution, 650,000 generators of hazardous waste, 27,000 abandoned hazardous waste dumps, 79,000 public water systems, and millions of cars, trucks, motorcycles, planes, and motorboats.[72] These parties differ in important ways: they produce different goods, emit different pollutants, are located on different terrain, and have widely varying pollution-control costs. It is frequently difficult to determine if a particular facility has in fact complied with existing rules.[73]

The EPA's resources have not kept pace with the accumulation of administrative tasks. Although the agency's responsibilities have grown substantially since 1981, its budget has dropped by at least 15 percent in real terms. The EPA has always had to rely on state and local governments to help it enforce federal rules. These agencies, as competent as many of them are, often have different priorities than the EPA and are subject to different political pressures.

Administrative overload has gone hand-in-hand with a climate of mistrust and suspicion. The most dramatic example of this was the effort of Reagan appointees to purge the agency of overzealous regulators. During Administrator Gorsuch's first year in office, the agency lost an astounding 40 percent of its personnel, including many of its most experienced em-

71 Quoted in Melnick, *Regulation and the Courts*, 244.
72 Richard J. Lazarus, "The Tragedy of Distrust in the Implementation of Federal Environmental Law," *Law and Contemporary Problems* 54 (1991), 322–28, and Rosenbaum, *Environmental Politics*, 207.
73 See Melnick, *Regulation and the Courts*, chaps. 6, 7, and 9.

ployees.[74] Soon, Gorsuch and her deputies were gone as well. Environmentalists and members of congressional subcommittee have repeatedly charged the EPA with being too slow, too tied to the White House, and too hesitant to impose costs on industry. Judges and reporters charge that it is too lenient in standard setting and too harsh in enforcement.

This "singular lack of trust," former Administrator Ruckelshaus argues, has produced "increasingly prescriptive legislation that strips away administrative discretion from EPA managers and often sets impossible goals for the Agency." The result, he maintains, "has been missed deadlines, unfulfilled promises of purity, a failure to achieve goals, and another round of EPA bashing, followed by even more stringent goals; and the spiral of mistrust continues."[75]

With so much to do, priority setting becomes crucial. And it tends to be outsiders rather than the agency's executives who establish the EPA's priorities. News stories and congressional hearings are two sources of the well-known "pollution of the week syndrome." Court decisions have become even more important; injunctions are hard to ignore.[76] This gives substantial leverage to environmental groups who can threaten to file suit to enforce a specific statutory deadline. By the late 1980s, many EPA officials had become convinced that the agency was devoting too much of its resources to relatively trivial problems. The efforts by Administrators Ruckelshaus, Thomas, and Reilly to make greater use of risk assessment was in part an effort by agency leaders to regain control over EPA's agenda.[77]

CONCLUSION

In his 1991 article exploring the causes of "adversarial legalism," Robert Kagan observed that Americans "have attempted to articulate and implement the socially transformative policies of an activist, regulatory welfare state through the legal structures of a reactive, decentralized, nonhierarchical governmental system. In the absence of a strong, respected national bureaucracy, proponents of regulatory change and social welfare measures have advocated methods of policy implementation that emphasize citizens' rights to challenge and prod official action through litiga-

---

74 Landy, Roberts, and Thomas, *The Environmental Protection Agency*, 250.
75 "Looking Back, Looking Ahead: EPA," *EPA Journal* 16 (January/February 1990), 14.
76 O'Leary, *Environmental Change*, 168–69.
77 Landy, Roberts, and Thomas, *The Environmental Protection Agency*, 252–59.

tion."[78] Over the past three decades, the responsibilities of agencies charged with protecting the environment have grown enormously, but policymaking has become ever more fragmented and contentious. Progressive Era conservationists would no doubt be pleased by our ability to reduce pollution and expand wilderness areas while our population grows and our economy expands. They would be pleasantly surprised at the extent of public control over private enterprise. But they would also discover that their efforts to build respected, powerful, expert administrative agencies to manage public lands and regulate corporate behavior have come to naught.

The failure of the Republican Congress to scale back environmental regulation demonstrates how deeply embedded in our political system are most current environmental policies. Federal programs unimaginable thirty years ago are unassailable today. But this has hardly produced political consensus. Environmentalists and the media always have new items to add to the government's agenda. A vocal minority of property owners, politicians, and entrepreneurs have yet to accept the new order. And most importantly, the vast American middle class remains uncomfortable with the government authority required to provide the environmental amenities and protections it demands. Our new environmental ethos coexists uneasily with our traditions of individualism, pluralism, and populism.

78 Kagan, "Adversarial Legalism and American Government," 392.

IV

Civil Rights

8

Since 1964: The Paradox of American Civil Rights Regulation

HUGH DAVIS GRAHAM

Civil rights policy differs in significant ways from the other broad areas of governance addressed in this volume. Compared to trade, conservation, immigration, and social welfare policy during the first half of the twentieth century, the civil rights field drew little national attention. Reformers were active in race relations but their agenda was local, conservative, and segregationist. National deference to the South's biracial caste system, reinforced by formidable defenses against change in the federal courts, Congress, the party system, and traditions of Anglo-American law, postponed the full emergence of civil rights as a major national issue until the second half of the century.

Between 1948 and 1964, the national government in a sense compressed seventy years of deferred debate into a second Reconstruction. The biracial civil rights coalition, mobilized under the liberal banner of equal individual rights, broke the back of the Jim Crow order. This we well know from a mountain of inspired literature, from powerful film and television specials, and from modern memory. This essay is about what happened next.

The three decades following the Civil Rights Act brought a transformation of social policy in the United States that was unprecedented in scope and authority and was unanticipated by any of the architects of the breakthrough legislation of 1964–65.[1] During the 1960s, Americans experienced one of those rare sea changes in our history that, like the New Deal, mark a watershed in our political and social life. These sudden shifts reflect what political scientists call a process of "punctuated equilibrium" in American politics, when relatively stable systems dominated by policy

---

1 Hugh Davis Graham, *Civil Rights and the Presidency* (New York: Oxford University Press, 1992).

elites break down.[2] Political leaders, having earned their posts by mastering the rules and structures of the old order, apply their formulas to novel circumstances.

Policies developed in such volatile periods are more likely to produce unintended consequences. In wartime, we complain, the admirals and generals attempt to fight the previous war, often with unfortunate results. Similarly, in moments of sharp transition a disjunction grows between the goals of policy, driven by new social forces, and the means of policy, tailored to the dynamics of the passing order.

I argue here that the shift in American civil rights policy from the nondiscrimination model enacted in 1964–68 to the affirmative-action or adverse impact model adopted during the Nixon presidency started a chain reaction with paradoxical consequences. The African American civil rights movement, ushering in a new era of social regulation, won strong remedies for past discrimination through group preferences derived from the nondiscrimination statutes, especially Title VI of the Civil Rights Act of 1964, and enforced administratively by federal contract-compliance officials, backed by federal judges. This regulatory leverage, which proved to be effective in redistributing employment and income, was soon demanded by rights-based advocacy groups representing women, Hispanics, the handicapped, the elderly, and other groups seeking the advantages of protected-class status. Congress and the presidency, traditionally responsive to organized interest-group demands, obliged during the 1970s by extending the affirmative-action model of rights regulation, designed to address the unique history of black Americans, to other petitioning clienteles. By the 1980s the civil rights coalition, politically powerful and expertly led, defeated most major efforts by the Reagan and Bush administrations to curtail civil rights regulation.

Paradoxically, however, the more institutionalized and effective the affirmative-action system became in redistributing benefits to an expanding array of protected clienteles, the weaker became the system's claims to fairness. The numerical standards of social regulation, generally accepted by most citizens as legitimate to protect customers, the environment, and workplace and transportation safety, were rejected by a majority of Americans as unfair when applied to minority group preferences. The advent of massive immigration, unanticipated when Congress in 1965 passed antidiscrimination reforms in immigration policy, weakened the moral claims

2 Frank R. Baumgartner and Bryan D. Jones, *Agendas and Instability in American Politics* (Chicago: University of Chicago Press, 1993), 3–24.

of preferences based on historic discrimination in the United States. The economic achievements of postwar civil rights reforms, by speeding the growth of middle-class and affluent minorities, strengthened the political base of the civil rights coalition while weakening the presumption that equated minority status with socioeconomic disadvantage.[3]

THE NEW SOCIAL REGULATION

To well-informed observers in 1965, the Civil Rights and Voting Rights acts appeared to crown a campaign of liberal reform that reached back at least to Franklin Roosevelt's wartime Fair Employment Practice Committee (FEPC) and arguably to Reconstruction. The civil rights reforms of 1941 to 1965 were based on the principle of nondiscrimination and hence rooted in liberalism's classic, negative, procedural admonition to harm no individual on account of race, national origin, or religion. They relied on statutes banning discriminatory acts, enforced judicially by civil courts in the tort tradition and administratively by antidiscrimination commissions. The commission device, modeled on the independent regulatory commissions of Progressive–New Deal provenance, linked civil rights enforcement to the long tradition of economic regulation. Reaching back to the creation of the Interstate Commerce Commission in 1887, this tradition embraced employment rights in the Wagner Act of 1935 and its National Labor Relations Board. In 1945, the commission device was used to police discrimination against minorities in New York's State Commission Against Discrimination; spreading throughout the urban-industrial states during the 1950s, it found national expression in 1964 when Title VII of the Civil Rights Act established the Equal Employment Opportunity Commission (EEOC).[4]

By the mid-1970s, however, the civil rights legislation of 1964–65 appeared to represent less the culmination of liberal nondiscrimination

---

3 The equation of race and sex discrimination, an important source of solidarity for the civil rights coalition, has been especially problematical. The complexities of the race-sex analogy, much discussed in feminist literature and addressed elsewhere in my own writing, are beyond the scope of this chapter. In the analysis that follows, I stress the importance in civil rights regulation of accumulating protected-class clienteles, such as women and the disabled, but I emphasize the role of minority group preferences in the debate over policy legitimacy.

4 See Morroe Berger, *Equality by Statute: The Revolution in Civil Rights* (rev. ed.; New York: Farrar, Straus, & Giroux, 1978); Hugh Davis Graham, *The Civil Rights Era: Origins and Development of National Policy, 1960–1972* (New York: Oxford University Press, 1990), 3–46.

than the founding charter of a new social regulation developed in Washington during the 1960s. What were the shared attributes that linked civil rights reform and social regulation? One was a common origin in social-movement mobilizations, first on behalf of African Americans, then on behalf of women, students, consumers and workers, and the environment. Second, these grassroots movements sought protection from an array of social evils that included employment discrimination, a polluted environment, dangerous products and services, and unsafe transportation and workplaces. Third, to provide this protection Congress established an array of new regulatory agencies—the EEOC (1964), the National Transportation Safety Board (1966), the Environmental Protection Agency (1970), the Occupational Safety and Health Administration (1970), the Consumer Product Safety Commission (1972), and others. Additional enforcement subagencies were established by the executive branch: the Office for Civil Rights (OCR) in the Department of Health, Education, and Welfare (HEW) and the Office of Federal Contract Compliance (OFCC) in the Department of Labor in 1965 and the Office of Minority Business Enterprise (OMBE) in the Department of Commerce in 1969.[5]

These new agencies embodied a model of social regulation that differed fundamentally from the older economic regulation. The latter emphasized independent, quasijudicial boards and commissions, responding to complaints (rate-fixing, anticompetitive practices, unfair labor practices) in adversarial proceedings, deciding cases with court-like decrees (complaint dismissal, rate approval, cease-and-desist orders, penalties, and relief). Social regulation, on the other hand, was proactive, emphasizing future compliance to reduce risk and eliminate hazards instead of emphasizing punishment for past misdeeds. The methods of social regulation, more legislative than adjudicatory, centered on notice-and-comment rulemaking and emphasized scientific expertise for setting standards of compliance. The agencies of social and economic regulation also differed structurally. Economic regulation was generally organized vertically, with agencies presiding over specific industrial sectors (surface transportation, communications, securities, airlines). Social regulation was organized

---

5 On the new social regulation see David Vogel, "The 'New' Social Regulation in Historical and Comparative Perspective," in Thomas K. McCraw, ed., *Regulation in Perspective* (Cambridge, Mass.: Harvard University Press, 1981), 155–86; Michael D. Reagan, *Regulation: The Politics of Policy* (Boston: Little, Brown, 1987), 86–111; Marc Allen Eisner, *Regulatory Politics in Transition* (Baltimore: Johns Hopkins University Press, 1993), 118–69.

horizontally, cutting across sector boundaries to clean the nation's air and water, eliminate employment discrimination, improve transportation safety, increase access for the handicapped, or combat consumer fraud.

Social regulators, empowered by the insurgent politics of the 1960s, needed to enforce their rulings in a way that quickly produced significant and measurable results. Because social regulation, unlike most economic regulation, was not sector-specific, effective regulation required authority that cut across industrial boundaries and government jurisdictions. For federal agencies setting standards of compliance for air and water pollution or for industrial and consumer safety, the legitimacy of broad congressional authority over interstate commerce had been established by the New Deal. But for federal agencies seeking to impose new nationwide controls on the hiring and promotion practices of private firms or state and local governments, or on the educational policies of public and private schools and colleges, the authority of Washington was greatly narrowed by the traditions of federalism. This was the decisive battleground for civil rights regulation in the 1960s.

THE WATERSHED OF THE 1960S: FEDERAL AID AND TITLE VI

The postwar development of regulatory and civil rights policy during the 1960s is anchored by two great policy changes, one occurring in 1964, the other at the end of the decade, in the first years of the Nixon presidency. The first of these events is the enactment of Title VI of the Civil Rights Act. The second is the shift in enforcement strategy from traditional non-discrimination policing, as exemplified by the antidiscrimination commissions in the northern industrial states and the original design of the EEOC, to minority preference requirements under the adverse impact standard adopted in 1969–71. In retrospect, each of these two watershed events marks a rare moment of decisive change in our history. On either side of them, during the years from 1945 to 1964 and later during the 1970s, important changes were occurring in the nature of civil rights enforcement and the American regulatory state itself; but they were more gradual and cumulative and their meaning was heavily determined by the sea changes of 1964 and 1969–71. After the 1980 election, the Reagan-Bush administrations mounted a counteroffensive that for the first time included civil rights regulation among the deregulatory targets. The outcome of the Reagan counterattack will be addressed later.

From the perspective of the 1960s, the heart of the Civil Rights Act was Title II (desegregating public accommodations) and Title VII (prohibiting job discrimination). From the perspective of the 1990s, it was Title VI (prohibiting discrimination in federally assisted programs). The efficacy of Title VI as an instrument of federal regulation rested on the increasing financial dependence of state and local governments and the private industrial economy on federal grants and contracts. For the postwar era this began in 1946 with the Hill-Burton Hospital Survey and Construction Act, when Congress began to build a comprehensive inventory of assistance programs to benefit local communities while requiring little from recipients in exchange. Between 1946 and 1963, the federal system underwent a fiscal revolution that increased the amount of federal aid to state and local governments from $701 million to $4.8 billion.[6] Washington's financial assistance took the form mainly of categorical grants-in-aid to help cities and states build roads, airports, hospitals, water systems, and other facilities to support rapid metropolitan growth.[7]

Because state sales and local property taxes were inadequate to pay for needed support services, Congress tapped the growing pool of federal income-tax revenue, voting frequently to add new aid programs while rarely needing to raise tax rates. Congress and the funding agencies attached few strings to the grant programs, other than standard technical requirements. In the vernacular of the mission agencies, the metaphor of the popular grant-in-aid programs was "leave it on the stump and run." As James Sundquist observed in a 1969 study of federalism, state and local governments are "subject to no federal discipline except through the granting or denial of federal aid"—a sanction that "is not very useful, because to deny the funds is in effect a veto of the national objective

---

6 Advisory Commission on Intergovernmental Relations, *Categorical Grants: Their Role and Design* (Washington, D.C.: U.S. Government Printing Office, 1978), 15–31. In 1990 dollars, federal aid to state and local governments increased from $4.7 billion in 1946 to $20.5 billion in 1963.

7 A distinction is made between federally *assisted* programs, where federal agencies provide grants of financial aid to assist state and local governments and other public entities in developing agriculture, building roads and airports, controlling floods, constructing hospitals, and improving education, and federal *procurement,* where agencies purchase goods and services through contracts with private firms to equip and provision military forces, construct U.S. government buildings, and supply government agencies. Title VI mainly concerned federally assisted programs, whereas procurement was regulated under the president's executive authority to define and enforce the terms of government contracts. In practice, however, there was considerable overlap. In civil rights policy after 1964, both categories involved contract compliance with affirmative-action guidelines.

itself."[8] The categorical grant programs were popular because they met local needs, were loosely administered by federal officials, and mutually served the political interests of Washington's triangular bargaining networks.

During the 1960s, the federal grant system expanded dramatically. In 1962 there were 160 categorical programs; in 1965 there were 330; by 1970 there were 530. Eighty percent of these were legislated after 1960—158 of them in 1965–66 alone, the bonanza year of the 89th Congress and the Great Society. In the "categorical explosion" of 1964–68, Congress poured money into the states and cities to aid education, rebuild urban areas and transportation networks, assist antipoverty programs, and reduce water and air pollution. Federal aid outlays to state and local governments, $2.3 billion in 1951, grew to $7 billion in 1960 and to $23 billion by 1970 ($77.5 billion in 1990 dollars). As a percentage of domestic federal outlays, grants amounted to 16.4 percent in 1960 and 21.9 percent in 1970.[9] The proliferation of grants, when added to billions in annual contracts awarded by federal agencies for goods and services, especially during the years of the Vietnam War and the space race, meant that, by 1970, federal assistance in the form of grants and contracts reached deeply into the recesses of 3,044 counties, 18,517 municipalities, 15,781 school districts, and 23,885 special districts. Federal contracts for goods and services funded the work of more than 100,000 businesses employing twenty million workers.

Accompanying this growth in the 1960s was a sharp increase in performance requirements for recipients of federal funds. The federal lunch had never been free, and the incremental attachment of strings to federal grants had a long history.[10] In Washington lore, the Golden Rule of Fiscal

8 James L. Sundquist, *Making Federalism Work* (Washington, D.C.: Brookings Institution, 1969), 12.
9 Michael D. Reagan, "Federal-State Relations During the 1960s: Unplanned Change," in Lawrence E. Gelfand and Robert J. Neymeyer, eds., *Changing Patterns in American Federal-State Relations During the 1950s, the 1960s, & the 1970s* (Iowa City: University of Iowa Press, 1985), 31–48.
10 Prior to the New Deal, most federal grants supported agricultural experiment stations and extension, forestry management, vocational education, and rural highway building. Congress as early as 1892 limited working hours for laborers and mechanics employed on public work by the U.S. government and its contractors and subcontractors. In 1931, the Davis-Bacon Act rewarded organized labor by requiring federally assisted contractors to pay the "prevailing wage" in their area. Prior to the 1960s, however, most federal "strings" or controls accompanying grants programs, such as those governing hospital construction and airports and interstate highways, concerned technical requirements.

Federalism was: "He who provides the gold sets the rules." Federal controls by tradition emphasized project-specific rather than cross-cutting requirements. Regulations binding aid recipients were tailored by agency experts to fit the specific practical needs of projects in agricultural experiment and extension, water control, biomedical research, road and airport building, and hospital construction. During the 1960s, however, the federal government made the most significant change in federal assistance programs and their control since the land-grant program was created in 1862. The instrument of this change was Title VI of the 1964 Civil Rights Act.

In light of the extraordinary consequences of Title VI, the gravity of this change can only be appreciated in hindsight. Its magnitude was not discernible at the time because such consequences were not intended and were not expected (especially by their proponents). Indeed, for most participants in the debates of 1963–64 the subsequent applications of Title VI were scarcely imaginable. In emphasizing unintended consequences, it is important to recognize that the most important consequence of the Civil Rights Act was its *intended* consequence: the destruction of the racial caste system in the South. For this reason most attention during the great debates of 1963–64 was riveted on Title II on public accommodations desegregation and Title VII on fair employment. I will concentrate here on two major *unintended* consequences of the great sleeper provision, Title VI. First, it provided the chief leverage for national enforcement after 1970 of an adverse impact standard in minority rights. Second, it created a model for comprehensive federal regulation through cross-cutting requirements reaching far beyond the arena of race relations that dominated the events of 1964.

As proposed in President Kennedy's original, post-Birmingham bill of 1963, Title VI would deny funds to federally assisted programs that discriminated against individuals because of their race, religion, or national origin. Its goal was to end federal subsidies for segregated southern schools, colleges, medical institutions, highway construction, and myriad other service programs run by state and local governments and partially funded by federal grant-in-aid dollars. Because Title VI was explainable to constituents in practical terms (preventing federal tax dollars from strengthening segregation), it won wide and bipartisan support from nonsoutherners in Congress. Title VI's sole substantive prohibition provides: "No person in the United States shall, on the basis of race, color, or national origin, be excluded from participation in, be denied the benefits of, or be subjected to discrimination under, any program or activity receiving federal financial assistance."[11]

Title VI was debated in Congress and was attacked by southern conservatives, most notably by senators Sam Ervin of North Carolina and Richard Russell of Georgia, who deplored its vagueness in not defining the term "discrimination" (Russell called Title VI "the realization of a bureaucrat's prayers"). In the negotiation process it was narrowed by various constraining amendments in the House and, in the Senate, by a "pinpoint" provision that confined its sanctions to "the particular program or part thereof in which noncompliance has been found." But Title VI retained its simple purpose and its enormous potential power. Given the deep attachment of Congress to traditional patterns of federalism in domestic legislation, it is difficult to imagine congressional approval of such a mighty sword for the executive branch in any circumstance less explosive than the civil rights crisis of 1963–64. The target seemed self-evidently confined to the no-longer tolerable world of Bull Connor.

In attacking segregated stores, hotels, and restaurants, Title II "tore old Dixie down" almost overnight. The Justice Department, working with Labor Department officials (especially the OFCC) and the EEOC, effectively used a combination of Title VI, President Johnson's Executive Order 11246, and Title VII to desegregate employment all over the South.[12] On the whole, the Civil Rights Act worked quickly and efficiently (low costs, high benefits) in achieving its goal of destroying the Jim Crow caste system in the South. In our racial angst of the 1990s, this is too easily forgotten. In this, the "longest debate" in the history of Congress, there is no evidence that the supporters of the major titles of the Civil Rights Act, including Title VI, were insincere in believing that its use would be largely confined to punishing racial discriminators in the South.[13] Nor is there any reason to believe Senator Hubert Humphrey insincere when he pledged to eat the civil rights bill page by page if Title VII ever led to racial preferences in public policy.

11 *Civil Rights Act of 1964* (Washington, D.C.: Bureau of National Affairs, 1964), 115–16.
12 Federal efforts to promote job desegregation in the South reach back to Roosevelt's wartime Fair Employment Practice Committee and achieved some success under the leadership of Vice President Lyndon Johnson during the Kennedy administration. See Graham, *Civil Rights Era*, 47–73.
13 Charles and Barbara Whalen, *The Longest Debate* (Cabin John, Md.: Seven Locks Press, 1985); Gary Orfield, *The Reconstruction of Southern Education: The Schools and the 1964 Civil Rights Act* (New York: Wiley-Interscience, 1969), 35–46.

THE ENIGMA OF RICHARD NIXON

The shift from the nondiscrimination or equal-treatment standard of 1964 to the adverse impact or proportional-results standard of the early 1970s is the second of the great changes in regulatory policy brought by the 1960s. There is no need to recapitulate here the story of the Philadelphia Plan, resurrected by Labor Secretary George P. Shultz in the early months of 1969 and escorted safely by the determined Nixon White House through a congressional counterattack led by an unusual coalition of southern Democrats, Republican conservatives, and organized labor. This was a decisive turning point in the development of federal civil rights policy, one unlikely to have occurred in the absence of Richard Nixon's surprising defense of the minority hiring formulas developed by the OFCC. Could such a controversial shift have occurred without Nixon's support? A plausible affirmative argument can be made, citing momentum supporting race-conscious affirmative action standards in the federal courts, especially in the school desegregation cases; in the enforcement agencies, where staffs increasingly reflected the interests of advocacy groups for the protected classes; and in Congress, where the Leadership Conference for Civil Rights was growing in membership and effectiveness. But the reality remains that a president who nominated G. Harrold Carswell to the Supreme Court, denounced racial quotas, and seriously proposed a constitutional amendment against school busing nonetheless institutionalized a system of minority preferences enforced by federal contract compliance officials acting under the authority of Title VI and executive orders (including Nixon's own).[14]

The causes of the national shift in rights-enforcement policy during 1969–1971 are complex. They include the urgency generated by the urban rioting of 1965–68, the skill of the civil rights coalition in lobbying legislators and agency officials and in staffing the new enforcement agencies, and the support provided by federal courts, especially in 1971 in *Contractors Association* and above all in *Griggs*.[15] Within the Nixon administration they include the president's determination to split the labor–civil rights alliance, speed the growth of a conservative black mid-

---

14 Graham, *Civil Rights Era*, 322–45; Joan Hoff, *Nixon Reconsidered* (New York: Basic Books, 1994), 89–113; Hugh Davis Graham, "Richard Nixon and Civil Rights: Explaining an Enigma," *Presidential Studies Quarterly* 26 (Winter 1996): 93–106.
15 *Contractors Association of Eastern Pennsylvania v. Secretary of Labor*, 404 U.S. 854 (1971); *Griggs v. Duke Power Co.* 401 U.S. 424 (1971).

dle class, associate "racial quotas" in the public mind with the liberal legacy of the Democratic party, and foster working-class resentment of court-ordered busing and "reverse discrimination."[16] These events helped produce a seismic shift in the American political landscape. It included, by the 1980s, the mass defection of southern and blue-collar whites from the New Deal coalition, the emergence of a Republican presidential majority and with it conservative trends in the executive and judicial branches, and a deep split in the civil rights coalition over the principle of constitutional color-blindness.[17]

REGULATORY EXPANSION IN THE 1970S: THE CLONING OF TITLE VI

Within a year following the passage of Title VI, Congress in the Elementary and Secondary Education Act authorized a billion-dollar aid program to local school districts. Soon thereafter, the newly established Office for Civil Rights in HEW issued cross-cutting school desegregation "guidelines" that linked southern school-aid requirements to northern de facto segregation.[18] In 1969, the OFCC, using the Philadelphia Plan, imposed a model requiring rough proportional representation in minority employment on federally assisted construction projects. Then, in 1970, the OFCC in Order No. 4 extended the Philadelphia Plan model to all government contracts. Cross-cutting regulation by contract-compliance officials won impressive employment and education gains for racial and ethnic minorities, and this was not lost on the leaders of other movements, most notably feminist groups, the physically handicapped, Hispanic activists, and advocates for the elderly. By 1975, advocacy groups representing all four constituencies had persuaded Congress to borrow the language of Title VI and apply it to their own regulatory needs:[19]

---

16 Graham, *Civil Rights and the Presidency,* 150–69.
17 Edward G. Carmines and James A. Stimson, *Issue Evolution: Race and the Transformation of American Politics* (Princeton, N.J.: Princeton University Press, 1989); Thomas Byrne Edsall with Mary Edsall, *Chain Reaction: The Impact of Race, Rights, and Taxes on American Politics* (New York: Norton, 1991); E. J. Dionne, Jr., *Why Americans Hate Politics* (New York: Simon & Schuster, 1991).
18 J. Harvie Wilkinson III, *From Brown to Bakke* (New York: Oxford University Press, 1979), 104–06.
19 U.S. Advisory Commission on Intergovernmental Relations, *Regulatory Federalism: Policy, Process, Impact, and Reform* (Washington, D.C.: Advisory Commission on Intergovernmental Relations, 1984), 70–91.

- Feminist groups such as the National Organization of Women (NOW) and the Women's Equity Action League (WEAL), having persuaded Lyndon Johnson in 1967 to include sex discrimination in the executive order program enforcing the Civil Right Act, in 1971 won affirmative-action protection for women in the OFCC's Revised Order No. 4.
- In 1972, Congress by voice vote passed Title IX, an amendment to the education statutes banning federal financial assistance to any educational program or activity that practiced sex discrimination. Replicating the language of Title VI, Title IX added "sex."
- The following year, 1973, Congress in Section 504 of the Rehabilitation Act reshaped the familiar language of Title VI to read as follows: "No otherwise qualified handicapped individual in the United States shall, solely by reason of his handicap, be excluded from participation in, be denied the benefits of, or be subject to discrimination under, any program or activity receiving Federal financial assistance."
- In 1974, Congress established an Office of Bilingual Education and authorized appropriations of $585 million in fiscal 1975–1978 for bilingual assistance to local school districts, and the following year the OCR under Title VI authority issued the "Lau Remedies," which required bilingual/bicultural education for elementary students with limited English proficiency in all federally aided school districts.
- In the Age Discrimination Act of 1975, Congress again borrowed the boilerplate language of Title VI and filled in the modifier blank with "age" discrimination.

These extensions of the Title VI device during the 1970s differed from the pioneering efforts of the 1960s in several respects. In each instance, a far-reaching expansion of cross-cutting regulation occurred with little grassroots pressure from constituency movements, little attention in the media, and little congressional debate. Grassroots constituencies do not understand the arcane workings of federal regulation. But policy entrepreneurs in Congress do. Working quietly with advocacy-group lobbies, they extended Title VI's cross-cutting formula to protect new groups—often, according to the U.S. Advisory Commission on Intergovernmental Relations, "with virtually no discussion or debate about the similarities and differences in the forms of discrimination faced by different groups and the types of remedies that might prove most effective in dealing with them."[20]

20 U.S. Advisory Commission on Intergovernmental Relations, *Federal Regulation of State and Local Governments: The Mixed Record of the 1980s* (Washington, D.C.: Advisory Commission on Intergovernmental Relations, 1993), 9.

Section 504 of the Rehabilitation Act, taken almost verbatim from Title VI and enacted even without hearings, demonstrated an important difference between regulatory laws on behalf of civil rights constituencies (racial and ethnic minorities, women, the elderly, the handicapped) and legislation governing other forms of social regulation (consumer fraud, health and safety, environmental protection). In the detailed statutes governing the clean air and water standards enforced by the EPA, for example, or the workplace safety standards enforced by OSHA, Congress stipulated precise numerical standards and compliance deadlines for agency enforcement. But in extending protected-class status to new civil rights constituencies by cloning Title VI, Congress delegated wide discretion to the enforcement agencies. In Section 504 of the Rehabilitation Act, for example, Congress surely did not mean what it appeared to say (that blind individuals could drive taxis so long as they were "otherwise qualified").[21] What Section 504 *did* require would be decided later, mainly by staff lawyers in contract-compliance offices, working in consultation with disability rights organizations. By 1975, the compliance regulations, following the path of federal contracts and grants, would cover sixteen thousand public school districts, three thousand colleges and universities, thirty thousand institutions and agencies delivering health and social services, sixteen million civilian government employees, and more than 150,000 private businesses employing twenty-five million workers.

STRENGTHS AND WEAKNESSES: FOUR MODELS OF CIVIL RIGHTS REGULATION

These impressive statistics of expanding regulatory reach imply an administrative coherence that reality rarely matched.[22] Conservative writers have often described the affirmative-action regime as a colossus, imputing to contract-compliance officials a unity and capacity for coercion inconsistent with the sprawling, fragmented, uncoordinated nature of the

---

21 On the origins and development of Section 504, see Richard K. Scotch, *From Goodwill to Civil Rights* (Philadelphia: Temple University Press, 1984); Edward D. Berkowitz, *Disabled Policy: America's Programs for the Handicapped* (New York: Cambridge University Press, 1987).

22 The political context for expanding statutory rights after 1964 is described in R. Shep Melnick, *Between the Lines: Interpreting Welfare Rights* (Washington, D.C.: Brookings Institution, 1994), 3–64.

American administrative state.[23] In modern civil rights regulation every president since Lyndon Johnson has grappled with the baffling jurisdictional puzzles posed by separation of powers and federalism. In attempting to bring greater policy coherence to civil rights regulation, Jimmy Carter was more successful than most. Carter in 1978 won agreement from fellow Democrats controlling Congress for a reorganization that consolidated enforcement responsibility within the EEOC for equal pay, age discrimination, and fair employment in government service. In the following year, Carter by executive order consolidated in the OFCC the functions of eleven contract compliance agencies scattered throughout the executive departments and renamed the already awkwardly named agency the Office of Federal Contract Compliance Programs (OFCCP). As a consequence of the Carter consolidation, both the OFCCP and the EEOC experienced an extraordinary expansion in personnel. Between 1978 and 1980 the OFCCP expanded from 68 full-time staff members to 1,304, and the EEOC expanded from 267 to 3,433.[24]

Nonetheless, by 1980 the enforcement machinery for civil rights remained uneven and poorly articulated. Four models of regulation can be discerned, ranging across the spectrum of authority and effectiveness. Three of the models reflect the behavior of leading enforcement agencies—the EEOC, the OCR, and the OFCC. The fourth, contract set-asides, involves a form of contractual obligation in civil rights policy that legislatures impose on mission agencies through the appropriations process. At the weaker end of the spectrum of regulatory authority stood the agency most familiar to the public, the EEOC. Though technically not a regulatory agency, the EEOC behaved like one, pressing for proportional employment results by issuing guidelines on employment testing and employee selection that resembled the rule-making of the regulatory agencies.[25] Structurally, however, the EEOC remained the quasijudicial commission of Title VII provenance. The commission processed complaints through a decentralized network of regional and district offices, produced

---

23 See, for example, Herman Belz, *Equality Transformed: A Quarter-Century of Affirmative Action* (New Brunswick, N.J.: Transaction, 1991), and Robert R. Detlefsen, *Civil Rights Under Reagan* (San Francisco: Institute for Contemporary Studies, 1991).

24 U.S. Commission on Civil Rights, *The Federal Civil Rights Enforcement Budget: Fiscal Year 1983* (Washington, D.C.: U.S. Government Printing Office, 1982), 14–54.

25 Unlike the OCR, OFCC, and smaller contract-compliance offices in a score of federal agencies, which could freeze or terminate federal funds, deny contracts, and debar bidders, the EEOC sought enforcement through court suits. The 1972 amendments to Title VII authorized the EEOC, previously limited to recommending lawsuits to the Justice Department, to bring suit directly in federal courts.

written findings of reasonable cause, sought conciliations, filed suits through an independent counsel (separately organized in regional litigation centers), and accumulated a complaint backlog that often delayed action for years.[26]

During the Carter years, the EEOC compensated for these procedural and structural constraints by adopting a carrot-and-stick regulatory strategy. Eleanor Holmes Norton, appointed by Carter to chair the EEOC in 1977, shifted the agency's enforcement emphasis from processing individual complaints to filing class-action lawsuits against large employers. In the wake of the 1978 consolidation, the EEOC issued the Uniform Guidelines on Employee Selection Procedures, a set of rules grounded in adverse impact theory that curtailed the use by employers of employee tests and other merit criteria. As Alfred Blumrosen observed, the EEOC's accelerated enforcement strategy under Norton, strengthened by the Carter reorganization, "precipitated an enormous pressure on employers."[27] Businesses were told, in effect, that the EEOC would ease enforcement pressures and provide immunity against reverse-discrimination lawsuits like *Weber* in exchange for employer adoption of "voluntary" affirmative-action plans.

The EEOC was a unique and not very satisfactory hybrid, child of the elaborate compromises attending the construction of Title VII in 1964. Title VI, on the other hand, had spawned regulatory enforcement agencies in eleven federal departments by 1978, the largest by far being the OCR, the second model of civil rights regulation. In theory, the OCR was armed with vast enforcement authority. Its bureaucrats policed discrimination by race, national origin, sex, and disability in the nation's elementary and secondary schools, institutions of higher education, agencies delivering health and social services, and all state and local government agencies holding federal government contracts.

In practice, the OCR faced formidable difficulties. First, OCR's original charge, school desegregation, was initially successful in the South. But school integration grew elusive as whites fled urban schools and the Supreme Court and Congress protected nonsouthern suburban constituencies from de facto desegregation. Second, agency capture by beneficiary clientele groups, a staple source of cohesion and coalition-building in civil

---

26 Hanes Walton, Jr., *When the Marching Stopped: The Politics of Civil Rights Agencies* (Albany: State University of New York Press, 1988).
27 Alfred W. Blumrosen, *Modern Law: The Law Transmission System and Equal Employment Opportunity* (Madison: University of Wisconsin Press, 1993), 167.

rights enforcement at the EEOC and the OFCC, produced intramural squabbling at the OCR, where the cloning process of Title VI protections energized successive waves of client groups competing for scarce resources.[28] Third, under pressure from competing clientele groups, OCR officials produced regulations that often backfired politically. In a few celebrated instances (school desegregation guidelines for Chicago, school dress codes and hair-length codes, school-busing requirements for racial balance), OCR regulations were repudiated even by Democratic-controlled Congresses. In others (banning boys' choirs and father-daughter school dinners), public ridicule forced bureaucratic retreat.[29]

Finally, the OCR got massively caught up in the explosion of public law litigation that spun out of *Brown v. Board of Education.* In 1970, the National Association for the Advancement of Colored People (NAACP) Legal Defense Fund sued HEW secretary Elliot Richardson, seeking federal court orders to accelerate the pace of school desegregation in the South. Thus began the extraordinary *Adams* case, a twenty-year saga in which the OCR essentially fell into receivership in the federal district court of Judge John Pratt of Maryland. Competing plaintiff groups jockeyed and bickered over OCR's enforcement priorities—first on behalf of African Americans (LDF), then women (WEAL), Hispanics (Mexican American Legal Defense and Education Fund), and the handicapped (National Federation of the Blind). Stephen Halpern, in *On the Limits of the Law,* presents a detailed study of the *Adams* case, which emphasized procedures and managerial efficiency over substantive results, and ended in collapse in 1990 when the frustrated and exhausted Judge Pratt and the Fourth Circuit Court of Appeals terminated the case.[30]

The third model of civil rights regulation is the OFCC. Armed with the awesome power of the federal purse, the OFCC stood between federal contractors and their livelihood. By finding, or threatening to find, contractors and bidders not "in compliance" with agency criteria for workforce participation by minorities and women, the OFCC held a mighty sword.[31] The OCR dealt mainly with government entities and hence got

28 Jeremy Rabkin, *Judicial Compulsions: How Public Law Distorts Public Policy* (New York: Basic Books, 1989), 147–81.
29 Joseph A. Califano, *Governing America* (New York: Simon & Schuster, 1981), 219–26.
30 Stephen C. Halpern, *On the Limits of the Law: The Ironic Legacy of Title VI of the 1964 Civil Rights Act* (Baltimore: Johns Hopkins University Press, 1995).
31 There was considerable overlap in responsibility and authority between civil rights enforcement agencies, and hence considerable confusion among regulated parties. Prior to 1964 the executive order tradition from Roosevelt's Fair Employment Practice Com-

entangled in the political snarls of federalism and in public law litigation like *Adams;* the OFCC dealt with the private, profit-seeking sector where agency officials enjoyed wide discretion. Congress and federal judges rarely interfered with its operations. Unlike the EEOC, which was obliged to seek enforcement through the federal courts, the OFCC controlled the government's paymasters.

By 1980, most private firms of significant size in the United States were bound by OFCC requirements. Employers seeking federal contracts understood the ageless wisdom of Omar Khayyam: "Whose bread I eat, whose wine I drink, his song I sing." The officials of the OFCC, in contrast, sensitive to charges of enforcing minority "quotas," exercised flexibility and discretion in negotiating goals and timetables for minority hiring and promotion. By 1981, when Ronald Reagan became president, the Labor Department scarcely resembled the small, unprestigious, union-captured mission agency of 1964. Reagan's Labor Department housed two of the most powerful and controversial enforcement agencies of the new social regulation: the OFCC and the Occupational Safety and Health Administration.

THE CONTAGIOUS WORLD OF MINORITY CONTRACT SET-ASIDES

The fourth model of post-1964 civil rights regulation, created unexpectedly by Congress in the Public Works Employment Act of 1977, was the contract set-aside requirement. Without committee hearings or reports, Congress adopted a floor amendment proposed by Representative Parren Mitchell, Democrat of Maryland, to set aside for minority business enterprises 10 percent of a $4 billion antirecession appropriation.[32] Mitchell, Chair of the Congressional Black Caucus, noted that minorities were 18 percent of the population but received less than 1 percent of federal con-

mittee through Kennedy's "affirmative action" directive of 1961 had lacked statutory authority in civil rights law. After 1964, executive orders drew authority from the Civil Rights Act, especially President Johnson's Executive Order 11246 of 1965. The OCR, the largest of the five contract-compliance agencies enforcing Title VI in cabinet-level departments, enforced Executive Order 11246 in educational institutions, medical and health institutions, social service agencies, and state and local public agencies holding federal government contracts. The Justice Department loosely coordinated agency enforcement under Title VI, leading in the 1970s to a unified adoption by contract compliance agencies of the "effects" test under the adverse impact theory approved by the Supreme Court in *Griggs* (1971).

32 Hugh Davis Graham, "Civil Rights Policy in the Carter Presidency," in Gary M. Fink and Hugh Davis Graham, eds., *The Carter Presidency: Policy Choices in the Post-New Deal Era* (Lawrence: University Press of Kansas, 1998), 202–23.

tracts.[33] Challenged by nonminority contractors as a quota violating the equal protection clause of the 14th amendment, the set-aside requirement was upheld by the Supreme Court in *Fullilove v. Klutznick* (1980).[34] *Fullilove* was a green light, inviting state, county, and especially city governments to adopt similar set-aside requirements.

The 1977 set-aside law opened the door for the expansion of government programs in two directions. First, mandates for set-aside programs were added to the authorizing legislation for federal agencies with significant contracting responsibilities. In 1978, Congress furnished a statutory basis for the Small Business Administration's 8(a) earmark program, begun administratively in 1968 against a background of urban riots, for business enterprises owned by "socially and economically disadvantaged persons."[35] In the 1980s, Congress—with cooperation from the Reagan White House—added set-aside provisions to most major agency appropriations.[36]

A second expansion of contract set-aside programs, more extensive and yet more diffuse, occurred at the state and local levels. The *Fullilove* decision coincided with the emergence of minority political power in the nation's major cities, including, by the 1980s, black mayors elected in

33 Women, excluded from the original, race-oriented set-aside program in 1977, much as they had been excluded from Title VI in 1964, again pursued a parallel catch-up strategy. In 1979, President Carter issued Executive Order 12138 to include women-owned businesses in federal assistance programs. The Women's Business Ownership Act of 1988 authorized the federal promotion of women business enterprises, which received $1.75 billion in federal contracts that year. See George R. LaNoue and John C. Sullivan, "Presumptions for Preferences: The Small Business Administration's Decisions on Groups Entitled to Affirmative Action," *Journal of Policy History* 6 (1994): 439–67.

34 Drew S. Days III, assistant attorney general for civil rights in the Carter administration, successfully defended the government set-aside in *Fullilove*. In 1987, Days, a law professor at Yale, wrote in the *Yale Law Journal:* "One can only marvel at the fact that the minority set-aside provision was enacted into law without having a committee report and with only token opposition." "Without a careful examination of the facts and alternatives," he observed, "the legislation may be misdirected and fail to assist those most deserving of aid, may harm others unjustifiably, and may operate . . . longer than necessary." Days, *"Fullilove,"* 96 *Yale Law Journal* (1987): 453, 469.

35 In 1978, more than 96 percent of the firms in the Small Business Administration's 8(a) program were owned by members of "presumptively eligible" groups (African Americans, Hispanics, Asians, American Indians, Eskimos, and Aleuts), and two-thirds of the participating firms were owned by blacks.

36 By 1990, the set-aside pattern for minority firms was common throughout the federal government. Appropriations bills for fiscal 1990 included set-aside requirements, for example, of 5 percent for defense procurement and research and development contracts, 8 percent of National Aeronautics and Space Administration contracts, and 10 percent of highway administration grants, international development grants, and construction contracts for U.S. embassies abroad. By 1990, federal agencies were awarding $8.65 billion in minority set-aside contracts.

Atlanta, Baltimore, Birmingham, Charlotte, Chicago, Cleveland, Detroit, Los Angeles, Newark, New Orleans, Richmond, Philadelphia, and Washington. When the Supreme Court in *City of Richmond v. Croson* (1989) sharply narrowed the scope of minority set-aside requirements below the federal level, at least 234 jurisdictions—states, cities, counties, and special districts—had established set-aside programs.[37]

By 1980, the cumulative process of Title VI cloning in Congress, regulatory expansion in the agencies, mostly favorable federal court decisions, and effective coalition-building by protected-class clienteles had forged a political consensus behind affirmative-action programs that seemed secure in the corridors of power. Public institutions such as state and local governments, public school districts, higher education systems, and health and social service agencies had transformed affirmative-action requirements into bureaucratic routines. American business leaders, faced with increasing EEOC complaint negotiations under Title VII, pressed by the strengthened OFCCP to meet proportional minority hiring goals, denied under the EEOC's Uniform Guidelines the use of traditional employee tests without expensive and vulnerable validation procedures, and fearing liability from reverse discrimination suits like those filed by Allan Bakke and Brian Weber, shifted toward the proportional representation model for employing minorities and women as a necessary way of doing business.[38]

These prudential adjustments to civil rights regulation by public and private employers, however, coincided with a rising chorus of complaints against excessive Washington regulation from the business community and from state and local governments.[39] By the early 1980s, the U.S. Advisory Commission on Intergovernmental Relations, established by Congress in 1959 to monitor the health of federalism, was describing the sprawling regulatory state as administratively fragmented, inflexibile, inefficient, inconsistent, intrusive, ineffective, and unaccountable.[40] The reverse-discrimination controversies over Bakke and Weber in the late

---

37 George R. LaNoue, "Split Visions: Minority Business Set-Asides," *The Annals* 523 (September 1992): 104–16.
38 For a critical view of this transformation see Belz, *Equality Transformed*, especially 111–33. For an approving view, see Blumrosen, *Modern Law,* especially 124–33, 161–81.
39 Martha Derthick, "Intergovernmental Relations in the 1970s," in Gelfand and Neymeyer, *Changing Patterns,* 54–59; David Vogel, *Fluctuating Fortunes: The Political Power of Business in America* (New York: Basic Books, 1988), 93–122.
40 Advisory Commission on Intergovernmental Relations, *Categorical Grants,* 287–293; Advisory Commission on Intergovernmental Relations, *Regulatory Federalism,* 10–18.

1970s underlined the spread of civil rights regulation in state and local government and in the larger enterprises of the private sector well beyond the requirements of federal officials.

THE REAGAN COUNTEROFFENSIVE AGAINST CIVIL RIGHTS REGULATION

The election in 1980 of Ronald Reagan, running on a platform hostile to minority preference policies, promised to expand the deregulation movement to include civil rights enforcement. As a presidential candidate, Reagan declared: "We must not allow the noble concept of equal opportunity to be distorted into federal guidelines or quotas which require race, ethnicity, or sex—rather than ability and qualifications—to be the principal factor in hiring or education."[41] Once elected, he appointed conservatives to executive departments and the federal bench and sought deregulation in voting rights law. At the end of his presidency, Reagan's record on civil rights was attacked in two books, one from the left and one from the right. In *Civil Rights Under the Reagan Administration,* Norman Amaker, a civil rights lawyer and former NAACP staff member, described it as a reactionary effort to overturn settled law and policy; in *Civil Rights Under Reagan,* Robert Detlefsen, an academic political scientist, saw an indecisive administration, weakened by internal disagreement in the face of a hostile liberal Congress and a liberal federal judiciary. Both agreed that Reagan had largely failed.[42]

Reagan was most successful, especially during his first term when Republicans controlled the Senate, in appointing conservatives to the federal courts and to senior posts in the regulatory and mission agencies. The judicial appointments matured slowly, providing their payoff after Reagan left the White House. Reagan's senior political appointees enlivened the news and raised the political temperature in Washington, but their legacy faded with their exit. The messy attempt by the Reagan White House to countercapture the nonregulatory Civil Rights Commission partially backfired, but he was more successful in curbing civil rights regula-

---

41 Quoted in Gary L. McDowell, "Affirmative Inaction: The Brock-Meese Standoff in Federal Racial Quotas," *Policy Review* 48 (Spring 1989): 32.
42 Norman C. Amaker, *Civil Rights and the Reagan Administration* (Washington, D.C.: The Urban Institute, 1988); Detlefsen, *Civil Rights Under Reagan.* Views similar to Amaker's are found in Walton, *When the Marching Stopped.* Detlefsen's disappointment in the Reagan record is echoed in Belz, *Equality Transformed.*

tion at the EEOC and, to a lesser extent, at the OFCC. At the EEOC, chairman Clarence Thomas deemphasized class-action, disparate impact lawsuits against large employers in favor of policing intentional discrimination and providing make-whole relief for victims. At the OFCC, a similar moderation of regulatory aggressiveness sped the rate of successful compliance reviews. In both agencies the change in regulatory policy was accomplished not through formal notice-and-comment procedures but through internal policy directives.[43]

More revealing of the political odds Reagan faced are three failed initiatives of the Reagan administration, two of them in Congress and one within the administration. They demonstrate the entrenchment and resilience of the civil rights coalition and the affirmative-action programs they had built. In 1981–82 the civil rights coalition in Congress overwhelmed Reagan's attempt to narrow the scope of Justice Department regulation under the Voting Rights Act. The voting rights amendments of 1982 extended for twenty-five years the Attorney General's preclearance authority and declared in Section 2 that discriminatory effects of electoral arrangements violated the act irrespective of their intent. Congress also overrode Reagan's veto of the Civil Rights Restoration Act of 1988, which reversed the Supreme Court's 1984 ruling in the *Grove City College* case. In that decision, the court held that agency regulations accompanying federal aid to public and private institutions applied only to the specific programs receiving the federal dollars (the college admissions office, a recipient of federal tuition aid), not to the entire institution.

In both congressional defeats the Reagan administration faced a bipartisan coalition swollen by Republican defectors. Despite increasing conservativism among Republican leaders, party solidarity broke down on voting rights, where challenging the Leadership Conference invited charges of racism. In the *Grove City College* case, Reagan's narrow view of regulatory jurisdiction unified the opposition of virtually all advocacy groups—racial and ethnic minorities, feminists, the physically and mentally disabled, and the immigration bar.[44]

The campaign within the Reagan administration to revise Lyndon Johnson's affirmative-action executive order of 1965, led by assistant

---

43 Blumrosen, *Modern Law,* 267–74; Belz, *Equality Transformed,* 181–207.
44 Hugh Davis Graham, "The Storm Over Grove City College: Civil Rights Regulation, Higher Education, and the Reagan Administration," *History of Education Quarterly* 38 (Winter 1998): 407–29; idem, "The Politics of Clientele Capture: Civil Rights Policy and the Reagan Administration," in Neal Devins and Davison Douglas, eds., *Redefining Equality* (New York: Oxford University Press, 1998), 103–19.

attorney general for civil rights William Bradford Reynolds and supported by attorney general Edwin Meese, died in a quiet collapse in 1986. Leading the cabinet-level opposition to any fundamental change in Executive Order 11246 was Labor secretary William Brock, whose department had risen in authority and esteem since 1965 largely on the strength of its status as the government's lead agency in contract compliance. Joining Brock in defending the affirmative-action status quo within Reagan's cabinet were the secretaries of State (George Shultz), Treasury (James Baker), Health and Human Services (Margaret Heckler), Transportation (Elizabeth Dole), and Housing and Urban Development (Samuel Pierce).[45] Their resistance to a radical change in the affirmative-action status quo reflected the reluctance of the nation's large employers to plunge into unknown waters. The Associated General Contractors and the small-business constituency of the Chamber of Commerce supported Reynolds's effort, but the National Association of Manufacturers opposed it. Strongly Republican and supporting deregulation elsewhere, big business preferred the known routines of underutilization analysis and minority hiring requirements to the unknown perils of reverse-discrimination lawsuits.[46]

Nor were the Republican administrations of Reagan and Bush consistent in their opposition to race-conscious affirmative action. Like Nixon and Ford, Reagan and Bush courted African American and Latino middle-class constituencies by offering minority set-asides. During the 1980s, both Republican presidents expanded earmarked aid to historically black colleges and increased set-aside requirements in agency budgets to support minority businesses. And by the late 1980s, Republican strategists had learned the partisan virtues of strict voting-rights enforcement. Republican-led Justice Departments pressed successfully for majority-minority districts whose increasingly bizarre configurations offered three partisan advantages: (1) they modestly increased the election of minority Democrats, (2) they rapidly increased the election of subur-

---

45 "The New Rights War," *Newsweek,* 30 December 1985, 66–8; Daniel Seligman, "It Was Forseeable," *Fortune,* 22 July 1985, 119; McDowell, "Affirmative Inaction," 32–37. According to these sources, Meese and Reynolds were supported by the secretaries of Education (William Bennett), Energy (John S. Herrington), Interior (Donald P. Hodel), and the director of the OMB (James C. Miller III).

46 Daniel Seligman, "Affirmative Action is Here to Stay," *Fortune,* 19 April 1982, 143–62; Anne B. Fisher, "Businessmen Like to Hire by the Numbers," *Fortune,* 16 September 1985, 26–30; Steven A. Holmes, "Affirmative Action Plans Are Part of Business Life," *New York Times,* 22 November 1991.

ban white Republicans, and (3) they sharply reduced the ranks of white Democrats.[47]

CIVIL RIGHTS IN THE BUSH ADMINISTRATION: THE AMERICANS WITH DISABILITIES ACT OF 1990 AND THE CIVIL RIGHTS ACT OF 1991

Finally, President George Bush, formerly chairman of Reagan's task force on regulatory relief, confirmed the apparent permanence of the government's comprehensive regulatory regime in civil rights by signing into law the Americans with Disabilities Act in 1990 and the Civil Rights Act of 1991. The legislative effort culminating in the Civil Rights Act of 1991, which featured Bush vetoing a "quota bill" in 1990 and Congress reversing a brace of conservative Supreme Court decisions led by *Ward's Cove* (1989), received far more attention than did the Americans with Disabilities Act (ADA). Yet both statutes are civil rights laws. Together, they reveal much about the regulatory regime built on the founding legislation of 1964. Both major parties, not just the Democrats, have responded to the pressures of client politics since the 1960s by supporting civil rights legislation to benefit well-organized constituencies. The ADA, affecting an estimated forty-three million Americans, dealt with the largest minority in the country—and, according to Edward Berkowitz, "the minority with the greatest propensity to vote Republican."[48] Disability cuts across lines of race, sex, class, and party, and rehabilitation emphasizes Republican virtues: mainstreaming deserving individuals who sought self-improvement, turning them into tax-paying citizens. Although the ADA was a civil rights law, resting on the civil rights section of the Rehabilitation Act of 1973 which in turn was a clone of Title VI of the mother law of

---

47 *New York Times,* 14 February 1994, 16 April 1994, 17 August 1994. Studies of electoral behavior in the 1990s support the view that majority-minority districts limit minority influence to a few safe districts while marginalizing the minority vote elsewhere, thereby weakening minority bargaining power and increasing Republican electoral success. Carol Swain, *Black Faces, Black Interests: The Representation of African Americans in Congress* (Cambridge, Mass.: Harvard University Press, 1993); Kevin Hill, "Does the Creation of Majority Black Districts Aid Republicans?" *Journal of Politics* 57 (May 1995): 384–401; Charles Cameron, David Epstein, and Sharyn O'Halloran, "Do Majority-Minority Districts Maximize Substantive Black Representation in Congress?" *American Political Science Review* 90 (December 1996): 794–812.

48 Edward D. Berkowitz, "A Historical Preface to the Americans With Disabilities Act," *Journal of Policy History* 6 (1994): 109, 96–119.

1964, the ADA appealed to conservative Republicans who otherwise thundered against government regulation.

In passing both civil rights laws, Congress continued the tradition of concentrating on rights and benefits while paying little attention to costs. Social regulation appealed to Congress because it redistributed benefits to well organized constituencies at small cost to the federal budget. The ADA contains provisions requiring special employment accommodations, non-discrimination against physically and mentally disabled workers and students, access to all public and private transportation, and removal of architectural barriers, provisions that carry enormous potential costs for private and government employers. The managers of the legislative hearings on the ADA, relying on assurances from President Bush and Attorney General Richard Thornburgh that the ADA would reduce Social Security payouts and increase tax revenues and consumer spending, decided not to invite expert testimony on the cost-saving nature of the ADA.[49]

The Civil Rights Act of 1991, by making available for the first time jury trials and compensatory and punitive damages in cases of intentional sexual and disability discrimination (including the ill-defined area of sexual harassment), also provided economic incentives for litigation with potentially vast consequences. The act, according to one commentator, "thereby fundamentally changes the legal model underlying federal employment discrimination laws. Whereas previously these laws focused on conciliation and the improvement of employer-employee relations, the Civil Rights Act of 1991 provides monetary remedies that have been traditionally associated with civil trials for tort damages."[50] Unfunded federal mandates, a staple of civil rights regulation, brought positive economic consequences to beneficiaries and employers alike during the 1960s and 1970s, when nondiscrimination destroyed barriers to the free flow of labor and talent. But by the early 1990s the economic costs of civil rights regulation, never a topic of much interest to Congress, remained largely unexplored.

In passing the Civil Rights Act of 1991, the political branches of government on the eve of a presidential election responded to lobbying from a formidable array of civil rights constituencies (racial and ethnic minorities, women, the disabled) and enacted a law grounded in contradictory interpretations of the statute's meaning. Unable to agree on substantial

49 Ibid., 113.
50 David A. Cathcart et al., *The Civil Rights Act of 1991* (Philadelphia: American Law Institute—American Bar Association, 1991), 9.

policy questions, such as a statutory definition of "business necessity," Congress accompanied the act with several conflicting memoranda of interpretation, authored by legislative leaders of both parties (senators John Danforth, Robert Dole, Edward Kennedy, Frank Murkowski; representatives Donald Edwards, Henry Hyde) and published in the *Congressional Record*. One of these, Danforth's Interpretive Memorandum of October 25, 1991, is cited in Section 105(b) of the law as having exclusive authority as a source of legislative history and congressional intent concerning the burden of proof in disparate impact cases. As one commentator observed: "This attempt within a statute to establish its own exclusive legislative history may be unprecedented in the United States Code."[51] Congress and the White House could not agree on a statutory meaning, but could not resist passing the act anyway, while accompanying it with contradictory official explanations of what the new law meant. The federal courts would decide, by default.[52]

Finally, the civil rights policymaking of 1990–91, by intensely engaging a national network of Washington-centered policy elites but drawing little on grassroots support from the general public, reflected a widening gap between the policy preoccupations of Washington and a souring national mood. This growing public alienation and distrust of government is profound and its causes extend far beyond disagreement over civil rights.[53] Unlike the 1960s, when the moral claims of protesting African Americans were unchallengeable, in the 1990s the American public is deeply divided over the new social regulation.

THE TENSION BETWEEN EFFECTIVENESS AND LEGITIMACY

As the web of government regulation has thickened since the 1960s, its requirements have grown nettlesome to citizens in areas far removed from civil rights policy. Government increasingly requires us to do this and not do that about auto-emission testing, smoking, trash recycling, AIDS prevention, land use zoning, gun ownership, dog leashing, and airport se-

---

51 Cathcart et al., *Civil Rights Act of 1991*, 8; Henry H. Perritt, Jr., *Civil Rights Act of 1991: Special Report* (New York: Wiley, 1992), passim.
52 Melnick, *Between the Lines*, 4–6.
53 According to the University of Michigan's National Election Study data, in 1964, 76 percent of Americans thought that "Washington can be trusted to do what is right" all or most of the time. In 1992, only 24 percent shared that view. Frank Luntz and Ron Dermer, "A Farewell to the American Dream?" *The Public Perspective* (September/October 1994): 12–14.

curity. We are irritated by safety-belt contraptions we must buckle, by aspirin containers we cannot open, by the need to strap our children into backseat harnesses, and to buy and wear bicycle and motorcycle helmets. We grumble about their necessity or wisdom or design. But citizens and voters do not, as a rule, question the legitimacy of government responsibility for clean air and water or safe transportation and consumer products. The standard-setting, rule-making model of social regulation that won acceptance during the 1960s and 1970s to reduce risk and harm from environmental, consumer, and safety hazards was unable to win public acceptance when it was used to enforce civil rights policy. The story of Title VI of the Civil Rights Act, and of the executive orders and contract-compliance extensions reshaped over three decades by enforcement agencies and federal courts to require or encourage minority preferences, is a story of increasing effectiveness—of institutionalized political security—purchased at the price of decreasing public legitimacy.

Supporters of civil rights regulation under the adverse impact standard offer powerful arguments that the affirmative-action regime developed since 1964 has been proactive, administratively flexible, moderately effective when measured by economic outcomes, increasingly accepted by Congress (even after 1994), and preferred to unknown alternatives by employers.[54] And they are right. Critics have replied that the affirmative-action regime is permanent regulation with a temporary rationale, exercised by captured agencies in the interest of selected clientele groups, with benefits accruing to advantaged parties, including millions of recent immigrants with no commensurate claims to past discrimination.[55] And *they* are right. There is enough truth on both sides of this accounting ledger to sustain indefinitely the polarization over civil rights policy that afflicted American society in the 1990s. Since the beginning of the Nixon administration the civil rights coalition has won most of the battles over establishing and defending a regulatory regime of affirmative action pref-

---

54 See, for example, Herbert Hill and James E. Jones, Jr., eds., *Race in America: The Struggle for Equality* (Madison: University of Wisconsin Press, 1993); William L. Taylor and Susan M. Liss, "Affirmative Action in the 1990s: Staying the Course," *The Annals* 523 (September 1992): 30–37.

55 For claims that affirmative-action preferences have chiefly benefitted advantaged individuals and firms rather than the most vulnerable minorities and women, see Paul Burstein, *Discrimination, Jobs, and Politics* (Chicago: University of Chicago Press, 1985); William Julius Wilson, *The Truly Disadvantaged* (Chicago: University of Chicago Press, 1987); David M. O'Neill and June O'Neill, "Affirmative Action in the Labor Market," *Annals* 523 (September 1992): 88–103.

erences. But unlike the nondiscrimination principles of 1964, and unlike social regulation to protect consumers, worker safety, and the environment, affirmative-action regulation has been rejected by most Americans as unfair.

Opinion surveys in the 1990s have shown broad public support for "soft" forms of affirmative action (recruiting outreach, job training programs, targeted internships). But whites of both sexes have shown growing resentment against the minority preferences of "hard" affirmative action (proportional hiring requirements, contract set-asides, minority scholarships and admissions preferences).[56] Typically, 80 percent of white men oppose "preferential treatment" to improve the position of blacks and other minorities. White women, who comprise 40 percent of the U.S. voting population, and who have benefitted greatly from nondiscrimination and soft affirmative action since the 1960s but little from gender preferences under hard affirmative action, agreed with the opinion of white men.[57] In 1996, California voters approved Proposition 209, the "California Civil Rights Initiative" that banned preferential treatment for minorities and women in state employment, contracting, and education programs. White and Asian voters supported Proposition 209 by large margins while black and Hispanic majorities opposed it.

In *The Scar of Race,* Paul Sniderman and Thomas Piazza, using experimental interview techniques to explore the dimensions of white racial prejudice, found that white attitudes toward blacks were diverse and pliable. Although white racial prejudice was still manifest regarding housing patterns and school resegregation, it is "simply wrong," they found, "to suppose that the primary factor driving the contemporary arguments over the politics of race is white racism."[58] By increasing margins, whites support not only government policies banning deliberate discrimination based on race but also government programs to provide income, services, and training to improve the economic and social circumstances of blacks.

---

56 Seymour Martin Lipset, "Affirmative Action and the American Creed," *Wilson Quarterly* (Winter 1992): 52–62; idem, *American Exceptionalism* (New York: Norton, 1996), 125–50. According to Lipset, whites overestimate the extent of reverse discrimination; blacks on the other hand underestimate the extent of black economic progress, "due in part to the reluctance of black leaders to admit it" ("American Creed," p. 60).

57 Peter A. Brown, "Ms. Quota," *New Republic,* 15 April 1991, 18–19; Thomas Byrne Edsall, "Rights Drive Said to Lose Underpinnings," *Washington Post,* 9 March 1991; Lipset, *American Exceptionalism,* 125–31.

58 Paul M. Sniderman and Thomas Piazza, *The Scar of Race* (Cambridge, Mass.: Belknap Press, 1993), 5.

On issues of school busing for racial balance and affirmative-action preferences, however, white Americans of both sexes are massively opposed.
As the regulatory state has extended its reach and increased its intrusiveness, it has met its stiffest resistance in the one area where the efficiency of
modern social regulation has clashed with a core conviction of most
Americans that individuals should not be harmed, especially by their government, on the basis of characteristics they were born with.[59]

There are many reasons for this growing resentment, including such
less highminded sources as persistent white racism, immigrant scapegoating in stiffening economic competition, and the natural human tendency
to blame others for one's own disappointments and shortcomings. But
high among the sources of disaffection has been the demoralizing effect
over a generation of a political process that has pulled into protected-class
status not only black Americans in the wake of urban riots but also new
groups with widely differing claims to preference.

Since the immigration reforms of 1965, approximately twenty-five
million immigrants have come to the United States, three-quarters of them
from Latin America and Asia. By the historical logic of affirmative action,
they have qualified, like African Americans, for protection from the
effects of past discrimination even when they were newly arrived and their
group had no significant history of oppression in America. Thus Cubans
and Taiwanese, irrespective of their income or education, were presumed
disadvantaged by government bureaucrats on the basis of cultural origin
and were provided remedies justified by historic rationales originally
based on African American slavery and southern segregation. The Small
Business Administration's 8(a) program approved minority preference
status for individuals on the basis of ancestry from Indonesia, Sri Lanka,
India, Pakistan, China, and Japan, ethnic communities whose history in
the United States varies widely but whose average family income and
education by the 1990s considerably exceeded that of "white" families.[60]

The controversy over proliferating beneficiary groups in affirmative-
action programs has increased tension between African American civil
rights organizations and Latino and Asian leaders. Rising criticism of
minority preferences by whites has also fueled resentment by middle-class
African Americans. Middle-income blacks see racial discrimination per-

---

59 Paul M. Sniderman and Edward G. Carmines, *Reaching Beyond Race* (Cambridge,
   Mass.: Harvard University Press, 1997).
60 Lawrence H. Fuchs, *The American Kaleidoscope: Race, Ethnicity, and the Civic Culture*
   (Hanover, N.H.: Wesleyan University Press, 1990), 453–57.

sisting despite a generation of civil rights reforms and interpret white attacks on affirmative action as racial insults.[61]

CONCLUSION

Our political system, in summary, has been well designed to accelerate an additive, pluralist process of program-building to serve organized clientele groups. But it is badly designed to restrain its excesses or balance competing claims against accepted norms of fairness. It has been geared to ratchet up, but not down.[62] In civil rights policy, no less than in farm or veterans or education policy, our postwar system of interest-group liberalism has seemed unable to sate its appetite. Politically, affirmative-action remedies could not be confined to African Americans. Peter Skerry points out (in Chapter 5) that Mexican American immigrant leaders saw no alternative to claiming victim-beneficiary status under the affirmative-action regime. Rationales and remedies based on past discrimination against long-resident Mexicans and Chinese could not be denied to newly arrived and prosperous Argentines and Indonesians. "Soft" affirmative-action remedies, easier to defend against quota charges, hardened and spread in the competitive environment of Title VI cloning.

In the course of this regime change in civil rights regulation since 1964, power shifted from the periphery to the center and from the private sector to public officials. Within government, power shifted from the courthouse and statehouse to the White House and Congress, then increasingly to regulatory and mission agencies backed by the federal courts. By the 1980s, the affirmative-action regime had taken root in the personnel and procurement systems of state and local governments, including school and

61 Jennifer L. Hochschild, *Facing Up to the American Dream: Race, Class, and the Soul of the Nation* (Princeton, N.J.: Princeton University Press, 1995), chap. 7.

62 A large literature documents the political bias of interest-group liberalism toward upward-ratcheting benefits, for example in agricultural commodities, veterans benefits, student loans, and university research support. In civil rights regulation, this tendency is seen for example in the creep of contract set-aside requirements. As the *Croson* litigation demonstrated, local governments established and raised the percentage requirements of minority set-aside contracts largely in response to political criteria. In Richmond, Va., the minority set-aside challenged in *Croson* was 30 percent of city contracts. In Washington, D.C., it was 50 percent. Ohio State University established a minority set-aside for painting contracts of 100 percent, meaning that white male painting contractors were banned. The growth of 100 percent minority set-aside requirements in low-skill sub-contracts, such as painting and highway guardrails, reflected the pressures on agency managers to meet set-aside goals when budgets were dominated by complex projects such as bridge-building and weapons procurement, where competing firms were large or technically sophisticated organizations not owned or controlled by a protected class.

higher education systems, and in business and professional firms. Because government regulators, unlike administrative managers, direct the expenditure of someone else's money, the agencies of civil rights regulation exerted great leverage with modest budgets and hence were less inhibited by the budget-cutting trends of the 1980s and 1990s. The expanding civil rights coalition, ably led and uniquely armed with constitutional protections not available to defenders of threatened programs for the poor (public housing, dependent children, Medicaid, legal services), extended the reach of affirmative-action regulation into the 1990s.

Because affirmative-action programs primarily aided not "truly disadvantaged" minorities on the basis of need but upwardly-mobile middle-class constituencies seeking advantages in college and professional admissions, appointments and promotions, and small-business contracts—advantages awarded by government officials on the basis of increasingly problematical criteria involving genetic and cultural traits—the affirmative-action regime lost moral authority in public opinion, even as it consolidated its power base.[63] As Jennifer Hochschild observes in chapter 9, even policies like affirmative action that build strong institutional structures and that diffuse costs among the public and concentrate benefits among the politically active may lose favor over time as economic conditions change and excluded constituencies grow resentful. The benchmarks of rising opposition to minority preference policies begin in 1989 when the accumulation since 1969 of more conservative presidential appointees on the federal bench produced a narrow but aggressive conservative majority on the Supreme Court. In decisions such as *Croson* (1989) and *Adarand v. Pena* (1995), which applied strict judicial scrutiny to minority preference programs in state and federal contracting, respectively, the federal courts sharply narrowed the reach of affirmative-action remedies. In 1994, Republicans won control of Congress in a conservative sweep, and the civil rights coalition was thrown on the defensive over minority preference policies for the first time since the "reverse discrimination" debates surrounding the *Bakke* case in the 1970s.

Yet the politics of the 1990s produced no decisive pendulum swing against civil rights regulation. The elections of 1996, affirming Republican control of Congress while returning Clinton to the White House, continued the tradition of the 1990s: divided government in Washington

---

63 Wilson, *The Truly Disadvantaged*, 109–18; Hugh Davis Graham, "Unintended Consequences: The Convergence of Affirmative Action and Immigration Policies," *The American Behavioral Scientist* 41 (April 1998): 898–912.

and ambiguous mandates from an electorate baffled by the complexities of the regulatory state.[64] For defenders of affirmative-action regulation, the continuity of American government and interest-group pluralism presents advantages useful in blunting threatening changes. With the exception of wartime and emergency control mechanisms, where interventionist bureaucracies and procedures were hastily constructed and rapidly dismantled, the American state has grown by administrative accretion. If American government organizations are not quite immortal, they are remarkably persistent and resilient.[65] The 185 member organizations in the Leadership Conference on Civil Rights are well-established players in the bargaining networks of interest-group politics. They mount a stout defense of affirmative action, bolstered by advantages that accrue to defenders of the status quo. Among these are the insider advantages of client politics, where the benefits of policy are concentrated on highly organized clientele groups and the costs of policy are widely distributed across a weakly organized mass of resentful taxpayers. Another advantage is the emotional power of the race issue, against a shameful history of slavery and segregation, and the related legal advantage of constitutionally protected classes.

Some of these advantages, however, cut both ways. The coalition-building that empowered the Leadership Conference also led to politically vulnerable practices: public policies determined by ancestry, beneficiary designations for some of America's most affluent groups, preferences for immigrants based on a history not experienced, racially based exclusions of individuals with strong claims to disadvantage. This trend in turn ultimately undermined the advantage of protected-class status because it highlighted a double standard in guaranteeing equal protection of the laws. Ironically, the tendency of affirmative-action programs to extend benefits to prosperous constituencies while excluding others on racial and gender grounds led the Supreme Court in 1989 to revive the standard of strict judicial scrutiny that Thurgood Marshall and the NAACP had won in the decade following *Brown* and that the Supreme Court had dropped in the 1970s in order to accommodate race-conscious school busing and affirmative-action remedies. Racial and ethnocultural classifications by

---

64 Marc K. Landy and Martin A. Levin, eds., *The New Politics of Public Policy* (Baltimore: Johns Hopkins, 1995).
65 Herbert Kaufman, *Are Government Organizations Immortal?* (Washington, D.C.: Brookings Institution, 1976); Paul C. Light, *Thickening Government* (Washington, D.C.: Brookings Institution, 1995).

government, whether devised by segregationist legislators or civil rights enforcement officials, were inherently suspect and merited the severe scrutiny of judges. This was the gravamen of Justice Sandra Day O'Connor's majority opinions in *Croson* and *Adarand*. These decisions, in some ways similar to the Supreme Court's abortion decisions since *Roe v. Wade*, narrowed the range of affirmative-action preferences while upholding their constitutionality.

This is the most likely scenario as American government enters the twenty-first century—a judicially mandated retrenchment but not a dismantlement. The Supreme Court will not return to a color-blind constitution because the court never proclaimed such a constitution. Congress, however, may reaffirm the classic language of nondiscrimination that anchors the Civil Rights Act of 1964, but in a gesture likely to be of greater symbolic than practical importance. Even under conservative Republican control Congress has shown little stomach for the legislative warfare required to dismantle affirmative-action preferences. The sharper contest will pit the compliance agencies and their protected-class clients against the judges, and there the U.S. Supreme Court will hold the trump cards. In this paradoxical scenario, the countermajoritarian Supreme Court would respond to majoritarian complaints of injustice in affirmative-action preferences while sparing minorities and elected officials the agony that a radical triage in civil rights protection would bring to centrist America.

9

You Win Some, You Lose Some: Explaining the Pattern of Success and Failure in the Second Reconstruction

JENNIFER L. HOCHSCHILD

White Americans believe on balance that the American racial structure has been successfully transformed since the 1950s and that, overall, African Americans have the same political, social, and economic opportunities as other Americans. For example, in a 1995 *Washington Post* survey, 55 percent of whites (compared with 29 percent of blacks) mistakenly agreed that "the average African American" is at least as well off as "the average white person" in terms of jobs and education. Over 40 percent of whites (and about 20 percent of blacks) held the same view with regard to housing and income.[1] Between one-tenth and one-third of whites believe that compared with whites, blacks have more opportunities, are less vulnerable to economic upheaval, receive better health care, are treated better in the courts and the media, and are more likely to obtain good jobs and be admitted to good colleges.[2]

Black Americans do not on balance share that belief. In some surveys, up to half claim that the situation of blacks has worsened since some reference point in the past. Although only a handful of whites think that more than half of whites share the attitudes of the Ku Klux Klan, a quarter of blacks see more than half of whites as Klan sympathizers. In that context it is not surprising that over half of blacks but only a quarter to a third of whites think our nation is still moving toward two separate and unequal societies.[3]

How can citizens of the same country, with the same national and shared local histories and with no apparent disparity in perceptual capacity, have such different—and *increasingly* different—views?[4] And how can our nation sustain any kind of shared culture, set of political

1 Washington Post et al. 1995. 2 Hochschild 1995: chap. 3.
3 Hochschild 1995: chap. 3. 4 Hochschild 1995: chap. 3.

practices, and social intercourse with a gap so wide, intense, bitter, and growing? I will not answer those questions in this chapter, but they provide the setting for the question that I do address. In particular, they suggest the urgency of understanding the historical trajectory of the movement for racial equality in the past few decades; if we can develop a clearer sense of what has and has not changed and why, perhaps we can work more effectively toward further reforms over the next few decades.

This chapter explores the recent history of struggles for African American civil rights, more schematically than most historians would but with the same focus on change over time as the central phenomenon to be understood. It thus uses the tools of social science in the service of both historical explanation and policy prescription. The chapter proceeds through several steps. I briefly provide evidence showing that white racial domination in the United States is declining in some ways but persisting or even growing in others. That pattern explains much of the disparity between white and black Americans' perceptions of movement toward racial equality. I then propose reasons for this pattern that center on governmental structures and policy processes.[5] Once the pattern is clear and its (proximate) explanations adduced, I conclude by suggesting what is needed for the pattern of racial policymaking to shift in the direction of more successes and fewer failures.

SUCCESS, PARTIAL SUCCESS, AND FAILURE

Recent policies to transform the American racial structure have had some indisputable and probably permanent successes.[6] These are manifesta-

---

5 A complete analysis would also consider the content and intensity of public opinion, the amount and kind of resources available to policy implementers, and the level and efficacy of social activism in shaping the array of policy possibilities and the effects of policy implementation. Given the theme of this volume, however, I focus in this chapter on institutional structures and policy processes as explanations for racial success and failure.

6 By "recent" I mean since roughly 1950. "Policies" range from overt decisions about race (such as civil rights laws, executive orders on affirmative action, and court decisions about school desegregation) to covert decisions such as choices about the tax structure, staffing and budgetary levels of regulatory agencies, or location of municipal boundaries that are not explicitly about race but have clearly predictable and important racial consequences. Arguably all policies, overt and covert, have racial implications, but I will focus here on those that a reasonable person would agree substantially affect the American racial structure (always recognizing the indeterminacy of those phrases).

By "the American racial structure" I mean all of the ways in which whites, institutionally as well as individually, dominate blacks. I will assume for the sake of simplicity that there is a meaningful social distinction between the white and black races, regardless of whether that distinction has any biological basis. I will also, for the sake of essential

tions of the abolition of state-endorsed racial segregation, discrimination, and domination. The political system no longer creates and supports overt racial hierarchies, and in principle it may no longer ignore or reinforce covert racial hierarchies. Included in this abolition are:

- Desegregation of public accommodations, such as public transportation, hotels and restaurants, gas stations, hospitals, recreational facilities, and other locations of transactions that are directly run by the state or serve public functions.
- Desegregation of housing choices, such that communities may no longer exclude residents of a disfavored race, public housing authorities may not discriminate by race, and private sellers or real estate agents may no longer discriminate against potential buyers who are members of a disfavored race.
- Illegality of employment discrimination, such that most employers may no longer refuse to hire or promote otherwise qualified workers because they are members of the disfavored race.
- Desegregation of the armed services, such that the acceptance of citizens into the armed services, living and occupational conditions of soldiers, and promotion may not be racially structured. Furthermore, some branches of the armed services, notably the army, have taken substantial steps to ensure the abolition of racially biased behaviors and to promote the success of black soldiers.[7]
- Ending of discrimination in political participation, such that citizens may no longer be excluded from voting or seeking office because of their race or justifications that are thinly veiled stand-ins for race. In addition, electoral systems may no longer be structured in order to dilute the effects of black electoral participation.
- Ending of discrimination among participants in professional sports and the entertainment industry, such that many of the nation's most successful, best paid, and highly adulated athletes, musicians, and actors are African American.

---

simplifying, ignore issues of ethnicity and races other than African Americans and white Americans.

"Success" is the hardest term in this sentence to define. In this chapter, a successful policy must have at least two characteristics: it has been enforced for several decades and shows no sign of being abolished or significantly watered down, and it has had a substantial positive impact on the quality of life, range of opportunities, or resources of many African Americans. A complete definition would have to give a precise meaning to "strongly," "substantial," and "many," but the main point here is to suggest a threshold that is high but not insuperable.

7 Binkin and Eitelberg 1982; Daula, Smith, and Nord 1990; Moore 1996; Moskos and Butler 1996. But see Smith (1996) for continued skepticism on this point.

None of these successes are complete; housing segregation, separate schooling, the absence of people of color in the management of sports and entertainment, and employment discrimination all persist. Nevertheless, the policy of racial equality is uncontroversially established in all of these arenas, and many African Americans have benefited from reductions in housing, school, and job discrimination since the 1960s. It is even arguable that recent policy initiatives, such as federal monitoring of discrimination in mortgage decisions, are accelerating the move from official policy to actual practice.

Partly as a consequence of these changes, the United States now enjoys a substantial and thriving black middle class.[8] In the 1960s, blacks enjoyed "a perverse sort of egalitarianism" of almost uniform poverty.[9] But by conventional measures of income, education, and occupation, about one-third of the African American population can now be called middle class (compared to about one-half of the white population). The best-off third of African Americans hold a larger share of their race's income than do the best-off third of white Americans, and the gaps between well-off and poor blacks are greater than the parallel gaps between well-off and badly off whites with regard to educational attainment, occupational status, likelihood of being a victim of a crime, and even mortality.[10] As far as I know, no other ethnic group in the history of the United States has achieved such a rapid and extensive growth of a middle class in one generation.

This is a long and impressive list of accomplishments. It would be misleading, however, without consideration of a comparable list of less complete successes and outright failures in the effort to end white racial domination. Partial successes include:

- School desegregation: Schools are no longer formally segregated, and overall the number of students attending school with students of another race has increased since the early 1960s. But racial separation in schools, with its attendant disparities in educational resources and social standing, was never eliminated and is now rising.[11] Since mandated school desegregation began, racial separation within each school, either through tracked classes

---

8 There are surprisingly few studies that directly link racial policy changes to outcomes for individuals. Among the best are studies by Heckman and Wolpin (1989), Leonard (1990), Card and Krueger (1992), and Massey and Denton (1993); they all show that appropriate policies are effective in narrowing racial gaps.
9 The phrase, and evidence, come from Hogan and Featherman 1978.
10 Hochschild 1995: chap. 2
11 Orfield et al. 1997; Boozer, Krueger, and Wolkon 1992.

or within classrooms, has always remained higher than racial separation across schools.[12] Few members of either the black or white communities now insist on desegregated schools. Conversely, there is considerable and increasing sentiment—sometimes backed by court orders—to eliminate extant school desegregation plans that rely on mechanisms other than voluntary student transfers or that use tax resources to increase the likelihood of voluntary student transfers.[13]

- Residential desegregation: Housing is no longer formally segregated, federal loan policies no longer encourage racial homogeneity in neighborhoods, and banks may not legally discriminate in lending for mortgages. But residential segregation is declining in most metropolitan areas at an extremely slow rate, and banking practices are changing slowly and reluctantly at best.[14] African Americans of all classes find it very difficult to move into white communities, and African Americans find it more difficult to do so than do members of any other racial or ethnic group.[15]

- Political empowerment: The proportion of blacks who voted rose dramatically in the 1950s and 1960s, stayed roughly even during the 1970s and 1980s, and has declined since then. The proportion of the voting population that is black has similarly risen, then fallen. Again, the proportion of elected offices held by African Americans rose dramatically and has recently leveled off.[16] Recent Supreme Court decisions make it unlikely or even impossible for voting districts to be newly designed in order to increase the number of black elected officials; redistricting in the foreseeable future may in fact reduce that number.[17]

- Affirmative action: The federal government committed itself and its contractors and grant recipients to a fairly robust program of affirmative action during the 1970s. The rules remained in place during the 1980s, but enforcement was lax or nonexistent. In the 1990s, many elected officials and some federal courts have backed off from even that low level of commitment. Voters in California and Washington State approved referenda to abolish affirmative action, although Houston's voters did not. The future of affirmative action policies and practices is uncertain.[18]

- The criminal justice system: Before the 1960s, African Americans in the South (the vast majority) could almost never serve on juries or appear in

---

12 Oakes 1985; Meier, Stewart, and England 1989.
13 *Freeman v. Pitts* 1992; *Missouri v. Jenkins* 1995.
14 Bradbury, Case, and Dunham 1989; Canner 1991; Massey and Denton 1993; Farley and Frey 1994; Goering and Wienk 1996.
15 Massey and Denton 1987; Frey and Farley 1996.
16 Farley 1992: chap. 7; Rosenstone and Hanson 1993: 219–24; Joint Center for Political and Economic Studies 1994; Thernstrom and Thernstrom 1997: 288–294.
17 *Shaw v. Reno* 1993; *Miller v. Johnson* 1995; *Bush v. Vera* 1996.
18 *Richmond v. Croson* 1989; *Adarand v. Pena* 1995; Clinton 1995; *Hopwood v. Texas* 1996; Hochschild 1999.

courtrooms as attorneys. They could be sure, whether as plaintiffs or defendants, to receive worse treatment than whites. That radical disparity has mostly been eliminated. In addition, legal reforms of the 1960s, including the provision of attorneys to the indigent and the implementation of the *Miranda* rule, have materially improved the chances in court of the poor, who are disproportionately people of color. Since the 1960s, affirmative action and antidiscrimination policies have made police departments and juries demographically more similar to residents of cities than at any time since the Irish dominated both the immigrant rolls and urban public offices. Nevertheless, African Americans still complain vigorously and often correctly of police brutality in the streets, malfeasance in the courtroom, and racial discrimination at all stages of the criminal justice process from writing laws to executing murderers to supervision of parolees.[19]

Among public policies intended to eliminate black subordination, the set of failures is most easily summarized by the phrase "inner cities." Components of that failure include:

- An atrocious school system: Although the overall dropout rate for African Americans has declined dramatically over the past few decades, in some large-city school systems more than half of black teens leave school before graduation. Fully half of black adults living in extreme poverty areas of large cities have not completed high school.[20] In fourteen schools in Hartford, Connecticut, fewer than 5 percent of fourth-graders have achieved grade-level mastery of reading, and "in 14 of the District [of Columbia]'s 18 high schools, more than 94 percent of the students tested were functioning below grade level in math."[21] School boards are sometimes corrupt, often motivated more by political ambition than by educational vision, and not infrequently ignorant about their charges.[22] Inner-city schools lack windows and basic plumbing; students and teachers must dodge falling plaster and puddles; coal-fired furnaces labor to provide enough heat to cope with New York winters.[23]

19 Jaynes and Williams 1989: chap. 9; Bell 1992: chap. 5; Dembo 1988; Greenwood 1992; Petersilia 1992.
20 Kasarda 1993: 172–73; Burbridge 1991: 7, 9.
21 Abernathy 1996; quotation from Milloy 1998.
22 In Boston, the School Committee was for decades a jumping-off point for a mayoral campaign. In New York City, a recent survey showed that over half of the district school board members did not know how many students were in their district, and over three-fourths could not tell the amount of their district budget, even though they had voted on it a few weeks before the survey (Sugarman 1996; see also Purdy 1996; Purdy and Newman 1996; Hendrie 1997).
23 Kozol 1991; Tomasky 1996.

- An overwhelmed social service system: Hospitals in New York City took care of almost thirteen thousand "boarder babies" during a thirty-one-month period in the late 1980s. Substantiated reports of child abuse rose from 500,000 in 1980 to more than 1 million in the early 1990s, and rates of child abuse are higher among the poor and African Americans than the rest of the population (although they are not higher among African Americans once social class is controlled for).[24] The foster care caseload in New York State doubled in the two years after 1987 and grew by 44 percent in California from 1985 to 1988. Foster children also are disproportionately poor, urban, and black.[25] Some of these problems eased in the more prosperous 1990s; nevertheless social service systems in many big cities confront horror stories of children who are murdered by their parents partly because case workers have no time for proper investigations and record-keeping systems are hopelessly outdated and inadequate.

- An inadequate or possibly counterproductive income support system: More than one-quarter of black children, compared with 6 percent of white children, lived below *half* of the poverty line in the late 1980s. During the past twenty years, about one-third of black children remained poor for six or more years, and until recently the number was rising. In the hundred largest central cities, the proportion of poor blacks living in neighborhoods where more than 40 percent of their neighbors were also poor rose from 28 percent in 1970 to 42 percent in 1990.[26] Between 1983 and 1992, the poorest fifth of whites gained only 5 percent ($570) over their previous income, but the poorest fifth of African Americans *lost* 12 percent ($558) of their meager income.[27] Many Americans believe (although the research evidence does not clearly substantiate the view) that dependence on Aid to Families with Dependent Children (AFDC) encouraged teens to bear children with no intention to marry and no capacity to support their children. Many also argue that "the welfare system" provided enough of a financial cushion to

24 On boarder babies (babies who remain in the hospital a long time after birth because they have no home to go to), see U.S. Dept. of Health and Human Services 1990: 2; U.S. Congress 1989: 120–31; Child Welfare League of America 1992. On child abuse, see Besharov 1996; National Center on Child Abuse Prevention Research 1994: 5; Ards 1989. Besharov, like virtually all analysts of child abuse and neglect, cautions about the unreliability of these figures either across race and class or over time.

25 Besharov 1996; National Center for Children in Poverty 1990: 60; National Black Child Development Institute 1989: 23–51; U.S. Congress 1989: 46–88; Wulczyn and Goerge 1992: 279–80;

26 Duncan and Rodgers 1991: 543; Eggebeen and Lichter 1991: 809; Kasarda 1993: 266–68.

27 During this period, the wealthiest fifth of both whites and blacks gained 15 percent over their previous income (Hochschild 1995: 49). Considerable evidence suggests that at least during the 1980s, governmental policies deliberately redistributed income upward, so it is perhaps an ironic misnomer to call persistent poverty a failure of governmental policy (see Gramlich, Kasten, and Sammartino 1993: 234–39).

inhibit adult parents from seeking or maintaining jobs.[28] Since the implementation of welfare reform under the program of Temporary Assistance to Needy Families (TANF), welfare caseloads have declined dramatically. However, "blacks now outnumber whites [on welfare]. . . . In addition, the remaining caseload is increasingly concentrated in large cities."[29]

- A deteriorating public infrastructure: Disparities in wealth and amenities between central cities and their suburbs have grown steadily since 1970.[30] Cities struggling to balance their budgets in the face of declining federal aid and growing proportions of poor residents frequently close branch libraries, hospitals, and fire stations, and defer maintenance on bridges and sewer systems. Some cities have "solved" the problems of high-rise public housing projects by dynamiting them into rubble; the waiting list for the relatively adequate public housing system in New York City has a backlog of almost a decade.

- An unevenly distributed criminal justice system: Although victimization from violence, theft, and household crimes steadily declined in the United States over the past few decades, victimization in cities rose as a proportion of all victimization.[31] More precisely, in 1976, 5 percent of poor blacks suffered from violence, compared with 4 percent of well-off blacks, 4 percent of poor whites, and almost 3 percent of well-off whites. By 1992, the affluent of both races were less likely to be victimized—violence rates had fallen to 3.5 percent among well-off blacks and 2 percent for well-off whites. However, the poor, and especially the black poor, had become *more* likely targets—victimization rates from violence had risen to 4.5 percent for poor whites and to fully 6 percent for poor blacks.[32] During the 1980s and early 1990s, violent and often fatal attacks by young black men on each other skyrocketed, primarily in large cities.[33] Crime rates have fallen since then, but homicide remains a chief cause of death among young black men. In some cities, young black men now fear violence from the police as much as from recognized "criminals."

And so on—the list could continue. The very cumulation of ills produces a dynamic of its own; each policy failure makes the others more harmful to citizens and harder for public officials to deal with, and the overall effect is "a process of social contagion that generates epidemics of social problems . . . [in] America's inner cities."[34]

28 Mead 1992.
29 De Parle 1998.
30 Nathan and Adams 1989; Ledebur and Barnes 1992.
31 U.S. Department of Justice 1994: 247, 248, 285, 288, 353, 363–64.
32 Hochschild 1995: 50.
33 Hochschild 1995: 47, 202.
34 Case and Katz 1991; Crane 1991: 319; DiIulio 1989.

Can these policy failures be legitimately considered a part of American racial policy? Not as obviously as school or housing desegregation, but I would nevertheless argue that they are intrinsic to it. This point is worth dwelling on for a moment, because how one answers that question reveals a lot about how one connects race and class, public and private, and overt and covert policymaking. The cumulative failure of public services in cities is not explicitly a matter of racial policy. After all, some poor European Americans, Latinos, and Asian Americans live in central cities, and almost half of African Americans do not.[35] In addition, one can explain the problems of inner cities in terms of poverty, mismanagement, inadvertence, culture, or the inexorable workings of advanced capitalism rather than in terms of racial domination. Finally, in this view the civil rights movement was aimed at ending official structures of racial domination, not at economic equality or the control of market forces.[36]

That view, however, seems too narrow and excessively formalistic. For one thing, residents of the most severely dysfunctional urban neighborhoods are disproportionately black, and African Americans are disproportionately harmed by the failures of cities to provide decent living conditions. In addition, the very boundaries between city and suburb that help to concentrate poverty, unemployment, and mismanagement as well as people of color within the city are themselves the result of deliberate policy choices that were made partly on racial grounds. Finally, African Americans involved in the drive for racial equality throughout the twentieth century never sharply separated civil and legal rights from political empowerment and social and economic betterment. On the contrary, black leaders have always firmly linked civil rights with social welfare and fought for both simultaneously.[37] Thus it seems appropriate to include

35 Just over 54 percent of African Americans and 22 percent of whites live in central cities; 23 percent of residents of central cities are African American and 54 percent are white. Roughly speaking, the larger the city, the higher the proportion of people of color among its residents.

36 John Goering of the U.S. Department of Housing and Urban Development argues, in response to an earlier draft of this chapter, that "by linking traditional civil rights program outcomes with 'inner city' social and policy dynamics you have set up a strawperson. . . . The broader American policy failure in addressing systematic, place-based inequalities gets unfairly placed at the door of the civil rights movement." I do not wish to blame the civil rights movement for failing to solve a problem that it did not set out to solve. But as I read the history of the movement, social and economic inequality, especially when disproportionately endured by black Americans, was one of the problems that many civil rights activists sought to solve—unsuccessfully. (Quotation from private communication, October 23, 1996.)

37 Hamilton and Hamilton 1997.

policy failures in large cities in the same domain as policy successes in the courts and military services.

Readers probably know, at least in general outline, all of what I have just rehearsed; I do not, in any case, see much that is controversial up to this point.[38] My reason for this rehearsal is to emphasize the wide range of outcomes in recent efforts to transform the American racial structure. Focusing on that range allows us to do several things. First, it helps us to understand the disparity in trajectories of white and black racial views described in my introduction.[39] Whites legitimately point to the impressive list of transformations, which after all have come at some cost to members of their race. Blacks equally legitimately point to the no less impressive list of partial transformations and failures, which persist at great cost to members of *their* race.[40]

Second, emphasizing the range of outcomes of efforts over the past four decades to transform the American racial structure leads us to ask why. Why have efforts in some policy arenas produced substantial and presumably permanent change for the better, whereas other efforts have produced transitory improvements and still others none at all (for the better, at least)? That is the question to which the remainder of this chapter is devoted.

"POWER TO . . .": EXPLANATIONS THAT INHERE IN THE POLICY

Some policies are easier to design, promulgate, implement, maintain, and measure than others.[41] As soon as one says that, caveats rush in: policy makers (and citizens) are poor judges of what will be easy to do; policies that seem easy to implement turn out to be, or are made to be, complicated; unanticipated consequences always abound and sometimes rule the

38 Except possibly for the inclusion of "inner cities" in the list of racial failures.
39 I say "*helps* us to understand" in response to an argument by John Goering that "many of the deeply held, patterned inconsistencies between black and white views of race relations precede the civil rights era and . . . [are more] determined by . . . a broader set of pressures" stemming from centuries of control and subordination. I agree, with two caveats. First, these views are not fixed on either side; in the 1960s, blacks were more optimistic than whites about the current state and future trajectory of American race relations. Second, members of both races point to particular policy successes and failures when expounding and explaining their racial views.
40 For a more formal and extensive analysis of why white and black Americans hold such disparate views of black racial progress, see Hochschild 1995: chaps. 3, 7.
41 Stone (1989, chap. 11) provides the best analysis of the distinction between "power over" and "power to." See also Hartsock 1983, esp. chapter 9.

day.[42] "Easy" policies to enable African Americans to become first-class citizens took more than a century to promulgate after slavery was abolished and required violence and death to move from promulgation to implementation. Nevertheless, if nothing is easy, some things are easier than others.

What kind of policy initiatives might be easier to promulgate and sustain than others? Put otherwise, what kind of policy initiatives contain within themselves the power to accomplish their end? One promising kind are policies that offset market distortions created by "inefficient" tastes, such that a market freed by government mandate from such artificial distortions will then automatically and successfully take over the enforcement effort. One inefficient taste is that for racial discrimination.[43] This explanation helps to explain the success of desegregation of public accommodations: once restaurant owners and bus companies were forced to be free of their own and their current customers' discriminatory preferences, they found it easy and profitable to accept the dollar bills of anyone who cared to proffer them. The same principle partly accounts for the partial success of affirmative action. Once corporate managers and foremen were forced to look beyond their assumptions about who makes a good worker, they found that African American employees could at least enhance their relations with surrounding communities and draw in new customers, and at most provide an almost untapped pool of talent and new perspectives.[44] The same principle accounts for the success of black athletes and singers; many are simply more talented than their white counterparts, and once the market was forced to operate according to criteria of merit and consumer preference for talent, the racial composition of stadiums and concert stages changed dramatically.

But the fact that a policy initiative corrects a market distortion is neither a necessary nor a sufficient condition for that policy to succeed.[45] Market corrections do not help to explain some successes in racial policy

---

42 Pressman and Wildavsky 1973; Bardach 1977; Mazmanian and Sabatier 1983; Hirschman 1991; Merton 1996 (1936); Tenner 1996.
43 Becker 1957.
44 Thus railroad owners were not enthusiastic about implementing the principle of "separate but equal" at the turn of the century—it was expensive, complicated, and reduced ridership and profits—and officials of large corporations are not enthusiastic about ending federal affirmative action policies. Among firms "with high levels of product market power, those that employ relatively more women are more profitable" (Hellerstein et al. 1997). For corporate enthusiasm on "diversity," see Conference Board 1997.
45 My logic of considering whether each policy's or policymaker's characteristic is either necessary or sufficient for policy success resembles, though it was not derived from, that of Rosenberg (1991).

such as voting rights, desegregation of the armed forces, and changes in the criminal justice system. And the claim that market corrections are always effective is contradicted by the fact that residential segregation persists even in affluent communities. One would expect a priori that once the government required a free market in home sales and rentals, the incentives for the real estate industry would be to seek out as many clients as possible and to encourage as many buyer-seller matches as possible. But that has not been the case.[46]

A second kind of policy that should be relatively easy to promulgate and sustain is one that is a "single-stage policy"—colloquially, one that can be created by a single stroke of the pen.[47] A single-stage policy has "no intermediate steps between adoption of the policy and production of the effects;" a classic example is a legislative change in the tax code. A single-stage policy can be distinguished from a multiple-stage policy, which implies a long causal chain from, say, prenatal health care through Head Start through raising teachers' salaries in order eventually to improve high school graduation rates.

Here is the most straightforward meaning of "power to": although no policy worth its salt is *very* easily implemented (think of the number of tax accountants and H. & R. Block employees needed to implement a change in the tax code), the fewer the stages that a new policy must go through the more likely it is to succeed.[48] Most of the clear successes in American racial policy are closer to single- than to multiple-stage policies. Once an end to discrimination against black would-be voters is required, it is fairly easy to figure out how to stop discrimination in registration and polling places. Once the owner of a baseball team decides to try a "racial experiment," he needs only to find a Jackie Robinson waiting in the wings.[49]

But many imaginable single-stage policies that would affect the racial structure in the United States have not been implemented, so this explanation too is insufficient to explain the full pattern of racial policy success

---

46 The failure of supposedly free markets to increase the pace of housing desegregation may be explained by the fact that when one buys a home one is buying so much else—a level and kind of status, self-image, schooling, social life, security, and convenience—that housing markets are exceptionally "sticky."

47 The quotation and explanation of the concept come from Arnold (1990: 19–20); the colloquial phrase was the language of President Kennedy's promise to end discrimination in public housing. For a similar idea, see Mazmanian and Sabatier 1983.

48 The classic demonstration of the problems of multiple-stage policies is Pressman and Wildavsky 1973.

49 Frommer 1982; Tygiel 1983; Rampersad 1997.

and failure. Examples range from reparations to African Americans whose ancestors lived in the United States before 1865, to redrawing school district or municipal boundary lines, to promulgating electoral mechanisms such as proportional representation or cumulative voting. Conversely, some multiple-stage policies have been successfully implemented, so having only one step in the policy process is also not necessary for success. After all, the armed services' efforts to move beyond abolishing discrimination to recruiting, training, and promoting black officers have required many steps and much reworking of old policy. They still have not succeeded completely. But they have not been abandoned, as have other complicated efforts such as mandatory school desegregation, and on balance they are effective enough to provide a model for the rest of the nation.

So far I have described policies in terms of their internal characteristics. One can also characterize policies with "power to" (be relatively easily implemented) in terms of the distribution of their intended effects. For example, a policy that diffuses costs among the public and concentrates benefits among the politically active is usually thought to be relatively easy to promulgate and sustain.[50] At first glance, this rule of thumb does little to explain the pattern of successes and failures in American racial policy. On the one hand, many successful transformations imposed clear costs on some citizens who were symbolically or substantively important to the electoral system; examples include desegregation of the armed forces and the abolition of discriminatory structures for voting and office holding. On the other hand, a few successful transformations provided benefits to citizens who were symbolically or substantively unimportant to the electoral system; one example is the provision of attorneys to indigent defendants. More importantly, the failure of policy structures in inner cities is a case of concentrated and highly visible costs to some voters (inner-city residents and people who live in suburbs but would prefer to live in the city), and no publicly legitimate benefits to any.

The converse of this principle, however, does help to explain why some apparent successes were only transitory. That is, a policy that imposes high costs on many people, with unclear or concentrated benefits for a few, will be very hard to sustain absent some form of powerful support. School desegregation was very costly to white citizens in their view, and

50 Wilson 1973: 330–37; Arnold 1990: 25–28.

seems increasingly costly to black citizens. Few whites and not many more blacks see clear benefits from it. It has thus lost most of what political constituency it had.[51] Affirmative action similarly seems to impose high costs on many white employees, with few beneficiaries except for "undeserving" blacks (and perhaps corporate managers and stockholders). As the economy appeared to worsen and white workers became more insecure in the early 1990s, the costs of affirmative action rose in their view, and their general dissatisfaction with the policy hardened in some cases to vehement opposition.[52]

A similar rule of thumb is that the most sustainable policies are those that allow citizens to engage in positive-sum, rather than zero-sum or negative-sum, games. That is, if most people can gain from the promulgation of a new policy, it is good politics as well as good policy. That is the theory behind the Laffer curve: lowering the rate of taxation on the wealthy will directly benefit them; they will invest more and more productively in the economy, which will produce more jobs and higher tax revenues, thus indirectly benefiting all citizens. High rates of taxation, conversely, illustrate a negative-sum game; they harm the wealthy who withdraw from the economy, thereby harming everyone else.

Racial policies that come to be understood as positive sum are among those on the list of successes. The best examples are the abolition of discrimination in public accommodations and in sports and entertainment. In parallel fashion, racial policies that come to be understood as zero sum or even negative sum are among those on the list of transitory successes or failures. For example, many whites fear that if their neighbors sell or rent their houses to African Americans, the value of their own property will decline or the quality of life in their community will deteriorate. They thus see residential desegregation as a gain to the seller but a loss to the rest of the neighborhood. Their pressure, either directly on their old white friends and new black neighbors, or indirectly through social networks and ties to real estate agencies, is enough to keep the 1968 Housing Act the least well implemented of the three big civil rights acts of the 1960s.

51 See Armor (1995) on "the harm and benefit thesis" in the context of school desegregation.

52 Although fewer than 10 percent of whites claim that they or a close connection have lost a job due to affirmative action, up to two-thirds believe it likely that a white will suffer such a loss (Hochschild 1995: 144; see, more generally, chap. 7 for a discussion of blacks' and whites' perceptions of the costs of racial change).

But once again, creating a positive-sum game is neither necessary nor sufficient to explain the pattern of success and failure in American racial policy. On the one hand, some zero-sum games have been sustained: the best examples are assertive policies of promotion of African Americans in the armed services and changes in local voting structures from at-large to single-member districts. White would-be military officers and political officeholders lost in both cases, and one would not have expected them to be without political influence. On the other hand, some positive-sum games have not been sustained or even begun: it would presumably be in everyone's interest for children in inner-city schools to be able to read and calculate, and yet the policies and practices of inner-city schools and the institutions of governance within which they are embedded contribute to the academic failure of many children.[53] So this policy characteristic, too, does not suffice to answer the puzzle posed at the beginning of the chapter.

So far I have described four characteristics of policies themselves that presumably explain why those policies were more likely to be promulgated and sustained than policies with the opposite characteristics.[54] All of these characteristics have to do with the "power to"—the ability to accomplish what one sets out to do because the policy is straightforward, accords with powerful market mechanisms, is politically attractive, or substantively benefits most citizens. Some evidence suggests the validity of each claim of "power to" but other evidence either contradicts each claim or suggests that that claim is irrelevant. So I have only part of the key to the puzzle of why some racial policies have mostly succeeded, others partly or temporarily succeeded, and others failed over the past four decades.

53 The claim that positive-sum games are more easily sustained than negative-sum ones does not even explain white hostility to school desegregation very well, since opposition to "forced busing" was not closely related to whether one's own child was involved in the desegregation program (Giles, Gatlin, and Cataldo 1974; McConahay 1982, n.d.). On current school practices that inhibit the success of inner city children, see Rich 1996; Stone 1998; Henig et al. 1999.

54 As I have noted already, Mazmanian and Sabatier (1983) structure their argument along somewhat similar lines; their category that comes closest to my "power to" formulation focuses on the "tractability of the problem." Their lists do not, however, fully address my puzzle in this chapter. For example, one of their four items in the "tractability" category, "target group as a percentage of the population," has no variance in the arena of racial policy, so it does not help to explain different rates of success and failure. In addition, Mazmanian and Sabatier do not take advantage of the analytic power of the power to/ power over distinction and they do not address the issue of necessity and sufficiency, which is central to the logic of my analysis. Thus our analyses overlap, but do not duplicate each other.

"POWER OVER . . .": EXPLANATIONS THAT ADHERE IN POLICYMAKERS

I turn now to potential explanations for the pattern of success and failure that focus on who is making the policy rather than on what the policy consists of. These explanations revolve around the question of "power over"—who has the capability and incentive to make and enforce new policy. Here too we have several plausible candidates.

First, policymakers who can create or build on strong institutional structures are more likely to be able to impose their preferences than policymakers who are flying without much of a net. Even if the origins of a robust institution are controversial, it is strengthened by virtue of the citizenry's eventual acceptance of its mission and activity. Officials located within such a robust institution typically are committed to the success of a policy initiative, understand that their salaries and professional prestige depend on the policy's success, and know how to attain the resources and shape the tools needed to implement, enforce, evaluate, and modify a new policy. Once a policy is firmly lodged within a robust institution, it is relatively easy to keep it going and to ensure that modifications are constructive rather than threatening. Thus, at any rate, goes the basic theory of institutional capacity and path dependency.[55]

The creation of strong institutions designed to change racial policy and to ensure the continuation of those changes does help to explain some racial successes. New laws and new agents of the Justice Department were needed to police voting regulations and practices and to create new boundaries for voting districts. Once those changes were in place, path dependency came into play: African Americans were increasingly elected to office and they attained the status, finances, and opportunities of incumbent in the (usually Democratic) party organization. From that point on, they had many resources besides their race to help them attain reelection, move to a higher office, and promote the prospects of more junior black candidates.[56] Similarly, once the Army reconfigured its barracks and other facilities to accommodate desegregation, created and staffed race relations training programs, and promoted many black officers, this

55 Nordlinger 1981; Skocpol 1992.
56 This point is stated historically, since the clearest case is the increase in black mayors and council members of cities since the 1960s. It also, however, fits the case of the five black members of Congress who gained office in newly drawn majority black districts in 1994, and were able to retain their seats in even-more-newly drawn majority white districts in 1996, largely due to the powerful effect of well-managed incumbency.

new set of structures, processes, and actors made it more likely that efforts toward racial equalization would persist and grow.

However, creation of an apparently strong institution is not sufficient to sustain a racial policy. After all, mandates to desegregate schools and engage in affirmative hiring generated complex and elaborated bureaucracies, with the committed personnel, budgets, and new procedures attendant on a robust institution. But school desegregation offices are being dismantled, and affirmative action offices are under attack. There is no institution stronger than the Federal Reserve Board, yet its repeated statements of commitment to the implementation of the Equal Credit Opportunity Act of 1974 had until recently very little impact on the practices of mortgage-granting bankers.[57]

Nor is the creation of a powerful institution necessary for success. Again, public accommodations provide the best example, in this case of a major change in one aspect of racial domination with essentially no institutional penumbra.

Consider next a more direct manifestation of "power over"—the ability of one political actor to require another to change its behavior, and to impose the costs of change on the one doing the changing. President Truman in Executive Order 9981 told the armed forces to desegregate; the Supreme Court in *Brown v. Board of Education* told southern educators and judges to desegregate schools; Northern members of Congress told southern election officials to desegregate voting booths; Judge Garrity remained in Wellesley while he told residents of Boston to desegregate their schools; Branch Rickey told the Brooklyn Dodgers to play ball with their new teammate. Each of these examples manifests "A getting B to do something that B would not otherwise do" without A having to do the same thing.[58] One branch of government gives an order to another, one region of the country imposes a change on another, one policy actor gives a command that he or she need not live under, an owner of a business imposes a new work rule on his employees.

But like the others I have discussed, this characteristic of policymakers does not by itself fully explain the pattern of the United States' racial successes and failures. Some policies imposed on reluctant recipients have stuck, whereas others have not; again contrast desegregation of the armed

---

57 Hochschild and Danielson (1998) analyze why an apparently very powerful agency—New York's Urban Development Corporation—could not attain its mission of desegregating public housing.
58 Robert Dahl's (1963, p. 40) classic formulation of influence.

forces and sports teams with desegregation of schools, or the persistent, if bumpy, reduction of employment discrimination with the faltering path of affirmative action. Why is that the case? Partly because some policies are easier to impose and implement than others, which takes us back to the "power to" characteristics already discussed. Partly because some policies cost a lot more than others (costs can be financial, organizational, or political), and even powerful policy actors face limits to the costs they can impose on others. And partly because powerful actors only sometimes persist in their decision to make other less powerful actors carry out and live under a new and unpopular policy. After all, many of the policies that have failed most severely in inner cities could succeed if an external authority imposed reform, provided some resources, and mandated that city officials pay the remaining costs. Consider social services for children: case workers are paid very poorly, they are drastically overworked, their offices are just edging into the computer age, and they are frequently overseen by political appointees with an eye for the next job. It is entirely predictable that under these circumstances some children who could have been helped will instead be injured or killed. Mayors or state legislatures could choose to reallocate funds, effective managers, and equipment into social service agencies, but they seldom do.

One could adduce a further array of explanations for why no one imposes improvement on social service agencies, starting with the fact that poor black children and their parents do not vote. But my point here is that we need that further array to understand fully why powerful actors do or do not impose changes. The claim that policies are likely to succeed when some policy actors have power to make others change their behavior is, in short, only partly true and only true for some policies.

A third form of "power over" focuses on characteristics of the policy's recipient rather than the promulgator. That is, policy mandates issued to organizations that are tightly hierarchical rather than loosely coupled are more likely to succeed.[59] Some recipients such as school teachers, homeowners, and criminals operate in an environment where their actions cannot or may not easily be controlled by external authorities. They can thus ignore a directive with relative impunity. Other policy recipients such as enlisted soldiers, baseball players, or government contractors operate in an environment where their actions are readily known to, and are easily

59 Weick 1970.

and legitimately controlled by, external authorities. They ignore directives only at their peril.

This characteristic of recipients helps to explain the relative success, on the one hand, of desegregation of the armed forces and affirmative-action hiring among government contractors during the 1970s, and the relative failure, on the other hand, of open housing policies, policies against second-generation discrimination in schools, efforts to control police brutality in violent encounters, and affirmative action among noncontractors. It does not explain the success of desegregating public accommodations (gas stations and restaurants are loosely coupled) or the failure to maintain the public infrastructure of cities (oversight agencies could have direct control over public hospitals, branch libraries, roads and bridges, and apartment buildings).

A final form of "power over" addresses the incentives of the actors, both policy makers and policy recipients. Policies are most likely to succeed if policy makers have strong enough incentives for success that they figure out how to overcome the inevitable obstacles to it.[60] In one sense, that observation is circular—policies succeed when policymakers work hard enough to make them succeed. Nevertheless, the observation offers an entry point into the vexed question of when policymakers are prepared to exercise their "power over" and when they are able effectively to do so. The military has worked so hard to desegregate the activities of the soldiers and the composition of the officer corps because it had to. The army needed black recruits in order to fill out the ranks, and once it had them it needed to ensure that they could fight and win battles. That was possible only if black soldiers were as well trained as white ones, and if members of both races were used to taking orders from members of both races—hence recruitment, education, aggressive promotions, and training in race relations. Similarly, the 1965 Voting Rights Act was promulgated and aggressively enforced partly because of the Democratic Party's need for new voters to replace the whites defecting to the Republican party as a consequence of the 1964 Civil Rights Act. Once a few African Americans were elected to office, the electoral imperative was strong enough to impel them to devote considerable resources to ensuring that there would continue to be black voters and black-majority districts.

Conversely, school administrators seldom see school desegregation as essential to their core mission, and real estate agents seldom see housing

---

60 Doig and Hargrove 1990.

desegregation as contributing to the attainment of what they most desire. Thus, even if administrators and agents desire racial equality, they lack a sufficiently strong incentive to pursue it through seemingly unending difficulties. That logic partly explains the failure of so many policies in inner cities; mayors are usually most responsive to constituencies for whom racial equality is not the first priority, whether they be downtown developers, taxpayers' organizations, municipal unions, or bondholders. The countervailing forces of social activists and poor African American voters are simply not strong enough to keep even well-intentioned mayors from placing other priorities ahead of racial and class equalization.[61]

CONCLUSION: THE ROLE OF POWER IN EXPLAINING RACIAL POLICY SUCCESS AND FAILURE

We have at this point eight potential explanations, in two clusters, for why some race policies have mostly succeeded over the past thirty years, some began to succeed but are now faltering, and some have failed or were never seriously attempted. Each explanation provides some leverage, but none is either necessary or sufficient to explain the pattern. That may be too stringent a criterion to apply to any social science explanation, but it seems equally true that no single combination of the potential explanations is either necessary or sufficient to explain the pattern of racial success and failure.

Instead I propose an alternative, looser, formulation. For a racial policy to succeed, it requires at least one "power to" characteristic to be combined with at least one "power over" characteristic across a period of time long enough to enable the policy to take deep root. This prix fixe menu formulation—choose two from column A and one from column B—lacks analytic elegance. Its only justification is that it works better than any alternative.

In short, among the many efforts over the past forty years to overcome the American racial hierarchy, policies thrived only if they were both amenable to implementation in one of the four ways specified and able to invoke strong and persistent backing from powerful policy actors. The first list, of successes, were all created by strong actors—the Supreme Court, the military brass, the Justice Department, the owner of a baseball team—and they all possessed some feature that allowed them to beat out their competitors in the polity or economy. Policies in the second list, of

---

61 Stone (1989) provides one of the best demonstrations of this dynamic.

partial or faltering successes, were promulgated by actors with just as much power over others as had the proponents of the first list—courts, the Justice Department, the Federal Reserve Board. But they did not enjoy the crucial features that generate success in the polity or economy, so they have not been able to sustain their initial gains.

The third list, of failures, lacks both "power to" and "power over" characteristics. Most of these policies are the responsibility of local or state actors, who are too politically dependent on their predominantly wealthy or white constituents to have the freedom of action sometimes enjoyed by the president, administrative agencies, or the Supreme Court. Most of these policies are also messy. They are complicated, they often seek to offset rather than to reinforce market forces, and—given the nature of city-suburban boundaries—they appear to benefit the few (poor urban blacks) at the expense of the many (the rest of the population). No wonder they fail. If this set of explanations for the pattern of success and failure in American racial policy is persuasive, three sets of questions remain. The historical questions are: what institutional and political configuration made it possible during a given period for powerful actors to promulgate policies that proved to be implementable? Conversely, why were other choices not made, other actors not so committed, and other conjunctions of institutions and politics less amenable to reform? The predictive questions are: will the supposedly firm successes remain so? Can the faltering successes be bolstered? Can the dismal failures be alleviated? That is, what should we make of the implication contained within the phrase "the second Reconstruction"—that most, if not all, of the changes in the American racial structure achieved since the 1950s will be reversed by policies designed to reestablish white domination? The prescriptive questions are: what must we do to create institutions and political contexts that will allow new policies to come to the fore? What new policies are available that combine enough features of "power over" and "power to" to give them a good chance of succeeding in reducing white racial domination? What can be done to create the essential mix of public opinion, social pressure, and political dynamic that will encourage potentially powerful actors to exercise their power in this arena?

Hugh Davis Graham's chapter in this volume contributes to answering the historical question, and I will not consider it further here. I will instead conclude, more like a social scientist than like a historian, with two observations on whether the United States is facing the end of the second

Reconstruction or whether, in contrast, we can design newly successful racial policies.

If my analysis is correct, there is little reason to expect new racial successes similar to those on my first list, or movement out of the second and third lists into the first. The relatively easy policies—policies that both contain within themselves the power to accomplish their goals and that enjoyed powerful and committed sponsors—have mostly been done. (Let me clarify a final time: they were not easy to accomplish—their ease is relative only to that of other racial policies.) The powerful and committed sponsors have, so far as I can predict the foreseeable future, mostly lost their will or are embedded in a political context that is too complicated to allow them to exert control. The few remaining policies that seem relatively easy by my substantive criteria—reparations, changing municipal boundaries, proportional representation, stringent forms of affirmative action—are political nonstarters. Thus the contours of public opinion interact with the nature of the remaining policy problems and the complexities of the American governance structure to set severe limits on future racial transformation.[62] If that argument is correct, the deepest problems of black poverty, alienation, and danger in the inner cities, and the continuing problems of discrimination in jobs, schools, and housing, are likely to persist.

Nevertheless, the racial configuration of the United States in 1999 is not the same as that of 1899, and in that sense the second Reconstruction has been a success. Our nation will not, I predict, return to Jim Crow apartheid. More whites now believe in, practice, and are prepared to work for racial equality than was the case a century ago. Immigrants who are neither white nor black have enough numbers and political and organizational resources to permit significant alliances among people of color. Most importantly, there now exists a substantial black middle class with enough wealth, education, professional standing, political clout, and determination to prevent Jim Crow from returning.

Where does this combination leave us? I see a growing class division within the African American community, not because middle-class blacks will choose in any straightforward way to distance themselves from poor

---

62 Within this framework, the precise causes of public opinion about racial policy—whether racism, ideological individualism, fiscal conservatism, mistrust of government, or whatever—do not much matter. What matters is whether the intersection between achievable policies, public willingness to pursue new policies, and leaders' will and capacity is or is not a null set.

blacks, but because they will have little choice in the matter. The racial successes on my first list will continue to propel some African Americans into the successful mainstream; the racially disproportionate failures on my third list will continue to prevent other African Americans from having any chance to move in the same direction. The direction in which the partial and faltering policies of the second list will move will be decided by political activity over the next few decades. That direction will largely determine the relative proportions of well-off and poor African Americans. I predict therefore that the second Reconstruction will end in a way that makes the black community resemble the white one at least in the ironic sense that it will add class divisions to already extant religious, regional, ethnic, and gender divisions.

WORKS CITED

Abernathy, Scott (1996) "Preliminary Capacity Study: Intra-district Vouchers and *Sheff v. O'Neill*" (Unpublished paper. Princeton University: Woodrow Wilson School of Public and International Affairs).

Adarand Constructors Inc. v. Pena, Secretary of Transportation et al. 115 S. Ct. 2097 (1995).

Ards, Sheila (1989) "Estimating Local Child Abuse," *Evaluation Review* vol. 13, no. 5: 484–515.

Armor, David (1995) *Forced Justice: School Desegregation and the Law* (New York: Oxford University Press).

Arnold, Douglas (1990) *The Logic of Congressional Action* (New Haven, Conn.: Yale University Press).

Bardach, Eugene (1977) *The Implementation Game: What Happens After a Bill Becomes a Law* (Cambridge, Mass.: MIT Press).

Becker, Gary (1957) *The Economics of Discrimination* (Chicago: University of Chicago Press).

Bell, Derrick (1992) *Race, Racism, and American Law,* 3rd edition (Boston: Little, Brown and Company).

Besharov, Douglas (1996) "Child Abuse Reporting," in Irwin Garfinkel, Jennifer Hochschild, and Sara McLanahan, eds., *Social Policies for Children* (Washington, D.C.: Brookings Institution): 257–73.

Binkin, Martin and Mark Eitelberg (1982) *Blacks and the Military* (Washington, D.C.: Brookings Institution).

Boozer, Michael, Alan Krueger, and Shari Wolkon (1992) "Race and School Quality since Brown v. Board of Education," *Brookings Papers: Microeconomics* (Washington, D.C.: Brookings Institution): 269–338.

Bradbury, Katharine, Karl Case, and Constance Dunham (1989) "Geographic

Patterns of Mortgage Lending in Boston, 1982–1987," *New England Economic Review,* Sept./Oct.: 3–30.

Burbridge, Lynn (1991) "The Interaction of Race, Gender, and Socioeconomic Status in Education Outcomes" (Wellesley College, Center for Research on Women).

Bush v. Vera 116 S. Ct. 1941 (1996).

Canner, Glenn (1991) "Home Mortgage Disclosure Act," *Federal Reserve Bulletin* vol. 77, no. 11: 859–81.

Card, David and Alan Krueger (1992) "School Quality and Black-White Relative Earnings: A Direct Assessment," *Quarterly Journal of Economics,* Feb.: 151–200.

Case, Anne and Lawrence Katz (1991) "The Company You Keep: The Effects of Family and Neighborhood on Disadvantaged Youths" (Boston: National Bureau of Economic Research).

Child Welfare League of America (1992) *The Youngest of the Homeless II* (Washington, D.C.: Child Welfare League of America).

Clinton, William J. (1995) Memorandum on Affirmative Action to Heads of Executive Departments and Agencies, July 19.

Conference Board (1997) "Managing Diversity for a Sustained Competitiveness" (New York: Conference Board).

Crane, Jonathan (1991) "Effects of Neighborhoods on Dropping Out of School and Teenage Childbearing," in Christopher Jencks and Paul Peterson, eds., *The Urban Underclass* (Washington, D.C.: Brookings Institution): 299–320.

Dahl, Robert (1963) *Modern Political Analysis* (Englewood Cliffs, N.J.: Prentice-Hall).

Daula, Thomas, D. Alton Smith, and Roy Nord (1990) "Inequality in the Military: Fact or Fiction?" *American Sociological Review* vol. 55, no. 5: 714–18.

Dembo, Richard (1988) "Delinquency Among Black Male Youth," in Jewell Taylor Gibbs, ed., *Young, Black, and Male in America: An Endangered Species* (Dover, Mass.: Auburn House): 129–65.

DiIulio, John Jr. (1989) "The Impact of Inner-City Crime," *Public Interest* no. 96: 28–46.

Doig, Jameson and Erwin Hargrove, eds. (1990) *Leadership and Innovation* (Baltimore, Md.: Johns Hopkins University Press).

De Parle, Jason (1998) "Shrinking Welfare Rolls Leave Record High Share of Minorities," *New York Times,* July 27: A1, A12.

Duncan, Greg and Willard Rodgers (1991) "Has Children's Poverty Become More Persistent?" *American Sociological Review* vol. 56, no. 4: 538–50.

Eggebeen, David and Daniel Lichter (1991) "Race, Family Structure, and Changing Poverty among American Children," *American Sociological Review* vol. 56, no. 6: 801–17.

Farley, Reynolds (1992) *The Changing Status of Blacks and Whites, Men and Women* (University of Michigan, Population Studies Center, manuscript).

Farley, Reynolds and William Frey (1994) "Changes in the Segregation of Whites From Blacks During the 1980s," *American Sociological Review* vol. 59, no. 1: 23–45.

Freeman v. Pitts 112 S. Ct. 1430 (1992).

Frey, William and Reynolds Farley (1993) "Latino, Asian and Black Segregation in U.S. Metropolitan Areas: Are Multiethnic Metros Different?" *Demography,* vol. 33 no. 1: 35–50.

Frommer, Harvey (1982) *Rickey and Robinson: The Men Who Broke Baseball's Color Barrier* (New York: Macmillan).

Giles, Micheal, Douglas Gatlin, and Everett Cataldo (1974) "The Impact of Busing on White Flight," *Social Science Quarterly* vol. 55, no. 4: 493–501.

Goering, John and Ron Wienk, eds. (1996) *Mortgage Lending, Racial Discrimination, and Federal Policy* (Washington, D.C.: Urban Institute Press).

Gramlich, Edward, Richard Kasten, and Frank Sammartino (1993) "Growing Inequality in the 1980s: The Role of Federal Taxes and Cash Transfers," in Sheldon Danziger and Peter Gottschalk, eds., *Uneven Tides: Rising Inequality in America* (New York: Russell Sage Foundation): 225–49.

Greenwood, Peter (1992) "Reforming California's Approach to Delinquent and High-Risk Youth," in James Steinberg, David Lyon, and Mary Vaiana, eds., *Urban America: Policy Choices for Los Angeles and the Nation* (Santa Monica Calif.: Rand Corporation): 207–25.

Hamilton, Dona and Charles Hamilton (1997) *The Dual Agenda: Race and Social Welfare Policies of Civil Rights Organizations* (New York: Columbia University Press).

Hartsock, Nancy (1983) *Money, Sex, and Power: Toward a Feminist Historical Materialism* (New York: Longman).

Heckman, James and Kenneth Wolpin (1989) "Determining the Impact of Federal Antidiscrimination Policy on the Economic Status of Blacks: A Study of South Carolina," *American Economic Review* vol. 79, no. 1: 138–77.

Hellerstein, Judith, David Neumark, and Kenneth Troske (1997) "Market Forces and Sex Discrimination" (Cambridge Mass.: National Bureau of Economic Research, Working Paper 6321).

Hendrie, Caroline (1997) "Politics of Jobs in City Schools Hinder Reform," *Education Week,* March 26: 1, 28.

Henig, Jeffrey, Richard Hula, Marion Orr, and Desirée Pedescleaux (1999 forthcoming), *Race, Politics, and School Reform* (Princeton, N.J.: Princeton University Press).

Hirschman, Albert (1991) *The Rhetoric of Reaction: Perversity, Futility, Jeopardy* (Cambridge, Mass.: Harvard University Press).

Hochschild, Jennifer (1999) "The Strange Career of Affirmative Action," *Ohio State Law Journal* vol. 59, issue 3: 997–1037.

Hochschild, Jennifer (1995) *Facing Up to the American Dream: Race, Class, and the Soul of the Nation* (Princeton, N.J.: Princeton University Press).

Hochschild, Jennifer and Michael Danielson (1998) "Can We Desegregate Public Schools and Subsidized Housing? Lessons from the Sorry History of Yonkers, New York," in Clarence Stone, ed., *Changing Urban Education* (Lawrence: University of Kansas Press): 277–295.

Hogan, Dennis and David Featherman (1978) "Racial Stratification and Socioeconomic Change in the American North and South," *American Journal of Sociology* vol. 83, no. 1: 100–26.

Hopwood v. Texas 84 F. 3rd 72 (1996).

Jaynes, Gerald and Robin Williams, eds. (1989) *A Common Destiny: Blacks and American Society* (Washington, D.C.: National Academy Press).

Joint Center for Political and Economic Studies (1994) *Black Elected Officials* (Washington, D.C.: Joint Center for Political and Economic Studies).

Kasarda, John (1993) "Inner-City Concentrated Poverty and Neighborhood Distress: 1970 to 1990," *Housing Policy Debate* vol. 4, no. 3: 253–302.

Kozol, Jonathan (1991) *Savage Inequalities: Children in America's Schools* (New York: Crown).

Ledebur, Larry and William Barnes (1992) *City Distress, Metropolitan Disparities, and Economic Growth* (Washington, D.C.: National League of Cities).

Leonard, Jonathan (1990) "The Impact of Affirmative Action Regulation and Equal Opportunity Law on Black Employment," *Journal of Economic Perspectives* vol. 4, no. 4: 47–63.

Massey, Douglas and Nancy Denton (1987) "Trends in the Residential Segregation of Blacks, Hispanics, and Asians, 1970–1980," *American Sociological Review* vol. 52, no. 6: 802–25.

Massey, Douglas and Nancy Denton (1993) *American Apartheid: Segregation and the Making of the Underclass* (Cambridge Mass.: Harvard University Press).

Mazmanian, Daniel and Paul Sabatier (1983) *Implementation and Public Policy* (Glenview, Ill.: Scott, Foresman).

McConahay, John (1982) "Self-Interest versus Racial Attitudes as Correlates of Anti-busing Attitudes in Louisville: Is It the Buses or the Blacks?" *Journal of Politics* vol. 44, no. 3: 693–717.

McConahay, John (n.d., c. 1978) "It Is Still the Blacks and *Not* the Buses: Self-Interest vs. Racial Attitudes as Correlates of Opposition to Busing in Louisville, a Replication" (Duke University, Institute of Policy Sciences, unpublished paper).

Mead, Lawrence (1992) *The New Politics of Poverty: The Nonworking Poor in America* (New York: Basic Books).

Meier, Kenneth J., Joseph Stewart Jr., and Robert England (1989) *Race, Class, and Education: The Politics of Second-Generation Discrimination* (Madison: University of Wisconsin Press).

Merton, Robert (1996 [orig. 1936]) "The Unanticipated Consequences of Social Action," in Robert K. Merton, *On Social Structure and Science* (Chicago: University of Chicago Press): 173–82.

Miller v. Johnson 115 S. Ct. 2475 (1995).

Milloy, Courtland (1998) "Low Test Scores Demand a Better Answer," *Washington Post,* Jan. 11: B1, B10.

Missouri et al. v. Kalima Jenkins et al. 115 S. Ct. 2038 (1995).

Moore, Brenda (1996) "From Underrepresentation to Overrepresentation: African American Women," in Judith Stiehm, ed., *It's Our Military Too!: Women and the U.S. Military* (Philadelphia: Temple University Press): 115–35.

Moskos, Charles and John Butler (1996) *All That We Can Be: Black Leadership and Racial Integration the Army Way* (New York: Basic Books).

Nathan, Richard and Charles Adams Jr. (1989) "Four Perspectives on Urban Hardship," *Political Science Quarterly* vol. 104, no. 3: 483–508.

National Black Child Development Institute (1989) *Who Will Care When Parents Can't?* (Washington, D.C.: National Black Child Development Institute).

National Center for Children in Poverty (1990) *Five Million Children: A Statistical Profile of Our Poorest Young Citizens* (New York: Columbia University, School of Public Health).

National Center on Child Abuse Prevention Research (1994) *Current Trends in Child Abuse Reporting and Facilities* (Chicago: National Committee to Prevent Child Abuse).

Nordlinger, Eric (1981) *On the Autonomy of the Democratic State* (Cambridge, Mass.: Harvard University Press).

Oakes, Jeannie (1985) *Keeping Track: How Schools Structure Inequality* (New Haven, Conn.: Yale University Press).

Orfield, Gary, Mark Bachmeier, David James, and Tamela Eitle (1997) "Deepening Segregation in American Public Schools" (Harvard University, Graduate School of Education, unpublished paper).

Petersilia, Joan (1992) "Crime and Punishment in California: Full Cells, Empty Pockets, and Questionable Benefits," in James Steinberg, David Lyon, and Mary Vaiana, eds., *Urban America: Policy Choices for Los Angeles and the Nation* (Santa Monica, Calif.: Rand Corporation): 175–205.

Pressman, Jeffrey and Aaron Wildavsky (1973) *Implementation* (Berkeley: University of California Press).

Purdy, Matthew (1996) "Web of Patronage in Schools Grips Those Who Can Undo It," *New York Times,* May 14: A1, B4.

Purdy, Matthew and Maria Newman (1996) "Students Lag in Districts Where Patronage Thrives," *New York Times,* May 13: A1, B4.

Rampersad, Arnold (1997) *Jackie Robinson: A Biography* (New York: Knopf).

Rich, Wilbur (1996) *Black Mayors and School Politics: The Failure of Reform in Detroit, Gary, and Newark* (New York: Garland).

Richmond VA v. J. A. Croson Co. 488 U.S. 469 (1989).

Rosenberg, Gerald (1991) *The Hollow Hope: Can Courts Bring About Social Change?* (Chicago: University of Chicago Press).

Rosenstone, Steven and John Hansen (1993) *Mobilization, Participation, and Democracy in America* (New York: Macmillan).

Shaw v. Reno 113 S. Ct. 2816 (1993).

Skocpol, Theda (1992) *Protecting Soldiers and Mothers: The Political Origins of Social Policy in the United States* (Cambridge, Mass.: Harvard University Press).

Smith, Earl (1996) "Serving Our Country: African American Women and Men in the U.S. Military Service," in Joyce Tang and Earl Smith eds., *Women and Minorities in American Professions* (Albany: State University of New York Press): 135–56.

Stone, Clarence (1989) *Regime Politics: Governing Atlanta* (Lawrence: University of Kansas Press).

Stone, Clarence, ed. (1998) *Changing Urban Education* (Lawrence: University of Kansas Press).

Sugarman, Rafael (1996) "Shocking Report on District School Boards," *New York Daily News*, May 30: pp. 1ff.

Tenner, Edward (1996) *Why Things Bite Back: Technology and the Revenge of Unintended Consequences* (New York: Knopf).

Thernstrom, Stephan and Abigail Thernstrom (1997) *America in Black and White: One Nation, Indivisible* (New York: Simon and Schuster).

Tomasky, Michael (1996), "All Fall Down," *New York Magazine*, Feb. 12: 44–49.

Tygiel, Jules (1983) *Baseball's Great Experiment: Jackie Robinson and His Legacy* (New York: Oxford University Press).

United States Congress (1989) House of Representatives, Select Committee on Children, Youth, and Families, *Born Hooked: Confronting the Impact of Perinatal Substance Abuse,* Hearing, April 27 (Washington, D.C.: U.S. Government Printing Office).

United States Department of Health and Human Services (1990) "OIG Management Advisory Report: 'Boarder Babies'," by Richard Kusserow (Washington, D.C.: U.S. Department of Health and Human Services).

United States Department of Justice (1994) *Sourcebook of Criminal Justice Statistics* (Washington, D.C.: U.S. Government Printing Office).

Washington Post, Kaiser Family Foundation, Harvard University (1995) *The Four Americas: Government and Social Policy Through the Eyes of America's Multiracial and Multi-ethnic Society* (Washington, D.C.: *Washington Post*).

Weick, Karl (1970) "The Twigging of Overload," in H. B. Pepinsky, ed., *People and Information* (New York: Pergamon): 67–129.

Wilson, James Q. (1973) *Political Organizations* (New York: Basic Books).

Wulczyn, Fred and Robert Goerge (1992) "Foster Care in New York and Illinois," *Social Service Review* vol. 66, no. 2: 276–94.

V

Social Welfare

10

From Beginning to End: Has Twentieth-Century U.S. Social Policy Come Full Circle?

THEDA SKOCPOL

Dropping in from Mars, a visitor from outer space arriving in the United States around 1900 and touching down again shortly before 2000 could be forgiven for believing that Americans repeat themselves when they debate public social policies. At the dawn of the twentieth century, critics of the federal government—including party opponents, independent reformers, and writers in the elite media—railed against "political corruption" that dispensed lavish Civil War pensions on old soldiers and dependents who didn't need or deserve benefits, the expense of which threatened to bankrupt the national treasury.[1] Almost a century later, similar sorts of critics denounce America's out-of-control "entitlements" as dire threats to the "future of our children and grandchildren."[2] The rhetoric of Mugwumps and Progressives before and after 1900, and the arguments of the Concord Coalition toward the end of the twentieth century, exhibit some uncanny similarities.

There are other apparent recurrences as well. Back in the early 1900s, many Americans, including reformist professionals and voluntary women's groups, argued that methods for aiding poor mothers and their offspring had to be fundamentally revamped to ensure good home care for all children and a healthy future for an otherwise threatened American civilization.[3] As the century comes to an end, poor mothers and children

---

1 Theda Skocpol, *Protecting Soldiers and Mothers: The Political Origins of Social Policy in the United States* (Cambridge, Mass.: The Belknap Press of Harvard University Press, 1992), chaps. 2 and 5.
2 Peter G. Peterson, *Facing Up: How to Rescue the Economy from Crushing Debt and Restore the American Dream* (New York: Simon and Schuster, 1993).
3 Skocpol, *Protecting Soldiers and Mothers*, chap. 8.

249

seem still to be a civilization-threatening problem in the United States.[4] Consequently, Americans have set out, once again, to "revolutionize" preexisting ways of aiding those mothers and children.

Of course those of us who study American history know that the first impression of the twice-visiting Martian is in many ways misleading. There are major differences between U.S. social politics at the dawn and at the twilight of the twentieth century. From another perspective, it looks as if Americans back then were just starting toward a modern welfare state, and now may be backing away from whatever approximation to a national welfare state was built up between the 1910s and the 1970s.

For example, during the 1910s, people who aimed to help poor mothers and children persuaded most U.S. states to authorize "mothers' pensions" so that worthy yet needy widows need no longer apply to private charity and could afford to keep their children at home rather than surrendering them, perhaps at the order of a judge, to foster homes or orphanages. In sharp contrast, late twentieth-century critics of Aid to Families with Dependent Children (AFDC)—the federally subsidized "granddaughter" of mothers' pensions—called for poor mothers to do full-time wage-work rather than stay at home to care for their children. If worst comes to worst, if the impoverished moms fail to get jobs or won't work, some conservatives today argue that poor children then would be better off in foster homes or orphanages, ideally run by private charities.

In other ways, too, attitudes toward governmental social provision in the United States seem to have flip-flopped. At the dawn of the twentieth century, elite and middle-class reformers may have been very skeptical of politicians and opposed to out-of-control federal spending on Civil War pensions. But most "progressive" reformers were simultaneously optimistic that local, state, and national government could be professionalized in "the public interest." Especially if staffed by well-trained people like themselves, new bureaucracies and regulatory agencies could successfully address many of the social disorders and inequities accompanying industrialization. Many reformers believed that public support for the unemployed, the sick, and the old could complement and help to realize long-standing U.S. ideals about individual initiative and market entrepreneurialism. Indeed, vanguard reformers assembled in the American Association for Labor Legislation (AALL)—a small group of professors and

---

4 Newt Gingrich, *To Renew America* (New York: Harper Collins, 1995), especially chap. 6, "Replacing the Welfare State with an Opportunity Society."

other professionals to be sure, but a vocal and confident one—were certain that all industrializing nations were on an irreversible, progressive road toward a regime of social insurance and labor regulations.[5] The United States, AALL members thought, would soon follow Germany, Britain, and other European pioneers along the road to what would later be called "the modern welfare state."

By contrast, as the United States approaches the end of the twentieth century, those calling most insistently for social policies to be revamped for the future are profoundly distrustful of government. Conservative and independent reformers alike seem determined to dismantle or fundamentally restructure many of the national or nationwide social programs that Progressive reformers and their cousins of the New Deal era succeeded in establishing in the United States.[6] American social insurance and welfare programs are seen by many as drags on national economic growth and threats to the moral integrity of families. Professionals and bureaucrats who staff public social programs, or run private charitable agencies tied to them, are portrayed as the enemies of market opportunity and mainstream moral values. The United States is said to have a destructively powerful "welfare state" that must be dismantled if Americans are to flourish in the twenty-first century. The air rings with apocalyptic rhetoric phrased in terms of generational trade-offs: our children and grandchildren will suffer, we are assured by the Concord Coalition and conservative Republicans, if we do not restrict aid to the poor, reduce federal expenditures, cut taxes, and restructure Social Security and Medicare. Even Democratic President Bill Clinton declared in his 1996 State of the Union Address that "the era of big government is over."

In some ways the "retrenchment politics" of the late twentieth-century United States resembles calls for cutbacks in social spending in other Western democracies. But American debates seem disproportionately hostile to governmental social provision, given that the United States has lower taxes, fewer social programs, and much healthier national finances than most other Western democracies. Conditions particular to U.S. history and politics are at work, along with broader trends that cut across nations.

---

5 Skocpol, *Protecting Soldiers and Mothers,* chap. 3.
6 Consider Gingrich, *To Renew America;* Peterson, *Facing Up;* and Ralph Reed, *Politically Incorrect: The Emerging Faith Factor in American Politics* (Dallas: Word Publishing, 1994).

What are we to make of both recurrent debates and apparent reversals over the course of twentieth-century U.S. social policy? In my view, we cannot get very far by looking simply for ideological continuities or cultural essences, although ideas and values do matter, as I shall suggest below. We cannot just trace social and economic transformations, although these certainly matter too—for example, the changing role of women in families and economic life. Nor can we merely trace the lineages of individual types of policies—such as welfare, health programs, or old-age pensions—because some transformations affect all types of policies or the relationships among them.

We need to get a sense of shifts over time in the big picture, in the connections of policies among themselves and in the groundings of programs and policy debates in the changing institutions and coalitions of modern U.S. politics. The peculiar twists and turns of social policies and debates about them are grounded in the distinctive formation of the American state and political parties, and in shifts across time in partisan and ideological alignments.

In the pages that follow, I first trace the major phases through which modern U.S. social policies have developed from the late nineteenth century to the present. Then I look back over the course of the past century to identify regularities and recurrent dilemmas or conflicts about America's peculiar version of the modern welfare state. Against this backdrop I return to the question of what may be happening now, at century's end, as Americans contend over the future shape of public social policies.

THE POLITICAL FORMATION OF U.S. SOCIAL POLICY

Modern "welfare states," as they eventually came to be called, had their start between the 1880s and the 1920s in pension and social insurance programs established for industrial workers and needy citizens in Europe and Australasia.[7] Later, from the 1930s through the 1950s, these programmatic beginnings were in certain countries elaborated into comprehensive systems of income support and social insurance encompassing entire national populations. In the aftermath of World War II, Great Britain rationalized a whole array of services and social insurance pro-

---

7 Peter J. Flora and Jens Alber, "Modernization, Democratization, and the Development of Welfare States in Western Europe," 37–80 in *The Development of Welfare States in Europe and America,* edited by Peter J. Flora and Arnold J. Heidenheimer (New Brunswick, N.J.: Transaction Books, 1981).

grams around an explicit vision of "the welfare state," which would ensure a "national minimum" of protection for all citizens against income interruptions due to old age, disability, ill health, unemployment, and family breakup. During the same period other nations—especially the Scandinavian democracies—established "full employment welfare states" by deliberately coordinating social policies, first with Keynesian strategies of macroeconomic management and then with targeted interventions in labor markets.

Comparative research on the origins of modern welfare states often measures the United States against foreign patterns of "welfare state development." America is often labeled a "welfare state laggard" because it did not establish nationwide social insurance until 1935. And many say that the United States has an "incomplete welfare state" because it never enacted national health insurance or established full-employment programs coordinated with social policies. Certain insights can be gained from cross-nationally inspired contrasts of this sort. But they overlook policies and patterns of politics distinctive to the United States.

Unlike most European countries, America did not experience centuries of rule by monarchs, aristocrats, and bureaucratic officials.[8] The United States was born of a late eighteenth-century rebellion against English colonial rule, following which Americans established a constitutional republic that deliberately divided governmental authority among states, localities, and a national government in which official powers were intricately dispersed and shared among the president, the Congress, and the courts.

Within a few decades after the American Revolution and the adoption of the constitution, the United States became what political scientist Stephen Skowronek has aptly dubbed a "state of courts and parties."[9] The new nation had few professionally run public bureaucracies. Along with the judges of the courts, party politicians held sway. They freely dispersed subsidies and favors through legislatures, while regularly competing for votes from virtually all of the country's white males. By the 1830s the United States had become the world's first mass democracy. Ordinary

---

8 Samuel P. Huntington, *Political Order in Changing Societies* (New Haven, Conn.: Yale University Press, 1968), 93–133.
9 This characterization of the original, nineteenth-century U.S. state comes from Stephen Skowronek, *Building a New American State: The Expansion of National Administrative Capacities, 1877–1930* (Cambridge and New York: Cambridge University Press, 1982), chap. 2.

workers and farmers, not just men of property, could participate fully in electoral politics, and throughout the nineteenth century most Americans who were eligible to vote regularly did so. Elections were frequent and often hotly contested.[10]

Only around 1900 did U.S. governments at local, state, and federal levels begin to develop significant bureaucratic capacities. This happened as patronage parties, voter participation, and electoral competition weakened. Yet public bureaucratization in the United States has always proceeded in fragmentary ways, and the nation has never developed a strong, well-paid, or highly respected stratum of national civil servants. Despite what many of today's conservatives believe, U.S. government is not highly centralized or "bureaucratic" by international standards. Divisions of authority among executives, agencies, legislatures, committees within legislatures, and state and federal courts are arguably even more pervasive within twentieth-century U.S. governance than they were in nineteenth-century party-dominated politics.

What is more, much of U.S. national politics has remained rooted in congressionally mediated coalitions of local (or locally active) interests. From party politics in the 1800s down to the more interest-group-centered politics of recent times, U.S. public programs are most viable when they distribute benefits, services, or regulatory advantages widely, across large numbers of local legislative districts. An institution quite different from the parliaments of other democracies, the U.S. Congress has always been, and remains, a pivotal institution for domestic policymaking.

Modern U.S. social policies did not start with the Social Security Act of 1935. Certain kinds of widespread and generous social policies flourished within the distinctive institutions and political arrangements of early American democracy, as we are about to note. From the nineteenth century onward, U.S. social policies simply took different forms, and developed in different phases, than those that grew up in what would eventually be called the "welfare states" of Europe and Australasia.

Before the Twentieth Century

The first major U.S. social policies were widespread schooling for many of the young, the foundations of which were well laid prior to the Civil War,

10 Michael E. McGerr, *The Decline of Popular Politics: The American North, 1865–1928* (New York: Oxford University Press, 1986).

and then surprisingly generous pensions for many of the nation's elderly, expenditures that burgeoned in the wake of Union victories in the 1860s conflict.

Americans were international pioneers when it came to educating their young. Starting early in the nineteenth century, hundreds of local communities outside the South devoted themselves to building the most extensive and inclusive system of primary, secondary, and higher education in the industrializing world.[11] U.S. federalism encouraged the competitive expansion of locally managed public education while allowing varieties of private schooling to flourish. Farmers and workers alike saw education as a way to participate fully in a democratic polity and market society. No aristocracy, established church, or national bureaucracy held sway in America, so schools and colleges and universities were free to proliferate competitively across localities and states. Public education was originally oriented more toward socializing majorities for shared citizenship than toward preparing elites for civil service careers.[12] During the Civil War the ascendant Republicans enacted land grant subsidies to encourage public higher education and agricultural research to benefit farmers across many states.

From the 1870s to the 1910s there was an enormous expansion of de facto old-age benefits for veterans of the Union armies of the Civil War.[13] By 1910, about 28 percent of all elderly American men, and nearly one-third of elderly men in the North, were receiving, from the U.S. federal government, pensions that were remarkably generous by the international standards of the day. Many widows and other dependents of deceased veterans were also pensioners, and extra aid was often available to Civil War veterans and survivors from state and local governments. Union soldiers and their dependents, it was argued, had "saved the nation" and should in return be cared for by the government to prevent the possibility of their falling into dependence on private charity or public poor relief.

Especially after the late 1870s, the expansion of federal benefits for Union veterans was fueled by electoral competition between patronage-

---

11 Arnold J. Heidenheimer, "Education and Social Security Entitlements in Europe and America," 269–304 in Flora and Heidenheimer; and Richard Rubinson, "Class Formation, Politics, and Institutions: Schooling in the United States," *American Journal of Sociology* 92 (1986): 519–48.

12 Ira Katznelson and Margaret Weir, *Schooling for All: Class, Race, and the Decline of the Democratic Ideal* (New York: Basic Books, 1985), chap. 2.

13 For full details and documentation, see Theda Skocpol, *Protecting Soldiers and Mothers*, chap. 2.

oriented political parties. Politicians used distributive policies to assemble cross-class and cross-regional support from a highly mobilized and competitive male electorate.[14] The old soldiers and those tied to them constituted critical blocs of voters, especially in those states of the East and Midwest where a few thousand votes could tip the balance toward Republicans or Democrats and determine the outcome of hotly contested presidential and congressional elections.

Public finances were not an obstacle to pension expansion, as the Republican Party in particular learned to combine high tariffs and generous pension expenditures. Tariffs catered to favored groups of northern industrialists and workers while raising plentiful revenues for the federal government. In turn, the revenues could be spent on pensions, applications for which could be manipulated in ways that helped the Republicans to appeal to people in competitive states just before crucial elections.[15] Along with party politicians, thousands of veterans' clubs federated into the Grand Army of the Republic became key supporters of pension generosity from mid-1880s onward, keeping congressmen across many northern legislative districts keenly interested in such social expenditures from the federal treasury.

Protections for Mothers, Not Workers

Around 1900, the U.S. "state of courts and parties" was undergoing major changes. The two dominant political parties, Democrats and Republicans, became less electorally competitive in most parts of the nation. Elite and middle-class groups were calling for political reforms that would weaken patronage-oriented parties and create nonpartisan, professional agencies of government.

At this juncture, reformers who wanted the United States to imitate early European social insurance and pension programs for workingmen and their families made little headway.[16] Informed publics did not believe that turn-of-the-century American governments could administer taxes and social spending honestly or efficiently. And reformers feared "corrup-

---

14 Richard L. McCormick, "The Party Period and Public Policy: An Exploratory Hypothesis," *Journal of American History* 66 (1979): 279–98.
15 Donald McMurry, "The Political Significance of the Pension Question, 1885–1897," *Mississippi Valley Historical Review* 9 (1922): 19–36; and Heywood Sanders, "'Paying for the Bloody Shirt': The Politics of Civil War Pensions," 137–60 in *Political Benefits,* edited by Barry Rundquist (Lexington, Mass.: D.C. Heath, 1980).
16 Skocpol, *Protecting Soldiers and Mothers,* Part 2.

tion" among politicians if huge new benefit programs—reminiscent to them of Civil War pensions—were created.

Yet the same set of political circumstances that discouraged social protection of workingmen in the United States opened up opportunities for reformers advocating social programs for mothers and children. Until 1920 (or a few years before in some states), American women lacked the right to vote. But they were hardly absent from politics more broadly understood.[17] Elite and middle-class women formed voluntary organizations to engage in charitable, cultural, and civic activities. By the turn of the twentieth century, nation-spanning federations of women's voluntary associations had formed, exactly paralleling the three-tier structure of local-state-federal government. Women's federations allied themselves with higher-educated female professional reformers, arguing that the moral and domestic values of married homemakers and mothers should be projected into public affairs. The nation should care for its people just as a good mother would; and all American mothers should be honored for their service to the community, just as the veteran soldiers of the Civil War were honored. Thus organized women appealed to established sentiments and values, but for new purposes.

Pressing arguments about motherhood, organized women urged legislators regardless of party to enact new social policies to help families, communities, and—above all—mothers and children. During a period when U.S. political parties were weakened and when male officials and trade unions could not readily take the lead in enacting social policies for workingmen, U.S. women's voluntary federations were uniquely well positioned to shape public debates in the 1910s and early 1920s across many local legislative districts.[18] Officials at both state and federal levels responded to the calls of women's organizations. The U.S. federal government established the female-run Children's Bureau in 1912, and expanded its mission in 1921 through the enactment of the Sheppard-Towner program partially to fund state and local health-care education to help American mothers and babies. Meanwhile, dozens of states enacted protective labor laws for women workers, arguing that their capacity for motherhood had to be protected. And forty-four states enabled local jurisdictions

---

17 Paula Baker, "The Domestication of Politics: Women and American Political Society, 1780–1920," *American Historical Review* 89 (1984): 620–47.
18 Skocpol, *Protecting Soldiers and Mothers*, Part 3; and Theda Skocpol, Christopher Howard, Susan Goodrich Lehmann, and Marjorie Abend-Wein, "Women's Associations and the Enactment of Mothers' Pensions in the United States," *American Political Science Review* vol. 87, no. 3 (1993): 686–701.

to provide "mothers' pensions" to impoverished caretakers of fatherless children. Mothers' pensions were the forerunners of what would eventually become Aid to Dependent Children (and later Aid to Families With Dependent Children).

The United States in the early twentieth century almost became a kind of "maternalist" welfare state, one in which benefits and protections for families were provided through the honored role of the homemaker mother. But this possibility did not come to fruition. Women's voluntary associations were more successful at setting agendas of civic debate and getting legislators to enact regulations or "enabling statutes" than they were at persuading various levels of government to adequately fund social programs. Mothers' pensions, in particular, were never adequately funded and soon degenerated into new versions of poor relief.[19]

Ironically, after American women were admitted to the formal electorate by the Nineteenth Amendment of 1920, the civic engagement of many women's groups weakened. For this and a variety of other reasons— including the mobilization of the American Medical Association to pressure Congress to cut funding for the Sheppard-Towner maternal health clinics—the expansion of maternalist social policies came to a halt by the later 1920s. In fact, earlier gains for mothers and children were partially reversed. Then came the Great Depression, bringing with it social and political upheavals that ushered in the next great era of U.S. social policy innovation.

Fashioning Social Security in Depression and War

The back-to-back crises of the Great Depression and World War II set the stage for the United States to construct its own version of national social insurance for employed citizens and the elderly. Emergency New Deal "relief" efforts were established for a time, and so were benefits for military veterans returning after World War II. Chiefly, however, America's modern social programs were launched by the Social Security Act of 1935, which included national Old Age Insurance (OAI), federally required and state-run Unemployment Insurance (UI), federal subsidies for optional, state-controlled Old Age Assistance (OAA), and Aid to Dependent Children (ADC, a continuation of the earlier mothers' pensions).

19 Aspects of this story are well told in Linda Gordon, *Pitied But Not Entitled: Single Mothers and the History of Welfare* (New York: Free Press, 1994).

A number of structural changes and political developments set the stage for the policy innovations of the 1930s and 1940s. The federal government—and within it the executive branch—came to the fore in the emergency of massive economic depression. State and local governments and charity groups, their resources exhausted, literally begged for federal intervention, even as business groups and other conservatives lost their ability to veto governmental initiatives. Economic crisis spurred the unionization of industrial workers as well as protests by organizations of farmers and the unemployed. The elderly were also aroused, as "Townsend Clubs" demanded generous pensions for retirees.[20] Economic crisis triggered electoral realignment, shifting votes from Republicans to Democrats—and transforming the Democrats from warring camps of southern "dry" Protestants versus northern "wet" Catholics into a nationwide conglomerate of local and state political machines hungry for new flows of economic resources.[21]

What the Depression, the New Deal, and even World War II did *not* accomplish, however, was the removal of contradictory local and state interests from "national" U.S. policymaking. Even at their strongest, President Franklin Roosevelt and the assorted New Deal reformist professionals who flocked into executive agencies during the 1930s all had to compromise with congressional coalitions rooted in state and local interests.[22] Above all, New Dealers had to respect southern Democrats' determination to protect their region's sharecropping agriculture and low-wage industries from actually (or potentially) unsettling "intrusions" by northern unions or federal bureaucrats. Southerners were happy to have resources from the federal government but did not want either centralized controls or benefits that might undermine existing southern labor and race relations. If the truth be told, congressional representatives of other localities and states in the nation felt pretty much the same protective way about the major labor and social relations of their areas. A broad congressional consensus throughout the New Deal and the 1940s sought to preserve a great deal of variety across states and regions in economic and social policy.

---

20 Abraham Holtzman, *The Townsend Movement: A Political Study* (New York: Bookman Associates, 1963).
21 Kristi Andersen, *The Creation of a Democratic Majority, 1928–1936* (Chicago: University of Chicago Press, 1979).
22 James T. Patterson, *Congressional Conservatism and the New Deal* (Lexington: University of Kentucky Press, 1967).

From this perspective, the shape and limits of the major social and economic programs of the 1930s and 1940s are not surprising. Federally run employment programs did not survive the mass unemployment of the Depression because efforts to institutionalize executive-run "full employment planning" and "social Keynesianism" ran afoul of congressionally represented southern, business, and farm interests.[23] The Social Security Act included only one truly national program—Old Age Insurance—enacted in an area where no states had previously established programs. Unemployment insurance was made federal rather than national not only because representatives of the South wanted their states to be able to establish terms of coverage, benefits, and taxation but also because representatives of Wisconsin and New York wanted their "liberal" states to be able to preserve the terms of the unemployment insurance programs they had established prior to the Social Security Act.[24] Public assistance programs for the elderly and dependent children were given federal subsidies under Social Security but were otherwise left entirely in the hands of the states.

During World War II, New Deal reformers tied to the National Resources Planning Board talked about permanently nationalizing and expanding both public assistance and unemployment insurance.[25] Their proposals got nowhere at all, and Congress disbanded the National Resources Planning Board soon after they were made. In the late 1940s, President Harry Truman championed national health insurance, but his efforts were defeated by congressional conservatives and the American Medical Association, which was influential in legislative districts across the country.[26] After the 1940s, health insurance coverage for many (but not all) working-aged Americans was provided by private employers, who

23 This point is developed in Margaret Weir and Theda Skocpol, "State Structures and the Possibilities for 'Keynesian' Responses to the Great Depression in Sweden, Britain, and the United States," 107–63 in *Bringing the State Back In,* edited by Peter B. Evans, Theda Skocpol, and Dietrich Rueschemeyer (Cambridge and New York: Cambridge University Press, 1985).

24 Edwin Amenta, Elisabeth Clemens, Jefren Olsen, Sunita Parikh, and Theda Skocpol, "The Political Origins of Unemployment Insurance in Five American States," *Studies in American Political Development* 2 (1987): 137–82; and G. John Ikenberry and Theda Skocpol, "The Road to Social Security," reprinted as chap. 4 in Theda Skocpol, *Social Policy in the United States: Future Possibilities in Historical Perspective* (Princeton, N.J.: Princeton University Press, 1995).

25 Edwin Amenta and Theda Skocpol, "Redefining the New Deal: World War II and the Development of Social Provision in the United States," reprinted as chap. 5 in Skocpol, *Social Policy in the United States.*

26 Monte M. Poen, *Harry S. Truman versus the Medical Lobby* (Columbia: University of Missouri Press, 1979).

received tax breaks from the federal government for offering this social benefit.[27]

On the governmental side of the social benefits ledger, only OAI tended to expand coverage and become more comprehensive after 1935. As Martha Derthick has shown, Social Security's administrators were unusually adept at managing relationships with Congress, presidents of both parties, and the public.[28] During the 1950s, benefits for disabled wage-earners were added to what was now known simply as "Social Security," and coverage was extended to more occupations. Thus "Social Security" for retired wage-earners and their dependents emerged as the centerpiece of such comprehensive public social provision as there would be in post–World War II America.

The only other truly generous and comprehensive postwar national social provision was the G.I. Bill of 1944, which featured employment assistance and educational and housing loans open to millions of military veterans returning from World War II.[29] Somewhat less generous benefits were subsequently made available to smaller veteran cohorts following the Korean and Vietnam conflicts. The G.I. Bill stands out in the history of U.S. social provision before and after, because it provided generous educational and economic benefits to young male workers and their families. By contrast, most previous and subsequent federal social benefits have gone to old people—including aging military veterans—and to widowed or otherwise single mothers and children.

Controversies over the Federal Social Role Since the 1960s

A new, federally directed period of innovation in U.S. social policy was launched in the aftermath of the civil rights struggles of the 1950s and 1960s as southern blacks gained the right to vote and liberal Democrats very temporarily gained executive power and majorities in Congress.[30] Liberals dreamed of "completing" the social and economic agendas left

27 Beth Stevens, "Blurring the Boundaries: How the Federal Government Has Influenced Welfare Benefits in the Private Sector," 121–48 in Margaret Weir, Ann Shola Orloff, and Theda Skocpol, editors, *The Politics of Social Policy in the United States* (Princeton, N.J.: Princeton University Press, 1988).

28 The expansion of Social Security is well chronicled in Martha Derthick, *Policymaking for Social Security* (Washington, D.C.: Brookings Institution, 1979).

29 Davis R. B. Ross, *Preparing for Ulysses: Politics and Veterans During World War II* (New York: Columbia University Press, 1969); and Keith W. Olson, *The G.I. Bill, the Veterans, and the Colleges* (Lexington: University of Kentucky Press, 1974).

30 James T. Patterson, *America's Struggle Against Poverty, 1900–1980* (Cambridge, Mass.: Harvard University Press, 1981), Parts 3 and 4.

over from the unfinished reform agendas of the 1930s and 1940s, and many activists hoped to rework U.S. social programs in ways that would aid and uplift the poor, particularly the politically aroused black poor. During this same period, the federal courts also became active in defining and enforcing new "rights" for minorities and new "entitlements" for welfare recipients and other clients of governmental programs.[31]

Despite the extravagance of liberal hopes and radical demands at the height of the War on Poverty and the Great Society, policy legacies and institutional features inherited from the New Deal era shaped and limited the openings available to policymakers. Liberals, unionists, and Civil Rights activists were not in a good position to create public full-employment programs that might have jointly benefitted the black poor along with white and black unionized workers. Instead, the institutional and intellectual legacy of the New Deal and the 1940s encouraged public policies that emphasized "commercial Keynesian" macroeconomic strategies supplemented by small federal programs designed to reeducate the poor to make them "employable."[32] Soon caught up in political controversies and squeezed for resources during the Vietnam War, federally sponsored employment-training efforts never really succeeded.

As the War on Poverty gave way to the Great Society and then legislation sponsored by President Richard Nixon, the emphasis shifted from job training and community development programs to helping the poor through new or expanded categorical social benefits such as AFDC, Food Stamps, and Medicaid. The reasons for this shift are many, but they include liberal demands for more spending on the poor, the after-effects of urban rioting, judicial decisions liberalizing the rules for federal welfare benefits, and the preference of the Republican administration of President Richard Nixon for spending on individual benefits rather than subsidies channeled to services and antipoverty agencies that were likely to be part of the Democratic Party's organizational base.

For a time, liberalized federal regulations and expanded social spending on targeted welfare programs helped welfare mothers and their children, as more needy single-parent families than ever before were added to the welfare rolls.[33] Yet during this same period the Social Security Admin-

---

31 R. Shep Melnick, *Between the Lines: Interpreting Welfare Rights* (Washington, D.C.: Brookings Institution, 1994).

32 Margaret Weir, *Politics and Jobs: The Boundaries of Employment Policy in the United States* (Princeton, N.J.: Princeton University Press, 1992).

33 Patterson, *America's Struggle Against Poverty,* chaps. 10 and 11.

istration took advantage of the heightened concern with antipoverty policy to put through long-laid plans for Medicare, nationalized Supplemental Security Income, and indexed Social Security benefits. As Jill Quadagno explains, "the 1972 amendments represented a turning point for Social Security, a watershed for U.S. welfare state development. The automatic cost-of-living increases removed benefits from politics and ensured older people that inflation would not erode the value of those benefits. . . . The 1972 amendments . . . solidly incorporated the middle class into the welfare state."[34] Thus, despite the focus of the rhetoric of the 1960s and early 1970s on poor working-aged and children, the most generous and sustainable innovations of the 1960s and early 1970s helped the elderly, including middle-class retirees as well as the elderly poor.

By the later 1970s and particularly during the 1980s, political backlashes set in against the welfare innovations and extensions of the 1960s and early 1970s. Leaving aside important exceptions and nuances, one can say that expanded "social security" provision for the elderly (poor and nonpoor alike) remained popular with broad, bipartisan swatches of American voters and politicians, while public "welfare" assistance to the working-aged poor became an increasingly contentious issue among politicians and intellectuals and within the electorate as a whole. The division between "social security" as a set of earned benefits and "welfare" as undeserved handouts to the poor had been built into the programmatic structure of federal social provision since the New Deal; in the wake of the policy changes of the 1960s and 1970s, this division became highly politicized along racial lines.[35]

Attacks on expansions of federally mandated or subsidized welfare programs for the poor aided the electoral fortunes of Republicans and conservative critics of governmental social provision.[36] Various reasons can be cited why such attacks were politically successful. Some would argue that they appealed to tacit racism in the U.S. white majority.[37] Others would argue that, racism aside, middle-class and working-class citizens were less and less willing to pay taxes for federal social transfers during a time of employment instability and declining real family wages.

34 Quadagno, "Generational Equity," 355–56.
35 Theda Skocpol, "The Limits of the New Deal System and the Roots of Contemporary Welfare Dilemmas," chap. 6 in Skocpol, *Social Policy in the United States.*
36 Thomas Byrne Edsall and Mary D. Edsall, *Chain Reaction: The Impact of Race, Rights, and Taxes on American Politics* (New York: W. W. Norton, 1991).
37 Jill Quadagno, *The Color of Welfare: How Racism Undermined the War on Poverty* (New York: Oxford University Press, 1994).

Still others would point to the changing roles of American women. Welfare policies that got their start back in the 1910s based on the presumption that mothers should stay at home lost much of their legitimacy in the eyes of most Americans from the 1970s onward, as more and more working-class and middle-class wives and mothers entered the paid labor force. Whatever the reasons, conservative Republican Ronald Reagan used antiwelfare appeals as part of his winning campaign for the presidency in 1980, and political attacks on welfare have deepened and spread ever since. Ronald Reagan was not the first politician to criticize welfare and he certainly spoke to doubts already widespread among Americans. Nevertheless, a president can do much to shape and reshape public "common sense" and agendas of policy debate. And Reagan certainly did this for welfare.

The Reagan presidency also changed the terrain of federal fiscal politics in America. A huge federal tax cut was enacted in 1981, leading to a burgeoning federal deficit that thereafter made it virtually impossible for new social programs to be funded. The Reagan ascendancy of the 1980s did not eliminate many programs or cut absolute domestic social spending but it did retard the growth of expenditures on targeted programs that had already lost considerable ground in the face of inflation during the 1970s. More important, the "Reagan Era" signalled an ideological sea change.[38] Both politicians' rhetoric and the actual squeezing and disrupting of governmental programs that occurred in this period helped to delegitimate governmental solutions to domestic social ills. Politicians became reluctant to discuss taxation as a positive means to the resolution of civic or individual concerns. And the huge federal budget deficit created by Ronald Reagan's tax cuts itself moved to the center of public discussion as supposedly the leading problem for the nation to resolve in the 1990s— neatly directing attention away from the increasingly acute difficulties faced by less educated working families in the U.S. national economy.[39]

Many of the supporters of Governor Bill Clinton of Arkansas hoped that the election of this moderate Democratic president in 1992 would suddenly undo the delegitimation of the federal social role that had progressed so far since the 1970s. It soon became apparent, however, that the

---

38 Sidney Blumenthal and Thomas Byrne Edsall, eds., *The Reagan Legacy* (New York: Pantheon Books, 1988).
39 Sheldon Danziger and Peter Gottschalk, eds., *Uneven Tides: Rising Inequality in America* (New York: Russell Sage Foundation, 1993); and Richard B. Freeman, ed., *Working Under Different Rules* (New York: Russell Sage Foundation, 1994).

policy initiatives of the 1993–94 Clinton administration could barely assemble congressional majorities and were invariably debated in a context of the continuing federal budget crisis and intense popular distrust of government.[40] The major initiative of Clinton's first year in office, his proposal to reform the national health care financing system to control costs and ensure "Health Security" for all Americans, ultimately boomeranged against the president and the congressional Democrats.[41] President Clinton designed his Health Security proposal with regulations rather than new taxes, trying to cut costs and reduce the federal budget deficit. But this ended up backfiring politically as interest groups in the existing health care system teamed up with insurgent antigovernment Republicans to fan popular anxieties about too much "government bureaucracy" in the health care system. Along with other early Clinton administration initiatives such as controls on assault weapons, the Health Security debacle of 1993–94 set the stage for the sweeping Republican congressional victories of November 1994. Although President Clinton maneuvered his way to a convincing reelection victory in 1996, Democrats were not able to displace Republicans in Congress. The boomerang of 1994 could not immediately be reversed by the Democratic party.

Generational Critiques at Century's End

New Deal reforms, eventually overlaid by the reforms of the War on Poverty through the early 1970s, culminated in an oddly structured configuration of social policies in the United States. Generous and relatively universal programs for the elderly coexist with much less generous, means-tested programs for very poor women and children. Groups "in the middle" tend to be left out, especially working-aged adults who are not very poor. Many bifurcations figure in the overall pattern of modern U.S. social policy, including those of race, gender, and middle-class versus poor. A bifurcation by life-course stage—elderly versus young—has also been implicit, ready to come to the fore in public discussions when political conditions became ripe—as they did starting in the 1970s and 1980s.

Against the backdrop of the generational imbalances in current U.S. social policies, we can understand why many debates in the 1980s and 1990s have been posed in terms of "helping America's children" or

40 Alan Brinkley, "Reagan's Revenge: As Invented by Howard Jarvis," *The New York Times Magazine,* June 19, 1994, 36–37.
41 Theda Skocpol, *Boomerang: Clinton's Health Security Effort and the Turn Against Government in U.S. Politics* (New York: W. W. Norton, 1996).

"doing what is best for our children and grandchildren." The generational critiques offered by groups such as the Concord Coalition, the Children's Defense Fund, and insurgent conservatives in and around the Republican Party make sense when we consider them in the light of the previous U.S. developments. Current debates are responding to disparities in social protections for old and young, disparities that are especially obvious now that the effects of the G.I. Bill have faded into the past, highlighting the absence of social programs for families in the middle of the age and class structure.

Political successes and failures from the 1960s to the 1990s also reverberate through current debates about the future of U.S. social policy. Although the rhetoric has changed, today's progressives and conservatives are carrying on old battles in new terms.

At the vanguard of today's liberal attempts to revive and extend Great Society social programs is the Children's Defense Fund, which was launched by Civil Rights activist Marian Wright Edelman between 1968 and 1973. Edelman was dismayed when the exhilarating political openings for liberals of the 1960s gave way to racial backlash and increasing conservatism. This happened just as she was establishing herself as a progressive policy researcher and agitator in Washington, D.C. She has made no secret that she decided to establish a nonprofit research and advocacy organization focusing on children "because we recognized that support for whatever was labeled black and poor was shrinking and that new ways had to be found to articulate and respond to the continuing problems of poverty and race."[42] In addition to talking about a wide array of children's problems, the Children's Defense Fund addresses the declining incomes of many young parents, black and white alike.[43]

Those on the conservative side of the political spectrum are also revisiting old battlefields with new tactics. In *Facing Up,* Peter Peterson of the Concord Coalition offers a scathing critique of Ronald Reagan and his policies of the 1980s.[44] During the Reagan era, fiscal conservatives hoped that "middle-class entitlements" would be restructured. But after briefly raising the possibility of such reforms, President Reagan and Budget

---

42 Marian Wright Edelman, *Families in Peril: An Agenda for Social Change* (Cambridge, Mass.: Harvard University Press, 1987), ix.

43 See, for example, Clifford M. Johnson, Andrew M. Sum, and James D. Weill, *Vanishing Dreams: The Growing Economic Plight of America's Young Families* (Washington, D.C.: Children's Defense Fund, 1988).

44 Peter G. Peterson, *Facing Up* (New York: Simon and Schuster, 1993), introduction and 87–89.

Director David Stockman quickly retreated from middle-class programs and concentrated most of their rhetorical and budgetary fire on means-tested social spending for the poor. Now Peterson and his fiscal conservative allies are taking a quite different approach to what they see as the problem of overly generous federal spending. Instead of appealing to middle-class hostility against blacks and welfare clients, Peterson and the Concord Coalition are appealing to middle-class anxieties about federal taxes and expenditures. Meanwhile, forces seeking to restructure broad social insurance programs point to the roaring stock market of the 1990s as a possible source of instant wealth, should Social Security taxes be diverted into individualized accounts.

Congressional conservative Republicans and their allies in the Christian Coalition are more careful about attacking Social Security than the Concord Coalition. They understand how popular this program is with middle-aged and older middle-class Americans and do not want to tackle it as long as Congressional Republicans face strong electoral competition from Democrats (who, for example, credibly portrayed themselves as defenders of Social Security and Medicare during the 1996 election). Yet the differences between the Concord Coalition and Congressional conservatives are more than just tactical, for the Republicans in Congress aim to revive and extend the "Reagan Revolution" as a tax-cutting enterprise. "Balancing the federal budget" is not a goal in and of itself for the conservative insurgents—certainly not to be furthered through tax increases of any kind. Rather, a balanced budget is a rhetorical and practical tactic for gaining middle-class support to shrink the federal government permanently.

Nor do the Congressional conservatives have any intention of redirecting what is left of federal social policy toward means-tested protections for the poor or "investments" in less privileged children. On the contrary, Republicans in Congress and forces on the Christian Right unabashedly wanted to cut taxes and regulations in ways that would directly benefit the wealthy and comfortable middle-class families. This might seem perverse, but not if seen from the perspective broadly shared by Republican Conservatives. As they see it, morally and economically successful Americans deserve to be rewarded by being allowed to keep more of what they earn for their own families. Better-off Americans will use their wealth to make the private market investments that will generate economic growth for the future; giving successful, privileged Americans extra resources will benefit everyone over time.

PATTERNS AND DILEMMAS

Although no one can predict the outcome of ongoing policy debates and political struggles, we can discern a number of interesting patterns across past eras of U.S. social policy and politics—patterns that cast light on today's alternative blueprints and on the constraints and possibilities that matter as we debate policies for the future.

The Popularity of Social Programs for the "Worthy" Many

It is often claimed that Americans are a people inherently opposed to taking "handouts" from the government. But the full historical purview we have taken here suggests that much depends on how benefits are understood and structured. Since the nineteenth century, large numbers of mainstream American citizens have been delighted to accept—and politically support—certain generous, governmentally funded social benefits. Public education, Civil War benefits, the Sheppard-Towner health program aimed at American mothers and babies, and Social Security insurance—all are examples of broad social programs that have done very well. They have been aimed at beneficiaries culturally defined (at any given time) as "worthy" because of their past or potential contributions to the nation. Children have been understood as potential citizens and economic contributors, and military veterans as those who served and "saved" the nation. By the 1930s, the elderly were seen as worthy of support after a lifetime of "contributions," through both taxes and work. And back around 1900, interestingly enough, mothers were celebrated as "serving the community" through child-bearing and rearing in the home.

The structure of public benefit programs as more or less universal also matters (along with cultural understandings as to which categories of people are worthy beneficiaries). Although middle-class and working-class Americans are typically reluctant to see public monies spent for the poor through welfare programs, they have repeatedly been willing to support politically and pay taxes for social benefits that are considered to be "earned" by citizens such as themselves. Aid to the poor has also been acceptable whenever it has been part of broader, more universalistic policies that also benefit middle-class citizens.[45] As Hugh Heclo has ex-

45 This argument is fully elaborated in Theda Skocpol, "Targeting Within Universalism: Politically Viable Policies to Combat Poverty in the United States," reprinted as chap. 8 in Skocpol, *Social Policy in the United States.*

plained, perhaps the best way to help the poor in America is to do so without talking about them, in the context of social services or benefits that have a broader, more universal constituency.[46]

Social Security and Medicare benefits for the retired elderly are the best contemporary examples of strong popular support for universal social policies that help both the poor and the middle class. Conservatives who are opposed to large governmental programs understand well that these programs will be hard to cut back as long as they enjoy middle-class support. It is therefore not incidental that contemporary conservative tactics for shrinking Social Security and Medicare take the form of efforts to convince young middle-class employees that these universal programs are a "bad deal" for them, while simultaneously suggesting that first Medicare and then Social Security are "bound to go bankrupt" as the post–World War II "baby boom" generation ages. If younger middle-class Americans can be taken out of Medicare and the Social Security system as taxpayers and beneficiaries, then retirement investments can be shifted into the private financial sector. What is more, U.S. political history suggests that without full middle-class participation, Medicare and Social Security would become "welfare" programs for the poor. It would then be politically easy to cut these programs again and again in the future.

The Problem of "Government Bureaucracy"

History also shows that arguments over particular social policies at given moments of U.S. history have been closely linked to perspectives on what U.S. government should do and to beliefs about what it apparently *can* do effectively. Americans are recurrently skeptical that government can administer programs well. And policy debates are influenced by the reactions of governmental officials, citizens, and politically active social groups to previous public policies. Prior policies may be seen as models to be extended or imitated; or they may be seen as "bad" examples to be avoided in the future. If policies that serve as an immediate referent for debates are seen as wasteful or corruptly or inefficiently administered, those perceptions can undermine efforts to create new or expanded policies along the same lines.

---

46 Hugh Heclo, "The Political Foundations of Antipoverty Policy," 312–40 in *Fighting Poverty: What Works and What Doesn't*, edited by Sheldon H. Danziger and Daniel H. Weinberg (Cambridge, Mass.: Harvard University Press, 1986).

Back in the early twentieth century, some politicians and trade union-ists wanted to imitate Civil War pensions, extending them into pensions for most elderly working Americans. But most politically active middle-class groups in that era viewed Civil War pensions as a negative precedent. They were trying to reduce the power of the kinds of elected legislators and party politicians who had worked to expand Civil War pensions in the first place. And they saw Civil War pensions not as social expenditures that legitimately aided many deserving elderly or disabled people but as sources of funding for "political corruption."

Social Security gained a good reputation from the 1950s on, not only because of its relative universality but also because it was nationally uni-form and seen as well-administered. During the Medicare battles of the 1960s, reformers were successful in invoking the prior Social Security model to mobilize support for similarly funded and administered medical insurance for all of the elderly, rather than benefits targeted on the poor elderly alone.[47] Today, however, the Social Security precedent may have less prestige, partly because Social Security has been attacked by the Con-cord Coalition as an extravagant "entitlement," and partly because conservatives—and many moderates, too—argue that the federal govern-ment bungles virtually any program it touches.

Throughout American history, certain proposed social policy reforms have been highly vulnerable to ideological counterattacks against govern-ment "bureaucracy." Although U.S. government has always been in many ways much less bureaucratic than the governments of other advanced-industrial nations, nevertheless there are understandable reasons why Americans fear federal regulation, which is what people often mean when they denounce "bureaucracy" in the United States. Precisely because the federal government in the United States lacks strong administrative agen-cies that can reach directly into localities or the economy, national-level politicians tend to enact programs that rely on a combination of financial incentives and legal rules to get things done. The federal government partly bribes and partly bosses around state and local governments and nongovernmental groups in order to get them to help the federal govern-ment do what it cannot do alone. Ironically, however, this sort of situation often gives rise to louder outcries against "federal bureaucratic meddling" than might exist if the national government were able to act directly. Such

47 Lawrence R. Jacobs, *The Health of Nations: Public Opinion and the Making of Ameri-can and British Health Policy* (Ithaca, N.Y.: Cornell University Press, 1993), chap. 9.

outcries are especially likely to occur if the federal government proposes to regulate more than to subsidize—something that has happened especially often since 1980, given the size of the federal budget deficit.

For example, in the 1993–94 debates over President Clinton's Health Security proposal, many interest groups—including insurance companies, but also hospitals and state governments—feared that federal regulations might financially squeeze and forcibly remodel their operations over time without giving them offsetting benefits in the form of generous federal subsidies to pay for currently uninsured groups of citizens.[48] This worry about the "bureaucracy" of the Clinton health care plan was enhanced by the fact that the president's declared objectives include "controlling costs" in the national health care system as well as extending coverage to all Americans. The President promised to do all of this without raising new general tax revenues, and opinion polls indicated that people were (rightly) skeptical about "getting something for nothing." Ironically, by trying to quell worries about taxation, President Clinton and his allies played into insurgent conservative hands by heightening even more deep-seated—and historically very predictable—worries about "governmental bureaucracy" in the United States.

Will Americans Pay Taxes for Social Programs?

American history gives the lie to a notion accepted as virtually sacrosanct in the early 1990s: that Americans will not pay taxes to fund social programs. At the same time, history highlights how crucial the issue of taxes is. If programs are not linked to reliable sources of funds, they cannot readily expand into the generous, cross-class programs that gain broad popular support in American democracy.

Civil War benefits in the late nineteenth century had the luxury of being linked to a politically complementary and very generous source of federal taxation. Republicans in that era were not only the party that had "saved the Union" and wanted to do well by the veterans and their relatives but were also supporters of high tariffs on U.S. industrial and some agricultural commodities. Those tariffs rewarded carefully fashioned alliances of businessmen, workers, and some farmers in the North, while in effect punishing southern farmers, who did not vote for the Republicans. At the same time, tariffs generated substantial funds for the federal treasury.

---

48 This argument is developed in Skocpol, *Boomerang*.

Actual "surpluses" emerged at key junctures, and the Republicans needed politically popular ways to spend them. One of the answers, from the Republican point of view, was Civil War benefits, because these tended to go to people in their northern electoral coalition—such as farmers or residents of small nonindustrial towns—who were likely to have served (or had family members or neighbors serve) in the Union armies but who did not necessarily benefit from tariff regulations.[49] For a time, the Republicans ended up in the best of all possible policy worlds; they could support and expand politically complementary taxation, regulatory, and spending programs.

Maternalist social policies ended up being very limited in the public funding they could mobilize, and thus in the benefits they could deliver to broad constituencies. As I pointed out earlier, the federated women's associations that had considerable success at influencing public opinion and the enactment of regulatory legislation in the states often could not persuade legislators to raise taxes and generously fund programs for mothers and children. This was an era of attacks on taxes by advocates of business competitiveness, and those attacks were especially likely to be effective in local and state governments, where funding decisions were made about mothers' pensions. At the federal level, tariffs were raising proportionately less revenue, and the income tax, instituted in 1913, remained marginal and focused only on the wealthy.

The only maternalist program that managed to tap into expanded funding for a time was the Sheppard-Towner program of the early 1920s. This was the one maternalist program structured as federal subsidies for a set of services open not just to the poor but to all American mothers; consequently, women's groups were able to ally with the Children's Bureau to persuade Congress to increase the program's appropriations over its first years. But by the mid-1920s, Sheppard-Towner had come under fierce attack from conservatives, including doctors, opposed to federally supervised and financed social services. The original legislation, enacted in 1921, expired 1926 and had to be reauthorized by Congress. While majority support still existed, opponents in the Senate were able to use the institutional levers available to determined minorities in U.S. governance to block reauthorization after 1928. Sheppard-Towner subsidies disappeared, and the Children's Bureau lost influence along with resources within the federal government.

49 Sanders, "'Paying for the Bloody Shirt.'"

It is well known, of course, that U.S. federal government revenues expanded after the Depression and World War II.[50] During the 1930s, all levels of government were strapped for resources in a devastated economy, but the federal government gained relative leverage over local and state governments because of its continuing ability to borrow. Although the Roosevelt administration tried to cut taxes and reduce government spending, it also raised and deployed "emergency funding" to cover many economic and social programs. Then, during World War II, the federal income tax was expanded to encompass much of the employed population. Automatic payroll withholding was instituted, a device that makes tax payments less visible to citizens, thus ensuring a regular and expanding flow of revenues to the federal government during the postwar economic expansion.

The various programs enacted in the Social Security Act of 1935 greatly benefited from the overall growth of federal revenues starting in the 1930s and 1940s. Yet OAI, the part of the 1935 legislation that eventually became popular and virtually universal—and usurped the label "Social Security"—carried its own source of funding: an earmarked payroll tax that was supposed to be used to build up a separate "trust fund" to cover future pension obligation. Because of President Roosevelt's fierce insistence on "fiscal soundness" for nonemergency social insurance programs, retirement insurance actually kicked in as a set of taxes well before any benefits were paid. After 1939, the program became more of a pay-as-you-go venture than it was originally.[51] Still, Social Security retirement insurance always benefited—ideologically as well as fiscally—from the existence of its earmarked payroll tax and nominally separate trust fund. Social Security taxes were deliberately labeled "contributions" and were treated as payments that built up individual "eligibility" for "earned benefits."[52]

---

50 John F. Witte, *The Politics and Development of the Federal Income Tax* (Madison: University of Wisconsin Press, 1985).

51 Andrew W. Achenbaum, *Social Security: Visions and Revisions* (Cambridge and New York: Cambridge University Press, 1986); and Edward D. Berkowitz, "The First Advisory Council and the 1939 Amendments," 55–78 in *Social Security After Fifty: Successes and Failures* (Westport, Conn.: Greenwood Press, 1987).

52 Derthick, *Policymaking for Social Security;* and Cheryl Zollars and Theda Skocpol, "Cultural Mythmaking as a Policy Tool: The Social Security Board and the Construction of a Social Citizenship of Self Interest," in *Political Culture and Political Structure: Theoretical and Empirical Studies,* edited by Frederick D. Weil for *Research on Democracy and Society,* vol. 2 (1994): 381–408.

As Social Security expanded to include more and more categories of employees, new taxes were collected ahead of the payment of benefits. Most retirees during the 1950s, 1960s, and 1970s actually did very well in terms of what they had paid into the system over their working lives. Increasing Social Security payroll taxes were accepted by majorities of American citizens as the system expanded toward near-universal coverage. And once the coverage became very broad, a majority of citizens— the elderly and their children—gained a stake in promised benefits. Even today, Americans do not object as much as one might expect to Social Security taxes, despite their regressiveness and the large cut they take from average incomes. The Social Security system's trust fund remains relatively solvent within an otherwise severely strained federal budget, and this affords some political protection in the face of determined conservative efforts to cut social spending.

At the same time, payroll taxes for Social Security and Medicare have become more obvious and relatively onerous as the income tax has receded in importance. For many small businesses, payroll taxes represent a substantial—and perhaps increasingly irritating—component of employment costs.[53] And many employees, especially the more privileged and highly educated, may be increasingly aware of the "cut" taken by these taxes, even as some feel that they could "get a better return" if they could channel these funds into private retirement savings.

Taxes are arguably the pivot on which the future of federal social policy may turn. Conservative advocacy groups, Congressional Republicans, and other advocates of eliminating the deficit and shrinking government are determined to cut severely both federal taxes and federal social spending. Their aim is to shift U.S. savings into private investment funds. Deficit cutters appeal to American middle-class citizens as taxpayers—especially as payers of property and income taxes—rather than as potential beneficiaries of existing or new broadly focused social programs. As I have already noted, conservatives are hard at work trying to reduce American middle-class faith in the viability and legitimacy of "middle-class entitlements" such as Social Security and Medicare. And of course conservatives are determined to block broad new federal commitments of any kind. Making discussion of taxes unthinkable is an important part of the contemporary conservative political agenda.

---

53 See the comments on small business in Milt Freudenheim, "Business May Pay More for Health Costs as Congress Cuts," *New York Times,* Saturday, November 4, 1995, 1, 49.

On the other side of the political spectrum, progressives want to increase governmentally funded "investments" not only in the economy but also in education, health care, and other social services. Progressives have already lost many battles to expand such social programs to the degree that they are narrowly targeted on the poor, on blacks, or on inner cities. They are still trying to expand programs for children but remain quite cautious about more generally addressing the needs of less privileged working families.

Many in the U.S. voting public remain suspicious that "children's programs" are a proxy for "welfare" expenditures or for make-work social service jobs.[54] One way out for progressives is to advocate, as the early Clinton administration did, either "tax credits" or universal "security" programs such as health care to aid the working middle class as well as the poor. But these progressive strategies are badly hampered by the unwillingness of politicians today, including many Democrats, to think creatively—or talk publicly—about taxes. After all, tax expenditure programs can hardly be expanded indefinitely as a tool of federal social policy in an era of shrinking overall tax revenues. And new social programs cannot work politically unless they have some federally mobilized resources behind them. Above all, new social programs cannot deliver significant help to less-well-to-do working and middle-class families unless they transfer resources in some significant way.

There is, in sum, no escaping the need to consider U.S. social policies in relation to sources of public revenue. In the future as in the past, successful social policies will have to be linked to well-accepted and sufficient sources of public revenue. Looking back over the history of modern U.S. social policies, we can see that the most expensive and inclusive benefit programs have flourished in the wake of America's biggest wars—the Civil War and World War II—and only when tied to inclusive electoral coalitions that supported postwar revenue-raising (through tariffs or income and payroll taxes) along with social spending for the middle class as well as the less privileged. By contrast, at the start of the twentieth century as well as at the end, U.S. governmental and electoral arrangements were/are in flux and public revenues sources were/are shrinking, shifting, and controversial. It is little wonder that fierce debates over the shape and future of social policies have raged at both watersheds.

54 Paul Taylor, "Plight of Children: Seen but Unheeded. Even Madison Avenue Has Trouble Selling Public on Aiding Poor Youth," *The Washington Post*, July 15, 1991, A4.

WHAT NEXT?

The United States at the turn of the twenty-first century is very much at a political and governmental crossroads. If antigovernment Republicans or conservative Democrats triumph, the country may permanently abandon national social provision altogether. If progressive Democrats somehow manage to give working-aged Americans a stronger stake in a federal social security system now very much skewed toward the elderly, then America's national social policies might gain a new lease on life. Finally, and perhaps most likely, there may be a period of prolonged governmental stalemate and political volatility, accompanied by the steady erosion of social programs but not their outright abandonment.[55] Let me close by briefly examining each of these possible scenarios.

A new breed of conservative Republicans, profoundly skeptical of any strong federal social role, made sweeping gains in the mid-term elections of November 1994. The election results in 1996 and 1998 trimmed the sails of this conservative "revolution" but left Republicans entrenched in Congress and in many states. Should Republicans revive in 2000, especially by gaining the presidency itself, then a truly conservative realignment might proceed. Federal regulations would be further dismantled in many areas, and core New Deal as well as Great Society social programs might be fundamentally restructured. Former Speaker of the House Newt Gingrich's vision of an "opportunity society" centered around individual efforts in competitive markets might well come to pass. Even sooner, the federal government may be further fettered by substantial tax cuts. With such structural changes in government accomplished, conservative nostrums could be locked into place, unless and until an overwhelming international or economic crisis spurred a sea change in national public opinion. Even then, entrenched minorities might be able to block new federal taxation.

But hard-line conservative Republicans probably will not triumph in 2000. Moderate Democrats may continue to hold sway, pursuing a politics of piecemeal economic regulation and social engineering through the tax code. This is the approach Bill Clinton and Al Gore have pursued of late. Its popularity depends very much on continuing robust economic

---

55 This possibility would continue the patterns documented in Margaret Weir, ed., *The Social Divide: Political Parties and the Future of Activist Government* (Washington, D.C.: Brookings Institution, 1998).

growth of the kind the United States has enjoyed through most of the 1990s. Under these circumstances, most Americans have been preoccupied with personal and family efforts at economic betterment, regarding government and politics with a mixture of contempt and disinterest.

Should economic circumstances turn sour and social problems become more apparent, the possibility remains that the United States could go in a very different, center-left direction. Yet for any gains by progressives in and around the Democratic Party to persist beyond one election, Democrats would have to do more than hold the line on Social Security and Medicare. They would have to address the very real fiscal and demographic pressures on those core, popular parts of late twentieth-century U.S. social provision while retaining their solidary and cross-class structure. While keeping federal spending in check, Democrats would have to devise new social benefits—perhaps education and family-oriented benefits—designed to give middle-class working-aged adults a direct stake in federal social provision.[56]

Needless to say, it will be very difficult for Democrats to do all of these things at once—bolster Social Security and Medicare, keep federal deficits from reemerging, *and* create new social programs for middle-class workers and parents—without finding new sources of federal revenue, not to mention stimulating new wellsprings of popular faith in the national government as an agent of social progress. Given the way U.S. electoral politics and public discussion work today—with low voter turnout, deepening public cynicism, and short attention spans encouraged by the constant need of the media to find new scandals and issues to feature—it is hard to imagine that Democrats can manage the political feats they would need to perform to renew broad public support for an inclusive federal social security state.

Indeed, volatility and governmental stalemate are the most likely immediate prognosis. Health "reform" efforts since 1990 are a good indication of what is to come. First, an apparent national consensus emerged in favor of "comprehensive" reforms that would use government to spread health insurance coverage to all Americans while moderating the rate of increase of health care costs. But within a year and a half, President Clinton's Health Security initiative, designed to meet the expectations of

---

56 This argument is developed in Stanley B. Greenberg and Theda Skocpol, eds., *The New Majority* (New Haven, Conn.: Yale University Press, 1997), and in Theda Skocpol, *The Missing Middle: Working Families and the Future of American Social Policy* (New York: W.W. Norton and The Century Fund, 1999).

this apparent national consensus, rose and fell with a resounding crash. Then conservative Republicans swept into office and claimed a national mandate to chop back federal regulations and social programs, including "reforming" Medicare health insurance for the elderly by rapidly reducing public spending in that area. Again, within months public opinion swung against much of what the conservative Republicans in Congress were trying to do. In the space of just three years, therefore, two radically opposite attempts at gargantuan changes in the federal social role emerged to popular and media acclaim, only to collapse within a short space. During 1996, some modest "incremental" health reforms finally passed Congress after much partisan bickering. But the Kennedy-Kassebaum legislation and new federal regulations regulating maternity stays in hospitals made only marginal adjustments in the rules covering already-insured Americans, leaving aside the question of coverage for those who have no employer health benefits at all.

Business interests have taken up part of the cause of "health reform" by transforming markets for employer-provided health benefits to encourage the expansion of profitable yet cost-conscious health maintenance organizations. The number of uninsured Americans continues to rise, and many physicians and middle-class patients are disgruntled by new fetters on their choices.[57] Meanwhile, insurance interests are mobilizing to take advantage of the looming stresses on Social Security and Medicare. They are funding broad media and advertising efforts to tout the advantages of "privatizing" these social programs by turning them into tax-subsidized individual investment accounts. Such reforms, if enacted, will likely make retirement protections more costly and less generous for most Americans. Yet partial steps in such a direction may be attractive to politicians in an era of budget deficits and skepticism about government, because they would reduce the stress on governmental budgets in the new century.

As America moves into the twenty-first century, the momentum will likely remain with those who doubt the capacity of government to deal with economic and social problems. Explicit changes in national or federal social programs may not occur as quickly as conservative Republicans would like. But if social programs are increasingly squeezed for funds, left unreformed in the face of changing social realities, and sub-

---

57 See the discussion of current and likely future trends in Henry Aaron, ed., *The Problem That Won't Go Away: Reforming U.S. Health Care Financing* (Washington, D.C.: Brookings Institution, 1996).

jected to unremitting attacks on their legitimacy, then more and more Americans—above all economically privileged citizens—will turn to private-market solutions to problems of retirement security and family well-being. Only the upper-middle classes and the wealthy, the upper fifth of the income distribution, would fare really well in this scenario. But they are the ones with increasingly disproportionate access to organized political clout and electoral voice.[58] Much like what happened in the 1920s, after many Progressive Era efforts at reforms fell short or were repudiated, there may be little to prevent economic polarization and a future piecemeal retreat from governmental social provision in the United States, at least for a time.

58 The increasing role of monetary contributions in U.S. politics is documented in the research of Sidney Verba, Kay Lehman Schlozman, and Henry E. Brady, *Voice and Equality: Civic Voluntarism in American Politics* (Cambridge, Mass.: Harvard University Press, 1995).

11

Governing More but Enjoying It Less

R. SHEP MELNICK

This volume's collaborators originally gathered in Washington, D.C., in November 1994, shortly after the Republican Party took control of both houses of Congress for the first time since 1952. The GOP's unexpected victory and strident antigovernment rhetoric led many of us to believe that the country was entering a period of significant political change. The long-awaited partisan realignment, it seemed, had finally arrived. Within two years, many predicted, the uniformly conservative Republican party would control the House, the Senate, the presidency, and the federal courts to boot. Republican leaders vowed to use their newfound power to roll back welfare programs, environmental regulation, affirmative action, and even Medicare and Social Security. Their attack on the power of the federal government was paired with paeans to state and local control and the virtues of free markets. To many of the gathered historians and political scientists the political situation in late 1994 was ominously analogous to the return to "normalcy" and Republicanism after World War I. In Theda Skocpol's words, "much like what happened in the 1920s," at the century's end "there may be little to prevent socioeconomic polarization and fundamental retreat from government social provision."[1]

As the authors of the essays in this book made their final revisions in 1998, though, the political landscape looked far different. Two years after the Clinton-Gore administration easily won reelection by promising to safeguard popular federal programs (most notably Medicare, Medicaid, education, and environmental protection), the Republicans nearly lost control of the House. Efforts to reduce environmental regulation

[1] Theda Skocpol, "From Beginning to End: Has Twentieth-Century U.S. Social Policy Come Full Circle?" in this volume.

280

withered on the vine, seriously damaging the appeal of Republicanism. After 1996 Congress passed incremental expansion of Medicaid and federal aid to education, and stood poised to impose significant new taxes and restrictions on tobacco and to expand federal regulation of health maintenance organizations. As the federal budget's red ink miraculously turned to black, even Republicans in Congress discovered new federal spending they could endorse. Pollsters detected growing public confidence in the federal government. Republican leaders prudently called off their frontal attack on entitlements and social regulation.

One could draw a variety of lessons from these events. For example: the American electorate is fickle, flitting quickly from requesting assistance from the federal government to expressing resentment over the attendant taxation and regulation. Or one could claim that newly elected presidents and speakers inevitably exaggerate their mandate, moving farther to the left or right than their constituents will go. Or this: writing and publishing an academic book takes so long that its discussion of political phenomena will be outdated before the work reaches the reader. Fortunately, this book was conceived and created in a broader context. Taken together, its essays offer a more important, less obvious lesson about the political events of the past several years: American politics has changed more profoundly during the twentieth century than either liberals or conservatives care to admit. The national welfare and regulatory state is deeply engraved in our politics, our culture, our economy, and our lives. It has not been foisted on an unsuspecting public by wily politicians, unaccountable judges, or a secularized cultural elite, as conservatives so often claim. Nor is our political system controlled or manipulated by corporate Political Action Committees (PACs) set on eliminating government regulation, by closet racists determined to undermine civil rights laws, by religious zealots set on reimposing Victorian morality, or by wealthy taxpayers anxious to dismantle the welfare state, as liberals habitually warn. Contrary to President Clinton's frequently repeated assertion, the "era of big government" is far from over because the public has not relinquished its great expectations of government protections and benefits. Perhaps the most valuable contribution of serious historic inquiry is to call into question the simplistic and misleading stories that so often dominate our political discourse.

PUBLIC POLICY, THEN AND NOW

As the introduction to this volume observes, it was in the first two decades of the twentieth century that Americans began to grapple with many of the issues that have dominated recent political debate. The Progressive Era also planted political seeds that have profoundly affected our age: party primaries and referenda; associations designed to organize and represent a wide variety of interests; the idea of the presidency as a bully pulpit; the image of an America willing and able to make the world safe for democracy. But the contrasts between governance at the beginning and the end of the century are at least as striking. Although many of the issues may seem familiar, the scale and character of the public programs of the two periods are worlds apart. Moreover, while progressive reformers may not have been able to create the political institutions they envisioned, they were remarkably successful in destroying the turn-of-the-century institutions they most despised—strong political parties.

Consider the tariff. Protectionism was solidly anchored in the political and economic fabric of the early twentieth century. The protective tariff was not just "the keystone of national economic policy," but played a key "party-defining role" in the political system. The Democratic and Republican positions on the tariff reflected the two parties' sectional bases and became "an important expression of the ideological differences between the parties."[2] The tariff produced nearly half of federal revenues, funding and justifying the era's major social welfare program, pensions for (Republican) veterans. Vigorous protectionism was the norm; free trade the transient and politically weak exception.

Since World War II, in contrast, American support for free trade has been remarkably durable. A mere three years after enactment of the Smoot-Hawley tariff, the United States embarked on a policy course that "fundamentally transformed American trade policy and the way it was made."[3] David Vogel's description of the economic, political, and intellectual underpinnings of the postwar regime not only shows how far we have come but why a return to the old protectionism is highly unlikely. International trade is just one part of America's involvement in world affairs. After winning World War I, the United States tried to retreat from the world. Neither victory in World War II nor the end of the Cold War produced such isolationism or demobilization. "America Firsters" con-

2 Morton Keller, "Trade Policy in Historical Perspective," in this volume.
3 David Vogel, "The Triumph of Liberal Trade," in this volume.

tinue to walk across the stage, but theirs are now cameo appearances: Pat Buchanan's "peasants with pitchforks" are no match for suburbanites with their Saabs and Sonys. Mass consumerism has been an unexpected source of support for elite internationalism. Moreover, what Vogel calls the "geographic dispersion of globally oriented firms"[4] has subjected almost all members of Congress to free-trade pressure. This is but one example of how the decline of sectionalism has transformed American politics and policy.

Just as importantly, trade policy no longer plays a party-defining role, or, indeed, much role at all in contemporary electoral politics. Democrats have become somewhat more protectionist than Republicans. Yet most Democratic presidents, including Bill Clinton, have been strong advocates of freer trade. It took a bipartisan coalition to pass the North American Free Trade Agreement (NAFTA) in 1993: 75 percent of House Republicans and 40 percent of House Democrats supported the President's proposal.[5] Over the past fifty years, trade policy has seldom been a central campaign issue. Despite Ross Perot's effort, NAFTA had little effect on the 1994 or 1996 elections. Although a few industries continue to push for protection, the recent "increase in business political mobilization was primarily motivated by opposition to the expansion of government social regulation and the power of trade unions," rather than trade issues.[6] In short, protectionism is no longer politically salient, culturally resonant, or intellectually respectable. Given American firms' recent success in adjusting to world markets, the free-trade regime seems more secure today than it has in many years.

Political and policy change is even more stark for civil rights. In the early years of the twentieth century, Jim Crow laws became more encompassing, more rigid, and more blatant. In most southern states, African Americans were virtually eliminated from the electorate. In 1913, a Democratic president brought segregation to the schools of Washington, D.C. Even the Progressive Party backed "states rights" in the area of race relations. Otherwise, race was off the national agenda, with both parties acquiescing to the racial caste system of the South.

Jennifer Hochschild's essay describes the enormous policy changes brought by the civil rights revolution of the 1960s: desegregation of public

4 Vogel, in this volume.
5 David Cloud, "Decisive Vote Brings Down Trade Walls With Mexico," *Congressional Quarterly Weekly Report* (November 20, 1993), 3174.
6 Vogel, in this volume.

accommodations, housing, and the armed services; elimination of overt racial discrimination in employment; removal of a variety of barriers to voting and other forms of political participation; substantial school de-segregation, especially in the South; and creation of a variety of affirma-tive action programs for employment, education, and government con-tracting. Hochschild reminds us that these policies have been successful in some respects but bitterly disappointing in others. Overt discrimination has become far less common. Indeed, "no other ethnic group in the his-tory of the United States has achieved such a rapid and extensive growth of a middle class in one generation."[7] Voter registration by African Amer-icans shot up after the 1965 Voting Rights Act. The number of black elected officials went from fewer than five hundred in 1965 to almost eighty-five hundred in 1996.[8] At the same time, these government pro-grams have not come close to solving the problems of poverty, social isolation, deteriorating school systems, declining urban employment op-portunities, and single-parent families that confront so many African Americans. But not—as in the early twentieth century—for want of effort by the national government.

Hugh Davis Graham emphasizes that the civil rights breakthrough of 1964–65 not only brought an abrupt end to state-sponsored segregation but also transformed relations between the states and the federal govern-ment. Little noted at the time, Title VI of the 1964 Civil Rights Act gave federal administrators a powerful tool for forcing desegregation on a resistant South. Federal judges adopted expansive interpretations of the "strings" attached to the growing number of categorical programs.[9] It did not take long for other interest groups, legislators, administrators, and judges to recognize the power of such federal mandates. The civil rights revolution not only discredited the old battle cry of states rights, but reinforced what Alice Rivlin has described as "the escalating perception . . . [that] states were performing badly even in areas that almost everyone regarded as properly assigned to them."[10]

Before the mid-1960s, the federal government provided states with money but few directions. Thereafter, the federal government pursued a

---

7 Jennifer Hochschild, "You Win Some, You Lose Some," in this volume.
8 Morris Fiorina and Paul Peterson, *The New American Democracy* (Allyn and Bacon, 1998), 650.
9 See R. Shep Melnick, *Between the Lines: Interpreting Welfare Rights* (Brookings Institu-tion, 1994), 48–51, 83–111, 164–75, and 245–49.
10 Alice Rivlin, *Reviving the American Dream: The Economy, the States, and the Federal Government* (Brookings, 1992), 86–7.

wide variety of objectives that conflicted with state and local priorities.[11] Throughout the 1970s and 1980s federal instructions multiplied as federal funds dwindled. Huge federal deficits made the strategy of passing costs along to the states even more appealing to Congress. Congress enacted no mandates in the 1940s or 1950s but created twelve in the 1960s, twenty-two in the 1970s, and twenty-seven in the 1980s.[12] Despite the Reagan administration's efforts, "the pace of administrative rulemaking and of new regulatory and preemptive enactments picked up as the decade progressed. The end result was an accumulation of new requirements roughly comparable to the record-setting pace of the 1970s."[13]

Meanwhile, the mechanisms used by the federal government to enforce its mandates have grown steadily more coercive. In their extended and often frustrating efforts to desegregate school systems and other state and local programs, federal courts and agencies developed new doctrines and techniques for forcing subnational governments to comply with federal policies. They found useful allies in the advocacy groups that grew up around these programs. As a consequence, Martha Derthick reports, "the rise of the affirmative command, occurring subtly and on several different fronts, constitutes a sea change in federal-state relations."[14] Although Republicans have recently increased the authority of states in some policy areas (most notably welfare), they have reduced state control on such varied matters as juvenile justice, telecommunications regulation and taxation, drunk-driving laws, and regulation of electric utilities.[15] The debate over state versus federal control continues, but the contemporary balance of power bears little resemblance to the pre–civil rights era.

Few policy areas remained untouched by the tidal waves set off by the civil rights explosion. The national origins quota system for immigration established in 1920 reflected the racist assumptions common in the early decades of the century. The national origins system came to an abrupt end in 1965. As Peter Skerry's chapter notes, concern for protecting the civil rights of Latinos has been a central feature of immigration politics over

---

11 Paul Peterson, Barry Rabe, and Kenneth Wong, *When Federalism Works* (Brookings Institution, 1986).

12 John J. DiIulio, Jr., and Donald F. Kettl, *Fine Print: The Contract with America, Devolution, and the Administrative Realities of American Federalism* (Brookings Institution, 1995), 40–44.

13 Timothy J. Conlan, "And the Beat Goes On: Intergovernmental Mandates and Preemption in an Era of Deregulation," *Publius* 21 (1991), 44.

14 Martha Derthick, "Federal Government Mandates: Why the States Are Complaining," *Brookings Review* (Fall 1992), 51–52.

15 Eliza Carney, "Power Grab," *National Journal* (April 11, 1998), 798–801.

the past decade. This is one reason why the "back door" of illegal immigration has remained ajar while the "front door" of legal immigration has been opened wider. Moreover, "post–civil rights institutions" have created incentives for Latinos to identify themselves as a discrete, insular, and stigmatized minority. Xenophobia regularly reappears but is now blocked or moderated by prohibitions, institutions, and sensibilities developed since the 1960s.[16]

In the early 1900s, the federal government took a few halting steps toward conserving natural resources. But asserting federal power and challenging producer interests was an uphill battle. In order to garner support for their forest policy, Theodore Roosevelt and Pinchot repeatedly bowed—and at times cravenly catered—to western grazing interests. According to Donald Pisani, "local interests repeatedly thwarted national conservation policies in the Progressive Era."[17] The conservation programs of the New Deal were more expansive and effective—so long as they were tied to job creation. As soon as the war put an end to the unemployment problem, Congress put an end to the Civilian Conservation Corps. The programs that survived remained highly responsive to local interests.[18]

When conservationism reappeared as environmentalism in the 1970s, national uniformity rather than local autonomy was the norm. The federal government substantially expanded its control over western lands, and extraction industries found that they could exert far less control over policy than in the past. For the first time in American history, the federal government established a plethora of detailed and demanding rules limiting pollution, regulations that affected nearly every business—and every driver—in the country. At the same time, it also developed an extensive administrative apparatus—not just the Environmental Protection Agency but the Occupational Safety and Health Administration, the Office of Surface Mining, an enhanced Fish and Wildlife Service, and many smaller agencies—capable of writing and enforcing these complex rules. The federal courts' interpretation of statutes both new and old was a key component of the drive for uniform federal regulation.

As important as the scope and complexity of these regulatory programs is the fact that they were established without long debate, presidential

---

16 Peter Schuck, "The Politics of Rapid Legal Change," in Marc Landy and Martin Levin, eds., *The New Politics of Public Policy* (Johns Hopkins University Press, 1995).
17 Donald Pisani, "The Many Faces of Conservation," in this volume.
18 Pisani, in this volume.

leadership, or partisan conflict. This was also true of post-1965 civil rights legislation and expansion of a variety of entitlement programs in the 1970s and 1980s. Clearly, public expectations of government in general, and the federal government in particular, had shifted significantly in the preceding years.

The growth of the federal welfare state has been just as dramatic as expansion of social regulation and much easier to quantify. In the early twentieth century, the central element of the national effort for social provision consisted of a corrupt, party-dominated pension system for (alleged) veterans of the Union army and their widows. One of the principal purposes of this distribution of funds to Republican voters was to suck up the fiscal surplus created by the Republican tariff. As these veterans and their dependents died, so did the pension system. Few mourned its passing. By the time of the Great Depression, only six states had enacted old age pension laws, and these covered only a few thousand retirees in toto. Except during World War I, the federal budget was less than 3 percent of the gross national product (GNP) for the first three decades of this century.[19]

Today, in contrast, federal spending is more than $1.5 trillion, nearly one quarter of GNP. Pensions and health care for retirees and the disabled cost the federal government almost $600 billion per year—more than one third of the federal budget and more than 7 percent of GNP.[20] Far from receding, this spending will increase steadily as the baby boom generation retires. By the year 2020, Social Security and Medicare alone could consume as much as 13 percent of GNP.[21] Social security taxes needed to pay for these pensions have risen substantially since the early 1970s, becoming unpopular and particularly burdensome to young families.

Surprisingly, means-tested programs, widely regarded as less politically popular than Medicare and Social Security, have grown even more rapidly over the past twenty years. Medicaid, Food Stamps, Supplemental Security Income, Temporary Assistance to Needy Families, the Earned Income Tax Credit, and a variety of smaller programs now cost more than $250 billion in federal funds plus another $100 billion in matching state and local funds. Controlling for both inflation and population growth,

19 Morton Keller, *Regulating a New Economy* (Harvard University Press, 1990), 208 and 219; and *Regulating a New Society* (Harvard University Press, 1994), 190.
20 House Ways and Means Committee, *1998 Green Book*, Appendix I, Table I-1.
21 Eugene Steuerle and John Bakija, *Retooling Social Security for the 21st Century* (Urban Institute, 1994), 56.

spending for means-tested programs rose at an annual rate of 4 percent during the Reagan and Bush years, and even more rapidly under President Clinton.[22] It is still too early to tell how the welfare reform act of 1996 will affect long-term spending levels. But it is highly unlikely that combined local, state, and federal expenditures will return to pre-Clinton levels. Today, unlike a century ago, entitlements—for the middle class, for corporations, and for the poor—are woven deeply into the fabric of American life.

THE DEMISE OF THE OLD REGIME

This extensive policy change was in part, of course, a response to the jolts of industrialization, depression, and war. Industrialization brought unparalleled concentration of economic power and, consequently, demands for countervailing political power. It produced mass markets for consumer goods and, in the long run, astonishing affluence. It also created new forms of risk—ranging from industrial accidents to labor unrest to such unusually dangerous products as the automobile and synthetic chemicals—which led to demands for new government regulation. The length and severity of the Great Depression was a necessary if not sufficient cause of the national government's new fiscal policy, jobs programs, regulation of banking, securities, power generation, transportation, labor relations, and income maintenance programs for the elderly and unemployed. Two hot wars and a long cold one produced for the first time in American history a large permanent military establishment and an enduring commitment to international engagement. Years of war also helped create an extensive national administrative apparatus, an income tax that required withholding and filing by average citizens, and a more vigorous sense of national citizenship. The economic preeminence of the United States after World War II set the stage for unprecedented growth and a global economy.

Taken individually, none of these changes required the creation of a permanent welfare, warfare, or regulatory state. In the past, the United States had fought costly, bloody wars, but demobilized and withdrew from world affairs soon thereafter. During Reconstruction, Congress passed extensive civil rights legislation and tried to redistribute economic and political power in the South. Yet by the 1880s, the political will to

---

22 House Ways and Means Committee, *1998 Green Book*, Appendix K, Table K-1.

reconstruct southern society had all but disappeared. Three decades after their creation, the progressive programs to aid mothers and children described by Theda Skocpol remained starved for funds. Government expansion and experimentation foundered on the shoals of American hostility to centralized government.

In the long run, though, the cumulative effect of all the changes listed above was to destroy the three reinforcing pillars of the old regime of limited government: federalism, sectionalism, and party politics. Slowly at first, then with surprising rapidity in the 1960s, the old regime crumbled. In retrospect, the long congressional debate over the 1964 Civil Right Act was the old guards' last stand. In 1964 and 1965—without a depression, a war, or a partisan realignment—Congress enacted the Voting Rights Act, Medicare, Medicaid, the Economic Opportunity Act, the Elementary and Secondary Education Act, and immigration reform. The periphery no longer held.

Describing governance in the United States at the beginning of the nineteenth century, James Sterling Young has written, "Almost all the things that republican governments do which affect the everyday lives and fortunes of their citizens, and therefore engage their interest, were in Jeffersonian times *not* done by the national government." The result was "a generalized or residual indifference among citizens toward the national government itself."[23]

Although decentralization of authority was not quite so severe a century later, control over most programs that affected the lives of Americans still lay with state and local governments. In 1860, the national government employed only thirty-six thousand civilians, 86 percent of whom worked for the Post Office. Over the next forty years, the federal government added 200,000 more civilian employees, 100,000 for the Post Office, 50,000 for weapons production, and almost all the rest in the Department of Agriculture and the Pension Office.[24] Despite the fact that the Constitution explicitly assigns to the federal government control over citizenship and naturalization, immigration policy remained in the hands of the states until the 1890s. Just as importantly, even when the federal government did act, its policies usually reflected local demands and regional differences.

23 James Sterling Young, *The Washington Community, 1800–1828* (Harcourt Brace Jovanovich, 1966), 31–32.
24 James Q. Wilson, "The Growth of the Bureaucratic State," in Nathan Glazer and Irving Kristol, eds., *The American Commonwealth—1976* (Basic Books, 1976), 81–88.

Behind this decentralization lay not just a deeply embedded constitutional vision but also intense sectional loyalties and extensive social and economic variation. Most distinctive was the South, with its racial caste system, backward economy, and peculiar politics. Per capita income in Dixie was about half of what it was in the rest of the country. The West, too, remained distinctive: sparsely populated, lacking water, reliant on extractive industries, and extraordinarily dependent on use of federal lands.

A variety of social, economic, and political changes slowly peeled away these sectional idiosyncrasies. The dislocation of war and depression; the mechanization of agriculture and black migration to the urban north; air conditioning, interstate highways, jet travel, and national television and radio networks; the emergence of national markets and mass marketing; the economic rise of the Sunbelt—just to list a few of the most obvious changes is to suggest the irresistible power of these nationalizing forces.

At the same time, policy "breakthroughs" such as regulation of the railroads and the trusts, passage of the Social Security and Wagner acts in 1935, and the civil rights legislation of the 1960s transformed public expectations about the role of government in general, and the federal government in particular. Each of these initiatives required long and heated debate, vigorous leadership, and significant electoral shifts. But each expansion of federal authority made the next a little easier. As James Q. Wilson has put it, "Once the 'legitimacy barrier' has fallen, political conflict takes a very different form. New programs need not await the advent of a crisis or an extraordinary majority, because no program is any longer 'new'—it is seen, rather, as an extension, a modification, or an enlargement of something the government is already doing. . . . Since there is virtually nothing the government has not tried to do, there is little it cannot be asked to do."[25] Eventually the ruling presumptions about government were reversed. The discovery of social problems now inevitably led to demands for public solutions. Today conservatives as well as liberals advocate aggressive federal policies to reduce crime, establish national education standards, promote employment, discourage litigation, and reduce smoking, drug use, family break-up, and welfare dependency. National uniformity has became the norm; it is now regional variation that requires special justification.

---

25 James Q. Wilson, "American Politics, Then and Now," *Commentary* (February, 1979), 41.

The nationalization of American politics has gone hand-in-hand with the destruction of the party system of the early twentieth century. For most of our history, national parties were little more than collections of state and local parties. According to E. E. Schattschneider, decentralization was "by all odds the most important characteristic of the American major parties."[26] The American party system stood as a bulwark against the centralization of authority, constantly blocking efforts to build an effective national administrative apparatus or to end institutionalized racism in the South.

Political reforms initiated in the Progressive Era contributed to what Joel Silbey describes as "the long secular trend that powerfully challenged, and then overthrew, the deeply rooted party ways of organizing and articulating American political life."[27] Primaries and open caucuses denied party organizations control over nominations. The Australian ballot, stiffer registration requirements, direct election of Senators, referenda and initiatives, reduction of patronage, and nonpartisan municipal elections deprived state and local parties of power and purpose.[28] These reforms combined with rising education levels and new forms of communication to reduce voters' ties to parties and parties' links to elected officials. By the 1970s, James Ceaser notes, "local parties had become mere shadows of their former selves."[29]

Many of the features of contemporary politics are consequences of this decline of the old party system: tepid party loyalty among voters, rampant ticket-splitting, the disappearance of presidential coattails, candidate- and media-centered elections, and year after year of divided government not just in Washington but in state capitals as well.[30] While we have managed to escape the corruption, parochialism, patronage, and inefficiency of traditional party politics, we have lost "a powerful aggregating center able

---

26 E. E. Schattschneider, *Party Government* (Rinehart, 1942), 129.
27 Joel Silbey, "Foundation Stones of Present Discontents: The American Political Nation, 1776–1945," in Byron Shafer, ed., *Present Discontents: American Politics in the Very Late Twentieth Century* (Chatham House, 1997), 9.
28 Stephen A. Salmore and Barbara G. Salmore, "Candidate-Centered Parties: Politics Without Intermediaries," in Sidney Milkis and Richard Harris, eds., *Remaking American Politics* (Westview, 1989), 216–20.
29 James Ceaser, "Political Parties—Declining, Stabilizing, or Resurging?" in Anthony King, ed., *The New American Political System*, 2nd version (American Enterprise Institute, 1990), 106.
30 Martin Wattenberg, *The Rise of Candidate-Centered Politics* (Harvard University Press, 1991), chap. 2; and Morris Fiorina, *Divided Government*, 2nd ed. (Allyn and Bacon, 1996), chaps. 1–2.

to overcome the fragmenting realities of the constitutional system, of the political economy, and of the political culture."[31]

The party system that survives is no longer dominated by state and local party organizations. Reinvigorated national parties and candidate-centered campaign organizations have stepped into the political void. Starting in the 1960s, the national Democratic Party became more aggressive in specifying the rules that states must follow for selecting delegates to national nominating conventions. In the 1970s and 1980s, the Republican National Committee had considerable success in fundraising, recruiting candidates for Congress and state legislatures, and defining conservative issues. Party leaders in Congress have expanded their efforts to discover and promote promising candidates and to offer campaign funds to their allies and acolytes. In the words of Sidney Milkis, "the traditional party apparatus, based upon patronage on state and local organizations, gave way to a more programmatic party politics based on the national organization."[32]

The nationalization of American politics became particularly apparent in 1994, when the ostensible party of decentralization—the Republicans—mounted a national congressional campaign on the basis of a specific party platform, the Contract with America. According to President Clinton's pollster Stanley Greenberg, "In 1994 Republicans and conservative voters set aside parochial concerns . . . [to] cast a nationalized vote against the 'Democratic Congress.'"[33] Unlike most previous efforts to nationalize congressional elections, this one worked. House Republicans defeated thirty-four Democratic incumbents without losing a single seat of their own, turning a 177–256 deficit into a 231–203 majority.

Partisanship intensified once the Republicans took control of the 104th Congress. In 1995, two-thirds of all roll-call votes pitted a majority of one party against the majority of the other—a forty-year high. Ninety percent of Republicans supported their party in these votes. Remarkably, House Republicans were unanimous on over half of the first 150 votes in 1995.[34]

This was no fluke: party unity in Congress has been rising for two and a half decades.[35] *National Journal* reports that its 1997 congressional vote

31 Silbey, "Foundation Stones," 24.
32 Sidney Milkis, *The President and the Parties* (Oxford University Press, 1993), 266.
33 Stanley Greenberg, *Middle Class Dreams* (Yale University Press, 1995), 268.
34 Janet Hook, "Republicans Vote in Lock Step, But Unity May Not Last Long," *Congressional Quarterly Weekly Report* (February 18, 1995), 495.
35 Kitty Cunningham, "With Democrat in White House, Partisanship Hits New High," *Congressional Quarterly Weekly Report* (December 18, 1993), 3432.

ratings "reveal continuing deep divisions between the two parties. If any-thing, the 1997 session featured a hardening of party lines on everyday votes. The partisan differences ran across the board on virtually all issues, whether they dealt with economic, social or foreign policy. Nary a Demo-crat was among the 40 percent of Senators who ranked as the most conservative in those areas. . . . Republicans were scarce among the 40 percent of lawmakers whose voting scores placed them at the liberal end of the scale in any issue category."[36]

Behind the rise of party unity in Congress and the Republicans' unex-pected victory in 1994 lies a key component of the nationalization of American politics: the political reconfiguration of the South. As the Civil Right Act of 1964 and the Voting Rights Act of 1965 destroyed the southern caste system, they also transformed the New Deal party system. In 1964, the Democrats lost the solid South at the presidential level. Republicans won five of the next six presidential elections. Thirty years later, the Democrats lost the South in congressional elections, and the Republicans regained the House for the first time since the early 1950s.

In 1955, Democrats held 110 of the 120 House seats in the thirteen states of the South, not to mention all twenty-six Senate slots. In 1994, Republicans captured seventy-three of 137 southern districts, fifteen Sen-ate seats, and a majority of the region's governorships. By 1996, Re-publicans held seventy-nine House and eighteen Senate seats in the region. Today, most Republican congressional leaders—including the Majority Leader and Majority Whip in the House and the Majority Leader in the Senate—hail from the former Confederacy. The Republican caucus has become more uniformly conservative as it has grown more southern. Only a handful of "Rockefeller Republicans" remain in Congress.

From the point of view of liberal Democrats in Congress, the gradual defection of southern voters had a silver lining: it allowed them to escape control by the Dixiecrat establishment. In 1955, southerners constituted half of the House and Senate Democratic caucuses; by 1975 they were less than one third.[37] As the number of conservative southern Democrats shrank, the liberal Democratic Study Group (DSG) finally gained control

36 Richard Cohen, "Business as Usual," *National Journal* (March 7, 1998), 4.

37 Rhodes Cook, "Dixie Voters Look Away: South Shifts to the GOP," *Congressional Quarterly Weekly Report* (November 12, 1994), 3231; and Kenneth Shepsle, "The Changing Textbook Congress," in John Chubb and Paul Peterson, eds., *Can the Govern-ment Govern?* (Brookings Institution, 1989), 248–50.

of the Democratic caucus. The DSG quickly used its newfound power to dethrone "Committee Barons" and to institute activist "subcommittee government."

The realignment of the South changed the character as well as the size of the southern Democratic contingent in Congress. Many of the Democrats elected in the new South were African American, Hispanic, or Anglos who managed to put together a biracial coalition. In 1997, the five states of the deep South sent only four white Democrats to the House.[38] Consequently, southern Democrats came to look more like their northern and western counterparts.[39] Congressional Democrats became more uniformly liberal as Republicans became more uniformly conservative. The nationalization of American politics thus produced ideologically polarized parties without an ideologically polarized or partisan electorate.

What these changes have not produced is a critical realignment or a dominant political party. Not only did the Republicans lose the presidency again in 1996, but their hold on the House is tenuous. In short, the Republicans have been no better at cementing their coalition than were the Democrats before them. The weak links between national parties and voters have contributed to the instability and unpredictability of American politics.

THE NEW AMERICAN EXCEPTIONALISM

Most Progressives and New Dealers believed that building a modern welfare and regulatory state required not just nationally coherent, principled parties but also an invigorated executive capable of subduing an inevitably parochial Congress and reactionary judiciary. They envisioned a president who served as both leader of public opinion and administrator-in-chief. They sought to construct a more autonomous, more professional federal bureaucracy. Progressive politics required "state-building," which in the end means creating a powerful, centralized executive branch.

Certainly strong, determined presidents played a key role in the expansion of federal power. But so did the reconstructed Supreme Court of the 1950s and 1960s and the resurgent Congress of the 1970s and 1980s. In a variety of ways the Warren Court increased federal control over state and local governments, establishing uniform national rules on such matters as

---

38 Lori Nitschke, "Political Trends Come Together to Diminish Coalition's Clout," *Congressional Quarterly Weekly Report* (January 3, 1998), 23.
39 Shepsle, pp. 256–9; and Dave Kaplan, "Southern Democrats: A Dying Breed," *Congressional Quarterly Weekly Report* (November 19, 1994), 3356.

criminal procedures, electoral participation, desegregation, welfare eligibility, obscenity, abortion, church-state relations, and conditions within state institutions. The Democratic Congress reasserted its authority, decentralized its operation, and created a plethora of regulatory and spending programs opposed by Republican presidents. One of the most remarkable features of American politics since the mid-1960s is how the growth of federal responsibilities has coincided with the dispersal of political power at the national level.

Rather than growing more autonomous, most federal agencies have been subject to increasing demands, constraints, and oversight. Once-powerful agencies such as the Social Security Administration, the Federal Bureau of Investigation, the Atomic Energy Commission, and the Forest Service found themselves under siege, saddled with unmanageable tasks, and subject to hopelessly conflicting pressures.[40] As Theda Skocpol notes, not only has the United States "never developed a strong, well-paid, or highly paid national civil service," but "divisions of authority among executives, agencies, legislature, committees within legislatures, and state and federal courts are arguably even more pervasive within twentieth-century U.S. governance than they were in nineteenth-century party-dominated politics."[41]

Nor has the long-standing American preoccupation with individual rights been jettisoned in favor of a more collectivist public philosophy. Rather, the traditional understanding of individual rights as limits on government authority has been amended to include rights to an array of government entitlements and protections. Over 70 percent of the public believe that health care should be considered a basic right of citizenship. Sixty percent could give this status to adequate provision for retirement, and about half to an adequate standard of living.[42] The right to an appropriate education, to adequate nutrition, to clean air, to accessible public transportation, to a discrimination-free workplace—all these are now firmly embedded both in statutes and in American political culture.[43]

---

40 Martha Derthick, *Agency Under Stress* (Brookings Institution, 1990); James Q. Wilson, *The Investigators* (Basic Books, 1978); Joseph Sax "Parks, Wilderness, and Recreation," in Michael Lacey, ed., *Government and Environmental Policy* (Woodrow Wilson Press, 1989).

41 Skocpol, in this volume.

42 William Mayer, *The Changing American Mind* (University of Michigan Press, 1993), 464, citing findings of Roper polls.

43 See R. Shep Melnick, "The Courts, Congress, and Programmatic Rights," in Milkis and Harris, 188–201.

The new understanding of individual rights was most clearly articulated by Franklin Roosevelt in his 1944 State of the Union Address.
Roosevelt's "Second Bill of Rights" was a modern supplement to the
"sacred Bill of Rights of our Constitution." It included "the right to earn
enough to provide adequate food and clothing and recreation"; the right
to "adequate medical care," "a decent home," and "a good education";
and "the right to adequate protection from the economic fears of old age,
sickness, accident and unemployment." Each of these rights, Roosevelt
added, "must be applied to all our citizens, irrespective of race, creed or
color." "What all this spells," he explained in 1944, "is security."[44]

Eighteenth-century liberalism promised security from civil war, anar-
chy, and arbitrary government action. Its cornerstone was the protection
of a realm of private autonomy from government intervention. Contemporary liberalism promises a broader security—security against the va-
garies of the business cycle and other hazards created by dynamic capitalism, against the prejudices of private citizens and the consequences of
three centuries of racism, against the risks of congenital handicaps and
inevitable old age, and against the consequences of poverty and of family
decomposition. Protecting traditional rights usually meant restraining the
growth of government. The new understanding of rights, in contrast, has
required expansion of the public sector and extension of federal authority,
subtly combining old institutional and rhetorical forms with new policy
substance.

The reinvigoration of separation of powers, the redefinition of individual rights, and the weakening of party ties together have produced a
political system that is more fragmented and individualistic than that of
the early twentieth century. If partisanship was the organizing principle of
politics in 1900, policy entrepreneurship is the touchstone of politics
today. One does not advance in politics in the 1990s by deferring to
authority or by working one's way up the organization, as was the case in
the days of the party machine. Instead, as Alan Ehrenhalt has noted,
"anybody starting a career at almost any level . . . confronts the problem
of how to express independence and individuality in a way that is appealing to the electorate."[45] No one selects, trains, or controls candidates for

44 Franklin D. Roosevelt, State of the Union Address, 1944, *Public Papers and Addresses,*
   vol. 13 (Random House, 1950), 41.
45 "Mayor Daley and Modern Democracy: What We Should Have Learned from Chicago
   in the 1950s," in Shafer, *Present Discontents,* 20.

public office. They select themselves, define themselves, market themselves, and create their own campaign organizations and even their own think tanks. Occasionally (as in 1994–95), these independent contractors find advantage in uniting behind a leader who shares their policy preferences. But they will not hesitate to distance themselves from such leaders whenever ideology or electoral considerations so dictate—as Newt Gingrich painfully learned.

Political independence and policy entrepreneurship are most readily apparent at the presidential level. No longer are presidential nominees selected by party elders. Instead, those who have sufficient "fire in their belly" to spend long months fundraising, barnstorming, and braving assorted media assaults compete in a series of unpredictable, often quirky primary battles. Once in office, presidents define their personal agenda and build their personal reelection organizations. Frequently they bolster their own position by challenging leaders of their own party in Congress.

Half a century ago, the Senate was run by an inner "club," whose members prized collegiality, disdained publicity, and made a habit—even a fetish—of championing parochial interests. "In the 1930s and 1940s," Nelson Polsby notes, "it was unusual for senators to run for president, to cultivate national constituencies in the pursuit of policy initiatives, or to go out of their way to court publicity." Today, in contrast, "as a matter of course, senators interest themselves in constituencies beyond those mobilized exclusively in their home states and seek to influence national policy on the assumption that it is politically useful to them to achieve national recognition and national resonance in their work." As a result "the Senate is now a place in which public policy ideas are tried out, floated, deliberated, and sometime parked as they await the proper constellation of forces leading to eventual enactment."[46]

A similar shift took place a few years later in the House. The subcommittee government that emerged in the 1970s provided most members of the majority party with a subcommittee chairmanship, considerable staff, and a license to legislate and investigate within their loosely defined jurisdiction. Efforts to make these powerful subcommittees representative of Congress as a whole were abandoned as each member sought a piece of the action and was allowed to choose the type of action he or she favored.

---

46 Nelson Polsby, "Political Change and the Character of the Contemporary Congress," in King, *New American Political System*, 36 and 33.

The influence of the more cautious and balanced "insider" committees plummeted. Using subcommittee resources, Congressmen initiated new programs and revised old ones, challenging the president for the title of "chief legislator." No longer would Congress write vague legislation asking the executive to "do something." Now it was writing detailed statutes that frequently deviated significantly from the president's program.

Environmental protection is a good example of this shift. Environmental legislation was the product of legislative entrepreneurship, first by Senator Muskie, then by members of the House such as Henry Waxman, James Florio, Al Gore, and John Dingell. Congressional committees carefully scrutinized agency action to ensure that it comported with their understanding of legislative intent. Despite opposition from Republican presidents, federal laws became more demanding and more detailed as Congress regularly rewrote the underlying legislation. In 1986 and 1990, the key deals on immigration policy were brokered by relatively junior members such as Senators Simpson and Representatives Morrison and Frank.[47] In the mid-1980s, comprehensive tax reform was set in motion by Bill Bradley and Jack Kemp, neither of whom were senior members of the revenue committees.[48]

Individualism and entrepreneurship are evident in the judicial branch as well. In the Supreme Court the number of dissenting and concurring opinions has steadily risen. According to David O'Brien, "the justices now care less about reaching a consensus on opinions of the court. Traditional norms supporting institutional opinions have been eroded." As a consequence "the Court's rulings and policy-making appear more fragmented, less stable, and less predictable."[49] The Warren Court was famous for its policy activism and willingness to jettison precedent. The allegedly conservative Burger Court was nearly as likely to enter uncharted legal water, and even more likely to do so in an ad hoc, unpredictable manner. Supreme Court control over the lower federal courts has declined as caseloads have mounted and lower court judges have discovered mechanisms for insulating their decisions from appellate review.[50] Deference—to higher courts, to administrative expertise, to precedent, to the sentiments

---

47 Schuck, "The Politics of Rapid Legal Change," 60, 67–69, 77.
48 Timothy Conlan, David Beam, and Margaret Wrightson, *Taxing Choices: The Politics of Tax Reform* (CQ Press, 1990).
49 David O'Brien, *Storm Center: The Supreme Court in American Politics,* 2nd ed. (Norton, 1990), 309–10 and 313. Also see Henry Abraham, *The Judicial Process,* 6th ed. (Oxford, 1993), 202–206.
50 Melnick, *Between the Lines,* 38–40 and 253–55.

of the court's majority—has lost its appeal among conservatives and liberals alike.

Uncoordinated entrepreneurship and unrestrained individualism can easily produce chaos and stalemate. In the late 1970s, Norman Ornstein reports, debate on the House floor was "often a free-for-all" in which members engaged in "making ideological points for national groups or constituencies, protecting the interests of particular groups, asserting an individual prerogative, or altering a broader policy direction."[51] This decentralized, atomistic system produced many notable legislative failures, ranging from Nixon's Family Assistance Plan and Carter's national energy proposals to repeated efforts to balance the budget in the 1980s and Clinton's health plan in 1993–94.

It would be a mistake, however, to conclude that such entrepreneurial activity produced only sound and fury without legislative significance. Congressional activism and divided government have stimulated bidding wars on environmental protection, social security, and tax reform. As Graham's essay shows, each branch contributed to the incremental expansion of affirmative action. Skillful advocates used victories in one institution to gain political leverage in another. One finds a similar pattern in school desegregation, food stamps and other nutrition programs, the earned income tax credit, and a variety of programs for the disabled.[52]

The conventional wisdom on separation of powers and federalism holds that these features of our political system create multiple "veto points" that either defeat or moderate efforts to expand the public sphere. But separation of powers and federalism also create multiple "opportunity points" where reformers can establish a policy beachhead. Such entrepreneurial politics tends to produce a wide array of small initiatives and incremental expansion of established programs rather than large, new comprehensive programs. This makes them less visible but not less important.

---

51 Norman Ornstein, "The House and the Senate in a New Congress," in Thomas Mann and Norman Ornstein, eds., *The New Congress* (AEI, 1981), 368–69.
52 See Stephen C. Halpern, *On the Limits of the Law: The Ironic Legacy of Title VI of the 1964 Civil Rights Act* (Johns Hopkins University Press, 1995); Christopher Howard, *The Hidden Welfare State: Tax Expenditures and Social Policy in the United States* (Princeton University Press, 1997), chap. 3; Melnick, chaps. 7–10; Robert Katzmann, *Institutional Disability* (Brookings Institution, 1986); and Thomas Burke, "On the Rights Track: The Americans with Disabilities Act," in Pietro Nivola, ed., *Comparative Disadvantage? Social Regulation and the Global Economy* (Brookings Institution, 1997).

PRESENT DISCONTENTS

The United States enters the twenty-first century economically prosperous, militarily secure, and politically stable, yet curiously and chronic-
ally dissatisfied with the quality of its public life. Over the past decade we
have won the Cold War, achieved (for the moment at least) a low inflation,
high employment economy, and even produced a balanced budget. The
energy crisis is gone and forgotten. Our air and water are getting cleaner.
Crime, drug use, and teen pregnancy are declining. The nation still faces
plenty of problems. But in light of recent developments, claims that our
political institutions are incapable of coping with them ring hollow.

 ˙ Why, then, do Americans have so little confidence in their government
and feel so alienated from politics? Polls uniformly show that public
confidence in government—and in almost every other institution—has
declined steadily over the past three decades. In the mid-1960s, three-
quarters of the American public thought the federal government would do
the right thing most of the time. Thirty years later, only two out of ten
offer this view. Eighty percent rate the value they get from federal taxes as
fair or poor. A recent CNN-Time magazine poll found that 55 percent of
the public agrees that "the federal government has become so large and
powerful that it poses a threat to the rights and freedoms of ordinary
citizens." About half the public believes that government policies increase
economic inequality; more than a third believe that government programs
have increased the number of single-parent families and the rate of violent
crime. Only one voter in ten believes that the federal government has
ameliorated these problems. Although prosperity has produced a small
uptick in public confidence in government (a rising stock market lifts all
approval ratings), a quarter-century of cynicism has left the generations
that came of political age in those years alarmingly devoid of political trust
and attachment.[53]

This lack of trust in government is evident in each of the policy arenas
explored in the preceding chapters. A driving force behind immigration

---

53 The best study of this problem is Seymour M. Lipset and William Schneider, *The Confi-
    dence Gap* (Johns Hopkins University Press, 1987). The more recent polling data is
    reported in DiIulio and Kettl, *Fine Print* 59 (citing data from the Roper Center for Public
    Opinion Research); Karlyn Bowman and Everett Carll Ladd, "Opinion Pulse," *The
    American Enterprise,* March/April (1995), 102; William Schneider, "When Politics As
    Usual Isn't Enough," *National Journal* (November 18, 1995), 2902; and Thomas B.
    Edsall, "The GOP Gains Ground as Trust in Government Erodes," *Washington Post
    National Weekly* (February 12, 1996), 12 (citing a poll conducted by Harvard and the
    Kaiser Foundation).

reform in the 1980s and 1990s has been the widespread frustration and disgust at the government's failure to "retain control of its borders." Nor does the public believe the government has been successful in forcing other countries to accept a "level playing field" in international trade. By the mid-1990s, more than two-thirds of Americans believed that "the welfare system does more harm than good, because it encourages the breakup of the family and discourages work."[54] A majority of 18–55-year-olds believe that Social Security will go bankrupt before they retire.[55] The Environmental Protection Agency is repeatedly attacked both for overregulating and for failing to protect the environment. Congress has responded by inserting multiple, conflicting constraints and deadlines into environmental statutes. According to Hugh Davis Graham, the history of affirmative action in the 1970s and 1980s "is a story of increasing effectiveness, of institutionalized political security, purchased at the price of decreasing public legitimacy."[56]

A peculiar feature of this American distrust of "big government" is that it is not based on hostility to identifiable government activities. By large margins Americans support major regulatory and entitlement programs. Indeed, they frequently demand more services, benefits, and protections. Although they loathe bureaucracy in the abstract, they report favorable opinions of those agencies with which they have contact. The only programs Americans oppose are foreign aid (whose cost they substantially overestimate) and something called "welfare." Yet most means-tested programs—including Medicaid, Supplemental Security Income, and nutrition programs—receive widespread public support. Even those who strenuously oppose "welfare" support "public assistance for needy families."[57]

A recurrent theme of the preceding essays sheds light on this paradox. Over the past half-century, the growth of the public sector has gone hand-in-hand with the decline of two institutions that previously linked citizens

54 R. Kent Weaver, Robert Y. Shapiro, and Lawrence R. Jacobs, "Public Opinion on Welfare Reform: A Mandate for What?" in Weaver and Dickens, eds., *Looking Before We Leap: Social Science and Welfare Reform* (Brookings Institution, 1995), 112.

55 Virginia Reno and Robert Friedland, "Strong Support but Low Confidence: What Explains the Contradiction?" in Eric Kingson and James Schulz, eds., *Social Security in the 21st Century* (Oxford, 1997), 178–94.

56 Hugh Davis Graham "Since 1964: The Paradox of American Civil Rights Regulation," in this volume.

57 Fay Lomax Cook and Edith J. Barrett, *Support for the Welfare State: The Views of Congress and the Public* (Columbia University Press, 1992); Weaver, Shapiro, and Jacobs, "Public Opinion on Welfare Reform: A Mandate for What?" 112–14, and Alan Wolfe, *One Nation After All* (Viking, 1998), 195–209.

and the state: political parties and local government. The nationalization of American politics reduced the importance of state and local institutions. Party loyalty and influence faded. The organizations that have subsequently become most visible and important in national politics for the most part do not command the allegiance or engage the passions of most Americans. The public has become more dependent on government but more detached from politics. Citizens fear they have little control over the government that has so much control over their lives.

Peter Skerry describes the effect of these changes on the political mobilization of immigrants. In the past, he notes,

immigrants and their families were drawn into politics not only by patronage jobs and the fabled Christmas turkeys, but also by the fellowship at neighborhood political clubs, where precinct captains and other familiar faces offered camaraderie along with an array of personalized services. In this fashion unsophisticated and, very likely, indifferent peasants were coaxed into the political process of a modern nation.

Today, in contrast,

face-to-face primary group relationships among immigrants are bypassed by a depersonalized and professionalized politics of campaign consultants, media buys, and computerized direct mail. This is not to say that politics is completely beside the point in today's immigrant communities. A few hardy souls are attempting to knit together political organizations from these dense social networks. Party officials and community activists do mount periodic voter registration campaigns, but these are episodic, often built around the campaigns of individual candidates, and almost by definition lack much, if any, organizational longevity.[58]

Despite the facts that a record number of Hispanics have been elected to public office in recent years and that the two parties are actively competing for the Hispanic vote, Skerry finds within the contemporary immigrant community "the almost total absence of any political organizational life."[59]

Virtually all the contemporary political organizations described in this volume are closer to the Mexican American Legal Defense and Education Fund (MALDEF) than to the traditional party machine. They tend to be geographically dispersed rather than locally based, to be staff-dominated rather than participatory or communal. As Robert Putnam has empha-

---

58 Peter Skerry, "The Racialization of Immigration Policy," in this volume.
59 Skerry, in this volume.

sized, the "members" of organizations such as the American Association of Retired Persons, the Environmental Defense Fund, the National Abortion Rights League, and the National Conservative Political Action Committee never meet to engage in face-to-face discussions. In fact, these organizations consist primarily of a staff with a mailing list. As a consequence, they do little to build social capital, civic engagement, or political trust.[60] Indeed, their adversarial, media-oriented, hyperbolic strategies often further erode trust in government. Many contemporary interest groups—corporate and ideological, liberal and conservative—build clout inside the Beltway by fueling popular hostility toward politics in Washington.

It is ironic that this decline in direct political participation has gone hand-in-hand with reforms that have made American politics more open, democratic, and responsive. Long-standing barriers to political participation by African Americans have been eliminated. Party competition has at last come to the one-party South. Today, most candidates are selected in open primaries rather than by a handful of party regulars. In many states, initiatives and referenda—legacies of our Progressive past—have become an important (in California's case predominant) form of policymaking. At the national level, a variety of new legal rules have encouraged group formation and representation. Examples include relaxed standing requirements in federal court, new public participation procedures and intervenor funding in federal agencies, and court-mandated due process hearings.

Combined with generous foundation support and the growth of an affluent, educated middle class, these changes have produced a wide array of new advocacy organizations. Of the many civil rights groups discussed by Graham and Skerry—including the NAACP, MALDEF, NOW, WEAL, the Leadership Conference on Civil Rights—only the NAACP dates back to the beginning of the century. Of the multitude of environmental rights groups now active in national politics, only the Sierra Club was engaged in conservation politics in the Progressive Era. The first wave of advocacy groups came from the left. Recent years have witnessed a flurry of activity by conservative organizations, ranging from the Moral Majority and anti-abortion groups to libertarian think-tanks and legal foundations. All have become adept at using new technologies and media savvy to mobilize (or

---

60 Robert Putnam, "The Strange Disappearance of Civic America," *The American Prospect*, Winter (1996).

threaten to mobilize) a previously inattentive public. This, in turn, has made politicians more attentive to shifting public moods.[61]

A variety of studies have also shown that the much-lamented expansion of political action committees and Washington lobbyists has spurred electoral competition and weakened seemingly indestructible "iron triangles."[62] As James Madison explained over two hundred years ago, increasing the number of interests engaged in politics tends to decrease the control any one of them has over policymaking. The multiplicity of competing interests was key to the surprising defeat of a horde of well-heeled business lobbyists in the "Showdown at Gucci Gulch," otherwise known as the Tax Reform Act of 1986.[63] Divisions within the ranks of business help explain the deregulation of the 1970s and 1980s.[64] In the 1950s, the American Medical Association (AMA) spoke for the medical community and singlehandedly delayed enactment of Medicare. Mark Peterson reports that in the 1990s, "The previous alliance of medical, business, and insurance interests that had always prevented the federal government from enacting comprehensive reform was split in every conceivable way.... Scores of specialty organizations with an invigorated Washington presence ... challenged the AMA's position on health care reform and its role as medicine's voice."[65] The multiplication of interests helps explain why the Clinton plan got as far as it did—as well as why it eventually died.

In an impressive study of interest group behavior, Heinz, Laumann, Nelson, and Salisbury note that these interests "confront pervasive uncertainty" in contemporary policymaking: "Despite historically unparalleled levels of investment in attempts to shape national policy, the return on

61 Lawrence R. Jacobs and Robert Y. Shapiro, "The Politicization of Public Opinion: The Fight for the Pulpit," in Margaret Weir, ed., *The Social Divide: Political Parties and the Future of Activist Government* (Brookings Institution, 1998).

62 Hugh Heclo, "Issue Networks and the Executive Establishment," in Anthony King, ed., *The New American Political System* (American Enterprise Institute, 1978); Jeffrey Berry, "Subgovernments, Issue Networks, and Political Conflict," in Milkis and Harris, *Remaking American Politics;* Robert Salisbury, "The Paradox of Interest Groups in Washington—More Groups, Less Clout," in King, *The New American Political System;* Frank Soraf, *Inside Campaign Finance: Myths and Realities* (Yale University Press, 1992); and sources cited in notes 60–66.

63 Conlan, Wrightson, and Beam; Jeffry Birnbaum and Alan Murray, *Showdown at Gucci Gulch: Lawmakers, Lobbyists, and the Unlikely Triumph of Tax Reform* (Vintage, 1987).

64 Martha Derthick and Paul Quirk, *The Politics of Deregulation* (Brookings Institution, 1985); Dorothy Robyn, *Braking the Special Interests: Truck Deregulation and the Politics of Policy Reform* (University of Chicago Press, 1986).

65 Mark Peterson, "The Politics of Health Care Policy," in Weir, *The Social Divide,* 184.

that investment is highly uncertain and often intangible. For many groups, including the most privileged and powerful corporate actors in this society, interest representation involves a game of running to stand still."[66] This is obviously quite different from the picture most Americans have of corporate lobbyists.

The mobilization of so many competing groups, combined with the institutional changes described above, has made American political life unusually contentious, unpredictable, and bitter. No one's electoral or budgetary base is as secure as it once was. Among those who devote their careers to politics, partisan and ideological lines have hardened. Unable to achieve a clear electoral mandate, liberals and conservatives, Republicans and Democrats, have frequently resorted to what Shefter and Ginsberg call "politics by other means": scandal-mongering, personal vilification, and endless investigation.[67] Elected officials spend more time campaigning and fund-raising and less time getting to know each other. Consequently, they are less likely than in the past to develop personal loyalties or a sense of camaraderie. No longer are political animosities suspended during an evening poker game, as they frequently were during Tip O'Neill's rise to power in Congress. For many combatants, politics is now a "blood sport" to be fought by all available means.[68]

The fragmented, individualistic American political system has always made it tempting, and frequently rewarding, to promote oneself by attacking everyone else. Members of Congress, Richard Fenno has taught us, run *for* Congress by running *against* Congress: "each member of Congress polishes his or her individual reputation at the expense of the institutional reputation of Congress." This strategy, Fenno laments, "is ubiquitous, addictive, cost-free and foolproof."[69] And it isn't limited to members of Congress. For years, Republicans ran for president by claiming that only they could protect the public from tax-and-spend Democrats in Congress and arrogant bureaucrats in federal agencies. President Clinton campaigned as the antidote to Neanderthals and zealots in the 104th Congress. United States Attorneys develop the groundwork for their political

66 John Heinz, Edward Laumann, Robert Nelson, and Robert Salisbury, *The Hollow Core: Private Interests in National Policy Making* (Harvard University Press, 1993), 5.
67 Benjamin Ginsberg and Martin Shefter, *Politics by Other Means: The Declining Importance of Elections in America* (Basic Books, 1990).
68 The term comes from James Stewart's *Blood Sport: The President and His Adversaries* (Simon and Schuster, 1996). Compare Stewart's description of politics in the 1990s with Tip O'Neill's description of politics in the 1950s and 1960s, *Man of the House: The Life and Political Memoirs of Speaker O'Neill* (Random House, 1987), chaps. 6–10.
69 Richard Fenno, *Homestyle* (Little Brown, 1978), 166 and 168.

advancement by accusing state and local officials of misconduct. Journalists burnish their reputations as watchdogs for the public by tarnishing the reputation of politicians of all persuasions. Nearly every elected official, however long he has been in office, claims to be an "outsider," opposes "business as usual," and encourages voters to "send a message to Washington."

In this environment it is hardly surprising that most citizens adopt a skeptical view of their political leaders. They have little direct political experience with which to compare the pictures painted by hyperventilating combatants. As much as they claim to admire principledness and outspokenness in their representatives, most Americans are uncomfortable with the inevitable contentiousness of politics. This, of course, is hardly new. Americans have long taken pride in expressing contempt for their leaders. In the past such contempt reinforced the nation's deep-seated commitment to limited government. Now it coexists uneasily with a deep-seated commitment to energetic government. Reconciling our expansive expectations of government with our low estimation of politics will be a central task of our next century.

Appendix

Major Environmental Statutes Enacted in the 1970s and 1980s

National Environmental Policy Act of 1969	Required environmental impact statements; created Council on Environmental Quality.
Clean Air Act Amendments of 1970 (Revised 1977 & 1990)	Required administrator to set national air quality standards and emission limits for new sources and for new automobiles; required states to develop implementation plans by specific dates.
Federal Water Pollution Control Act (Clean Water Act) Amendments of 1972 (Revised, 1977 & 1987)	Set national water quality goals; established pollutant discharge permit system; increased federal grants for waste treatment plants.
Federal Environmental Pesticides Control Act of 1972 (amended the Federal Insecticide, Fungicide, and Rodenticide Act of 1947)	Required registration of all pesticides in U.S. commerce; allowed administrator to cancel or suspend registration.
Marine Protection Act of 1972	Regulated dumping of waste into the oceans and coastal waters.
Coastal Zone Management Act of 1972	Authorized federal grants to the states to develop coastal zone management plans under federal guidelines.

Adapted from *Environmental Policy in the 1990s*, ed. Norman J. Vig and Michael E. Kraft (Washington, D.C.: Congressional Quarterly Press, 1990).

Endangered Species Act of 1973	Broadened federal authority to protect all "threatened" and "endangered" species; required coordination among all federal agencies.
Safe Drinking Water Act of 1974 (Revised, 1986 & 1996)	Authorized EPA to set standards to safeguard the quality of public drinking water supplies and to regulate state programs for protecting underground water sources.
Toxic Substances Control Act of 1976	Authorized pre-market testing of chemical substances; allowed EPA to ban or regulate the manufacture, sale, or use of any chemical presenting an "unreasonable risk of injury to health or environment"; prohibited most uses of PCBs.
Federal Land Policy and Management Act of 1976	Gave Bureau of Land Management authority to manage public lands for long-term benefits; officially ended policy of conveying public lands into private ownership.
Resource Conservation and Recovery Act of 1976	Required EPA to regulate treatment, storage, transportation, and disposal of hazardous waste.
National Forest Management Act of 1976	Set new standards for management of national forest lands; restricted timber harvesting to protect soil and watersheds; limited clearcutting.
Surface Mining Control and Reclamation Act of 1977	Established environmental controls over strip mining; required restoration of land to original contours.
Alaska National Interest Lands Conservation Act of 1980	Protected 102 million acres of Alaskan land as national wilderness, wildlife refuges, and parks.
Comprehensive Environmental Response, Compensation, and Liability Act of 1980	Authorized federal government to respond to hazardous waste emergencies and to clean up chemical dump sites; created $1.6 billion "Superfund"; established liability for cleanup costs.

Nuclear Waste Policy Act of 1982; Nuclear Waste Policy Act Amendments of 1987	Established a national plan for the permanent disposal of highly radioactive nuclear waste and authorized the Energy Department to site and construct repositories for spent fuel.
Hazardous and Solid Waste Amendments of 1984	Strengthened EPA procedures for regulating hazardous-waste facilities; prohibited land disposal of certain hazardous liquid wastes.
Superfund Amendments and Reauthorization Act of 1986	Provided $8.5 billion through 1991 to clean up the nation's most dangerous abandoned chemical dumps; set strict standards and timetables for cleaning up such sites; required that industry provide local communities with information on hazardous chemicals used or emitted.
Ocean Dumping Act of 1988	End all ocean disposal of sewage sludge and industrial waste by December 31, 1991; established dumping fees, permit requirements, and civil penalties for violations.

Contributors

Hugh Davis Graham is Holland McTyeire professor of history and professor of political science at Vanderbilt University. His books on civil rights and national policy include *The Civil Rights Era, Civil Rights and the Presidency,* and *Civil Rights in the United States.* Graham has held fellowships from the John Simon Guggenheim Foundation, the Woodrow Wilson International Center for Scholars, and the National Endowment for the Humanities. His most recent research has been on the developing relationship since 1960 between civil rights and immigration policy.

Jennifer L. Hochschild is the William Stewart Tod Professor of Public and International Affairs at Princeton University, with a joint appointment in the Department of Politics and the Woodrow Wilson School of Public and International Affairs. She is author of *Facing Up to the American Dream: Race, Class, and the Soul of the Nation; The New American Dilemma: Liberal Democracy and School Desegregation; What's Fair: American Beliefs about Distributive Justice;* and coeditor of *Social Policies for Children.* Hochschild is a fellow of the American Academy of Arts and Sciences, a former vice president of the American Political Science Association, and a member of the board of trustees, the Russell Sage Foundation. She has also served as a consultant or expert witness in several school desegregation cases, most recently the ongoing case of *Yonkers Board of Education v. New York State.*

Morton Keller has been Spector Professor of History at Brandeis University since 1964. He has previously taught at the University of North Carolina at Chapel Hill and the University of Pennsylvania. He was Harmsworth Professor of American History at Oxford, and has also been

311

visiting professor at Harvard, Yale, and the University of Sussex. His books include *The Life Insurance Enterprise, 1885–1910; The Art and Politics of Thomas Nast; Affairs of State: Public Life in Late Nineteenth Century America;* and *Regulating a New Society: Public Policy and Social Change in Early Twentieth Century America, 1900–1933.* He coedited *The Encyclopedia of the United States Congress,* 4 volumes. Keller is an elected member of the American Academy of Arts and Sciences, the Society of American Historians, and the Massachusetts Historical Society.

R. Shep Melnick is Thomas P. O'Neill, Jr., Professor of American Politics at Boston College. He is author of *Between the Lines: Interpreting Welfare Rights; Regulation and the Courts: The Case of the Clean Air Act,* and numerous articles on social regulation, welfare policy, and the federal courts. He has taught at Harvard and Brandeis and served on the research staff of the Brookings Institution. He is co-chair of the Harvard Program on Constitutional Government.

Donald J. Pisani is Merrick Professor of History at the University of Oklahoma, Norman. He has written widely on the history of natural resources and the law, and his books include *From the Family Farm to Agribusiness: The Irrigation Crusade in California and the West, 1850–1931; To Reclaim a Divided West: Water, Law, and Public Policy, 1848–1902;* and *Water, Land, and Law in the West: The Limits of Public Policy, 1850–1920.* He is currently president of the American Society for Environmental History.

Peter Skerry teaches political science at Claremont McKenna College and is senior fellow at the Brookings Institution, where his research focuses on immigration policy and the politics of the U.S. census. His book *Mexican Americans: The Ambivalent Minority* was awarded the 1993 Los Angeles Times Book Prize. His writings on politics, racial and ethnic issues, and social policy have appeared in a variety of publications including *Society,* where he serves on the Board of Advisory Editors; *New Republic; Slate; Public Interest; Wilson Quarterly; National Review; New York Times; Los Angeles Times; Wall Street Journal;* and *Washington Post.* Skerry was a fellow at the Woodrow Wilson International Center for Scholars and was a Research Fellow at the American Enterprise Institute. He was director of Washington Programs for UCLA's Center for American Politics and Public Policy, where he also taught political science.

Theda Skocpol is Victor S. Thomas Professor of Government and Sociology at Harvard University. She has written extensively on the history and politics of American social policy. Her books include *Protecting Soldiers and Mothers: The Political Origins of Social Policy in the United States,* which won the Woodrow Wilson Prize of the American Political Science Association, and the Ralph Waldo Emerson Award from Phi Beta Kappa; *Boomerang: Clinton's Health Security Effort and the Turn against Government in U.S. Politics;* and *Civic Engagement in American Democracy* (co-edited with Morris Fiorina).

Reed Ueda is professor of history at Tufts University and a former visiting professor at Harvard University and Brandeis University. He was research editor of the Harvard Encyclopedia of American Ethnic Groups. His books on immigrant acculturation and social mobility include *West End House, 1906–1981; Avenues to Adulthood: Origins of the High School and Social Mobility in an American Suburb;* and *Postwar Immigrant America: A Social History.* Ueda has been a fellow of the American Council of Learned Societies, the National Endowment for the Humanities, the Charles Warren Center of Harvard University, and the Woodrow Wilson International Center for Scholars.

David Vogel is George Quist Professor at the Haas School of Business and professor of political science at the University of California at Berkeley. He has written extensively on business-government relations in the United States and other countries. His books include *Kindred Strangers: The Uneasy Relationship between Business and Politics in America; Trading Up: Consumer and Environmental Regulation in a Global Economy; Fluctuating Fortunes: The Political Power of Business in America;* and *National Styles of Regulation: Environmental Policy in Great Britain and the United States.*

INDEX

AARP (American Association of Retired Persons), 303
ADA (Americans with Disabilities Act), 209–10
Adams, Henry, 61
Adams v. Richardson, 202–3
Adarand v. Pena, 216, 218
ADC (Aid to Dependent Children), 258. *See also* AFDC
Addams, Jane, 64–65, 75
adverse impact standard. *See* affirmative action
Advisory Commission on Intergovernmental Relations, 198, 205
AFDC (Aid to Families with Dependent Children), 225, 250, 258, 262
affirmative action: and black-Latino rivalries, 101, 116–18; deregulation of, 205, 206–8, 213, 216, 217–18; evolution of from nondiscrimination, 188–89, 191, 194, 196–99, 201, 202–3n31; executive orders about, 195, 202–3n31, 207–8; expansion of minorities covered by, 83, 188, 197–99, 209; judicial cases about, 196, 202–3n31, 216, 218; opposition to, 205–6, 212–15, 213n56, 216, 232, 301; perpetuation of minority problems by, 83, 94, 100–101; regulatory entrenchment of, 207–8; and reverse discrimination, 201, 205–6, 213n56, 232, 232n52; successful and unsuccessful aspects of, 212, 223, 229, 231, 232, 235, 236–37; third party interest in, 97n67, 116. *See also* EEOC; OCR; OFCC; set-asides
AFL (American Federation of Labor), 29, 64

AFL-CIO (American Federation of Labor and Congress of Industrial Organizations), 42, 51
African Americans. *See* black Americans
age discrimination, 197, 198
Age Discrimination Act, 198
agriculture: and family farms, 125, 126, 132, 133; on public land, 124–25; and subsidized water and power, 124–25, 132, 133; and tariffs, 15, 16, 17, 24, 25, 28, 29, 33, 36, 271–72. *See also* livestock industry
Aid to Dependent Children, 10–11, 258. *See also* Aid to Families with Dependent Children
Aid to Families with Dependent Children, 225, 250, 258, 262
air quality: Clean Air Act, 164–66, 168, 169, 171, 177; regulation of before Clean Air Act, 163, 163n14
Alaska Lands Conservation Act, 180
Aldrich, Nelson, 22, 24, 25
AMA (American Medical Association), 260, 304
Amaker, Norman, 206
American Association for Labor Legislation (AALL), 250–51
American Association of Retired Persons, 303
American Banker's Association, 29
American Business and Public Policy, 38
American Medical Association, 260, 304
American racial structure, 227–28, 238–41; definition of, 220–21n6. *See also civil rights headings*
American Sugar Refining Company, 25

Americans with Disabilities Act, 209–10
American Wildlife Institute, 140
antiachievement values, 106–10
antitrust, 27
arable lands. *See* Bureau of Reclamation; irrigation
Archer Daniels Midland, 177
ARCO, 177
Argentina, 85
Arieli, Yehoshua, 70
armed forces, 221, 231, 234–35, 237, 284
Army Corps of Engineers, 128, 133, 179
Artesian Well Survey, 143
Asian Americans: and black Americans, 116, 116n133; intermarriage among, 88, 104; population of, 116n134. *See also* Asian immigrants
Asian immigrants, 6–7; and affirmative action, 214, 215; and California Proposition 209, 213; employment and wages of, 104–5; quotas, restrictions and exclusions of, 57, 59, 60, 62–63, 66, 69, 75–76; residential segregation of, 103–4n88; socioeconomic mobility of, 103–4, 103–4n88
Association of General Contractors, 208
Association of Local Air Pollution Control Officials, 177–78
Atomic Energy Commission, 179
Audubon Society, 153
Australasia, 252
Australia, 85
autarky, 2, 27, 31, 34

Baker, James, 208
Baldwin, Stanley, 27
Bardach, Eugene, 165
Bazelon, David, 172–73
Beck, James B., 19
Bennett, William, 208n45
Berkowitz, Edward, 209
Bernstein, Marver, 156–57, 158
Berry, Jeffrey, 93
Beveridge, Albert, 24
Bhagwati, Jagdish, 41
Big-Thompson Project, 133
Bingham, Hiram, 29
black Americans: in the armed forces, 221, 231, 234–35, 237, 284; and Asians, 116, 116n133; class division among, 240–41; and criminal justice, 223–24, 226, 231, 236; Democratic Party courting of, 234, 234n56, 237; discrimination against, 105, 108–9,

223, 224, 232, 240, 284; in elected office, 204–5, 223, 234, 234n56, 237, 284, 294; intermarriage among, 104; and Latinos, 101, 115–18, 116n135, 117n139, 214; population of, 116n134; poverty among, 222, 225–26, 225n27, 284; on racism and inequalities, 213n56, 214–15, 219–20, 228, 228n38, 228n39; Republican Party courting of, 208–9, 209n47; and residential segregation and desegregation, 103–4n88, 221, 223, 230; and set-asides, 204n35, 229; Small Business Administration support of, 204n35; socioeconomic mobility of, 103–4, 103–4n88, 222, 240–41, 284; violence against and among, 224, 226; voting among, 213, 223, 233, 283, 284; white Americans on equality of, 213–14, 219–20, 228, 228n39, 232n52. *See also* affirmative action; *civil rights headings*; public accommodations segregation and desegregation; school segregation and desegregation
Blumrosen, Alfred, 201
Board of Irrigation, 144
Boone & Crockett Club, 131
Bourne, Randolph, 64–65
Bradley, Bill, 298
Brewer, David J., 71
Bridges, Horace J., 73
Briseno, Theodore, 116n135
Brock, William, 208
Brown, Jerry, 37
Brown v. Board of Education, 202, 217, 235
Bryan, William Jennings, 23, 33
Buchanan, Patrick, 37, 52, 114, 283
Bundy, McGeorge, 94
Bureau of Biological Survey, 135–36, 146, 147
Bureau of Immigration/Bureau of Immigration and Naturalization, 59, 71
Bureau of Land Management, 172, 180
Bureau of Reclamation, 128, 130, 132–33, 145. *See also* dams, reservoirs and canals; hydroelectric power; irrigation; Reclamation Act
Burke-Hartke Bill, 44
Bush, George: and civil rights, 209–11; and environmental policy, 167, 168
business deregulation, 39
business lobbies and PACs: overall influ-

ence of, 281, 303–5. *See also specific subjects*
business schools, 39
business trusts, 23

California Civil Rights Initiative, 213
California Proposition 187, 92, 98–99, 112
California Proposition 209, 213
Canada: immigration to, 85; trade agreement with, 46
Carey, Henry C., 15
Carlisle, John, 18
Carnegie, Andrew, 17
Carnegie Foundation, 174
Carson, Rachel, 154
Carswell, G. Harrold, 196
Carter, Jimmy, 200, 201, 204n33
CCC (Civilian Conservation Corps), 130–32, 131n11, 145, 150, 236, 286
Ceaser, James, 291
Central Valley (CA), 132, 133
Chamber of Commerce, 208
child abuse, 225, 225n24
Children's Bureau, 257, 272
Children's Defense Fund, 266, 275
China: floods and deforestation in, 138; U.S. trade with, 47
Chinese Exclusion Act, 59, 66, 69, 75–76
Chinese immigrants. *See* Asian immigrants
Chittenden, Hiram Martin, 137
Christian Coalition, 267
citizenship. *See* immigrant citizenship
Citizens Trade Campaign, 38
City of Richmond v. Croson, 205, 215n62, 216, 218
Civilian Conservation Corps. *See* CCC
Civil Rights Act of 1964: intent of, 189, 192, 194–95; Title II (public accommodations desegregation), 192, 194, 195; Title VI (prohibit discrimination in federal programs), 189, 194–96; Title VII (prohibit job discrimination), 189, 192, 194, 195; Title IX (prohibit sex discrimination in federal programs), 198, 204n33; unintended consequences of, 188–89, 194–95, 199. *See also* affirmative action; armed forces; criminal justice; EEOC; OCR; OFCC; public accommodations segregation and desegregation; residential segregation and desegregation; school segregation and desegregation; set-asides; *other civil rights headings*

Civil Rights Act of 1991, 209–11
Civil Rights Commission, 206
civil rights deregulation, 205, 206–8, 213, 216, 217–18
civil rights policymaking, 9–10; and business interests, 208; and Congressional coalitions, 196, 203–4, 207; "power over" policies, 234–38; "power to" and "power over" policy combinations, 238–40; "power to" policies, 228–33, 233n54; and public interest groups, 197–99, 202, 210, 249, 251, 266–67, 270, 274; and public opinion, 188–89, 202, 211–15, 211n53, 216, 219–20, 223, 232, 232n52, 233n54, 240; and states' loss of rights, 164, 284–85. *See also other civil rights headings*
civil rights regulation: before 1964, 189, 192–94, 192n6, 192n7, 193n10, 195n12, 202–3n31, 235; breadth of effect of, 187–91, 199, 215–16, 283–84; the future of, 218, 239–41; measurement of success versus failure of, 220–21n6, 220n5, 222n8, 227–28, 227n36, 229n45, 233n54; and minority status definition, 188–89, 189n3, 197–99, 201, 204n, 204n33, 204n35, 209–10; models of enforcement of, 200–206; self-perpetuation of, 215–18, 215n62. *See also* EEOC; OCR; OFCC; *other civil rights headings*
Civil Rights Restoration Act, 207
Civil Rights Under Reagan, 206
Civil Rights Under the Reagan Administration, 206
Civil War pensions, 10, 11, 249, 250, 255–56, 258, 270, 287
Clark-McNary Act, 149
Clayton Antitrust Act, 27
Clean Air Act, 164–66, 168, 169, 171, 177
Clean Water Act, 171
Cleveland, Grover, 18, 65
Clinton, William, 3; and health care, 265, 271, 277–78; and piecemeal legislation, 276–77; presidential campaign of, 305; on "the era of big government," 251, 281; and trade policy, 31, 32, 41, 46–47, 282
Cold War, 47, 48
Commission on Immigration Reform, 112, 113
Commission on Naturalization, 72
Common Cause, 93, 96

Competitiveness Council, 168
Concord Coalition, 249, 251, 266–67, 270, 274
Congressional Black Caucus, 203–4
Congress's Leadership Conference for Civil Rights, 196, 207
Connally, John, 37
conservation policymaking: and business and agriculture interests, 127–28, 133, 150–51, 154–55n68, 286; centralization attempts, 154–55; and conservation groups, 131, 140, 153; emotional aspects of, 137–38; and the executive branch, 152–53; and the Great Depression, 129–31, 133–34; and interagency rivalries, 141–48; and local and regional needs, 127–28, 132, 133, 143, 150–51, 150n64, 286; local and state government involvement in, 148–51, 149n61, 155, 156; and natural disasters, 129, 131; and the New Deal, 128, 131–32, 140–41, 142, 145. *See also* environmental policymaking; *other conservation headings*
conservation policy objectives, 8; economic development, 124–25, 132, 151–52; grazing and logging access, 124–28, 132; job creation, 129, 130–31, 149–50, 152, 155; preservation of nature and wildlife, 131–32, 140, 151, 154; recreation, 131–32, 140
conservation projects and programs. *See* dams, reservoirs and canals; hydroelectric power; irrigation; national forests; national parks; wildlife conservation and preservation
conservation science, 134–41; deforestation, 136–38, 136n25, 138n33; ecology, 139–40; forests and rainfall, 134–35, 134–35n21; soil erosion, 137, 141; wildlife conservation, 135–36. *See also* environmental science
Consumer Product Safety Commission, 190
consumer safety, 190. *See also* public health
Contractors Association of Eastern Pennsylvania v. Secretary of Labor, 196
contract set-asides. *See* set-asides
Contract with America, 292
Cooperative Wildlife Research Program, 140
Court of International Trade, 32
crime, 226

criminal justice, 223–24, 226, 231, 236
Croly, Herbert, 70
Cubberley, Ellwood P., 62
Cummins, Albert B., 23
customs duties. *See* tariffs

dams, reservoirs and canals, 124–26, 132–33
Danforth, John, 211
Danish Brotherhood of America, 67
Darling, Jay N. "Ding," 140, 142
Darrow, Clarence, 33
Daughters of America, 67
Davis-Bacon Act, 193n10
Days, Drew S. III, 204n34
defense industry, 132, 133
deforestation, 136–38, 138n32, 138n33, 154
DeLay, Tom, 170
Democratic Party: and civil rights, 237; courting of black Americans, 234, 234n56, 237; and the Democratic Study Group, 293–94; and environmental policy, 167–68, 170–72; nationalism of, 90–91; and social policy, 261–62, 264–65, 271, 276–77; and trade policy, 5, 18–20, 22–23, 25, 31, 36, 38, 282, 283. *See also* political parties; *specific subjects*
Democratic Study Group, 293–94
Denton, Nancy, 103
Department of Agriculture. *See* USDA
depressions: of 1890s, 125. *See also* Great Depression
Derthick, Martha, 261, 285
Destler, I. M., 40–41
Detlefsen, Robert, 206
Dewey, John, 70
Dingell, John, 298
Dingley Tariff, 22, 23
disabled persons: civil rights of, 197, 198, 199, 209–10; Social Security coverage of, 261
discrimination: against black Americans, 105, 108–9, 223, 224, 232, 240, 284; black versus white American opinions about, 219–20, 220n5, 228, 228n39, 232n52; against immigrants, 105, 107–10, 110n112, 110n113; against Latinos, 105–10, 110n113; against women, 189n3. *See also* civil rights *headings*
Divine, Robert A., 65
Dole, Elizabeth, 208
Dole, Robert, 171, 211
Downs, Anthony, 156–57

droughts, 129
Dust Bowl, 129, 141
duties. *See* tariffs

Earned Income Tax Credit (EITC), 287
Earth Day, 156, 157
ecology: origins of, 139–40. *See also* conservation science; environmental science
Edelman, Marian Wright, 266
Edmonston, Barry, 86, 104
education: bilingual, 198; and illegal aliens, 94n54; and immigrants, 72–74, 106–10; unequal access to, 224, 233. *See also* educational assistance; school segregation and desegregation
educational assistance: bilingual, 198; federal guidelines for, 197; foundations of, 254–55; and the G.I. Bill, 261. *See also* school segregation and desegregation
Edwards, Donald, 211
EEOC (Equal Employment Opportunity Commission): affirmative action approach of, 200–201, 205; establishment of, 189, 190; nondiscrimination approach of, 191, 195, 207; as one model of regulation, 200–202, 200n25. *See also* affirmative action
Ehrenhalt, Alan, 296
EIS (environmental impact statement), 178–79
elderly persons: equal rights of, 197, 198. *See also* Social Security; veterans' programs
Elementary and Secondary Education Act, 197
Ellis Island (NY), 81
emigration, 68, 86
employee safety, 190, 203
employment and unemployment: and immigrants, 63, 84, 100, 116–17; and trade policy, 19, 42, 43, 52, 53
employment assistance: failure of, 262; unemployment insurance, 235; for veterans, 261. *See also* CCC; set-asides
employment discrimination, 226; before 1964, 189, 195n12, 202–3n31. *See also* affirmative action; EEOC; set-asides
Endangered Species Act, 157, 171, 178–79
England. *See* Great Britain
Enlarged Homestead Act, 127–28
Environmental Action, 174

Environmental Defense Fund, 174, 303
environmental groups, 174–76; litigation by, 153–54, 165, 172, 178–79, 180, 183. *See also* environmentalism
environmental impact statement, 178–79
environmentalism: diverse interests in, 160–61; and economic conditions, 154, 157–58; and environmental consciousness, 158–59, 160; for health of ecosystem versus public health, 8–9, 152, 154, 161–62; as a lifestyle, 155; and the media, 152, 175, 175n53; staying power of, 8–9, 156–58, 172; and trade policy, 41, 47, 48, 52, 53
environmental policymaking, 8–9; and business interests, 166–68, 171, 172, 174, 176–77; legislative-executive battles over, 154–53, 166–74; and legislative subcommittees, 153, 166–70, 173, 178, 179, 181, 183, 297–98; nationalization of, 152, 153, 161, 163, 163n14, 166, 286; partisanship in, 167–68, 170–72; and public opinion, 8–9, 152, 154, 159–61; and regulatory bureaucracy, 154–55, 178–83; and "regulatory ratcheting," 165–66; state and local involvement in, 163, 163n14, 164, 180, 182. *See also* air quality; conservation policymaking; EPA; water quality; *other environmental headings*
environmental science, 154; ecology, 139–40; uncertainty in, 162, 180–81. *See also* conservation science
EPA (Environmental Protection Agency), 190; and air quality standards, 164–65; and business interests, 158, 178; cost/benefit analysis and risk assessment by, 171, 181–82, 183; and environmental groups, 158, 165, 172, 178, 183; and the executive branch, 164–65, 167–68, 178; and the judiciary, 158, 165, 172–74, 178, 183; and the legislature, 158, 167–72, 178, 183; public opinions about, 301; resource and staffing problems in, 155, 181–83, 190; standard setting by, 164–65, 169, 171–73, 181–82, 183; and state agencies, 155, 164, 182. *See also environmental headings*
Equal Credit Opportunity Act, 235
Equal Employment Opportunity Commission. *See* EEOC
Erie, Steven, 91
Ervin, Sam, 195
ethnic identity, of Latinos, 102–3, 103n85

ethnic predeterminism, 57, 58, 60–64, 65–66, 79–80, 87–88
Europe: social services of, 251, 252–53; tariffs of, 27
European immigrants: distinctions between, 57, 60, 61–62, 65–69, 76–77; preference for, 79–80
European Union (U. E.): trade with, 46–47
Everglades National Park, 140
exports: economic importance of, 16–17, 26, 31–32, 42–43, 49–50; from Great Britain to U.S., 19; to subsidiaries of U.S. companies, 50; subsidies of, 32; U.S. share of, 42. *See also* trade gaps

Facing Up, 266
Fair Employment Practice Committee (FEPC), 9, 189, 195n12, 202–3n31
Family Assistance Plan, 299
farming. *See* agriculture; livestock industry
Farrakhan, Louis, 80
federal aid, grants and contracts: expenditures for, before Civil Rights Act, 148–49, 192–93; gender requirements for, 198, 204n33; minority requirements for, 189, 194–96; minority requirements for, expanded, 188, 197–99, 209–10; requirements for, before Civil Rights Act, 148–49, 192–94, 192n6, 192n7, 193n10. *See also* set-asides
federal deficits, 264, 265, 267, 274, 285
federal government expansion, 162–63, 284–88, 290; Civil War effect on, 16; Clean Air Act as example of, 164–66; Great Depression effect on, 37, 259; lack of debate about, 286–87, 290; legislation of 1970s and 1980s, 307–9; and loss of states' rights, 164, 284–85; and regulatory entrenchment, 211–12, 215–16, 281. *See also specific subjects*
Federal Reserve Board, 26, 235
federal taxes and taxation: business taxes, 39, 273–74; and future social programs, 274, 275; income taxes, 37, 148, 272, 273; payroll, Social Security and Medicare taxes, 273–74, 287; reform of, 298; tariffs, 15, 37, 256, 271–72, 287; taxation theories, 37, 232; tax credits, 275; tax cuts, 264, 267
Federal Trade Commission, 26
Fenno, Richard, 305

Fernow, Bernhard, 134–35n21, 137
fertility rates, 86
Field Foundation, 174
Fiorino, Daniel, 161
First Quota Act, 66, 68
floods, 129, 136–37; and deforestation, 136–38, 138n32, 138n33
Florio, James, 298
Food Stamps, 262, 287
Ford, Gerald, 168
Ford, Henry, 27
Ford Foundation, 92, 94, 174. *See also* MALDEF
Fordney-McCumber Act, 27–28, 34, 36
foreign competition, 17, 19–20
foreign investments, 49–50
Forest Homestead Act, 127
forests: and deforestation, 136–38, 138n32, 138n33, 154; private, 149n61; scientific beliefs about, 134–38, 134–35n21, 136n25, 138n33; state and local, 149. *See also* national forests
foster children, 225
Fourth Wave immigration, 85–86, 85n12
France: embargo against, 35; tariffs of, 21
Freeman, Gary, 110, 111
free trade. *See* liberal trade
Free Trade Agreement, 46
Frey, William, 118
Friends of the Earth, 174
Fullilove v. Klutznick, 204, 204n34

Game Management, 139
Garfield, James A., 18
GATT (General Agreement on Tariffs and Trade), 35, 38, 40, 43, 46, 47, 48. *See also* World Trade Organization
gender issues. *See* women's rights
General Agreement on Tariffs and Trade. *See* GATT
General Land Office, 143
Gentlemen's Agreement with Japan, 66
Geological Survey. *See* USGS
Gephart, Richard, 37
German-American Citizens League, 67
Germany, tariffs of, 21
G.I. Bill, 11, 261
Gingrich, Newt, 171, 276, 297
Ginsberg, Benjamin, 89, 90, 305
GNP (Gross National Product): and imports/exports, 16–17, 49; and pollution abatement, 157; and social programs, 287
Godkin, E. L., 19
Goering, John, 227n36, 228n39

Golden Rule of Fiscal Federalism, 193–94
Gore, Al, 32–33, 276–77, 298
government, expansion of. *See* federal government expansion
Graham, Hugh, 9, 10, 83, 284, 301
Grand Army of the Republic, 256
Grand Canyon, 135–36
Grand Coulee Dam, 132, 133
Grant, Madison, 64
Grazing Office, 147
grazing rights: bureaucratic rivalries over, 146–47; environmentalists' opposition to, 180; establishment of, 126–27; local autonomy over, 150–51
Great Britain: economics of, 31; embargo against, 35; exports of, 19; social services of, 251, 252–53; trade policy of, 17, 21, 26, 27
Great Depression: and conservation, 129–31, 133–34; and government expansion, 37; and protectionism, 28–29; and science, 138–39; and states' rights, 129; and trade policy, 6, 29–30, 39; and urbanization, 129
Greeley, William B., 137
Greenberg, Stanley, 292
Greenpeace, 174
Gregg, Frank, 181
Griggs v. Duke Power Co., 196, 202–3n31
gross national product. *See* GNP
Grove City College v. Bell, 207
Guggenheim Foundation, 139
Guinier, Lani, 97

Hall, Prescott F., 62
Halpern, Stephen, 202
Hancock, Winfield Scott, 18
handicapped persons. *See* disabled persons
Hartford Convention, 35
Hawley, Ellis, 155
Hawley, Joseph, 76
Hayes, Samuel, 160–61
health care assistance: and AMA, 260, 304; and Clinton, 265, 271, 277–78, 304; future of, 277–79; privatization of, 260–61, 278, 279; and public opinion, 295, 301. *See also* Medicaid; Medicare; Sheppard-Towner program
health maintenance organizations, 278
Heckler, Margaret, 208
Heclo, Hugh, 89, 268–69
Heinz, John, 304–5
Henderson v. Mayor of New York, 58–59
Herrington, John S., 208n45
Hetch Hetchy reservoir, 161

Higham, John, 78–79
Hill-Burton Hospital Survey and Construction Act, 192
Hirschman, Albert, 96
HMOs, 278
Hoar, George Frisbie, 76
Hochschild, Jennifer, 10, 216, 283–84
Hodel, Donald P., 208n45
Homestead Act, 125
Hoover, Herbert, 28, 29, 67
Hoover Dam, 132
Horowitz, Donald, 88
Housing Act, 232
housing assistance, 226, 261
housing discrimination, 221, 223, 232. *See also* residential segregation and desegregation
Hull House, 75
human rights, and trade policy, 47
Humphrey, Hubert, 195
Hunter, Mark, 80
Hyde, Henry, 211
hydroelectric power, 132–33, 155
hypersegregation, 103–4

Ickes, Harold, 130, 140, 145, 146, 150
immigrant assimilation: and citizenship, 69–74; and English literacy, 99, 99n71; and ethnic predeterminism, 57, 58, 60–64, 65–66, 79–80, 87–88; and local politics, 81–82, 91, 94–96; and race or skin color, 7–8, 87–88, 99, 101, 115–16, 116n133; of school children, 106–10; speed of, 84; and voting, 90, 91, 302
immigrant citizenship: and assimilation, 69–74; barriers to, 90; and local politicians, 91; process of, 69, 71–74; second generation birthright, 69
immigrants: and affirmative action, 212, 214, 215, 217; and antiachievement values, 106–10; and anti-immigration sentiment, 7–8, 98–99, 112, 113n124; discrimination against, 105, 107–10, 110n112, 110n113; and education, 94–95n55, 94n54, 104, 105, 106–10; emigration of, 68, 86; fertility of, 86; Fourth Wave, 85–86, 85n12; and housing, 103–4n88, 105; intermarriage among, 104; and the labor market, 63, 84, 100, 116–17, 116n134; and local politics, 90–92, 91n42, 95–98, 95n58, 95n59, 96n61, 96n62, 98n68, 302; minority status of, 82, 83, 87–88, 94, 97–98, 99, 100–102, 105–10, 115, 188–89,

immigrants: and affirmative action (*cont.*)
212, 214, 215, 217–18; mobility of,
94–95n55; numbers of, 85–87,
85n13, 86n18, 111, 214; and reclamation programs, 125, 155; rivalries
between, 67; and social problems, 23,
62–64, 80; and tariffs, 23, 27; voting
by, 98, 98n68; wages of, 84, 95, 100,
104–5; and welfare, 86–87, 86n19,
104. *See also* Asian immigrants; Latino immigrants; *other immigrant and
immigration headings*
immigrants, illegal: and affirmative action,
83; and California Proposition 187,
92, 98–99, 112; and civil rights, 285;
discrimination against, 70–71; education of, 94n54; and employer sanctions, 110–15; identification of, 112–
13; motives of, 87n21; numbers of,
85n13, 86n18, 112, 112n121
Immigration Acts, 68
Immigration and Naturalization Service,
59, 60
immigration policymaking, 6–8, 82n4; bi-
partisanship of, 65; and ethnic predeterminism, 7, 57, 58, 60–64, 65–
66, 79–80, 87–88; and the judiciary,
58–59, 69, 94n55; and labor unions,
64, 96, 100, 110n112; and multiculturalism, 77–80; nationalization
and professionalization of, 58–59,
65–66, 71–72, 81–82, 89–92; and
public interest groups, 62, 92, 92n44,
94, 94n54, 96, 100, 102, 113, 115,
302, 303; and public opinion, 62, 64–
65, 67–68, 75–77; and scholarly
opinion, 61–62, 64, 75. *See also* immigration quotas and restrictions
immigration quotas and restrictions, 6;
abolishment of, 77, 285–86; of
Chinese and other Asians, 57, 59, 60,
62–63, 66, 69, 75–76; Chinese Exclusion Act, 59, 66, 69, 75–76; of Europeans, Middle Easterners and
Russians, 57, 60, 61–62, 65–67, 76–
77; exceptions to, 58, 68–69; First
Quota Act, 66, 68; Immigration Acts
of 1800s, 68; Immigration Reform
and Quota Act, 112–14, 115; National Origins quota system, 66–68,
76–77; Second Quota Act, 65, 66, 68;
and unfit persons, 59, 68. *See also* immigrants, illegal
Immigration Reform and Control Act,
112–14, 115
Immigration Restriction League, 62

Imperial Valley (CA), 132
imports: economic role of, 16–17, 19, 31–
32, 33, 42, 45; and foreign subsidiaries, 50; quotas on, 32, 42, 43–45,
46. *See also* tariffs; trade gaps; trade
quotas, restrictions and sanctions
income assistance. *See* poverty programs;
Social Security; unemployment insurance; veterans' programs
income taxes. *See* federal taxes and
taxation
Industrial Areas Foundation, 95n59
inland waterways, 128
Inland Waterways Commission, 128
inner cities, problems in, 224–28,
224n22, 227n35, 227n36, 228n39,
233
Interior Department: turf battles with
USDA, 142–47
intermarriage, 88, 104
internationalism, 282–83
International Trade Administration (ITA),
32
International Trade Commission (ITC), 32,
33, 45
Interstate Commerce Commission, 26
Irish Democrats, 19
irrigation: projects, 124–26, 132, 133,
135; regulation and management of,
127, 143–44
Irrigation Office, 144
Irrigation Survey, 143
Isle Royale, 140
"issue-attention cycle," 156–57
Izaak Walton League, 131

Japan: Gentlemen's Agreement with U.S.,
66; trade with U.S., 41, 43, 44, 46
Jefferson, Thomas, 19, 35
Jim Crow system, 187, 195, 240, 283. *See
also civil rights headings*
job training. *See* employment assistance
Johnson, Lyndon B., 163n14, 195,
195n12, 202–3n31
Jordan, Barbara, 112
judicial system, 2; and affirmative action,
196, 201, 202–3, 202–3n31, 207,
209, 216, 218; Burger Court, 298;
and conservation, 149n61; entrepreneurship in, 298–99; and environmental issues, 153–54, 165, 166–67,
172–74, 179, 181, 183, 286; and expansion of government, 294–95; and
immigration, 58–59, 69, 71, 94n55;
and reverse discrimination, 201, 205;
and school desegregation, 202, 217,

235; and set-asides, 204, 204n34, 205, 215n62, 216, 218; and social welfare, 235–36; and trade issues, 17–18n4; Warren Court, 298
Junior Order of United American Mechanics, 67

Kagan, Robert, 165, 183–84
Kasson, John A., 22
Keller, Morton, 5, 40
Kellor, Frances, 73, 75
Kemp, Jack, 298
Kennedy, Edward, 211
Kennedy, John F., 194, 202–3n31
Kennedy-Kassebaum legislation, 278
Khayyam, Omar, 203
King, Rodney, 116n135
Kings' Canyon, 140
Kinkaid Act, 127
Ku Klux Klan, 219

labor unions: and federal contracts, 193n10; formation of, 259; and immigration, 64, 96, 100, 110n112; and trade policy, 29, 38, 42, 51, 52
Laffer curve, 232
LaFollette, Robert, 24
laissez-faire, 17
land reclamation. *See* dams, reservoirs and canals; irrigation
Lash, William III, 41
Latino immigrants, 6–7; and affirmative action, 214; and civil rights, 285–86; employment of, 100, 104–5; and housing, 103–4n88, 105; socioeconomic mobility of, 103–4n88, 103–5
Latinos: and black Americans, 101, 115–18, 116n135, 117n139, 214; discrimination against, 105, 107–10, 110n113; in elected office, 96–97, 96n62, 294, 302; intermarriage among, 88, 104, 105; and local politics, 90n36, 95n58, 95n59, 96–98, 302; minority status of, 82, 83, 87–88, 94, 97–98, 99, 100–102, 105–10, 115, 214–15, 286; population of, 116n134; and public interest groups, 92, 92n44, 94, 94n54, 96, 100, 102, 113, 115, 202; racial self-identification of, 102–3, 103n85; Republican Party solicitation of, 208–9, 209n47; voting among, 98, 98n68, 213. *See also* Latino immigrants
Laumann, Edward, 304–5
Leadership Conference on Civil Rights, 115, 196, 217, 303

League of United Latin American Citizens, 92n44
Leone, Richard, 176
Leopold, Aldo, 139
liberal trade, 5; and Democrats, 18–20, 22–23, 25, 36, 282; and episodic protectionism, 33, 40–41, 43–45; future of, 52–53; and Great Britain, 17, 21, 26, 27; and the Great Depression, 39; and individual freedom, 19; and mass consumerism, 32; and the New Deal, 29–30; and progressivism, 20, 22–23, 24, 25–27; and reciprocity, 24, 30; and Republicans, 24, 31. *See also* multilateral trade agreements; trade policymaking; trade quotas, restrictions and sanctions
Lippmann, Walter, 70
livestock industry: and grazing rights, 126–27, 150–51, 161, 180; and public land transfers, 127–28
Lodge, Henry Cabot, 61
logging rights, 126, 157, 161, 180, 181

Madison, James, 304
MALDEF (Mexican American Legal Defense and Educational Fund), 92, 94, 94n54, 96, 100, 102, 113, 115, 202
Mann, Arthur, 77
market driven social policies, 229–30
mass consumerism, 32, 283
Massey, Douglas, 103
materialism, 155, 158–59
Matute-Bianchi, Maria Eugenia, 107–10
Mazmanian, Daniel, 233n54
McKinley Tariff, 21–22
Mead, Elwood, 144–45
the media, and policymaking, 2, 152, 175, 175n53
Medicaid, 262, 287, 301
Medicare, 11, 263, 269, 274, 277–79, 287
Meese, Edwin, 208, 208n45
Melnick, Shep, 8, 152, 153, 154
Merriam, C. Hart, 135–36
Merriam, Charles E., 70
Mexican American Legal Defense and Educational Fund. *See* MALDEF
Miles, Herbert E., 23–24
Milkis, Sidney, 90–91, 292
Miller, James C. III, 208n45
Mills, John Q., 19
Mills tariff, 18
mineral leasing, 150n64
Miranda rule, 224
Mitchell, Parren, 203–4

Model T, 27
Moral Majority, 303
Morrill Tariff, 20, 30
Morton, Sterling, 143
mothers' pensions, 10–11, 249–50, 257–58, 268, 289
Muir, John, 161. *See also* Sierra Club
multiculturalism, 78–80
multilateral trade agreements: and Democrats, 38; economic effects of, 45; and the executive branch, 43, 44–45, 49; Free Trade Agreement of 1989, 46; GATT, 35, 38, 40, 43, 46, 47; and industry, 32, 33, 46, 49–53; and labor unions, 38, 51, 52; NAFTA, 31–34, 38, 43, 46, 52, 283; reciprocal, 22, 24, 30, 35, 50–51, 53; and Republicans, 38; U.S. leadership in, 35, 41, 46, 48; and World War II, 42
Multiple Use Sustained Yield Act, 181
Murkowski, Frank, 211
Muskie, Edmund, 153, 167–68, 298
Myers, William Starr, 28

NAACP (National Association for the Advancement of Colored People), 94, 202, 303
Nader, Ralph, 175
NAFTA (North American Free Trade Agreement), 31–34, 38, 43, 46, 52, 283
National Abortion Rights League, 303
National Association of Manufacturers (NAM), 23–24, 208
National Conservative Political Action Committee, 303
National Council of La Raza, 92n44, 115
National Environmental Policy Act, 157, 178, 179, 181
National Federation of the Blind, 202
National Foreign Trade Council, 26
national forests: blister rust in, 131; establishment of, 126; expansions of, 129–30, 140, 142, 149, 157, 180, 181; grazing in, 126–27, 161, 180; logging of, 126, 157, 161, 180, 181; and the Multiple Use Sustained Yield Act, 181; predator management in, 135–36. *See also* forests; National Forest Service/Bureau; national parks; wilderness areas
National Forest Service/Bureau, 149; and grazing and logging regulation, 127, 146–47, 161, 180–81; land purchases by, 129–30; litigation against, 172,

180–81; loss of autonomy, 178, 180–81; and predator elimination, 135; and private lands, 149n61; publications of, 154n68; rivalry with Park Service, 146, 147; and tree planting, 141. *See also* national forests
National Governor's Associations, 172
nationalism, 15, 16, 21, 23, 27, 65
National Labor Relations Board, 90, 189
National Organization of Women, 198, 303
National Origins quota system, 66–68, 76–77
national parks, 126, 140, 157, 180. *See also* national forests; National Park Service; wilderness areas
National Park Service: establishment of, 129; and job creation, 131; litigation against, 172; loss of autonomy, 178; rivalry with Forest Service, 146, 147. *See also* national parks
National Resources Planning Board, 148, 260
National Tariff Institute, 27
National Transportation Safety Board, 190
nativism, 58, 62–64, 65, 67, 70–71, 79–80
naturalization. *See* immigrant assimilation; immigrant citizenship
Naturalization Act, 71
Natural Resources Defense Council, 174
Near East and Middle East immigrants, 60, 69
Nelson, Robert, 304–5
NEPA (National Environmental Policy Act), 157, 178, 179, 181
New Deal: and bureaucracy expansions, 145, 154–55; and conservation jobs, 123, 129–31, 149–50, 152, 155; and conservation policy, 128, 140–41, 142, 145; and nationalization of politics, 90–91; and science, 139, 139n34; and social policy, 258–62; and trade policy, 29–30
Newell, Frederick H., 144
Newlands, Francis G., 128, 138n33
New Zealand, immigration to, 85
Nineteenth Amendment, U.S. Constitution, 258
Nivola, Pietro, 33, 40
Nixon, Richard: and environmental policy, 166–68; and minority hiring, 196; political motives of, 196–97; and welfare, 262
North, David, 114–15
North American Civic League, 73

North American Free Trade Agreement.
See NAFTA
Norton, Eleanor Holmes, 201
NOW (National Organization of Women),
198, 303
nuclear power, 178, 179
Nuclear Regulatory Commission, 178, 179

O'Brien, David, 298
Occupational Safety and Health Admin-
istration, 190, 203
O'Connor, Sandra Day, 218
OCR (Office for Civil Rights), 190, 197,
198, 200, 200n25, 201–2, 202–3n31
OFCC (Office of Federal Contract Com-
pliance), 190, 195, 196, 198, 200,
200n25, 202–3, 202n31, 207
Office for Civil Rights. *See* OCR
Office of Bilingual Education, 198
Office of Federal Contract Compliance.
See OFCC
Office of Irrigation Inquiry, 143–44
Office of Minority Business Enterprise,
190
Office of the U.S. Trade Representative
(USTR), 32
Ogbu, John, 108, 109
Okeefinokee Swamp, 146
Old Age Assistance, 258
Old Age Insurance, 258, 260, 261, 273.
See also Social Security
Olympic National Forest, 140
O'Neill, Tip, 305
Ornstein, Norman, 299
OSHA (Occupational Safety and Health
Administration), 190, 203

PACs. *See* business lobbies and PACs
panic of 1907, 24
Park, Robert, 119, 119n145
Passel, Jeffrey, 86
Patriotic Order Sons of America, 67
Patten, Simon N., 19–20
Payne, Sereno, 24–25
Payne-Aldrich Tariff, 22, 24–25, 36
Penick, James L., 127
pension programs. *See* mothers' pensions;
Social Security; veterans' programs
Perot, Ross, 2, 31, 32–33, 37, 38, 52,
274, 283
Peterson, Mark, 304
Peterson, Peter, 266–67
Philadelphia Plan, 196, 197
Piazza, Thomas, 213
Pierce, Samuel, 208

Pinchot, Gifford: and grazing/logging
rights, 126–27, 161, 286; and interagency rivalries, 141–42, 145–46,
154–55n68; scientific beliefs of, 136–
38, 136n25, 138n32, 162
Pisani, Donald, 8–9, 162, 286
Plyler v. Doe, 94n54
Political Action Committees. *See* business
lobbies and PACs
political participation: among black Americans, 204–5, 213, 223, 233, 234,
234n56, 237, 283, 284, 294; among
immigrants, 81–82, 90–92, 95–98,
100; among Latinos, 90n36, 95n58,
95n59, 96–98, 96n62, 98n68, 100,
213, 294, 302; and civil rights, 221,
223, 230, 231, 234–35, 234n56, 284;
and empowerment, 96–98
political parties: electoral disloyalty to, 2,
175–76, 291, 293–94, 302; ideological convergence of, 32, 37–38, 282–
83, 296; ideological distinctions between, 5, 18–20, 22, 25, 33–34, 36,
282, 292–94; individualism within,
296–98, 299; and intraparty unity,
292–94; local control of, 253–54,
259; nationalization and professionalization of, 81–82, 89–92, 91n42,
166, 254, 291–92, 301–2; patronage
in, 90n36, 91, 95, 255–56, 292, 302;
sectionalism in, 17–18, 19, 22, 35–
36, 51–52, 259, 283, 289, 290, 293–
94. *See also* Democratic Party; Republican Party
politicians: entrepreneurship of, 296–98,
299; self-interest of, 305–6
pollution: abatement costs, 157, 165; by
government agencies, 178; rights,
165. *See also* air quality; *environmental headings;* water quality
Polsby, Nelson, 297
Pomper, Gerald, 89
Portes, Alejandro, 87–88
positive-sum social policies, 232–33,
233n53
poverty, 222, 225–26, 225n27, 284
poverty programs: failures of, 225–26,
225n27; future of, 287–88; growth
of, 262, 287–88; historical comparison of, 249–52; immigrants' use
of, 86–87, 86n19, 104; public opinions about, 249–50, 263–64, 301. *See
also* AFDC; CCC; Children's Defense
Fund; Earned Income Tax Credit;
Food Stamps; Medicaid; mothers'
pensions; poverty; Supplemental

poverty programs (*cont.*)
  Security Income; Temporary Assistance to Needy Families
Powell, John Wesley, 134–35
"power over" policies, 234–38
"power to" and "power over" policy combinations, 238–40
"power to" policies, 228–33, 233n54
Pratt, John, 202
pregnancies, teenage, 225
President's Council of Economic Advisors, 41
Progressive Party, 283. *See also* progressivism
progressivism, 282, 291; and conservation policy, 126, 286; and immigration, 57–58, 64–65, 70, 73–74, 77, 90; and trade policy, 20, 22–23, 24, 25–27
protectionism, 5; and classical economics, 17–18n4, 19; and economic security, 15, 16, 19–20, 23, 39, 52, 53; episodic, 33, 40–41, 43–45; and Great Britain, 27; and the Great Depression, 28–29; and immigration, 31–32; and nationalism, 21, 27; origins of, 16; and Republicans, 18, 19–20, 21–22, 36, 282; and xenophobia, 21, 27, 34. *See also* tariffs; trade policymaking
Protestant morality, 20
public accommodations segregation and desegregation, 105, 192, 194, 195, 221, 226, 229, 229n44, 232, 235, 237, 284
public health, 152, 154, 161–62, 173, 181–82
public interest groups: depersonalization of, 92–94, 92n44, 93n46, 93n47, 96–99, 97n67, 302–4; effectiveness of, 304–5; funding of, 92–93, 92n44, 96; self-interests of, 91–92, 100–101, 102, 112–15, 113n124. *See also* specific organizations; specific subjects
public lands: purchases of for job programs, 129–30, 149–50; sales of, 15, 124, 125; transfers of to private interests, 127–28; transfers of to states, 149–50. *See also* national forests; national parks; wilderness areas; wildlife conservation and preservation
Public Lands Commission, 127
public opinion. *See* public opinion, of federal government; *specific subjects*
public opinion, of federal government: public confidence in, 163–64, 281; public distrust of, 211, 211n53, 212,

250, 251, 256–57, 269–71; public expectations of, 281, 287, 288, 290, 295–96, 301; public lack of confidence in, 158, 163–64, 300–301, 302, 306. *See also* specific subjects
Public Works Administration, 130
Public Works Employment Act, 203–5, 204nn33–36
punctuated equilibrium, 187–88
Putnam, Robert, 90, 93, 302–3
PWA (Public Works Administration), 130

Quadagno, Jill, 263
Quetico-Superior Reserve, 140
Quota Board, 66
quotas. *See* immigration quotas and restrictions; trade quotas, restrictions and sanctions

racial identity, of Latinos, 102–3, 103n85
racial structure, 220–21n6; black versus white American opinions about, 219–20, 220n5, 228, 228n39, 232n52; future of, 239–41; and public policy, 227–28, 227n36, 228n39
Randall, Samuel J., 18
RAND Corporation, studies by, 101, 104–5, 107
raw materials, 16, 17
Reagan, Ronald: and civil rights, 191, 206–9; and environmental policy, 159, 180; and public opinion, 164; and welfare programs, 264, 266–67
Reciprocal Trade Agreements Act, 30, 35
reciprocal trade policies, 22, 24, 30, 35, 50–51, 53. *See also* multilateral trade agreements
Reclamation Act, 124, 127, 132, 133, 145. *See also* Bureau of Reclamation; dams, reservoirs and canals; hydroelectric power; irrigation
Reclamation Service. *See* Bureau of Reclamation
Red Apple Boycott, 116n133
Reed, David, 29
Rehabilitation Act, 198, 199, 209
Reinhold, Robert, 111
Republican Party: and deregulation, 163; and environmental policy, 167–68, 170–72; minority groups, courting of, 208–9, 209n47; and protectionism, 18, 19–20, 21–22, 36, 282; and social policy, 263–64, 266–67, 274, 276–78; and trade policy, 5, 18–20, 22–23, 24–25, 38, 256, 271–72, 282,

287; and welfare, 263–64, 274. *See also* political parties; *specific subjects*
Resettlement Administration, 131–32
residential segregation and desegregation, 223, 230, 230n46, 232, 237–38; of black Americans, 103–4n88, 221, 223, 230; of immigrants, 103–4n88, 105. *See also* housing discrimination
Resources Conservation and Recovery Act, 169
reverse discrimination, 201, 205–6, 213, 213n56, 216, 218, 232, 232n52
Reynolds, William Bradford, 208, 208n45
Ricardo, David, 39
Richardson, Elliot, 202
riots, 101, 119, 196
Rivlin, Alice, 284
Rockefeller Foundation, 139, 174
Roosevelt, Franklin D.: and conservation bureaucracy, 146, 147–48; and conservation job programs, 130–31, 149–50; and forests, 138n32, 141; and grazing land management, 150; and national forests and wildlife refuges, 129–30, 131–32, 140; and water policy, 133
Roosevelt, Theodore, 2; and conservation policy, 126–28, 131, 138, 138n32, 141–42, 144, 154n68, 286; and immigration, 64–65, 74, 90; and local political interests, 259; "Second Bill of Rights," 296; and social services, 273, 296; and trade policy, 24
Root, Elihu, 24
Rosenbaum, Walter, 169–70
Ruckelshaus, William, 175n53, 183
Rudolph, Lloyd, 78
Rudolph, Susanne, 78
Rugg, Harold, 75
Rumbaut, Rubén, 109
Russell, Richard, 195
Russia: immigrants from, 61; U.S. trade with, 47

Sabatier, Paul, 233n54
Safe Drinking Water Law, 169
safety. *See* consumer safety; employee safety; public health
Sage Brush Rebellion, 180
Salisbury, Robert, 304–5
Sax, Joseph, 180–81
Schattschneider, E. E., 38, 291
school segregation and desegregation, 202, 217, 222–23, 231–32, 233n53, 235, 236, 237–38, 283–84

Schultz, George P., 196, 208
Schurman, Jacob Gould, 64
science. *See* conservation science; environmental science
Scopes trial, 33
"Second Bill of Rights," 296
Second Quota Act, 65, 66, 68
sectionalism: demise of, 289, 290, 293–94; and social policy, 259, 289; and trade policy, 17–18, 22, 35–36, 51–52, 283
Select Commission on Immigration and Refugee Policy, 112
set-asides, 203–5, 204nn33–36, 208, 215n62, 216, 218. *See also* affirmative action
sex discrimination. *See* women's rights
sexual harassment, 210
Shaler, Nathaniel, 61
Shasta Dam, 132, 133
Shefter, Martin, 89, 90, 305
shelterbelt, 141
Sheppard-Towner program, 257, 258, 268, 272
Sherman, John, 62–63
Sherman Antitrust Act, 27
Sierra Club, 153, 161, 174, 303
Silbey, Joel, 291
Silent Spring, 154
Skerry, Peter, 7–8, 215, 302
Skocpol, Theda, 10–11, 280, 287, 295
Skowronek, Stephen, 253
Small Business Administration, 204, 204n35, 214
Smith, Al, 67–68
Smith, Henry Lester, 75
Smoot, Reed, 28, 29
Smoot-Hawley Tariff, 20, 27, 28–29, 30, 31, 34, 36, 49
Sniderman, Paul M., 213
social policies, types of: cost/benefit, 231–32; incentive to act, 237–38; judicially or politically supported, 235–36; market driven, 229–30; positive-sum, 232–33, 233n53; "power to," 228–33, 233n54; "power to" and "power over" combination, 238–40; robust institution-based, 234–35; single-stage, 230–31, 230n47; structured or controlled recipient, 236–37
Social Security: and the ADA, 210; expansions of, 11, 263; funding and costs of, 273–74, 275, 278, 287; future of, 277–79, 287; generational imbalances in, 251, 265–66, 269; and immi-

Social Security (*cont.*)
grants, 90; indexing of benefits, 263; middle class coverage by, 263, 266–67, 269, 274, 277, 288; privatization of, 267, 274, 278–79; public opinion about, 270, 295, 301. *See also* Medicare; Old Age Assistance; Old Age Insurance; Social Security Act; Supplemental Security Income

Social Security Act, 10, 11, 258, 260, 273

social services: bureaucratization of, 190–91; in the early versus late twentieth century, 10–11, 249–52; earned versus unearned, 10–11, 255, 257, 263–64, 268–69, 273; entrenchment of, 281, 288; in Europe, 251, 252–53; future of, 276–79, 287–288; public distrust of government role in, 250, 251, 256–57, 269–71; public expectations of, 295–96, 301; and public interest groups, 249, 250–51; public support for, 190, 249–50, 269, 301; spending on, 271–72, 273–75, 287. *See also* educational assistance; health care assistance; poverty programs; social policies, types of; Social Security; unemployment insurance; veterans' programs

soil conservation, 151. *See also* Soil Conservation Service; Soil Erosion Service

Soil Conservation Service, 146; and job creation, 130, 131, 150; and research, 139n34

Soil Erosion Service, 147

Sons of Norway, 67

Sons of the American Revolution, 67

South Africa: immigration to, 85; U.S. trade with, 47

Soviet Union, trade with, 47

Spencer, Herbert, 61

sportsmen's organizations, 131–32

Spreckels, Claus, 25

stagflation, 157

State and Territorial Air Pollution Program Administrators, 177–78

state parks, 149–50

states' rights, 164, 284–85, 289

Stockman, David, 267

subcommittee government, 166–67, 168–70, 173, 297–98

suburbanization, 2–3

Sumner, William Graham, 61

Sundquist, James, 192

Superfund, 177

Supplemental Security Income, 287, 301

Swain, Donald, 133

Taft, William Howard, 24, 25, 36, 65

Tariff Board, 24

Tariff Commission, 25, 28, 30

tariffs: and agriculture, 15, 16, 17, 24, 25, 28, 29, 33, 36, 271–72; and business interests, 18–19, 20, 23–25, 28–29, 33, 36, 271–72; and the Civil War, 16; Dingley Tariff, 22, 23; duty rates, 22, 28, 29, 32, 36, 45; economic effect of, 16–17; and the executive branch, 22, 26, 28, 30; and federal revenues, 15, 37, 282; Fordney-McCumber Act, 27, 28, 34, 36; and Great Britain, 21; and labor, 19, 20, 23, 24, 28, 29, 30, 38, 271–72; McKinley Tariff, 21–22; Méline Tariff (France), 21; Mills tariff, 18; Morrill Tariff, 20, 30; multinationalization of, 21; and the New Deal, 29–30; Payne-Aldrich Tariff, 22, 24–25, 36; Reciprocal Trade Agreements Act, 30, 35; replacement of, 40; Smoot-Hawley Tariff, 20, 27, 28–29, 30, 31, 34, 36, 39, 49, 282; of 1883 to 1897, 18; Underwood Tariff, 22, 25–26, 36; and World War I, 26–27. *See also* protectionism; trade policymaking; trade quotas, restrictions and sanctions

taxes. *See* federal taxes and taxation

Tax Reform Act, 304

Taylor Grazing Act, 146–47, 150

Teapot Dome, 145

Teller, Henry, 63

Temporary Assistance to Needy Families (TANF), 226, 287

Tennessee Valley Authority, 128, 130

"The Dirty Dozen," 175

The Scar of Race, 213

Thomas, Clarence, 207

Thornburgh, Richard, 210

timber depletion myth, 136–37, 136n25

timber industry, 126, 157, 161, 180, 181

Townsend Clubs, 259

Trade Expansion Act, 38, 51

trade gaps, 40, 42–43, 46, 157

trade policymaking, 4–6; and business interests, 23–24, 25, 26–27, 29, 33, 38–39, 40–41; depoliticalization of, 5, 32, 33, 34, 35, 36–39, 43, 49; and the executive branch, 26, 41, 45, 46–47; nonpartisanship in, 5, 30, 32, 36–38, 52, 283; partisanship in, 5, 18–20, 22, 24–25, 28, 35–36, 256, 282; and public opinion, 37–38, 43, 301; and sectionalism, 17–18, 22, 35–36,

51–52, 283. *See also* exports; imports; liberal trade; multilateral trade agreements; protectionism; tariffs; trade quotas, restrictions and sanctions

trade quotas, restrictions and sanctions: Burke-Hartke Bill, 44; and business interests, 39, 43–45, 46, 47; and environmental issues, 41, 47, 52, 53; and human rights, 47; and organized labor, 42; as political weapon, 41, 46–48; as redress, 33, 41, 43–45; as retaliation, 41, 44, 51; Trade Expansion Act, 38, 51; and trade imbalances, 40, 42. *See also* liberal trade; multilateral trade agreements; tariffs; trade policymaking

Train, Russell, 167–68

Truman, Harry, 235, 260

trusts, business, 23

TVA (Tennessee Valley Authority), 128, 130

Tyson, Laura, 41

Ueda, Reed, 7–8, 88

Underwood Tariff, 22, 25–26, 36

unemployment and employment: and immigrants, 63, 84, 100, 116–17; and trade policy, 19, 42, 43, 52, 53. *See also* employment assistance; unemployment insurance

unemployment insurance, 258, 260

Uniform Guidelines on Employee Selection Procedures, 201

United Farmworkers Union, 100

United Steelworkers of America v. Weber, 201, 205–6

urbanization, 2–3, 129, 132

USDA (U.S. Department of Agriculture), 30; turf battles with Interior Department, 142–47

USGS (U.S. Geological Survey), 128, 134–35, 142–44

U.S. v. Wong Kim Ark, 69

Vannest, Charles Garret, 75

Vasa Order of America, 67

veterans' programs: Civil War pensions, 10, 11, 249, 250, 255–56, 258, 270, 287; G.I. Bill, 261

Vietnam, trade with, 47

Vogel, David, 5, 176, 282–83

voting: among black Americans, 213, 223, 233, 283, 284; among Latinos, 98, 98n68, 213; and women's rights, 258. *See also other voting headings*

voting districts, 208–9, 209n47, 221, 223, 233, 234, 234n56

Voting Rights Act (VRA): and Asian Americans, 97n66; and black Americans, 237, 284; and Democrats, 237; extension of, 207; and immigrants, 96–98, 97n66; and Latinos, 94, 96–97; and racialization of immigration, 94, 98–99, 100–101

wages: and immigration, 84, 95, 100, 104–5; and trade policy, 19, 20, 27, 52, 53

Wagner Act, 189

Walcott, Charles D., 142

Walker, Jack, 93, 99

Wallace, Henry, 146, 147

Wall Street, on tariffs, 29

Ward's Cove Packing Co. v. Antonio, 209

War Production Board, 133

Warren, Francis E., 127, 144

War Trade Board, 26, 27

Washington Post, survey by, 219

water management, 128, 133. *See also* floods; hydroelectric power; irrigation; reclamation; water quality; water rights; wetlands

water quality, 169, 171

Water Quality Act, 169

water rights, 144, 151

Watt, James, 180

Waxman, Henry, 168, 298

WEAL (Women's Equity Action League), 198, 202, 303

Webb-Pomerene Act, 26–27

Weeks Act, 129–30, 142, 149

Weisbrod, Burton, 99

welfare. *See* social services

Wells, David Ames, 19

Western Governor Policy Office, 177

Western Range, 146–47

wetlands, 129, 148

Wharton, Joseph, 39

Who's Bashing Whom?, 41

Wilderness Act, 180

wilderness areas, 140, 146, 157, 180, 181

wildlife conservation and preservation: Endangered Species Act, 157, 171, 178–79; scientific foundations of, 135–36, 139; wildlife refuges, 126, 131–32, 140, 157

Wilson, James, 143

Wilson, Pete, 112

Wilson, William Julius, 118

Wilson, William L., 19

Wilson, Woodrow: on immigration, 64–65, 75; and trade policy, 25, 26, 36

Woll, Matthew, 29

women's and children's programs: in the early 20th century, 257–58. *See also* AFDC; mothers' pensions

Women's Business Ownership Act, 204n33

Women's Equity Action League, 198, 202, 303

women's rights, 189n3, 197–98, 202, 204n33, 207, 210, 213

women's special interest groups: in the early 20th century, 257–58, 272; in the late 20th century, 198, 202, 303

Wood, Gordon S., 78–79

Works, John D., 145

Works Progress Administration, 130, 131–32

world trade: U.S. share of, 16–17, 31, 42; value of, 40

World Trade Organization (WTO), 47, 48

World War I: and immigration, 65, 72; and tariffs, 26–27

World War II: and immigration, 6; and trade policy, 6, 42

Worster, Donald, 134

WPA (Works Progress Administration), 130, 131–32

Wright, Carroll, 17

Wright, Skelly, 172–73

xenophobia: and immigration, 7, 76, 79–80, 286; and protectionism, 21, 27, 34

Yellowstone National Park, 140

Yosemite National Park, 140

Young, James Sterling, 289

Zhou, Min, 87–88

Other books in the series (*continued from page iii*)

Deborah S. Davis, Richard Kraus, Barry Naughton, Elizabeth J. Perry, editors, *Urban Spaces in Contemporary China: The Potential for Autonomy and Community in Post-Mao China*

William M. Shea and Peter A. Huff, editors, *Knowledge and Belief in America: Enlightenment Traditions and Modern Religious Thought*

W. Elliott Brownlee, editor, *Funding the American State, 1941–1995: The Rise and Fall of the Era of Easy Finance*

W. Elliott Brownlee, *Federal Taxation in America: A Short History*

R. H. Taylor, editor, *The Politics of Elections in Southeast Asia*

Sumit Ganguly, *The Crisis in Kashmir: Portents of War, Hopes of Peace*

James W. Muller, editor, *Churchill as Peacemaker*

Donald R. Kelley and David Harris Sacks, editors, *The Historical Imagination in Early Modern Britain: History, Rhetoric, and Fiction, 1500–1800*

Richard Wightman Fox and Robert B. Westbrook, editors, *In Face of the Facts: Moral Inquiry in American Scholarship*